CONTEMPORARY ART IN
EASTERN EUROPE

CONTEMPORARY ART IN EASTERN EUROPE

black dog
publishing

london uk

FOREWORD

As with the other books in the ARTWORLD series, assembling a survey of contemporary art from a particular region is a challenging exercise—a statement which carries particular relevance when considering the case of contemporary Eastern European art. As a region, it is characterised by continuing political and social turbulence, even today, and as a result Eastern European art history has remained largely undiscovered, or misrepresented as censored Socialist Realism. *Contemporary Art in Eastern Europe* attempts to move away from stereotypes such as these, instead presenting the rich diversity of work emerging from the region, opening the subject up to further debate and discussion.

To begin with, the concept of 'Eastern Europe' must be discussed. Once again, the title of the book, and map within, appear to propose a geographically defined area, presumably in opposition to 'Western Europe'. However, to define this region by borders is a difficult task—as discussed in the reprint of Piotr Piotrowski's essay "The Grey Zone of Europe"—and in compiling a survey such as this, it must remain guided by fluid geographical definitions. Elaborating upon this point, Boris Groys asks whether it is possible for art from this region "to possess a distinctive character?" within his intuitive introductory essay "Haunted by Communism", highlighting the core issues and themes that pervade throughout Eastern European art today, in light of the region's recent history.

Contemporary Art in Eastern Europe features a broad range of artists, working in various disciplines—from the realist painting of Polish artist Wilhelm Sasnal, to the socially historic work of Lithuanian video artist Deimantas Narkevičius; and the infamous performance art of Russian artist

Oleg Kulik, to the Sots Art of Komar and Melamid—all of whom have been included on account of their reputation on the international contemporary art scene, decided upon with the expert guidance of two of the series' advisors Neil Gall and Rut Blees Luxemburg. For each artist we have tried to show a selection of their work that best represents the breadth of their practice—from pieces that have become synonymous with the artist's name, to others that are lesser known. The work is subsequently arranged by medium, rather than country of origin, paying testament to the fluidity of borders and geographical regions that the book looks to highlight, and furthering creative discussion through the juxtaposition of artist's nationalities and works. It must also be mentioned that whilst we have tried to be wholly representative of the region depicted in the map, there have, however, been some omissions—Belarus, Latvia, Montenegro and Macedonia—for the reason that whilst artists from these counties are becoming increasingly prevalent, their presence internationally is yet to be felt. In addition to the artist's profiles, the volume also includes reprints of essays by a number of leading academics in the field that attempt to contextualise the works featured.

Reaching beyond the region's recent history, *Contemporary Art in Eastern Europe* engages in discussion on a subject that has remained largely undocumented; and whilst attempting to present a comprehensive enquiry into a subject such as this remains a difficult task, it is hoped that this survey goes some way in articulating the issues and concerns central to contemporary Eastern European art, providing a platform from which further exchange and debate can be fashioned.

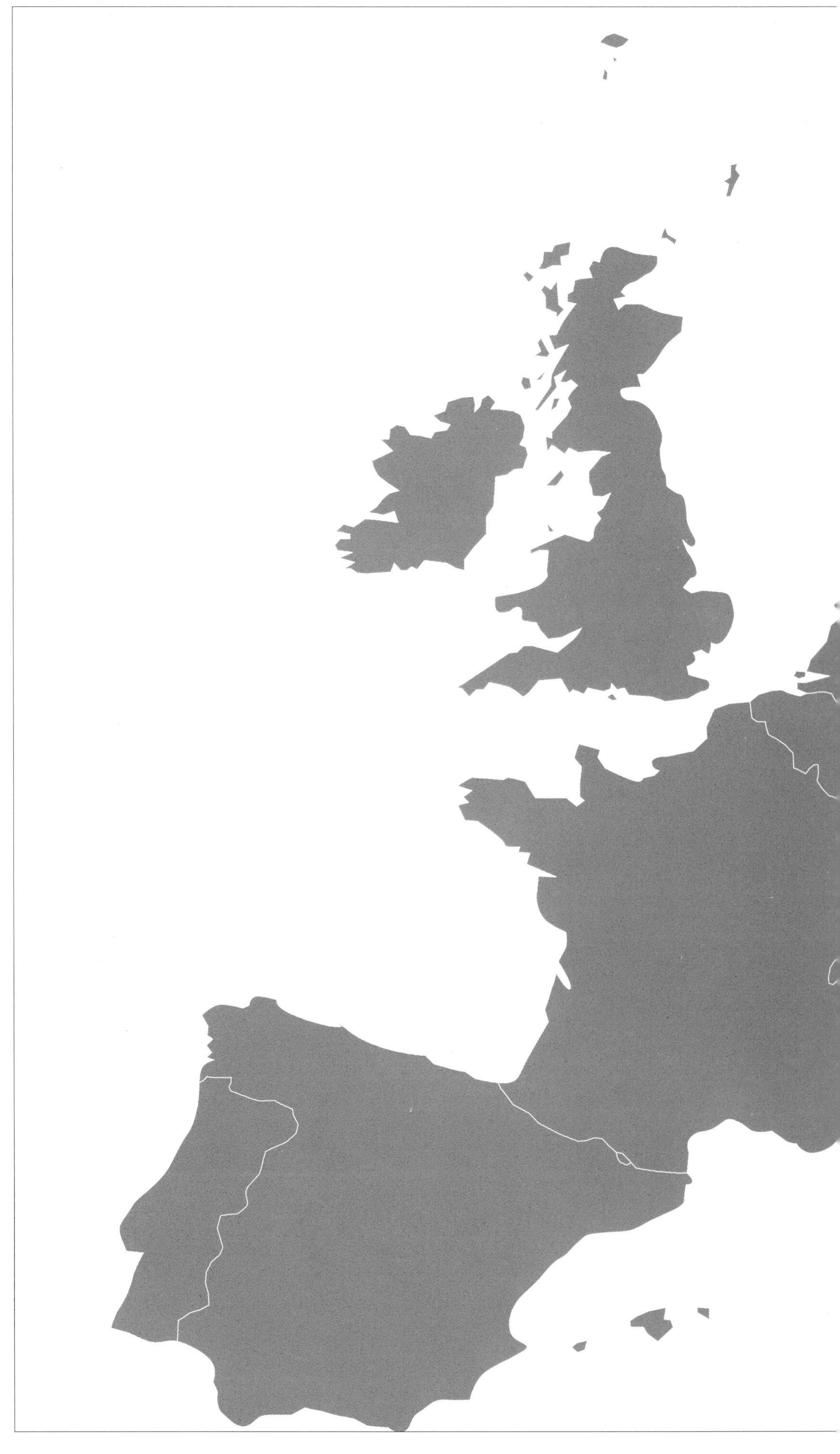

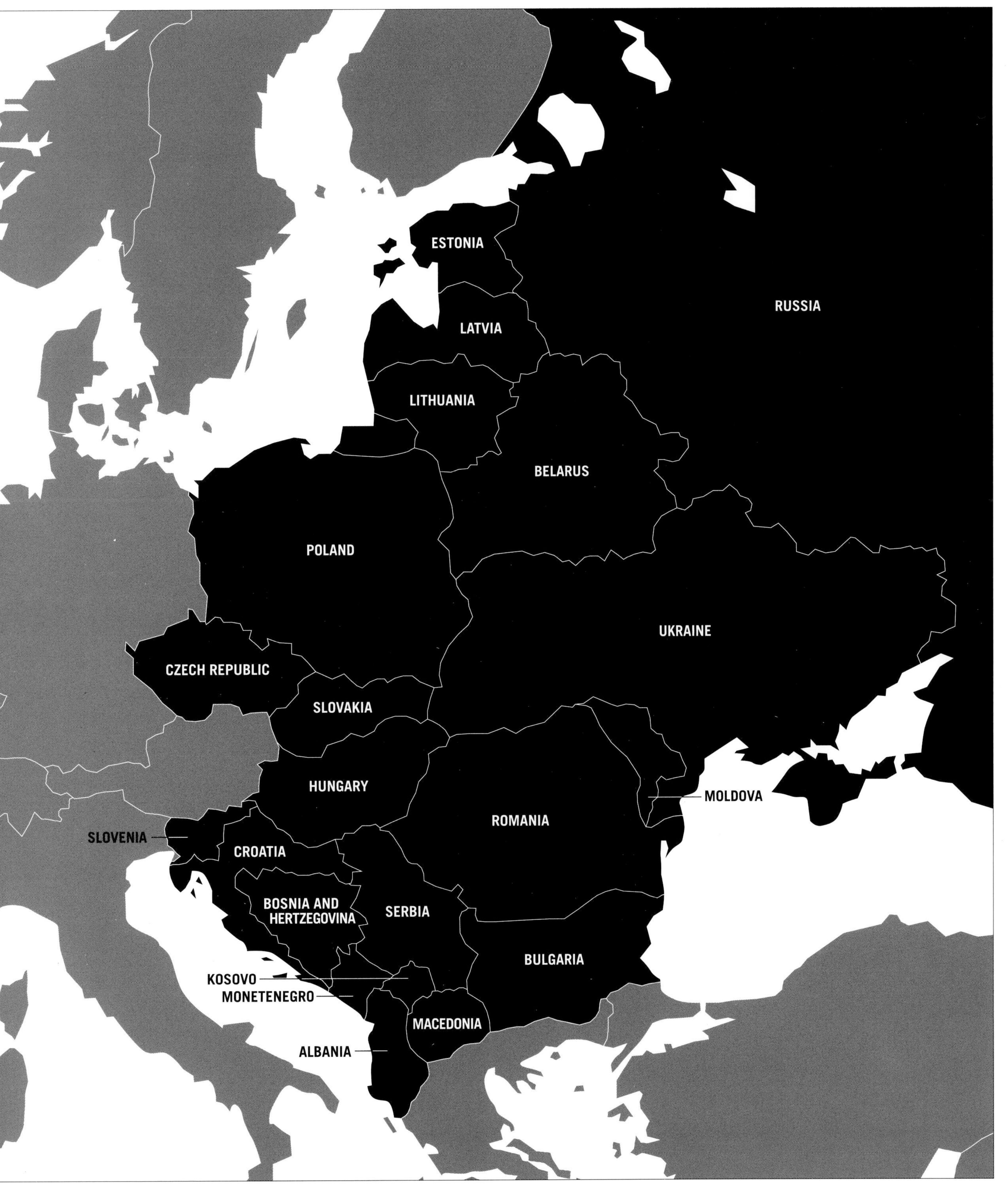

ESTONIA
RUSSIA
LATVIA
LITHUANIA
BELARUS
POLAND
UKRAINE
CZECH REPUBLIC
SLOVAKIA
HUNGARY
MOLDOVA
SLOVENIA
ROMANIA
CROATIA
BOSNIA AND
HERTZEGOVINA
SERBIA
KOSOVO
MONETENEGRO
BULGARIA
MACEDONIA
ALBANIA

TIMELINE

1930s

MAY 1935
—Russian artist Kazimir Malevich, pioneer of the Avant-Garde Suprematist movement, dies aged 57.

MAY 1937
—Eastern European countries are given sections at the Paris International Exhibition for the first time.

SEPTEMBER 1939
—Nazi Germany invades Poland.

OCTOBER 1939
—The Soviet Union invades Poland.
—Poland annexed by Germany and the Soviet Union.

1940s

SEPTEMBER 1940
—Germany, the Soviet Union and Japan sign the Tripartite Pact. Consequently joined by Hungary, Romania, Slovakia, Bulgaria over the following year.

APRIL 1943
—Warsaw Ghetto Uprising in Poland.

AUGUST 1943
—Warsaw Uprising in Poland.

NOVEMBER 1943
—Socialist Federal Republic of Yugoslavia established.

APRIL 1945
—Hitler commits suicide.

MAY 1945
—Germany surrenders to Western Allies and the Soviet Union.

JULY 1945
—Potsdam Conference. Germany is divided into four military occupation zones controlled by Britain, France, the Soviet Union and the USA.

AUGUST 1947
—The Academy of Arts of the Soviet Union is created.

MAY 1949
—The Federal Republic of Germany is established in West Germany.

OCTOBER 1949
—The German Democratic Republic is established in East Germany.

1950s

JULY 1950
—The first Documenta exhibition of contemporary art is held in Kassel, Germany.

MARCH 1953
—Joseph Stalin dies.

MAY 1955
—The Warsaw Pact is established between the Soviet Union, Poland, East Germany, Czechoslovakia, Hungary, Romania, Bulgaria, and Albania.

OCTOBER 1956
—Władysław Gomułka, leader of the Polish United Workers' Party, comes to power in Poland, ending the era of Stalinisation.
—Hungarian Revolution.

NOVEMBER 1956
—Soviet forces invade Hungary and quash the Revolution.

OCTOBER 1957
—The Soviet Union launch the world's first Earth-orbiting satellite.

1960s

APRIL 1961
—The Soviet Union sends the first man into space, Major Yuri Alexeyevich Gagarin.

JUNE 1961
—Soviet ballet dancer Rudolf Nureyev defects to the West.

AUGUST 1961
—East Germany closes frontier between East and West Berlin and erects the Berlin wall.

DECEMBER 1961
—The Soviet Union severs relations with Albania.

JANUARY 1962
—Soviet-Cuban trade treaty signed.

NOVEMBER 1962
—Aleksandr Solzhenitsyn's *One Day in the Life of Ivan Denisovich* is published.

JUNE 1963
—The Soviet Union sends the first woman into space, Lieutenant Valentina Tereshkova.

OCTOBER 1964
—Leonid Brezhnev replaces Kliment Voroshilov as leader of the Soviet Union.

MARCH 1965
—Soviet Cosmonaut Alexei Leonov becomes the first man to walk in space.

APRIL 1966
—Soviet spacecraft orbits the moon.
—The Foksal Gallery, Warsaw, Poland, opens.

DECEMBER 1967
—Nicolae Ceauşescu becomes President of Romania.

JANUARY 1968
—Alexander Dubček becomes leader of Czechoslovakia, marking the beginning of the "Prague Spring", a period of reform and political liberalisation.

AUGUST 1968
—Warsaw Pact tanks and troops invade Czechoslovakia.

APRIL 1968
—Gustáv Husák replaces Alexander Dubček as leader of Czechoslovakia.

SEPTEMBER 1968
—Albania formally withdraws from the Warsaw Pact.

NOVEMBER 1968
—At the fifth congress of the Polish United Worker's Party, Brezhnev outlines what will come to be known as the Brezhnev Doctrine, justifying Soviet military involvement in the affairs of constituent Eastern Bloc countries.

1970s

DECEMBER 1970
—Dissident Soviet author Alexandr Solzhenitsyn wins the Nobel Prize for Literature.

JULY 1971
—Josip Broz Tito is re-elected as the President of Yugoslavia.

AUGUST 1972
—20th Olympic Games is held in Munich.

AUGUST 1975
—35 states, including the USA, Canada, and all European states, except Albania and Andorra, sign the Helsinki Accord in an attempt to improve relations between the Eastern Bloc and the West.

SPRING 1976
—The first edition of American art and theory journal *October* is published.

OCTOBER 1978
—The Archbishop of Kraków, Karol Wojtyła, is elected Pope, taking the name John Paul II.

NOVEMBER 1978
—The Soviet Union signs a 25-year friendship treaty with Vietnam.

DECEMBER 1978
—Polish author Isaac Bashevis Singer wins the Nobel Prize for Literature.

JUNE 1979
—US President Jimmy Carter and Soviet Leader Leonid Brezhnev sign Strategic Arms Limitation Talks II treaty.

1980s

MAY 1980
—Josip Broz Tito dies. A presidency of nine members assumes power.

SEPTEMBER 1980
—Founding of the Independent Self-Governing Trade Union of Solidarity in Poland, with Lech Wałęsa elected as its chairman.

NOVEMBER 1982
—Soviet leader Leonid Brezhnev dies.

JULY 1984
—Soviet Cosmonaut Svetlana Saitkaya becomes the first woman to walk in space.

MARCH 1985
—Mikhail Gorbachev is elected Leader of the Soviet Union.

APRIL 1985
—Albania's Communist leader Elver Hoxha dies.

NOVEMBER 1985
—Mikhail Gorbachev and Ronald Reagan hold the Geneva summit.

APRIL 1986
—Fire breaks out at the Chernobyl Nuclear Power Plant in the Ukraine, causing massive radioactive fallout to spread across much of Europe.

FEBRUARY 1987
—Scandal breaks out when a poster designed by artist collective Neue Slowenische Kunst for the Yugoslavian Day of Youth is revealed as an appropriation of a painting by Nazi artist Richard Klein.

MAY 1987
—19 year old West German Mathias Rust flies a single-engine Cessna light aircraft from Helsinki, Finland, through the Soviet Union's air defences and lands in Moscow's Red Square.

JUNE 1987
—Komar and Melamid become the first Russian artists to be invited to exhibit at Documenta 8, Kassel, Germany.

SEPTEMBER 1987
—Reform of the Serbian Constitution.

MARCH 1988
—Marina Abramović and Ulay perform *The Great Wall Walk* along the Great Wall of China.

DECEMBER 1988
—Branko Mikulić's Yugoslavian government resigns.

—A massive earthquake devastates Armenia, killing as many as 100,000 people.

FEBRUARY 1989
—In response to public dissatisfaction the Central Committee of the Hungarian Socialist Worker's Party agree to a multi-party system and the holding of free elections.

MAY 1989
—Slobodan Milošević becomes President of Serbia.

JUNE 1989
—Semi-free elections are held in Poland. General Wojciech Jaruzelski becomes the first President of Poland and Tadeusz Mazowiecki of Solidarity becomes Prime Minister.

OCTOBER 1989
—The ruling Hungarian Socialist Worker's Party change their name to the Hungarian Socialist Party and adopt a new programme advocating social democracy and a free-market economy.
—Inauguration of the Third Republic of Hungary.

NOVEMBER 1989
—Velvet Revolution in Czechoslovakia. The Communist Party of Czechoslovakia announces it will relinquish power and dismantle the single-party state.
—Berlin Wall is opened.

DECEMBER 1989
—Romanian Revolution sweeps Nicolae Ceauşescu from power. He and his wife Elena are caught and executed while trying to flee the country.

DECEMBER 1989
—Dissident playwright Václav Havel is elected President of Czechoslovakia.

DECEMBER 1989
—Mikhail Gorbachev and Ronald Reagan sign arms treaty.

1990s

JANUARY 1990
—The Communist party of Yugoslavia
is dissolved.

FEBRUARY 1990
—The Croatian parliament change laws to
allow a multi-party system.
—The Central Committee of the Communist
Party of the Soviet Union agree to give
up their monopoly of power over Eastern
Bloc countries.

MARCH 1990
—To proceed with reforms opposed by
the majority of the Communist party,
Gorbachev consolidates power into
the new position of President of the
Union of Soviet Socialist Republics
and is elected first Executive President.
—Lithuania declare the restoration
of independence.
—Free elections held in East Germany.
Lothar de Maizière is elected Prime
Minister of the German Democratic
Republic and forms a government
under a policy of expeditious unification
with West Germany.

APRIL 1990
—First free elections held in Croatia.

MAY 1990
—Free elections held in Romania. Ion
Iliescu is elected Head of State with
Petre Roman as Prime Minister.
—Free elections held in Hungary. József
Antall, leader of the Hungarian Democratic
Forum, becomes the first democratically
elected Prime Minister of the Republic
of Hungary.

JUNE 1990
—Russian Soviet Federative Socialist
Republic declare State Sovereignty.
—Free elections held in Czechoslovakia.

JULY 1990
—The Ukrainian parliament issues
a Declaration of State Sovereignty
of Ukraine.
—The Belarusian government issues a
Declaration of State Sovereignty of the
Belarusian Soviet Socialist Republic.

OCTOBER 1990
—East and West German states
enter into a formal political union.
The German Democratic Republic is
dissolved into five states, which
become part of the Federal Republic
of Germany.
—Free elections are held in Georgia.
Zviad Gamsakhurdia becomes head of
the Supreme Council of the Republic
of Georgia.

DECEMBER 1990
—German Federal Election. Richard
von Weizsäcker becomes first President
of reunified Germany.
—Milošević wins first Serbian multi-party
election for President.
—Jaruzelski resigns as Poland's President
and is succeeded by Lech Wałęsa.

JUNE 1991
—Slovenia declares independence
from Yugoslavia.

JUNE 1991
—Boris Yeltsin is elected President of the

Russian Soviet Federative Socialist
Republic (no longer the Soviet Union).

JULY 1991
—Czechoslovakian president Václav Havel
formally ends the 1955 Treaty of Friendship,
Cooperation and Mutual Assistance, and
so disestablishes the Warsaw Pact.

AUGUST 1991
—Moldova declares independence.
—Estonia declares independence.

OCTOBER 1991
—Croatia declares independence
from Yugoslavia.

DECEMBER 1991
—The Soviet Union is dissolved into a
Commonwealth of Independent States.
—Gorbachev resigns as President of
the Union of Soviet Socialist Republics,
declaring the office extinct and ceding
all its remaining powers to the President
of Russia, Boris Yeltsin.

JUNE 1992
—IRWIN perform *Black Square on Red
Square*, covering Red Square, Moscow,
with a square black cloth.

MARCH 1992
—Beginning of the Bosnian War.

APRIL 1992
—Formal end of Socialist Federal Republic
of Yugoslavia. Proclamation of a new
constitution for Federal Republic of
Yugoslavia, which consists of Serbia
and Montenegro.

1990s

JANUARY 1993
—Czechoslovakia is separated into the Czech Republic and Slovak Republic.

SEPTEMBER 1993
—In a struggle for power and disagreements over economic reform, Yeltsin dissolves the Russia's legislature, initiating the Russian Constitutional Crisis.

MAY 1994
—The Europa, Europa exhibition opens at the Kunst-und Ausstellungshalle, Bonn.

OCTOBER 1994
—Helmut Kohl is re-elected as Chancellor of Germany.

DECEMBER 1994
—Beginning of the First Chechen War.

AUGUST 1995
—NATO bombing campaign in Bosnia and Herzegovina.

FEBRUARY 1996
—Opening of the Interpol Exhibition at the Färgfabriken Center for Contemporary Art and Architecture, Stockholm, where Alexander Brener and Oleg Kulik infamously destroyed other artists work.

JUNE 1996
—Manifesta, the new European Art biennale is held in Rotterdam.

JANUARY 1997
—Widespread unrest in Albania after the collapse of the economy due to a financial system dominated by Ponzi schemes and pyramid investment funds.

JULY 1998
—Opening of the Body and the East exhibition at the Moderna Galerija, Slovenia.

AUGUST 1998
—Russian Financial Crisis: Russian stock, bond and currency markets collapse.

MARCH 1999
—The Czech Republic, Hungary and Poland join NATO.
—NATO bombing of Yugoslavia.

AUGUST 1999
—Beginning of the Second Chechen War.

OCTOBER 1999
—One of the first comprehensive contemporary Eastern European art exhibitions—After the Wall: Art and Culture in post-Communist Europe—opens at the Moderna Museet, Stockholm.

DECEMBER 1999
—Yeltsin resigns from the Russian Presidency. Vladimir Putin is named acting President.

2000s

MARCH 2000
—Vladimir Putin wins the Russian Presidential Election.

OCTOBER 2002
—Chechen separatists take over a Moscow theatre with over 700 people inside demanding the immediate withdrawal of Russian forces from Chechnya.

FEBRUARY 2003
—The Federal Republic of Yugoslavia is reconstituted as the State Union of Serbia and Montenegro.

APRIL 2003
—Treaty of Accession signed; Czech Republic, Estonia, Cyprus, Latvia, Lithuania, Hungary, Malta, Poland, Slovenia and Slovakia enter the European Union.

APRIL 2004
—Bulgaria, Estonia, Latvia, Lithuania, Romania, Slovakia and Slovenia join NATO.

NOVEMBER 2005
—Angela Merkel becomes the first female Chancellor of Germany.

JUNE 2006
—Montenegro declares independence.

JULY 2006
—Serbia declares independence, thus ending the State Union of Serbia and Montenegro.

JANUARY 2007
—Bulgaria and Romania join the
European Union.

JUNE 2007
—American President George W Bush
visits Albania, the first sitting US
President to do so.

FEBRUARY 2008
—Kosovo declare independence from Serbia.

AUGUST 2008
—Georgia clash with Russia, South
Ossetia and Abkhazia in the South
Ossetian War.

SEPTEMBER 2008
—Polish artist Goshka Macuga is
nominated for the Turner Prize for
her solo exhibition Objects in Relation,
Art Now at the Tate Britain and her
contribution to the 5th Berlin Biennial
for Contemporary Art.

APRIL 2009
—Albania and Croatia join NATO.

MAY 2009
—Russian and Eastern European
contemporary art gallery Calvert 22
opens in London.

OCTOBER 2009
—Mirosław Bałka's *How It Is* opens at
the Tate Modern's Turbine Hall, London.

NOVEMBER 2009
—Jeanne-Claude Denat de Guillebon of
Christo and Jeanne-Claude dies aged 74.

MARCH 2010
—Marina Abramović retrospective 'The
Artist is Present' opens at The Museum
of Modern Art, New York.

APRIL 2010
—Regina Gallery London opens
specialising in Russian art.

ESSAY

HAUNTED BY COMMUNISM
BORIS GROYS

Anyone wishing to speak about present day Eastern European art has no choice but to once again take sides on the inevitable question: can this art be said to possess a distinctive character? Is it possible to speak about Eastern European art as a cultural phenomenon that crosses the borders of individual national cultures and unifies, to a certain degree, the Eastern European cultural space—being at the same time distinctive from the art of other regions? Indeed, the Eastern European cultural space is extremely heterogeneous. Historically, there is not so much common ground between, let's say, Estonian, Hungarian or Albanian cultures. Their ethnic roots, languages and cultural traditions do not unite, but separate them from each other. In fact, there is only one cultural experience that unites all Eastern European countries and at the same time differentiates them from the outer world—it is the experience of Communism of the Soviet type. The notion of Eastern Europe is a legacy of the Cold War. Now, many observers inside and outside Eastern Europe argue that this legacy should be forgotten and erased—so that Eastern European countries can return to their individual cultural identities that were violently suppressed by the Communist rule.

And, indeed, frequently the impression arises that Communism, now defunct, represented nothing more that a temporary interruption to the continuous 'normal' development of Eastern European countries—an interruption which, once it was over, left no traces other than a certain appetite to 'make up for lost time'. Seen from this perspective, Communism appears once again as the spectre of Communism that at some point in time simply evaporated into thin air. This effect of the disappearance of Communism is, actually, quite understandable. The Communist Movement was—and still is—an international one. This international character of the Communist event explains why in the context of any individual national history it can be treated as a mere pause or interruption.

Every historical event is within a particular history which requires a protagonist if it is to be narrated. Today we are still living in a system of nation states—our historiography can only function as a narrative if its protagonist is a nation or a nation state; the history of mankind manifests itself merely as the sum of all national histories. So for us, an event only becomes historical once it can be narrated as an episode in the history of a nation. Communism, on the other hand, was not only programmatically international but, actually, anti-national. Its aim was to overcome traditional national differences, to do away with existing national cultural identities and in their place foster a new, global, Communist humanity as the protagonist of a new history. But this new post-national humanity never came about—or rather it dissolved at the same time as Communism did. The event of Communism lost its historical subject, the historical protagonist to whose history it could have belonged.

Hence, a positivist, realistic historiography aspiring to grapple with concrete facts and not spectres finds no place for Communism as such. Instead, it generally prefers to proclaim Communism as a mere facade intended as a camouflage for solid national interests. Accordingly, it has now become characteristic for historical narratives dealing with the recent Eastern European history to treat Communism simply as an ideological facade for Russian imperialism. During the last years this perspective was increasingly adopted also by Russian historiography. Thus, the event of Eastern European Communism came to be gradually nationalised—as a part of Russian national history. At first glance, this development let the Communist event appear as something obsolete and irrelevant for contemporary art practices. And, indeed, there is a strong tendency in all the Eastern European countries, including Russia, to interpret their contemporary art practices solely in terms of individual cultural traditions and identities— ignoring their common ground in the Communist past.

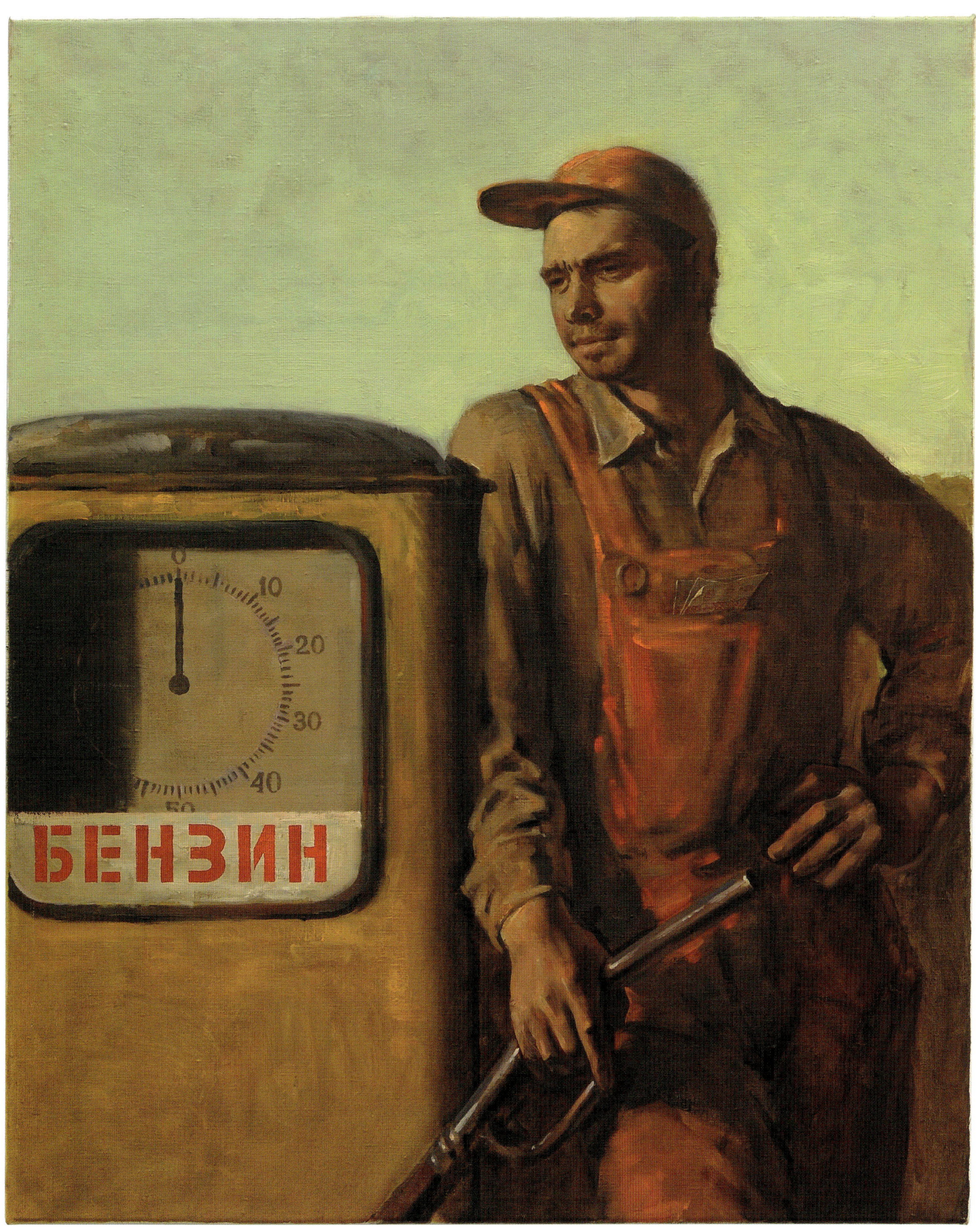
0
10
20
30
40
50
БЕНЗИН

However, at the same time this Communist past increasingly haunts Eastern European and Russian art. The reason for that development is the increasing internalisation of Eastern European art. Indeed, the end of the cultural isolation caused by the Cold War led to the inclusion of Eastern European art within the global art context—a process mediated primarily by the art market, from which the commercialisation and commodification of Eastern European art became the most immediate result of the end of the Cold War. In fact, the emergence and growing dominance of the art market was a traumatic experience for many Eastern European artists. One should not forget that during the period of Communist rule there was no art market in Eastern Europe—because under Socialism there was no market at all. Many generations of Russian artists and some generations of the Eastern European artists operated beyond the art market—under the regime of production, evaluation and distribution of art that was non-commercial but ideological. Indeed, under the Communist regime the value of a work of art was determined not by the rules of the market economy but by the rules of the symbolic economy that governed life under the Socialism of the Soviet type. They were rules of social recognition and political relevance as formulated by the official ideology that determined the value of every work of art. And this was not only true for the officially supported art. It was also true for unofficial, dissident, oppositional, critical art. Its value was also an ideological value. One can say that the ideological value circulated in the symbolic economy of the Soviet type just as money circulates in the Western market economy. Now, the memory of this non-commercial mode of art existence is still fresh in Eastern Europe—and that maybe constitutes the most obvious specificity of Eastern European art. Even now, two decades since the fall of the Berlin Wall, Eastern European art remains ideologically charged in a way in which Western art does not.

But, of course, the protest against the laws of the art market and the commercialisation of art was and still is *lingua franca* of the whole of international and, especially, Western art throughout its modern history—and also now. The most successful avant-garde and neo-avant-garde artistic movements were initially motivated by the rejection of the art market and the system of preferences that was imposed by it. But, of course, the art market, notwithstanding all the protests, remained the only functioning mechanism for evaluation and distribution of art in the West. Its power was many times criticised but never really challenged. Thus, one can say, that on the international contemporary art scene only Eastern Europeans and Russian artists have historical memories of non-Capitalist, non-market modes of art production. These memories are not always positive ones. But at the same time they have complexity and depth that utopian abstractions are lacking. Thus, the globalisation of Eastern art means not only its submission under the rules of the international art market but also a reactualisation of the experiences of its Socialist past. That makes it inevitable and at the same time justified to speak about Eastern European art in the first place as a post-Communist art. Of course, such a strategy leaves many developments in various Eastern European countries unmentioned and undescribed—especially, in respect to their specific national identities. But on the other hand, it offers the only possibility to speak about Eastern European art as a whole—as a unified and at the same time distinctive phenomenon.

In a certain way the current art situation, not only in Eastern Europe, but everywhere in the world, reminds the spectator of the beginning of the nineteenth century. After the end of the French Revolution and Napoleonic wars, Europe came to a certain stability and peace—under the conditions of a partial restoration of the pre-revolutionary modes of life. The age of political transformations and ideological battles seemed to be finally overcome. At that historical moment the Romantic artistic movement that emerged throughout the whole European continent became a 'place' where utopias were dreamt, revolutionary traumata were remembered and alternative life projects were lived. Today the art scene is a place of emancipatory projects, participative practices, radical political attitudes but also a place of memories of the social catastrophes and disappointments of the revolutionary twentieth century. In this context Eastern European art plays an important role because this revolutionary past is its own past. Just as the demise of Eastern European Socialist regimes left a vast territory and resources for private appropriation, the simultaneous death of Socialist humanity left a vast empire of feelings, a huge emotional estate released for individual artistic appropriation.

Now, these post-Communist feelings are highly ambivalent. For the post-Communist artists the socialist alternative is not only a utopian, idyllic dream projected into the future but also a nostalgic and simultaneously traumatic memory of their recent past. For the Romantic poets of the nineteenth century—from Byron to Goethe—a project of self-liberation mostly took the form of contract with Lucifer, the Devil, or Satan. The revolt against the restoration of the *ancien regime* is mixed here with the memory of the Revolutionary terror. In the same vein, today's artistic visions of emancipatory alternative are utopian and dystopian at the same time. Thus, Pavel Pepperstein combines in his recent series of drawings and paintings under the general title *Gorod Rossiya*, translated as "Russia City", the non-objective, abstract forms taken from the repertoire of the Russian avant-garde art with the images of human faces— creating modern centaurs consisting of non-objective, evolutionised, transformed bodies and pretty traditional- looking human heads. These series can be understood as proof that Pepperstein does not believe in the 'organic' resolution of the conflict between new humanity and 'old' individuality. The project of cohabitation between abstract forms and human faces reveals itself as utopian and dystopian at the same time: one does not know if the human heads are attached to the non-objective bodies and thus constitute a utopian promise of a new humanity or simply float in the empty space being cut from the organic bodies and left to die.

In a different way the same ambivalence of the utopian desire is demonstrated by Artur Żmijewski in his videotaped performance *Them*, 2007. Members of four different political groups, representative of today's Polish political landscape, are put in the same space where they are invited to express their ideological convictions by means of art. Thus, Żmijewski puts his protagonists in the utopian situation of being able to manifest their convictions solely by means of artistic creativity. But this utopian situation reveals itself as being liberating and destructive at the same time. The common artistic creative practice does not unite these groups but, rather, more

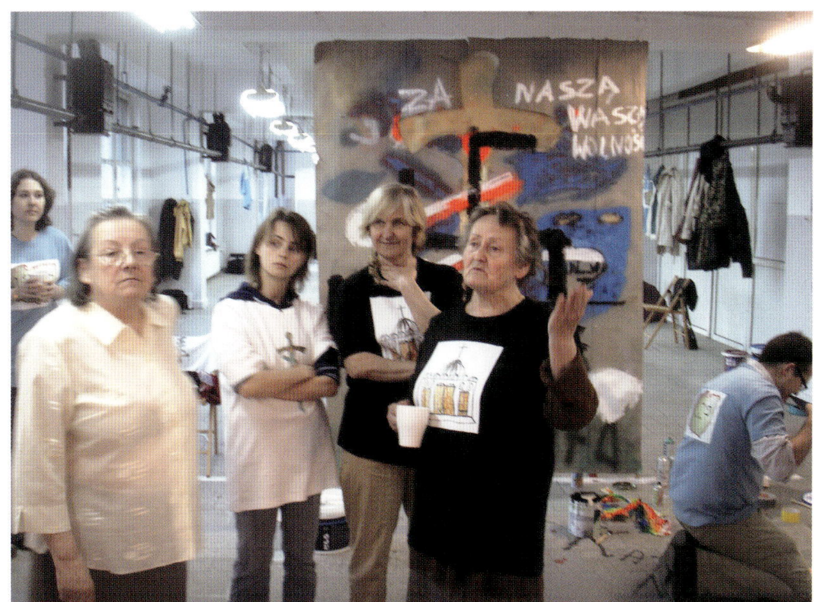

Once in the XXth Century
**2004, video beta cam SP film transferred
to DVD, 8 minutes**
Courtesy gb agency, Paris and Jan Mot, Brussels

radically, separates them from each other—so that the
whole project of expression and liberation through
art ends in complete disarray. Here again contradictions
remain unresolved—and the attempt to resolve them
looks utopian and dystopian at the same time. The same
ambivalence is demonstrated in a very elegant way by
Deimantas Narkevičius in his video *Once in the XXth Century*,
2004, in which the removal of a Lenin statue in Vilnius after
1991 is shown in reverse—so that the joyful crowd seems to
celebrate the installation of the statue and not its removal.

These examples also indicate an answer to an often-
formulated question concerning the originality of Eastern
European art. Time and again, one hears the same question:
is the art of Eastern Europe original or is it simply a sum of
imitations and repetitions of artistic trends that originally
emerged in the West? Now, if this question expresses the
suspicion that Eastern European artists began to work "like
in the West" after the fall of the Berlin Wall so as to be able
to achieve a success on the international art market, then
the answer is simply no. Contemporary Eastern European
and Russian artists work in a tradition of their own
avant-gardes of the first half of the twentieth century—but
also in the tradition of the alternative, unofficial, neo-avant-
garde art that emerged in these countries immediately after
the death of Stalin, e.g. already in the middle of the 1950s.
In the Soviet Union all the important Russian artists of
the older generation began to work in the late 1950s. They
had a restricted audience and reduced public visibility,
but they could work independently. The conditions for the
artists in Yugoslavia, Poland or Hungary were even more
comfortable. That means that neo-Modern and neo-avant-
garde trends in Russian and Eastern European art had
already emerged under Socialist conditions—without and
beyond the art market in the Western sense of this word.
And these artistic practices were developed for a long time
under these conditions, and these were quite different
from those of the West. One should not forget: the divisions
of the Cold War interrupted the flows of information from
both sides of the Iron Curtain, leaving Eastern European
art in a particularly isolated position that meant it was not
officially supported and therefore popularised. To properly
understand contemporary Eastern European art, one has
to know its genealogies reaching back into the 1950s and

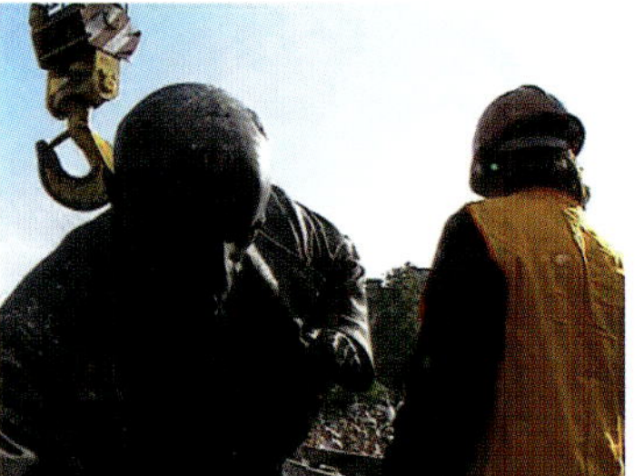
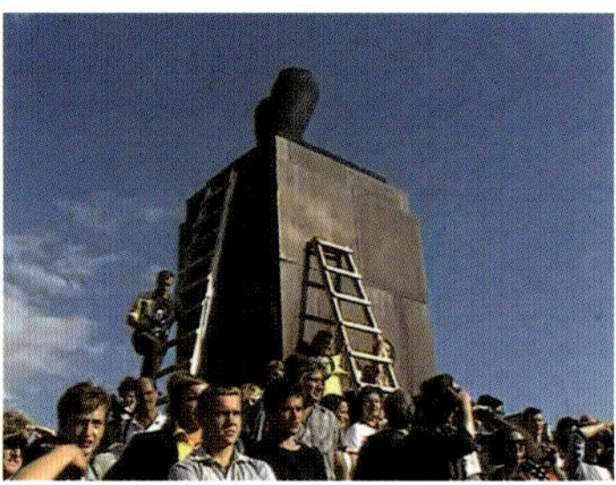
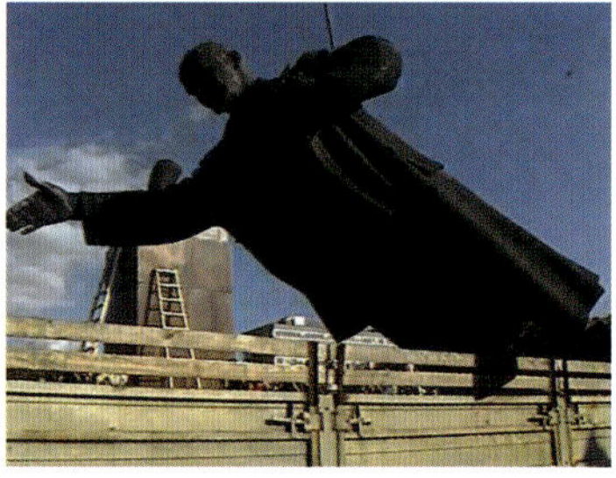
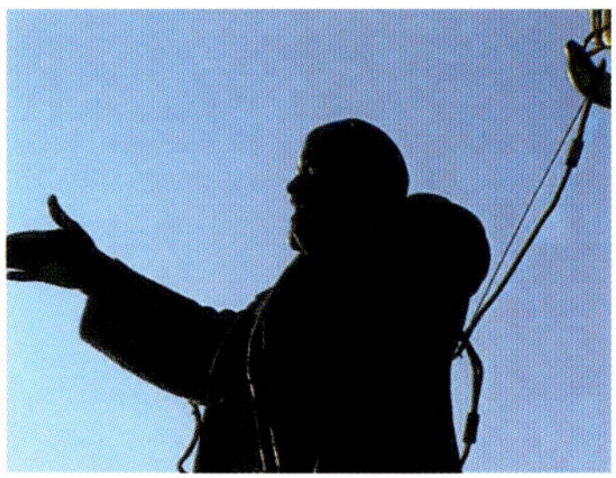
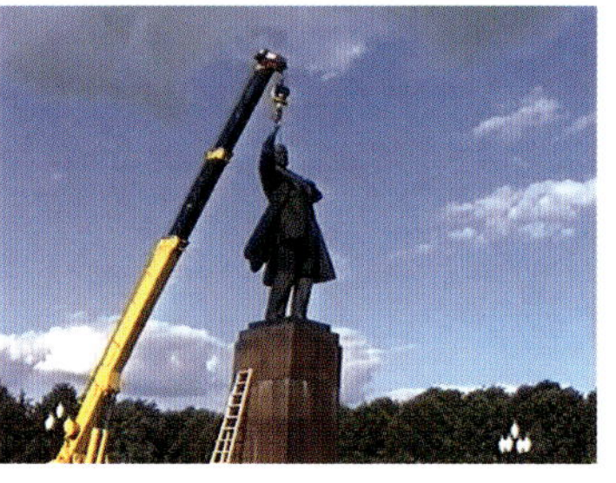

1960s. Until these genealogies become fully investigated and accessible to the international art community Eastern European art is doomed to remain *terra incognita* for its external spectators.

It is true that the initial impulse for the emergence of the Eastern European neo-avant-gardes of the 1950s and 1960s came from the West. But this impulse was understood precisely as a license for non-imitation of Western art. Indeed, traditional modernism pursued the ideal of a trans-cultural, autonomous artwork. As long as non-Western, including Russian and Eastern European, artists shared this pursuit they were condemned to remain secondary and imitative in relationship to the history of Western modernist art. The situation changed as Western art itself betrayed this modernist ideal. American Pop Art was the most radical manifestation of this betrayal. It abandoned the universality of Abstract Expressionism and became interested in the specificity of American mass culture. In this way, American Pop Art signalled to the artists from other parts of the world that they could also abandon their imitative pursuit of the modernist ideal—and turn for inspiration to their own national, social and political contexts. In this sense the imitation of the West became—for Russian, but also for many of Eastern European artists—an imitation of non-imitation.

Already at the beginning of the 1970s Russian artists such as Vitali Komar and Alexander Melamid, Ilya Kabakov and Erik Bulatov began using the framework of their own artistic practice, images and texts of official Soviet propaganda. This use was neither explicitly critical, nor affirmative. Rather, it reflected the decision of the artists to use privately the same visual language that occupied and controlled the public space. If this gesture was critical to a certain degree then this critique was directed against the modernist attitude of 'high art' that prevailed in unofficial Russian dissident art circles of that time. Komar and Melamid characterised their own art as "Sots Art"—referring both to official Soviet Socialist Realism and Western Pop Art. Around the same time Polish artists KwieKulik developed their own version of Sots Art—combining visual signs of Communist propaganda with the performance and installation art of

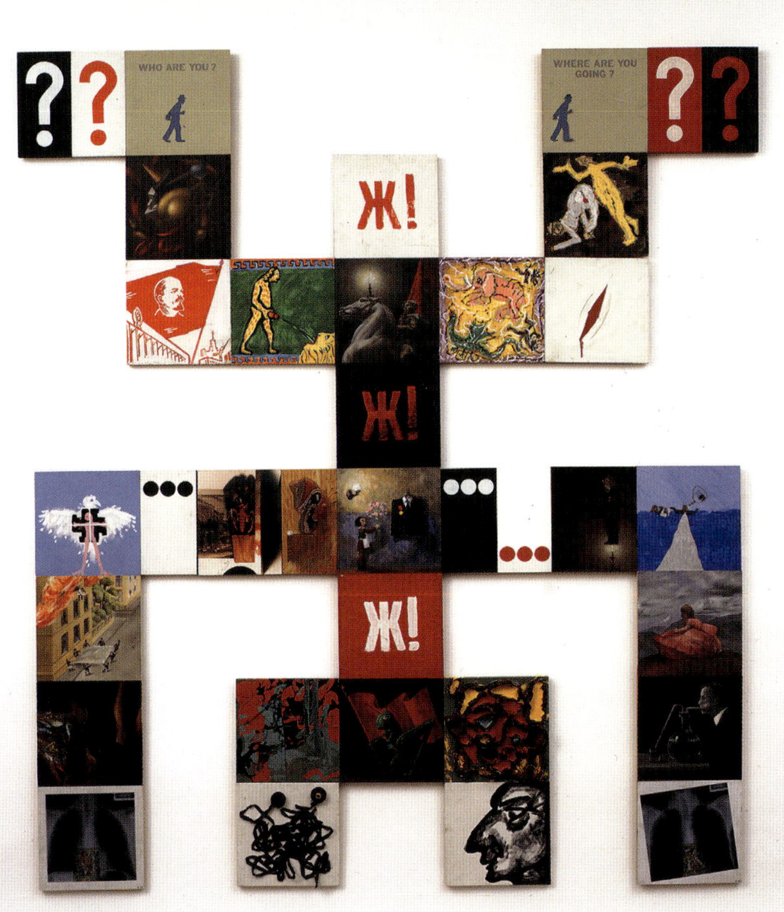

a Western type. Komar and Melamid were quite aware of the fact that their art produced parodistic and blasphemic effects by using the language of the official propaganda outside its own institutional and political context. KwieKulik, instead, wanted to substitute their own version of Sots Art to the language of the official political propaganda—with the goal of updating and modernising this language. But in both cases a certain irony could not be overlooked. For the artists, this irony was a means to distance themselves from the official ideology and, at the same time, to refer to its almost forgotten utopian, avant-gardistic potential. The same ironic attitude to the ideological languages of different types one finds in

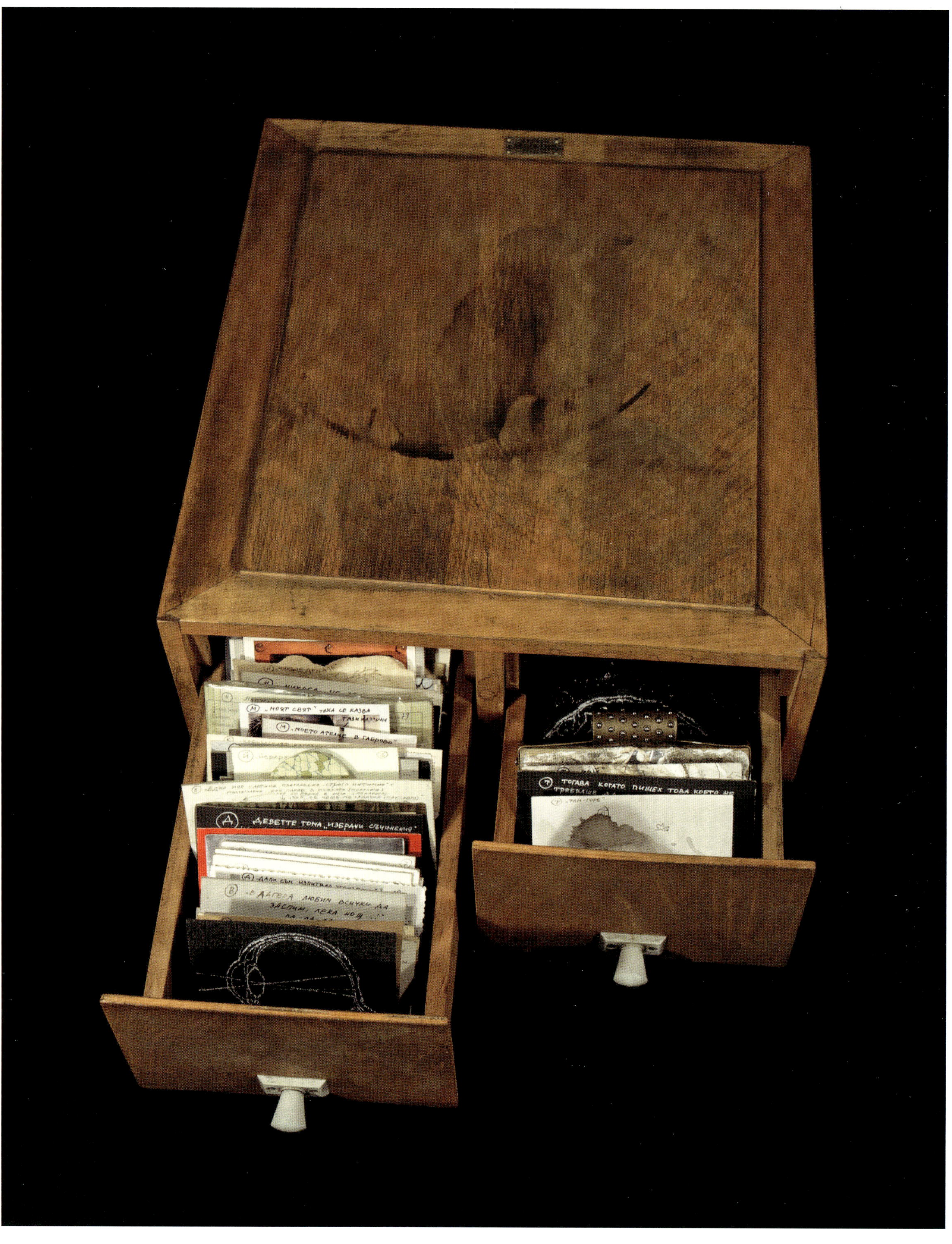

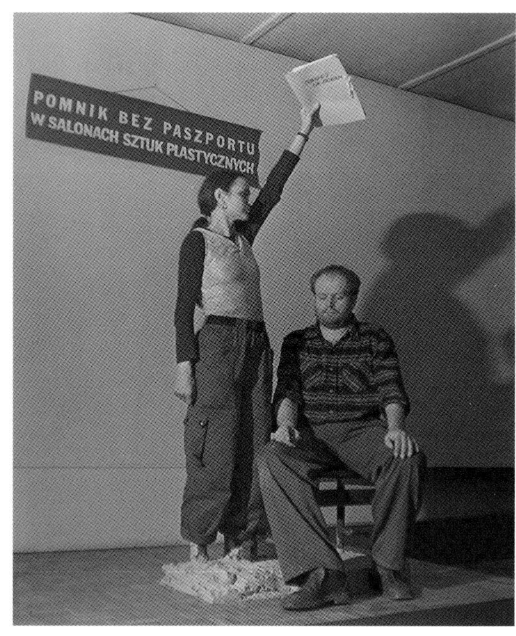

the artistic practice of the Slovenian Irwin group—in their works from the 1970s and 1980s. These ironic attitudes already announce the ambivalent artistic attitudes of the post-Communist period.

Of course, the reaction of contemporary Eastern European artists to their Communist past cannot be reduced to irony and ambivalence; thus, for example, Bulgarian artist Nedko Solakov and Albanian artist Anri Sala thematise the moral dilemmas and responsibilities that they inherited from the past. In his video *Intervista*, 1998, Anri Sala confronts his mother with a record of a speech that she gave during the Communist time that was conforming to the official Party line; and Nedko Solakov in *Top Secret*, 1989–1990, documents a short period of his own collaboration with the Bulgarian secret police as he was a student during Communism. Now, if these artists tend to look at the Communist past through the prism of moral accusation, then other contemporary artists try to remobilise the Communist ideology for the critique of the present capitalist conditions. This is especially characteristic of the Russian artistic groups such as Lifshitz Club—organised by Dmitri Gutov—and the group Chto delat? Or "What is to be done?" These and other artistic groups move from irony and ambivalence toward a revival of the early, pre-Stalinist collectivist, Communist projects. In this case the artists do not so much reflect on the ambivalences of the utopian politics as they attempt to purify it from its historical distortions. But whatever form the artistic reaction to the Communist project and its past realisations take, in every individual case, contemporary Eastern European artists still return to this project when they try to transcend the borders of their particular cultural identities.

1 Groys, Boris, *History Becomes Form: Moscow Conceptualism*, MIT Press, 2010.

2 Ronduda, Lucasz, *Polish Art of the 70s*, Warszawa, 2009, p. 224.

ARTISTS

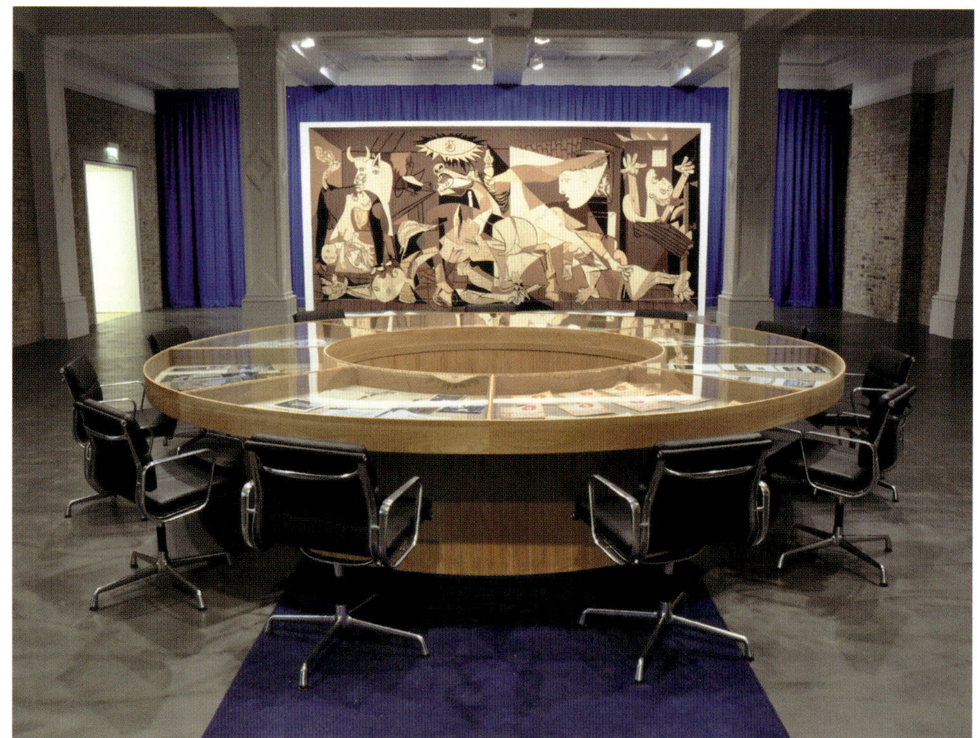

GOSHKA MACUGA

Goshka Macuga's installations evince a purposeful collapsing of the distinctions between artistic and curatorial practice. Often working in response to a particular site, Macuga assembles collections of found objects, archival extracts and works by other artists, creating intelligent and considered organisations that reorientate established meanings, disrupt historical classifications and render alternative narratives intelligible. In so doing, she exercises a command over the produce of culture and history, and fosters space for a multitude of subjective positions.

For her 2007 installation *Objects in Relation*, which earned her a nomination for the Turner Prize the following year, Macuga drew on the archive at Tate Britain, piecing together a survey of the British landscape artist Paul Nash and the group he formed in 1933—Unit One—which included the artists Ben Nicholson, Barbara Hepworth and Henry Moore, amongst others. Rather than renegotiate their art historical position, Macuga focused on extracting a human presence from fragments of a marginalised moment in history. Works by the artists, correspondence between them and other found objects were thus organised to create a sense of the personalities that stood for "the expression of a truly contemporary spirit, for that thing which is recognised as peculiarly today in painting, sculpture and architecture".

The Nature of the Beast, realised in 2009, saw a large, glass-topped, circular conference table installed in the ground floor of London's Whitechapel Gallery, along with a life-size tapestry copy of Pablo Picasso's *Guernica*, previously hung in the United Nations Security Council chamber and famously shrouded when Colin Powell stated his case for the Iraq war. The space thus housed a confluence of histories: as well as referencing the Whitechapel Gallery's 1939 exhibition of the original *Guernica*, Macuga produced a free newspaper that contrasted the content of Picasso's painting with Powell's infamous speech.

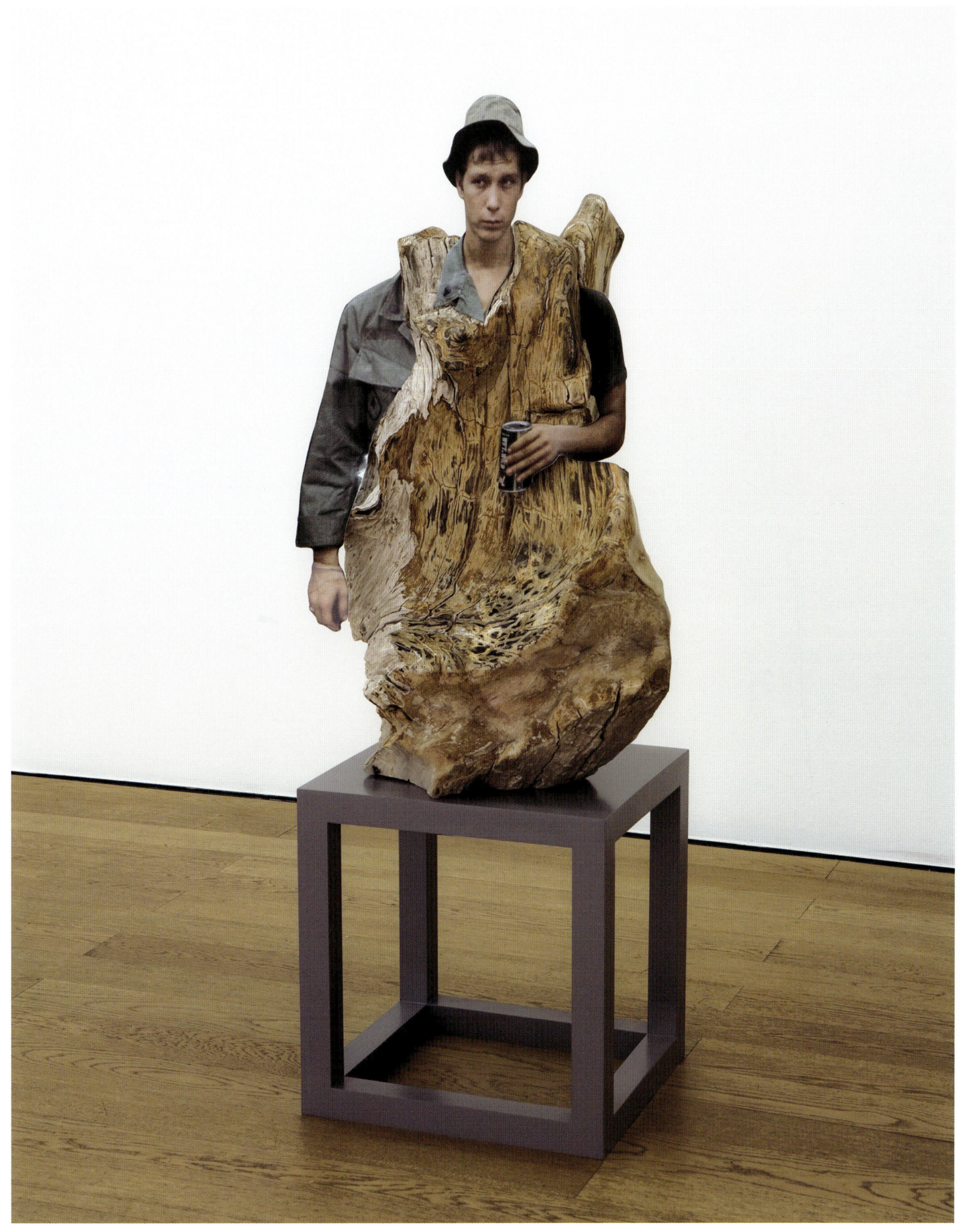

GOSHKA MACUGA
Installation view, Turner Prize 2008, Tate Britain
Courtesy of Kate MacGarry, London, photo: Andy Stagg

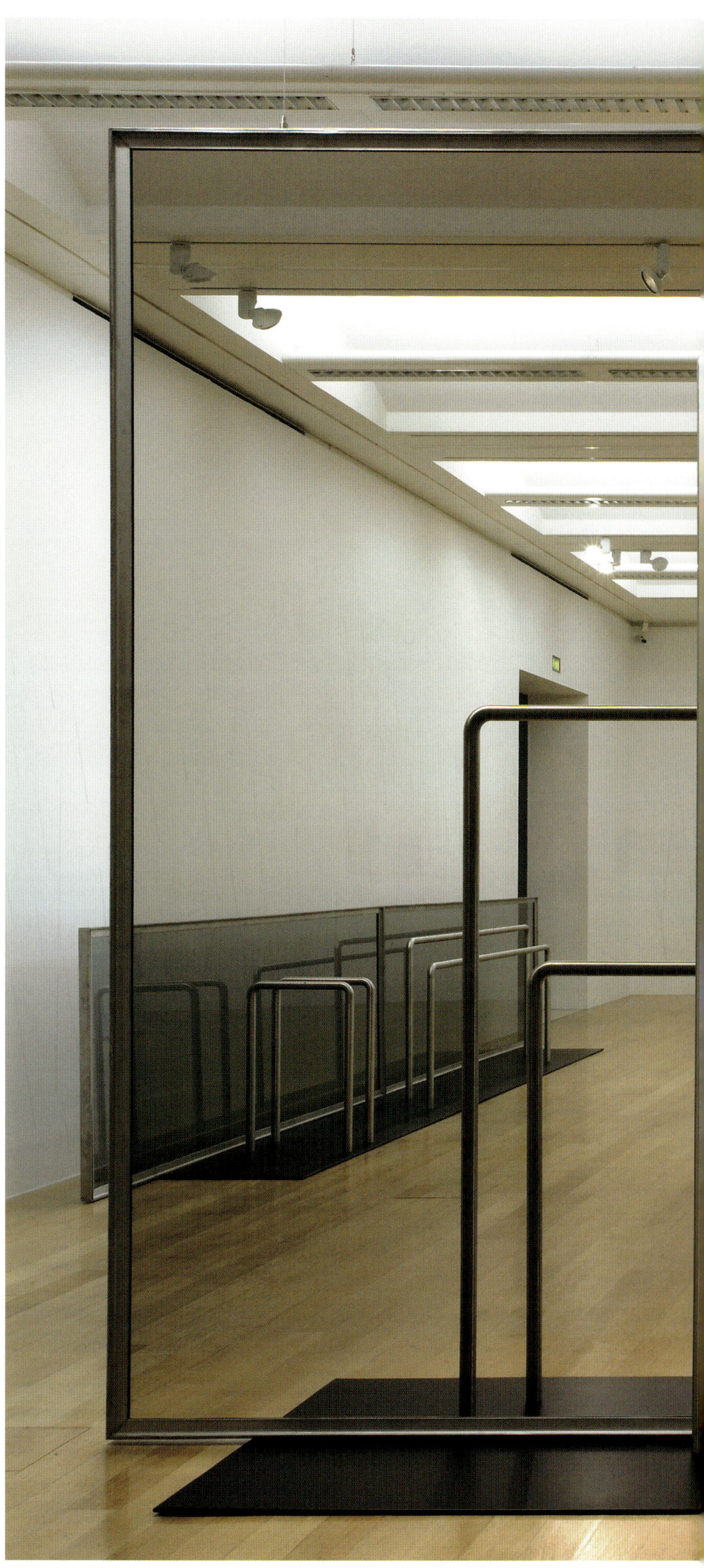

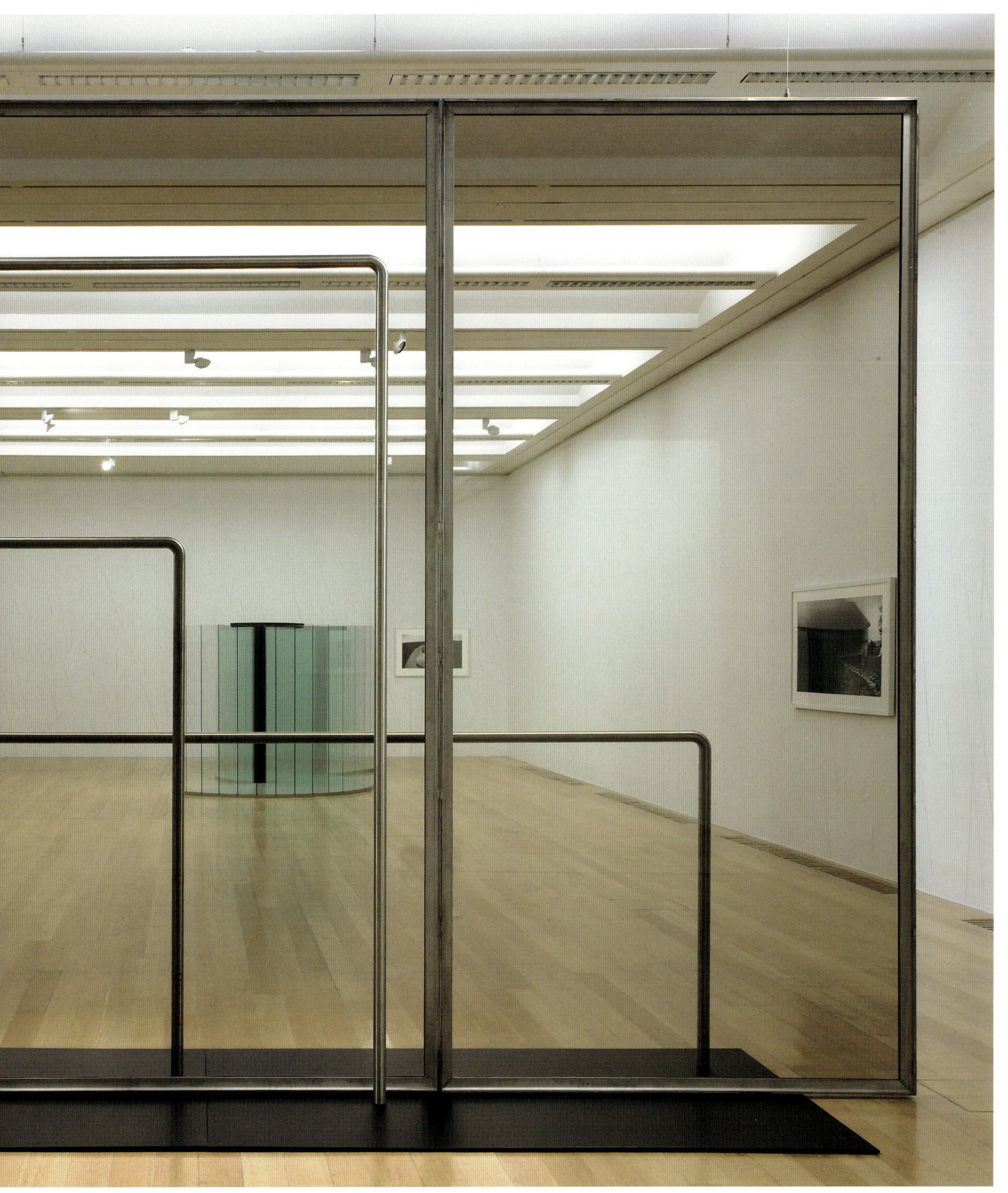

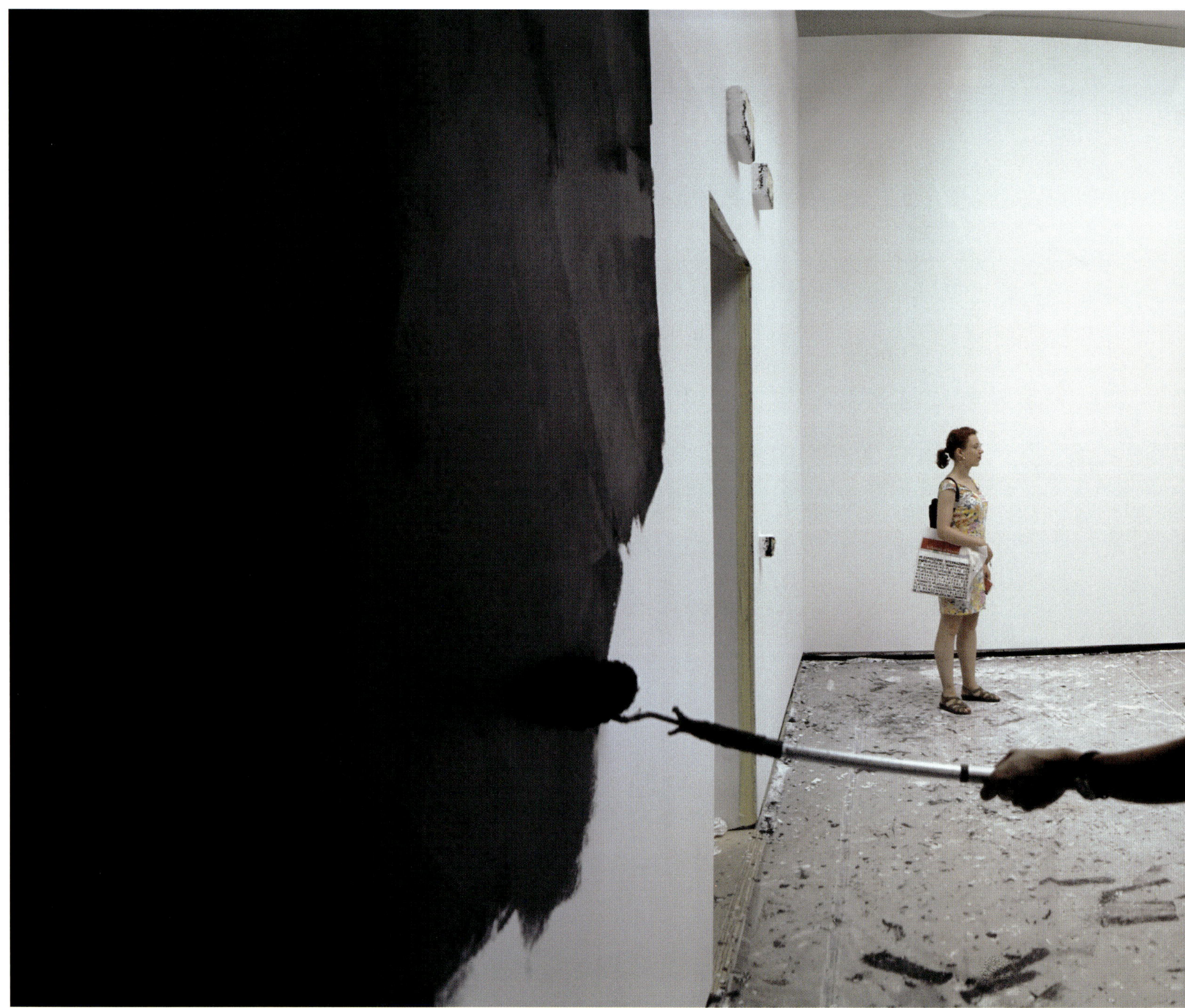

NEDKO SOLAKOV
A Life (Black & White)
1998, black and white paint; two workers/painters
constantly repainting the walls of the exhibition

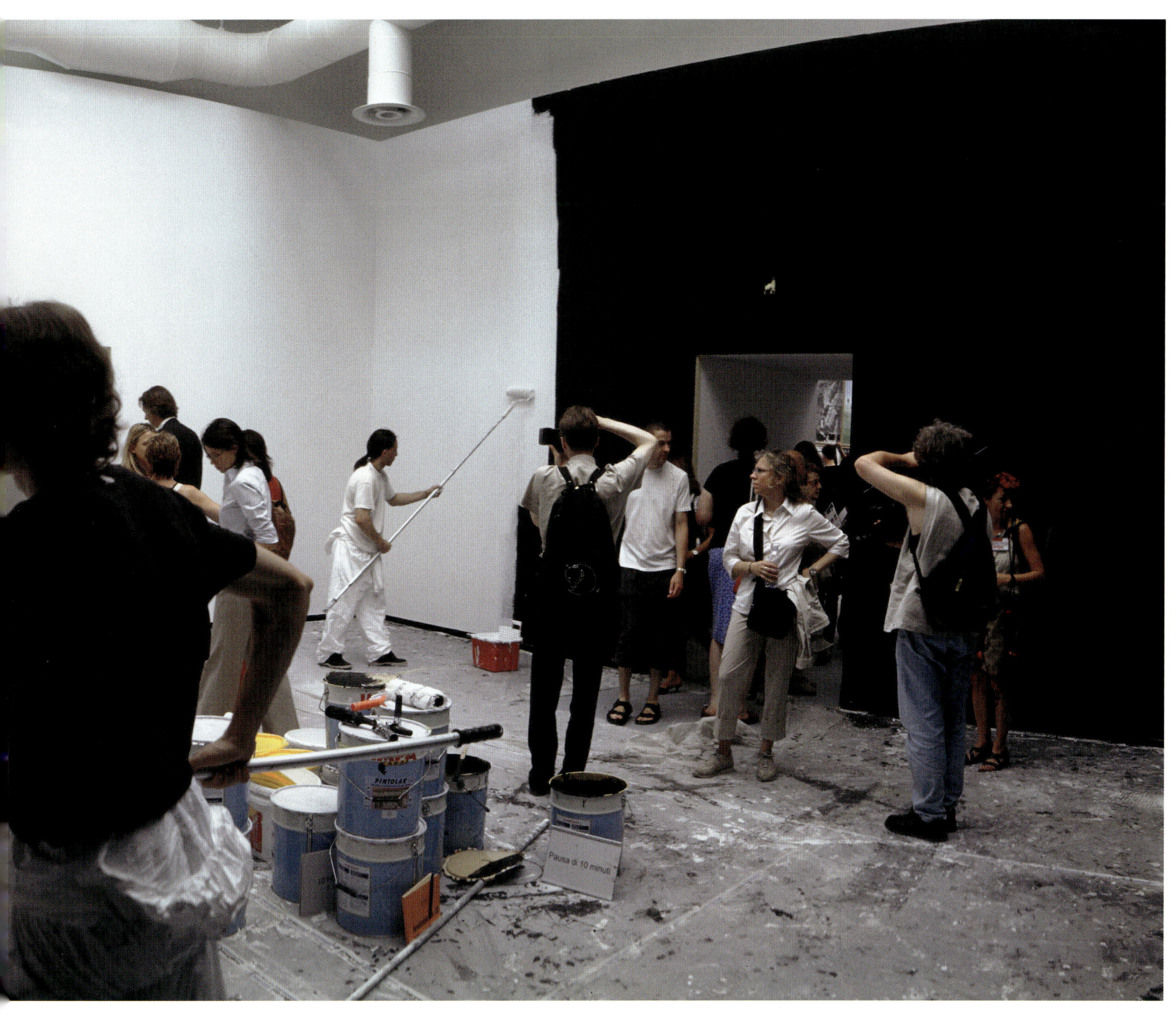
Pausa di 10 minuti
PINTOLAK

JAN MANČUŠKA

The work of Jan Mančuška ostensibly presents us with the substance of human experience and perception. His text-based installations are formed from fragments of real lives, allowing the viewer to intimately engage with a space where private thoughts are made manifest and personal experiences are recounted in a tangible form.

The objective sensibilities and minimalist aesthetics of artists such as Joseph Kosuth and the Art & Language group are clearly evidenced in Mančuška's practice, and furthermore in his use of text, which contributes a measure of formal self-reflexivity to his work. However, rather than allow for narratives to evolve with an expected linearity, Mančuška's installations render them all at once, separated and re-assembled as physical objects to be considered in their entirety. As such, the focus of Mančuška's work shifts from the substance of human experience and perception to the apparatus through which this substance is made intelligible, and the ways in which we resolve and appropriate our ideas around concepts that are housed within language.

While I Walked in my Studio in ISCP, 323 W 39th Street #811, New York presents a space that is largely bare, the only feature a thin section of black tape, just below eye-level, which skirts along and stretches between the blank, white walls. A text, travelling the length of the black tape in a clear, white font, appears to give a description of someone's movement around some sort of living space; an interior monologue that flows as they negotiate various objects and items of furniture. In itself, in the passive banality of its content, the text betrays very little purpose. However, it reflects back to us the movements we make as we read it. Our journey about the space therefore appears mapped out before us, and as the black tape doubles back and crosses over itself, new combinations of words are created, destroying the construction of meaning that finds order in the original text. The work thus disrupts the organisational procedures inherent to narrative forms, and undermines the authority that language exercises over human perception and experience.

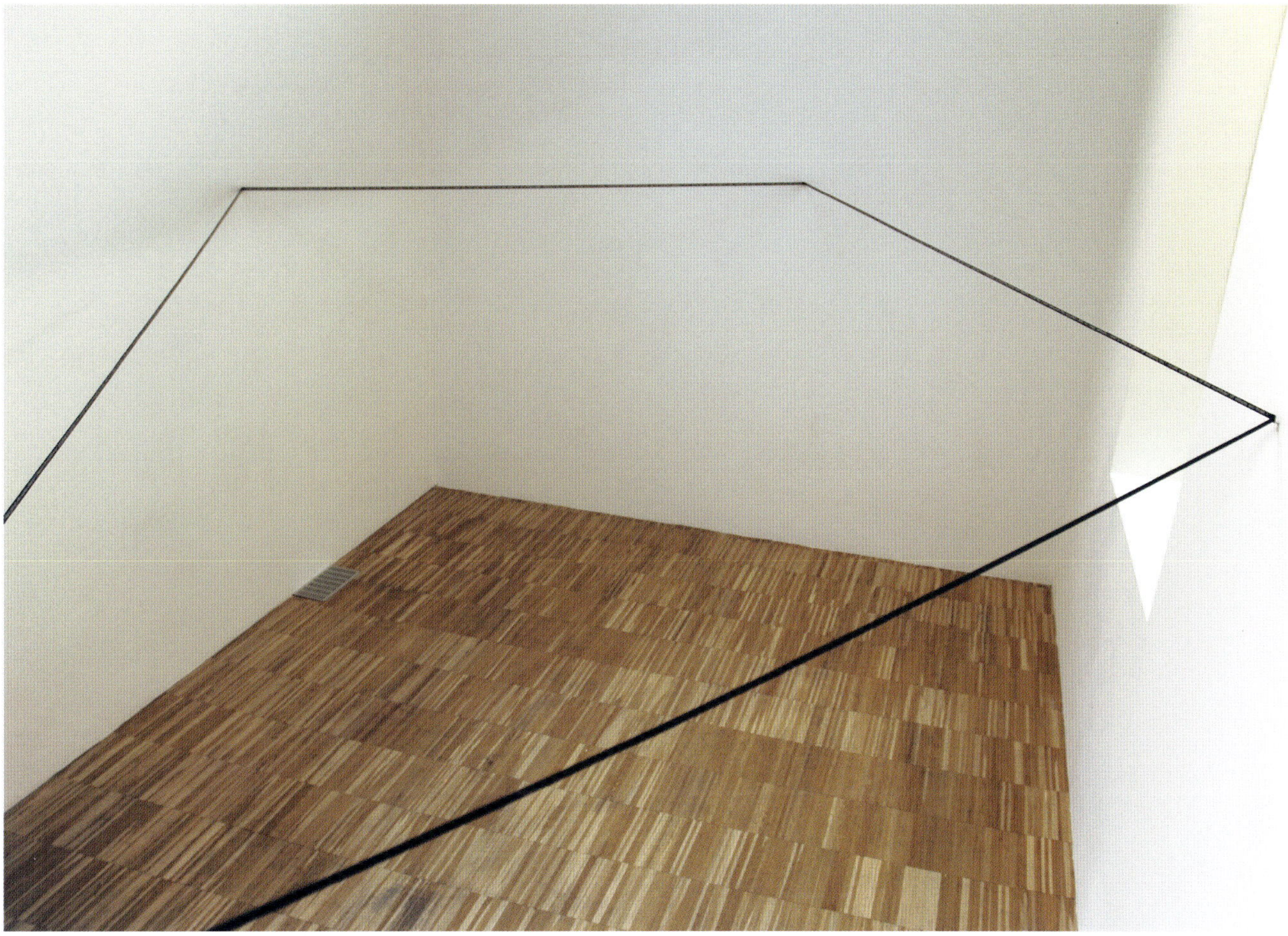

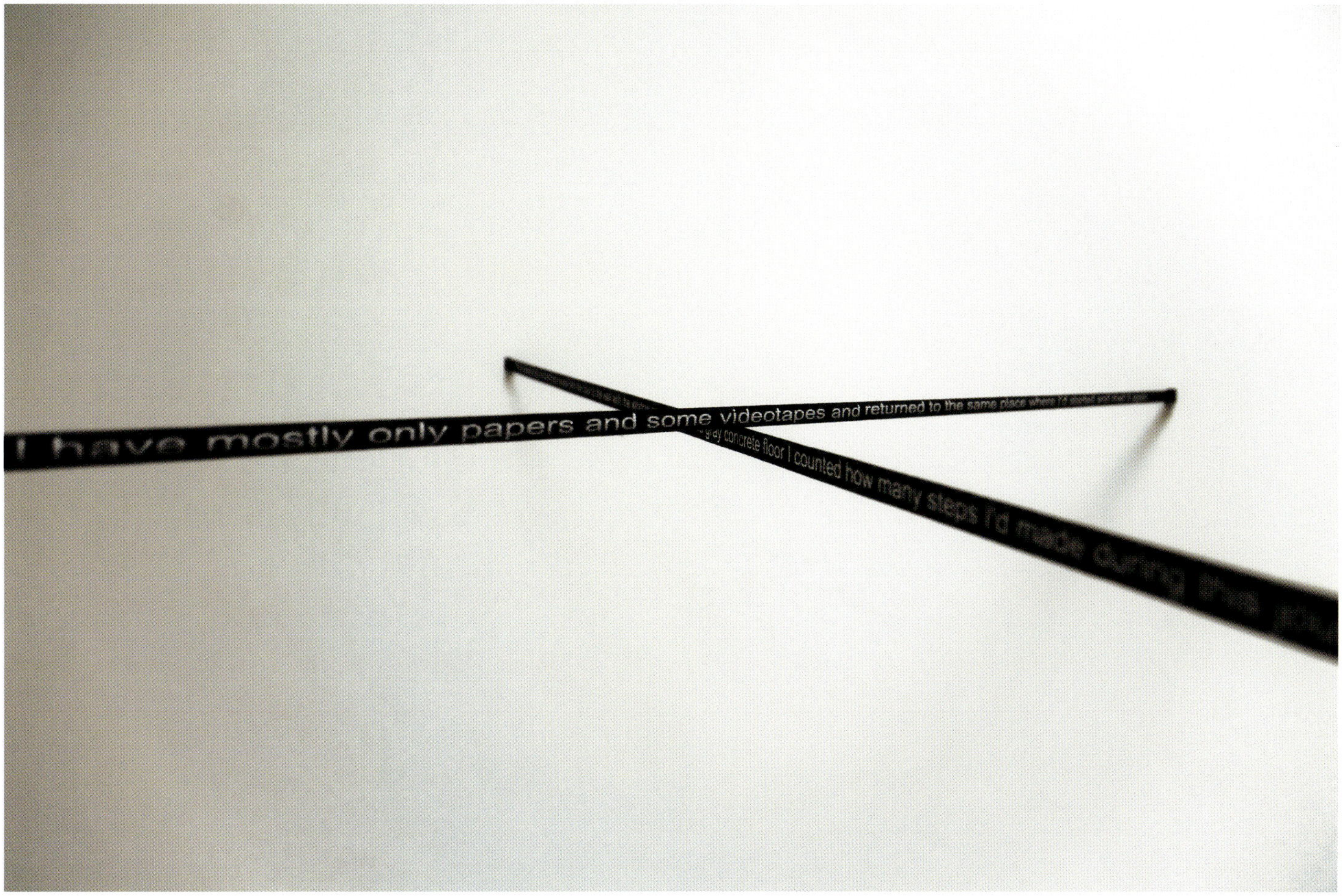

I have mostly only papers and some videotapes and returned to the same place where I'd started
gray concrete floor I counted how many steps I'd made during

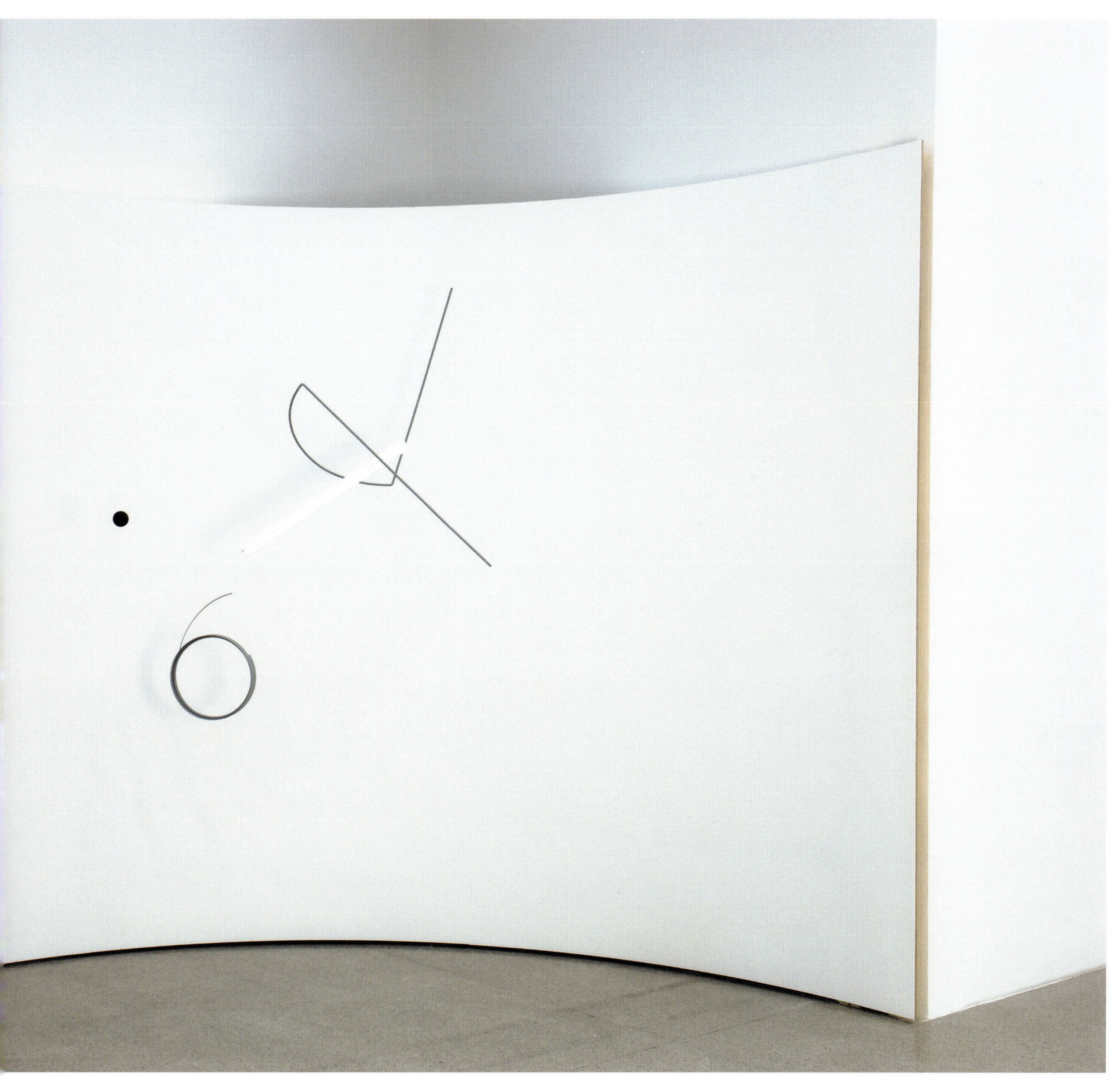

STANO FILKO

Stano Filko is widely recognised as one of the founders of conceptual art in Slovakia, experimenting with the formal artistic boundaries previously attributed to his home country's artists. Filko played a significant role in Bratislava art circles in the 1960s and 1970s, where he studied at the city's Fine Arts Academy. Following this he spent 20 years in the USA, where his work evolved in an alternative direction—away from the conventional art practice he had developed in Slovakia, in favour of uncharted methods, such as the installation work he has become recognised for today.

Filko's work is frequently concerned with space and boundaries, as explored in pieces such as those included in his ongoing series *White Space in a White Space*, initiated in 1973, which explores various metaphysical ideas, most notably the notion of infinite space. This series demonstrates Filko's prolonged preoccupation with spatial concepts, involving a complex range of ideas, in which he attempts to transcend traditional art values that continue to confront him as an Eastern European artist, in favour of something more radical. Best described as "environments", Filko's pieces explore concepts such as that of never-ending, non-physical emotion; supremacy; and the state and its involvement with artistic concerns—all of which he explored in *White Space in a White Space*, represented by the work's lack of colour and spatial experimentations.

The installation *Flight to the Moon and Back*, 1968–1969, demonstrates Filko's interest with the universe—an obvious direction in which to take his spatially aware work. This installation piece is a combination of blue perspex, scaffolding, mirrors, and aluminium panels, the latter of which Filko engraved with the details of space flights since 1959, used to symbolise outer space—the perspex representing the night's skies. Filko's fascination with man's race to space during the 1960s became highly influential in his work, where he considered his artistic practice as uniting science and spirituality.

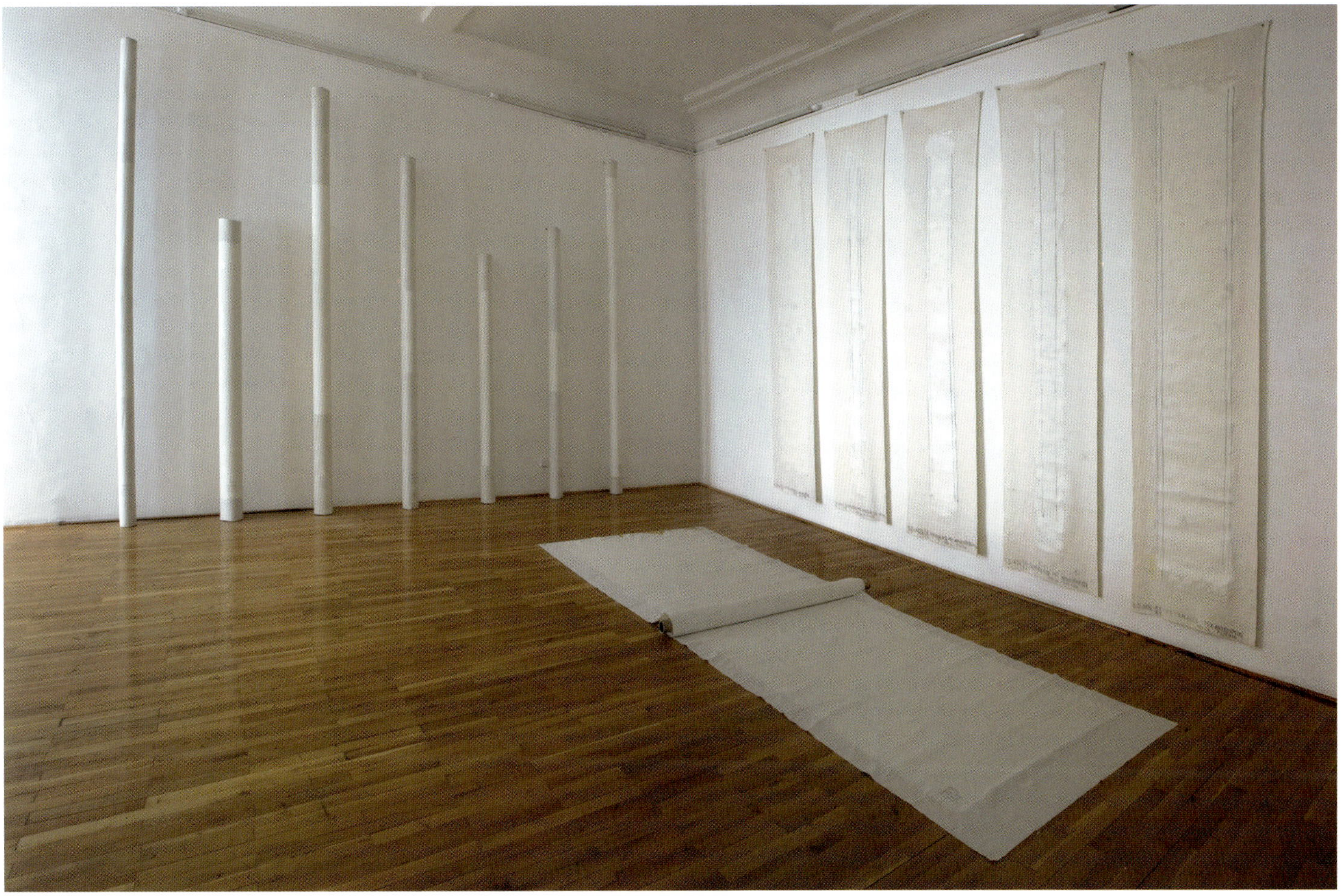

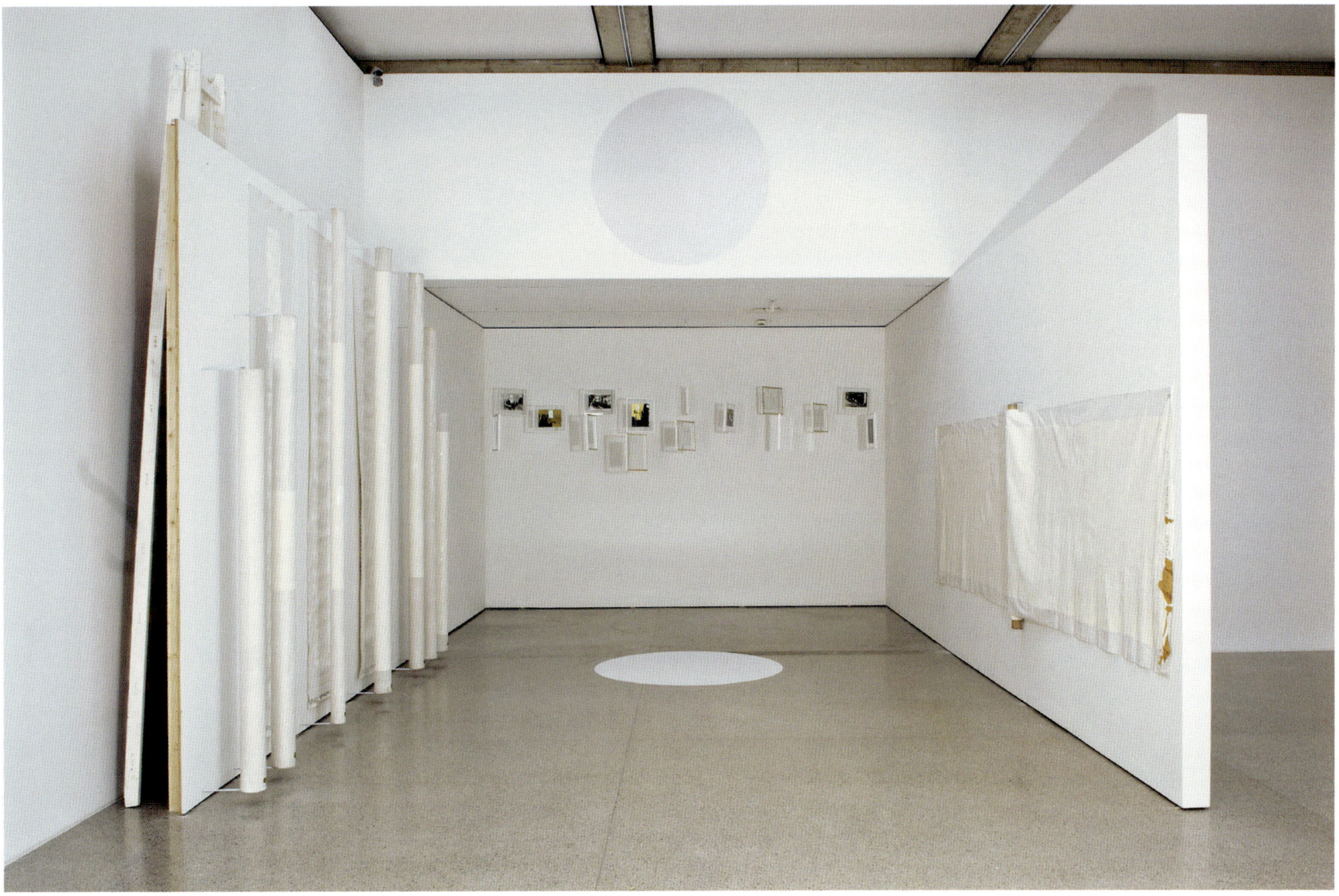

ROMAN ONDÁK
Two Mars Stories
2004–2006, four tables, drawings, newspaper, magazine
and book cut-outs, plexiglass, 74 x 195 x 75 cm
Private collection, Italy. Courtesy gb agency, Paris

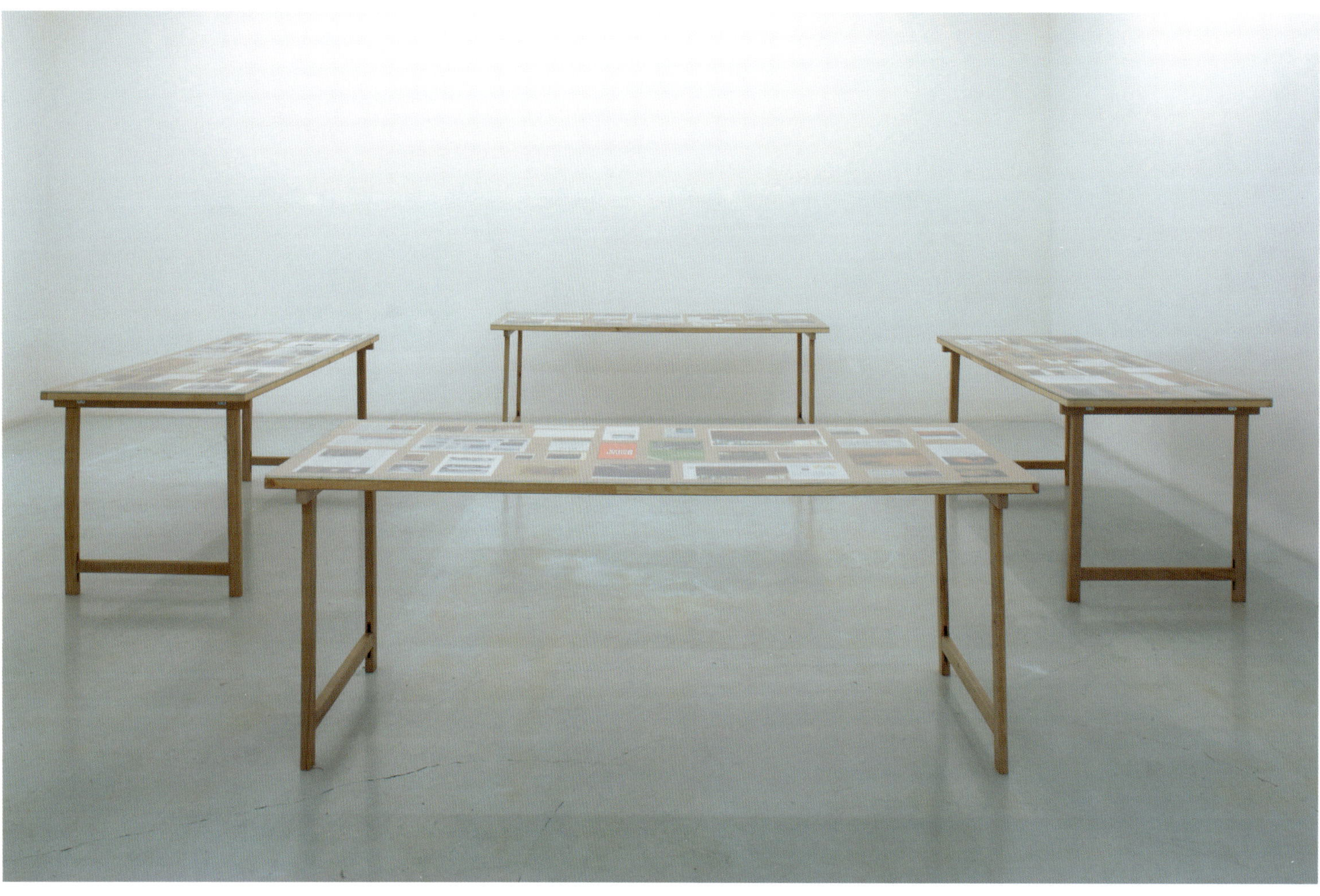

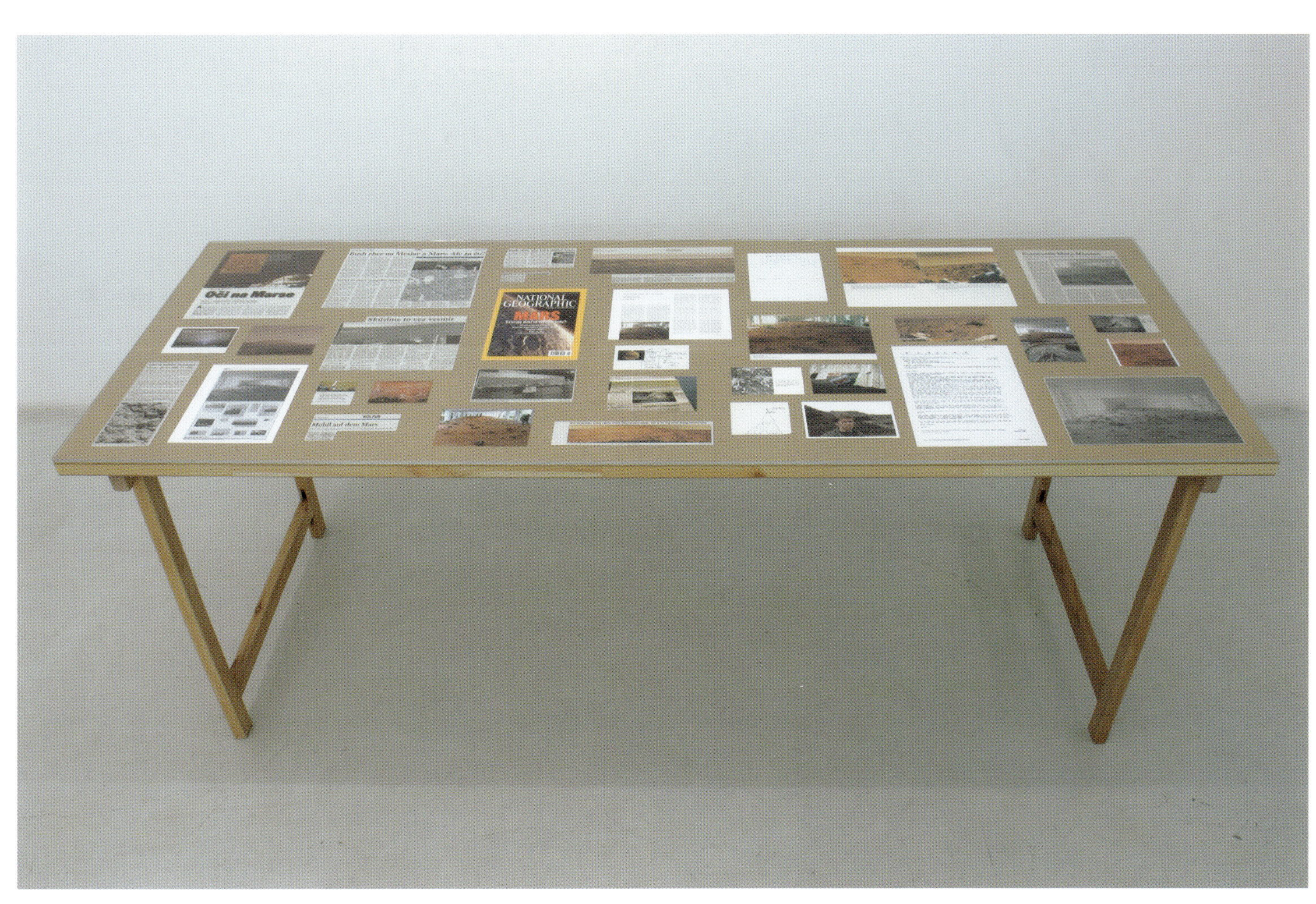

ANDREI MOLODKIN

Hope (below)
2009, acrylic block filled with crude oil,
19 x 59 x 11 cm
Courtesy Galerie Kashya Hildebrand

New Architecton (opposite)
2010, transparent tubes filled with crude
oil, neon tubes, 350 x 250 x 14 cm
Courtesy the artist

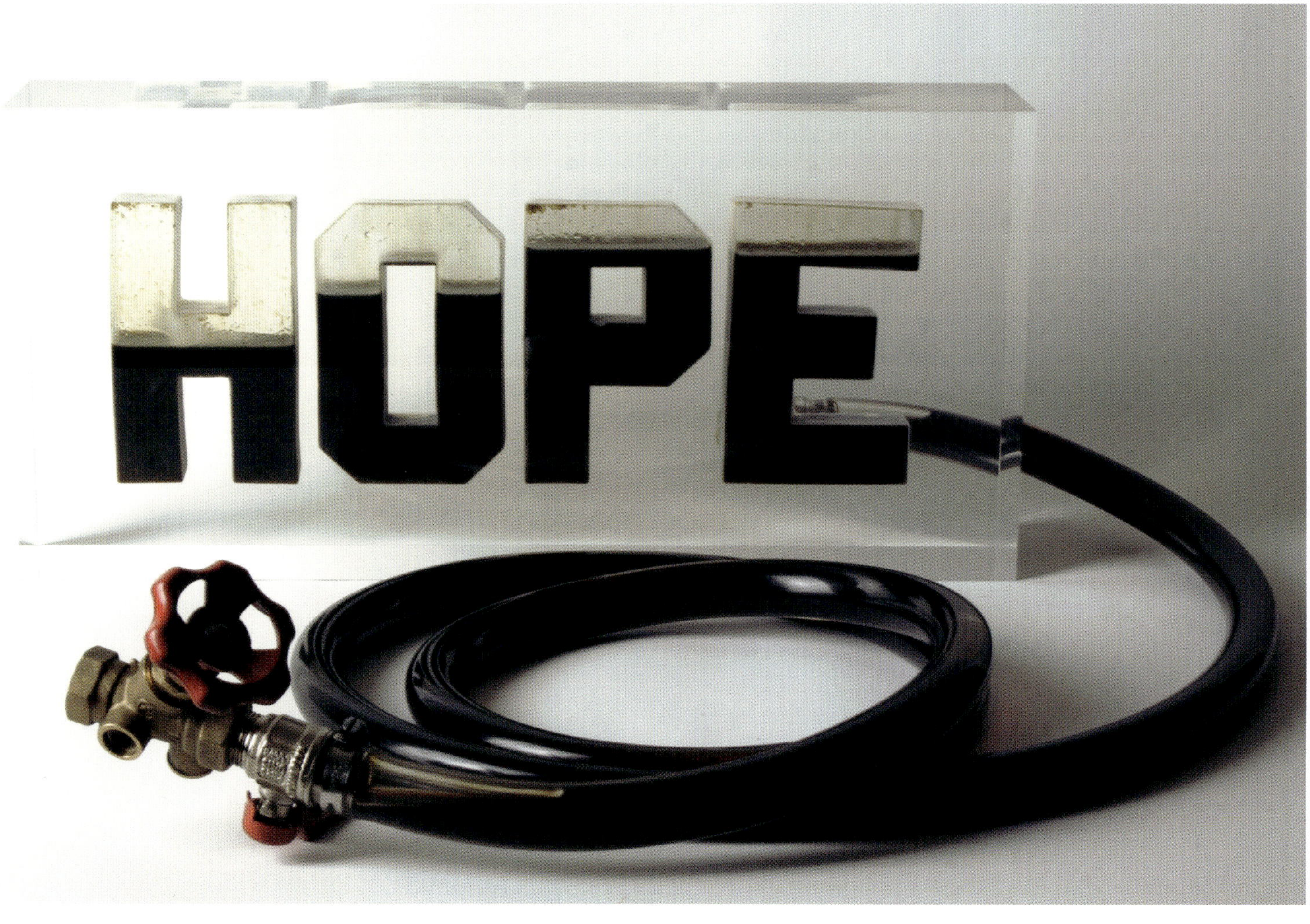

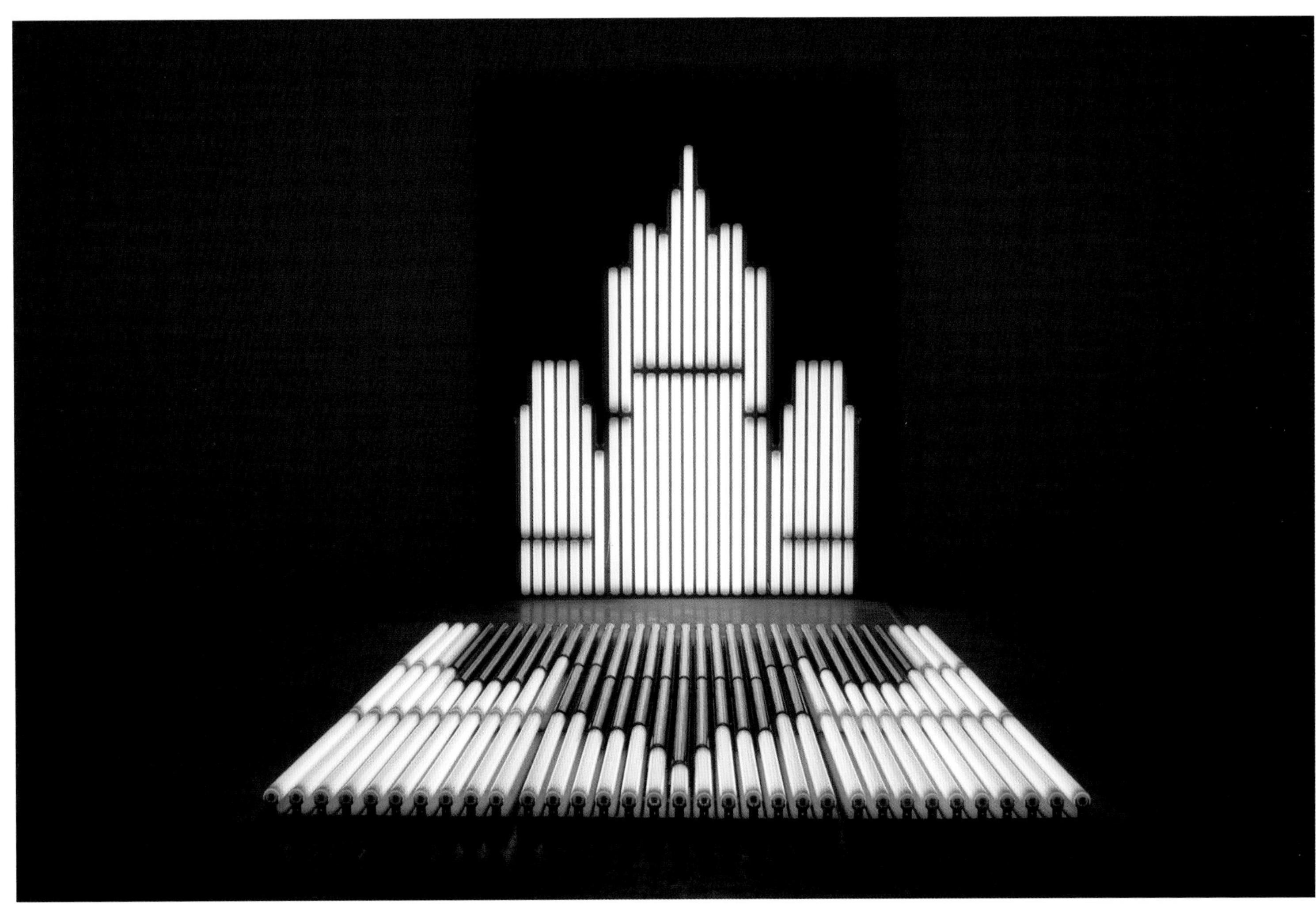

Path (right)
2007, sculpture projects Münster
Courtesy Foksal Gallery Foundation

Self-Portrait (opposite)
1993, mixed media, grass, hemp fibre, animal
intestine, wax and hair, 189 x 76 x 70 cm
Courtesy Foksal Gallery Foundation

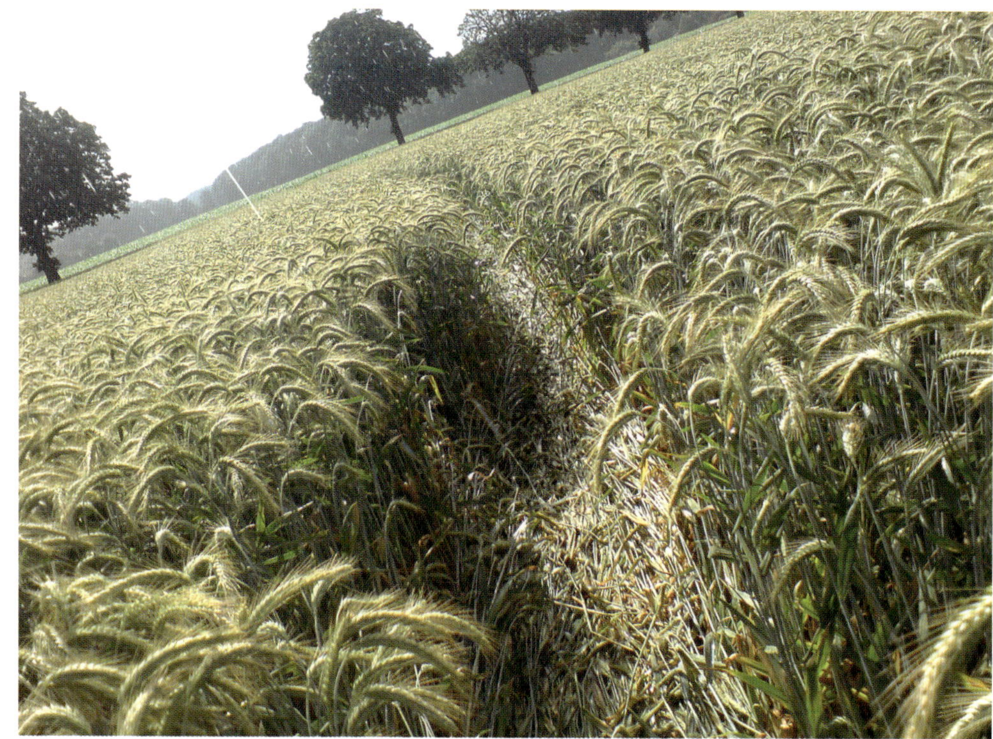

PAWEL ALTHAMER

Despite his firm grounding in the discipline of sculpture—due to his early training at the Warsaw Academy of Fine Arts—Pawel Althamer's practice has been eclectic in nature from the very beginning of his career. Restlessly and intuitively, his ideas have found form and expression across a range of different media and at the same time have complicated the boundaries that render these media sensible, as in his 1993 *Self-Portrait*—a life-size sculpture made from grass, hemp fibre, animal intestine, wax and hair.

Perhaps this is natural for an artist whose work often accommodates a concept of transgression, however. Althamer aims to breach the limits of our conceptual apparatus and challenge the strategies we employ for making sense of our place in the world. But he posits this breach as a natural, even primitive state within a social space of predetermined, rigid structures, a state we are encouraged to explore so as to encounter reality afresh and be surprised by it again. Althamer has explored this notion further by challenging stereotypical notions of place, as when he transformed the Neugerriemschneider Gallery, Berlin, into a picturesque ruin in 2003.

The evidence of process in Althamer's work—whether through an organic material and its gradual decay, or a path trodden step by step into a wheat field as in *Path, 2007*—offers up the existence of time and its passing for consideration. Sculpture also remains a premise for Althamer's actions, present in his tactile relationship to his working materials; the artist seems almost obsessed with creating things that are concrete, real, and which stand as discreet states and tangible signifiers for an otherwise impermanent temporal process.

In more recent work, Althamer has emphasised his concerns with human activity and societal relationships. For his 2000 project *Brodno 2000* he worked with the residents of a tower block in Warsaw's Brodno district, getting them to turn on or off their lights so as to illuminate "2000" on to the buildings facade. This tactic of "delegated performance" allows his practice to serve as a site for the inscription of social experience. A sense of community and inclusion is promoted and works to dispel the myth of the artist as an isolated individual, instead situating him firmly within a web of relationships: Althamer's work and actions simply become the product of an individual—one of many.

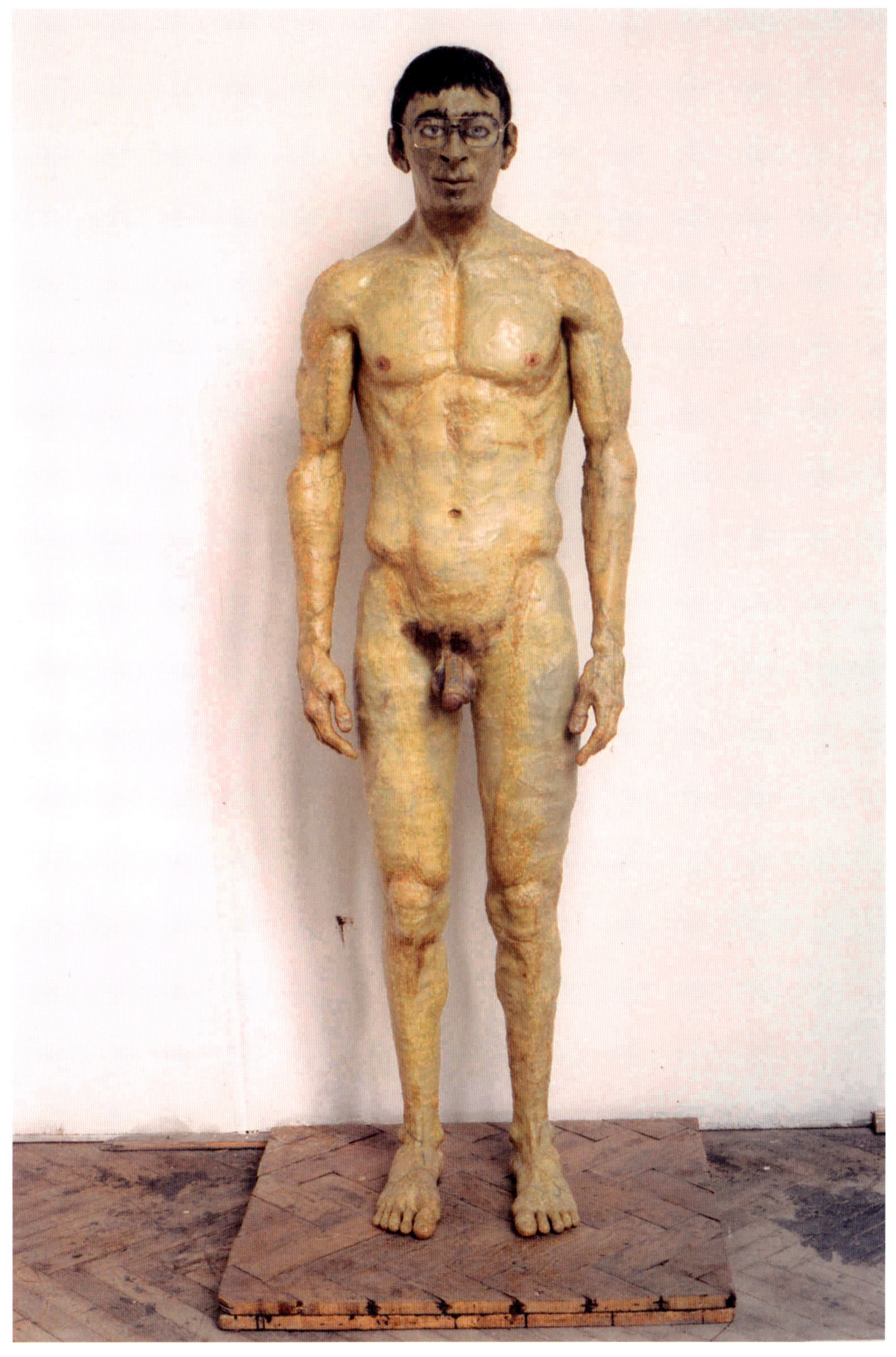

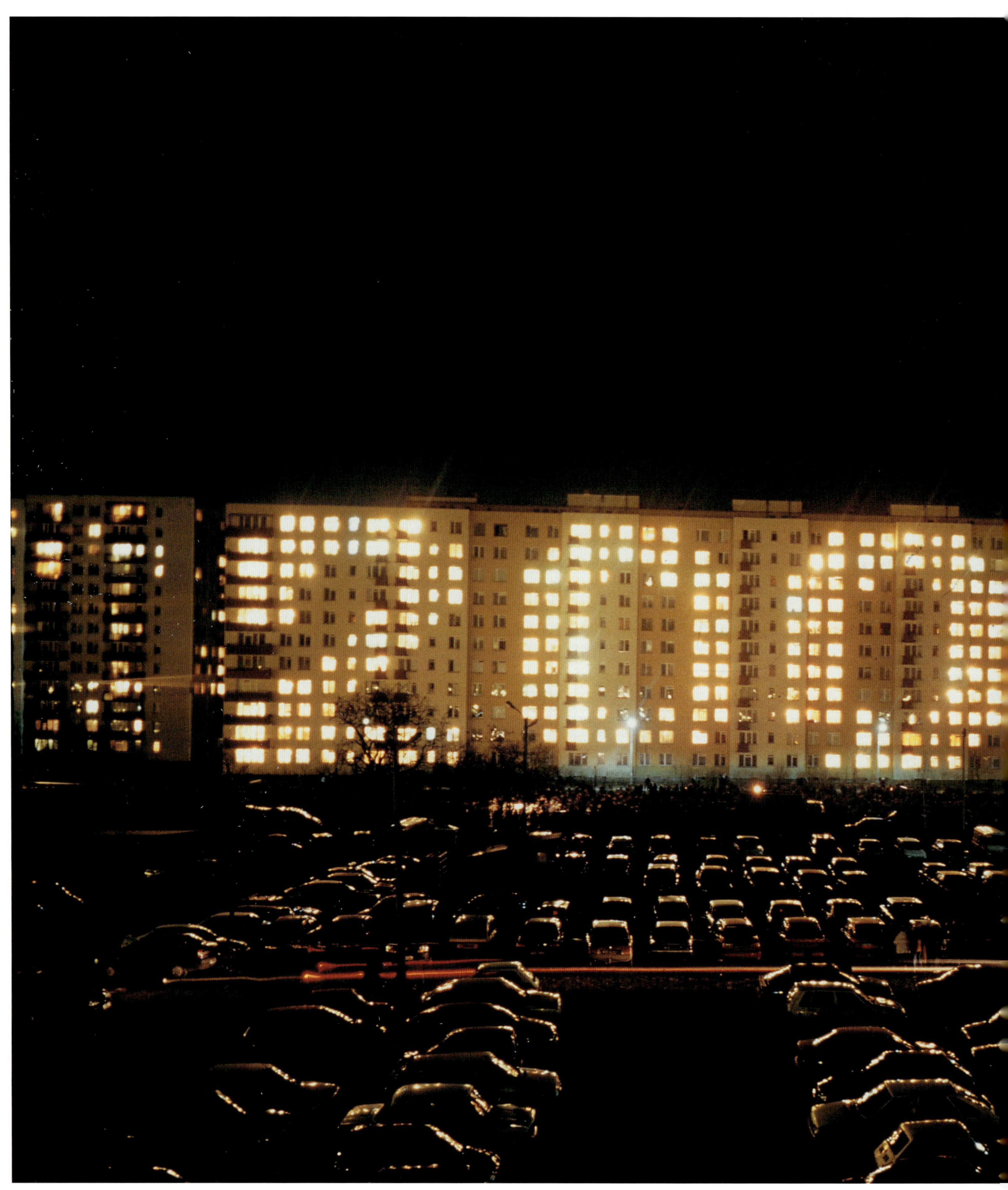

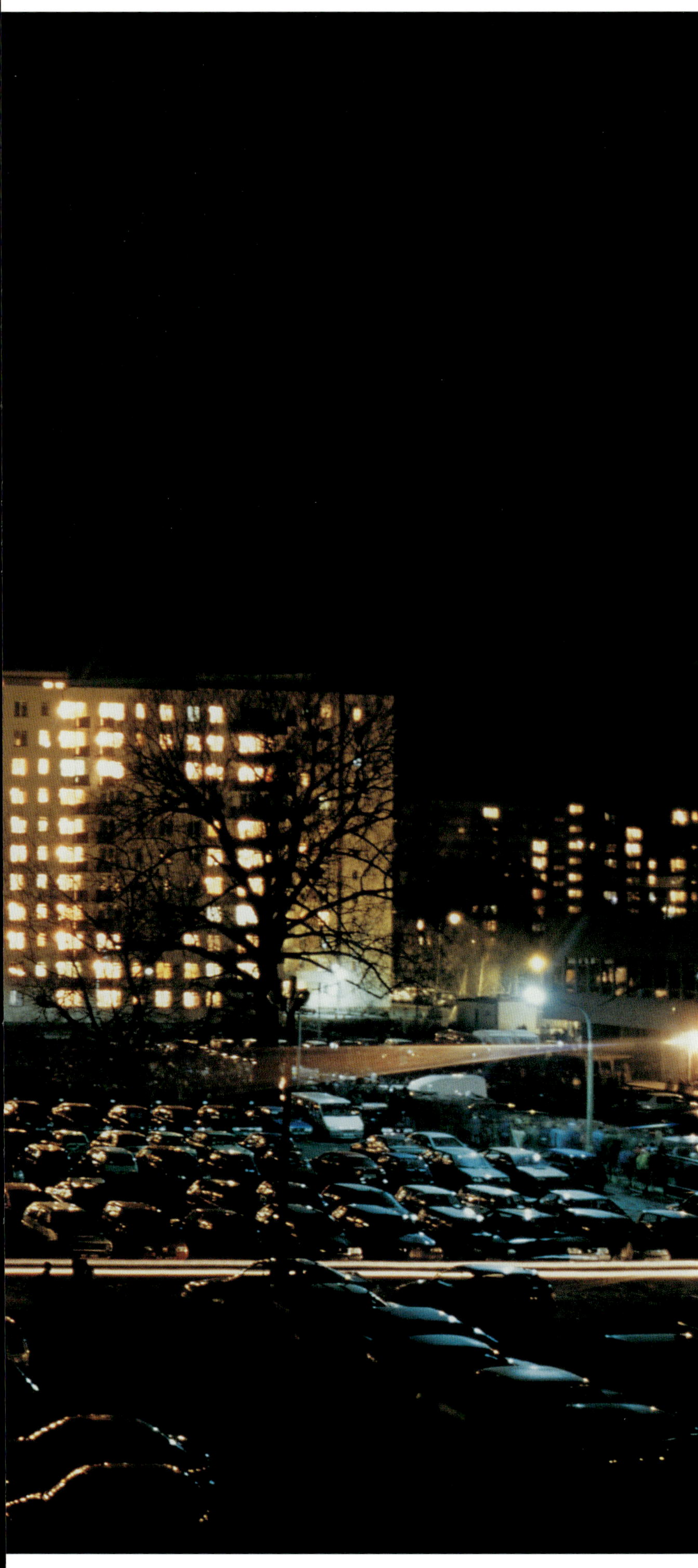

PAWEL ALTHAMER
Brodno 2000
2000, Warsaw
Courtesy Foksal Gallery Foundation

PAWEL ALTHAMER
Untitled
2003, mixed media
Courtesy Foksal Gallery Foundation

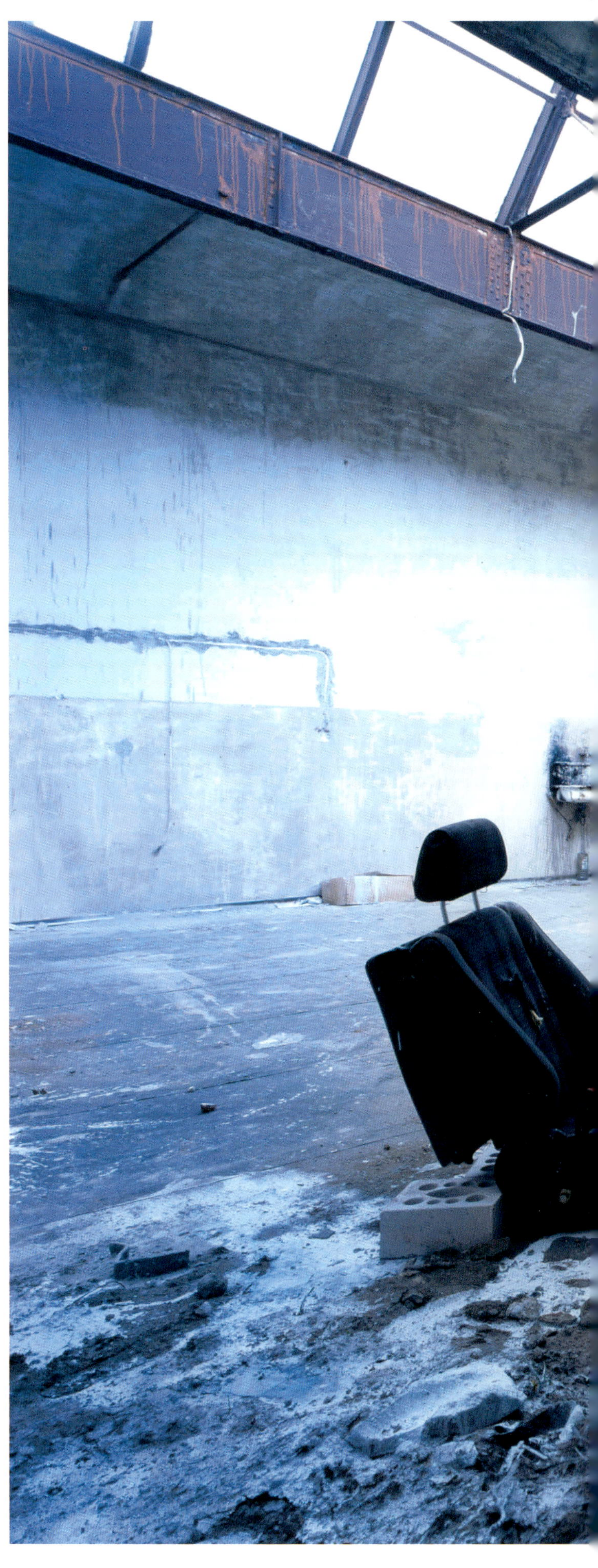

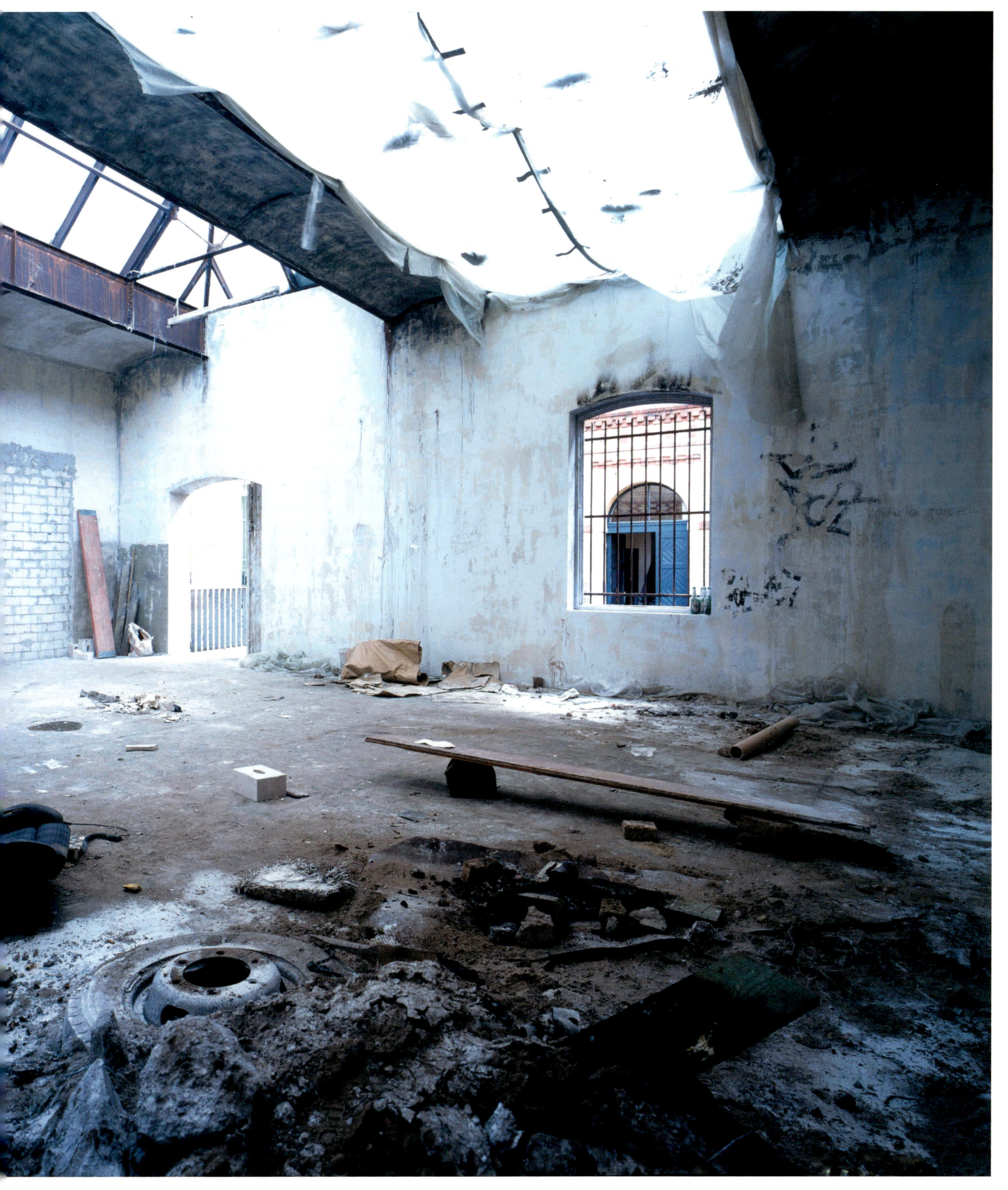

Wagon (opposite above)
2006, paper, cardboard, wood, clay,
300 x 280 x 1000 cm
Courtesy Foksal Gallery Foundation

Paris-Luxembourg-Leipzig (opposite below)
2003, photograph
Courtesy Foksal Gallery Foundation

ROBERT KUŚMIROWSKI

Famed above all for his painstakingly crafted replications of historical settings, Robert Kuśmirowski is one of Poland's most dynamic young artists. After studying sculpture at University of Lubin in South East Poland, Kuśmirowski gained critical acclaim for his atmospheric installations involving carefully fashioned structures and objects. Working with modest materials such as cardboard, and described as a genius counterfeiter and manipulator of reality, his works are characterised by their detail and precision.

At the beginning of his career Kuśmirowski began to duplicate small objects such as postage stamps and even photographs, which then evolved into highly ambitious large-scale installations such as *The Ornaments of Anatomy*, 2005–2006. In this we see Kuśmirowski take on the character of enigmatic scientist Dr Vernier and assemble his laboratory, consisting of a huge library and warren of forged artefacts and remnants. In this work the artist's obsession with gathering and collecting items is apparent; with genuine relics also being placed amongst the fake. Attempting to stir up the doctor's spirit, Kuśmirowski hid behind Vernier's portrait at the opening of the exhibition, and spied on the gallery visitors like a mischievous ghost. From this to his piece *Wagon*, 2006, for the 4th Berlin Biennial, a train carriage modelled on those used to ship detainees to Auschwitz, Kuśmirowski's works consistently revolve around the themes of recollection.

Kuśmirowski's practice could often be regarded as performance, with projects such as *Paris-Luxembourg-Leipzig*, 2003, involving the artist embarking on significant journeys. In this case, Kuśmirowski completed a 1,200 kilometre trip on a bicycle, beginning in Paris and ending in Leipzig at the Galerie für Zeitgenössische Kunst where the exhibition opened. Riding a bicycle dating from the 1920s, and dressed in sporting apparel from the same decade, he attempted to document the trip using photographs, aiming to resemble those of the time. The process is reminiscent and alike his other works confronts reality, uniting it with personal memory and his own mind's eye.

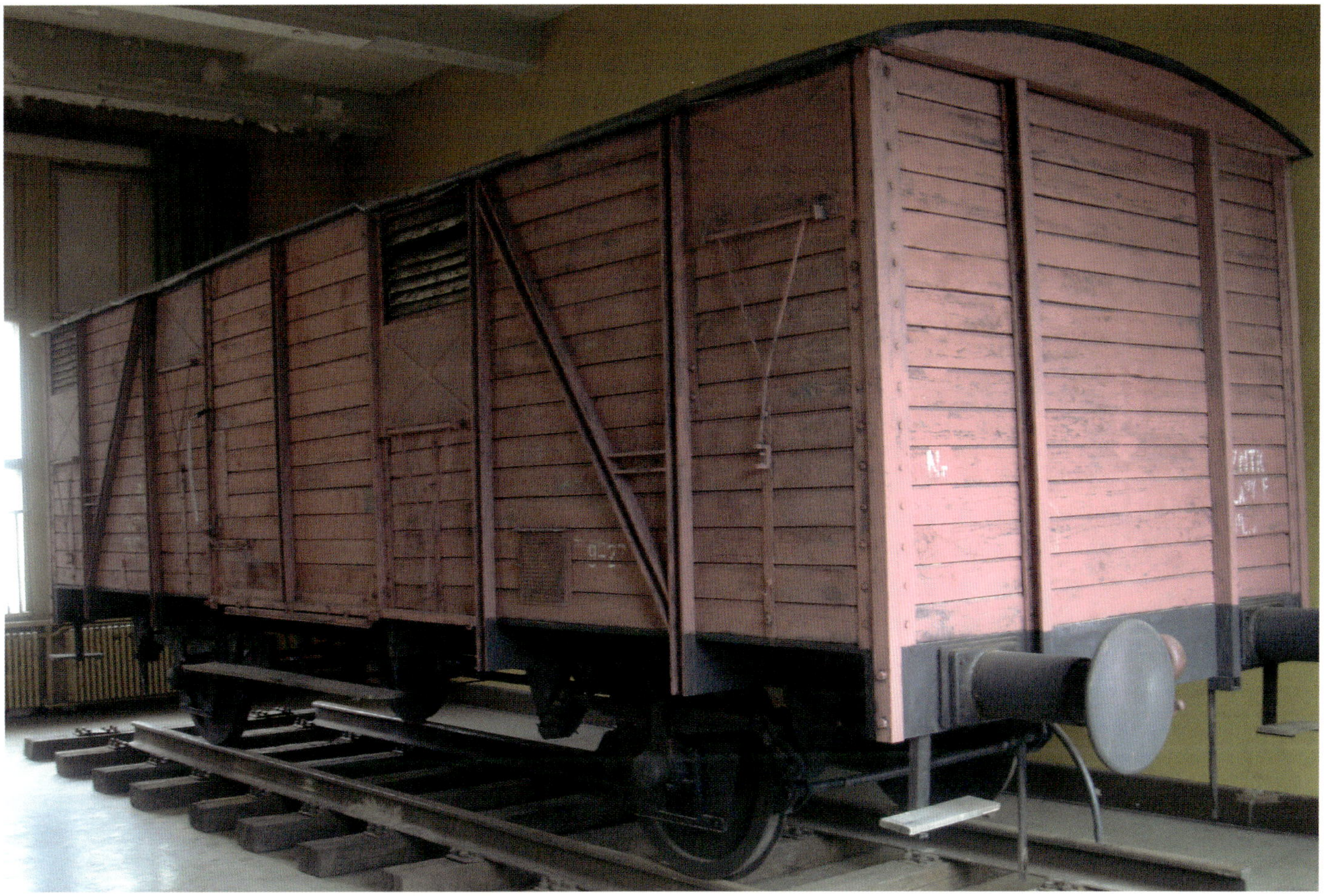

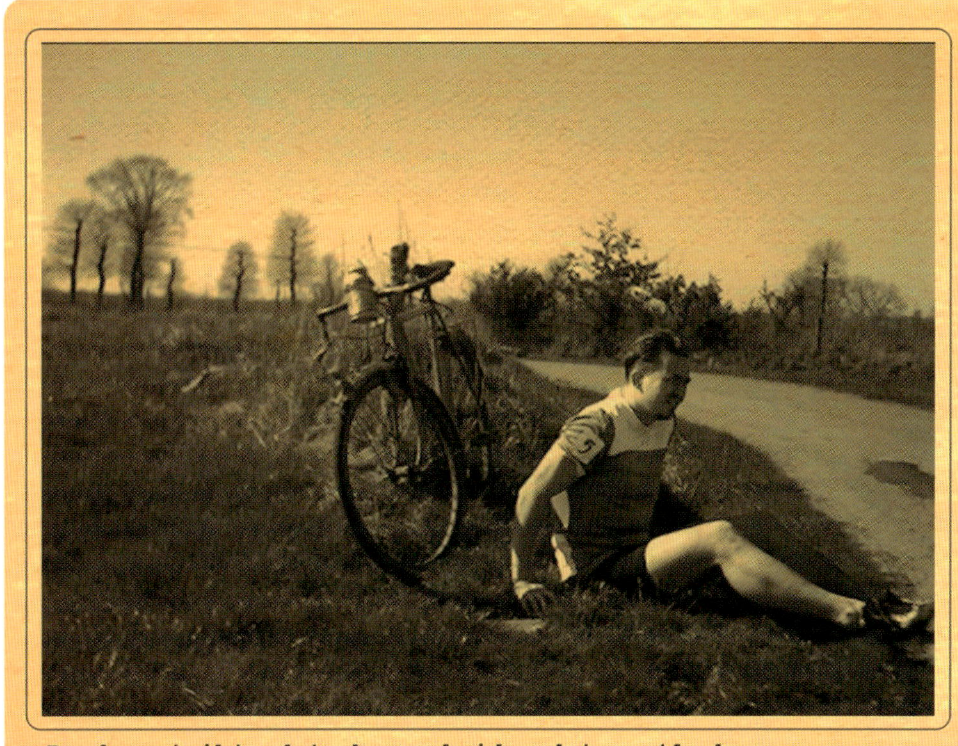

Bardzo ciężki odcinek a z każdym dniem sił ubywa.

ROBERT KUŚMIROWSKI
Ornaments of Anatomy
2005–2006, mixed media
Courtesy Foksal Gallery Foundation

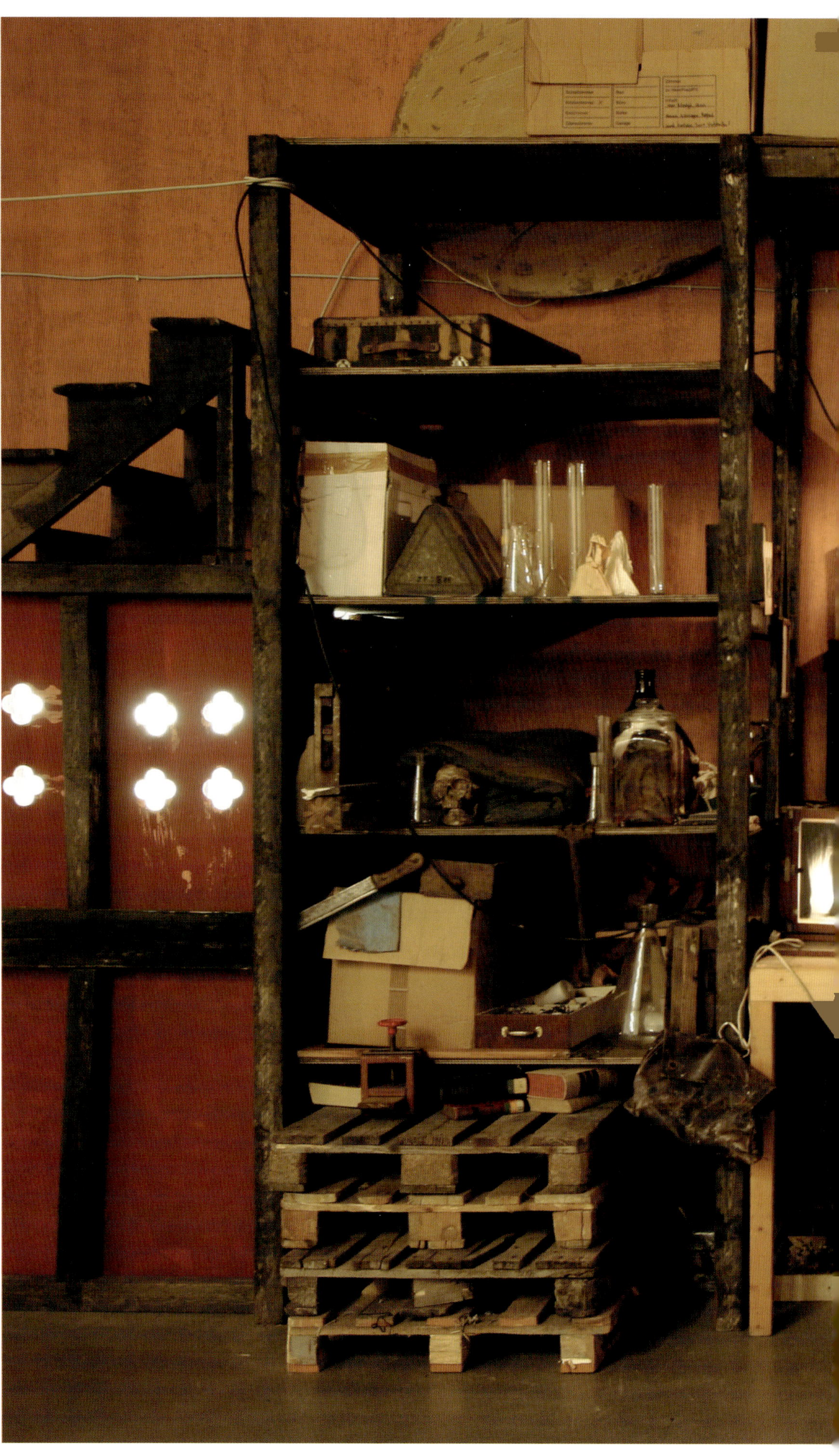

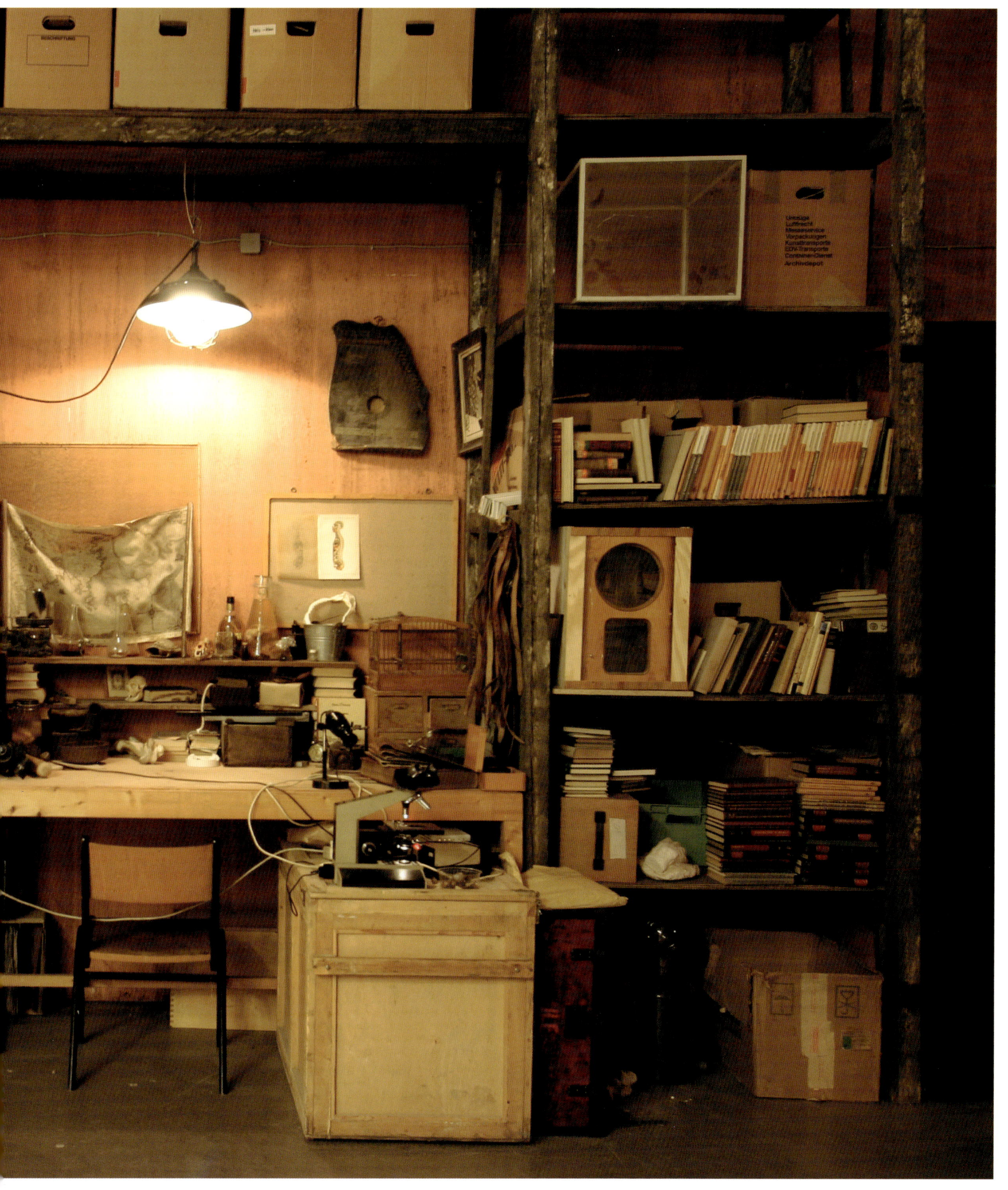

CHRISTO AND JEANNE-CLAUDE

Whilst residing in America for a number of years, the experience of growing up in Eastern Europe remains with Bulgarian born Christo, and the work he created with his late wife, herself of French descent, Jeanne-Claude.

Best known for their large-scale ephemeral works, created in urban and rural sites internationally, Christo and Jeanne-Claude combine elements of painting, sculpture, architecture and urban planning to explore a continued interest in the temporal quality of textiles and their relationship with different landscapes. Recognised for their use of fabric, the artists 'wrapped' highly recognised landmarks such as the Reichstag, Berlin, and the Pont Neuf, Paris, with swathes of fabric. Alongside projects such as these, islands have been surrounded and coastlines wrapped with metres of brightly coloured fabric, including 11 islands in Biscayne Bay and the coastline of Little Bay, Australia. Each project involves months of meticulous planning, followed through to completion with the help of a dedicated team of workers.

It is via this international stage, along with the artists' invested interest in distinctly diverse geographic locations, that ironically link Christo with his Bulgarian heritage —an underlying sense of displacement and nostalgia pervading throughout each project, as each landscape adopts a different facade. One of the couple's early works, *Wall of Oil Barrels-Iron Curtain-Rue Visconti, Paris*, 1962—an 'art barricade' that closed the Rue Visconti, Paris, for eight hours on the evening of 27 June 1962—can be considered a direct reference to Christo's Eastern European upbringing under Communist rule, with the iron barrels explicitly referring to the 'Iron Curtain', built just a year previous to the installation's creation: "This Iron Curtain can be used as a barricade during a period of public work in the street, or to transform the street into a dead end. Finally its principle can be extended to a whole area or an entire city."

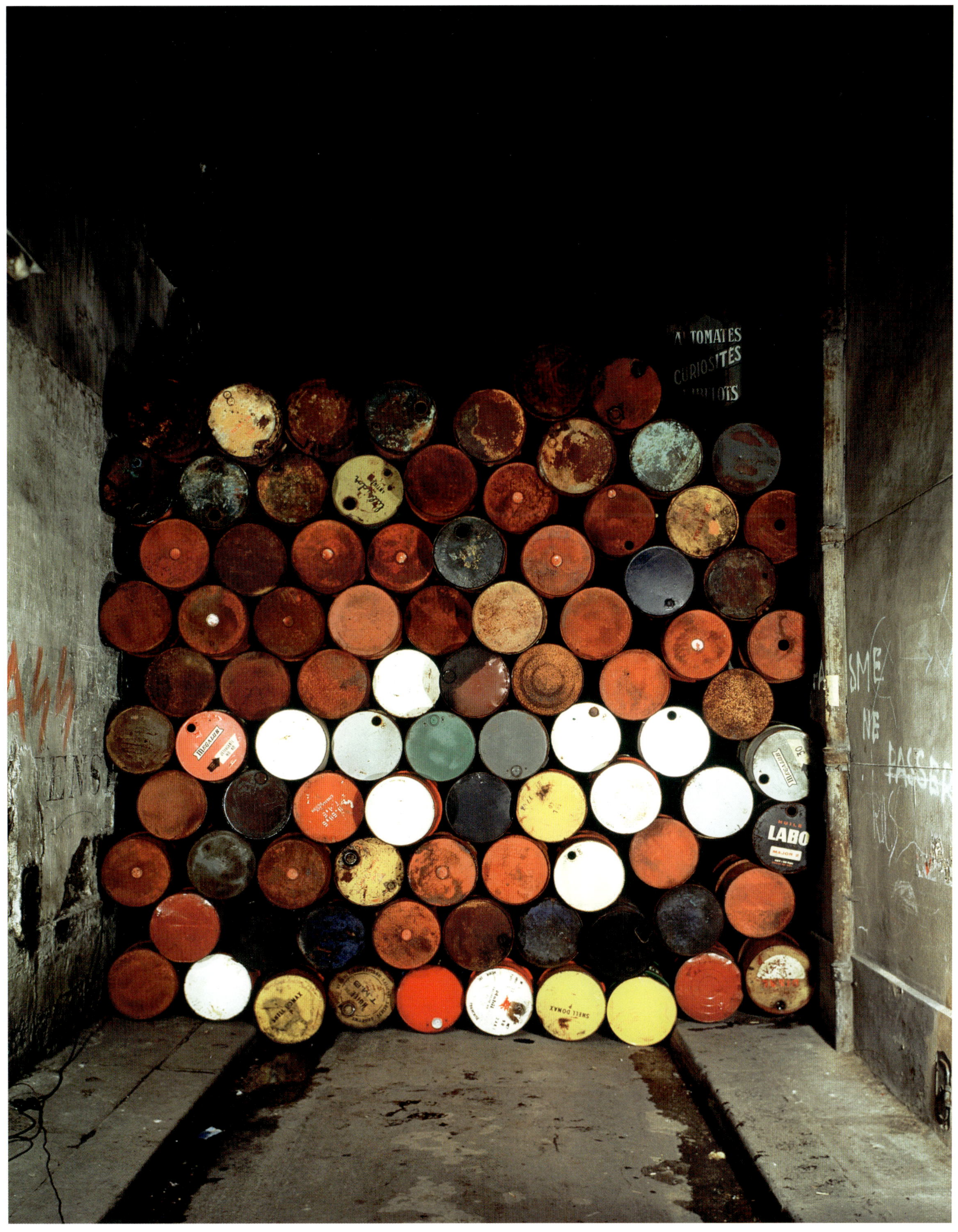
A TOMATES
CURIOSITES
LABO

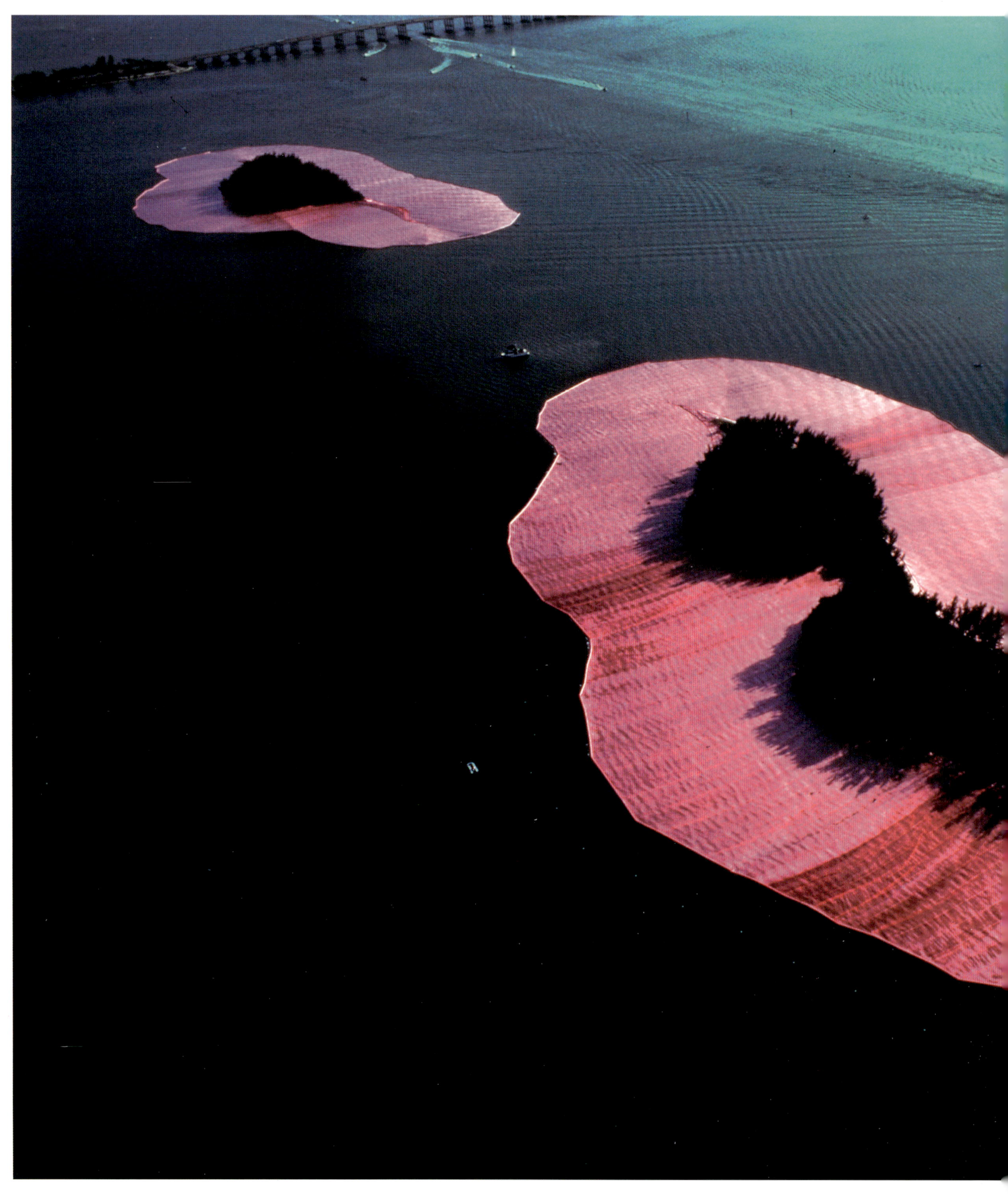

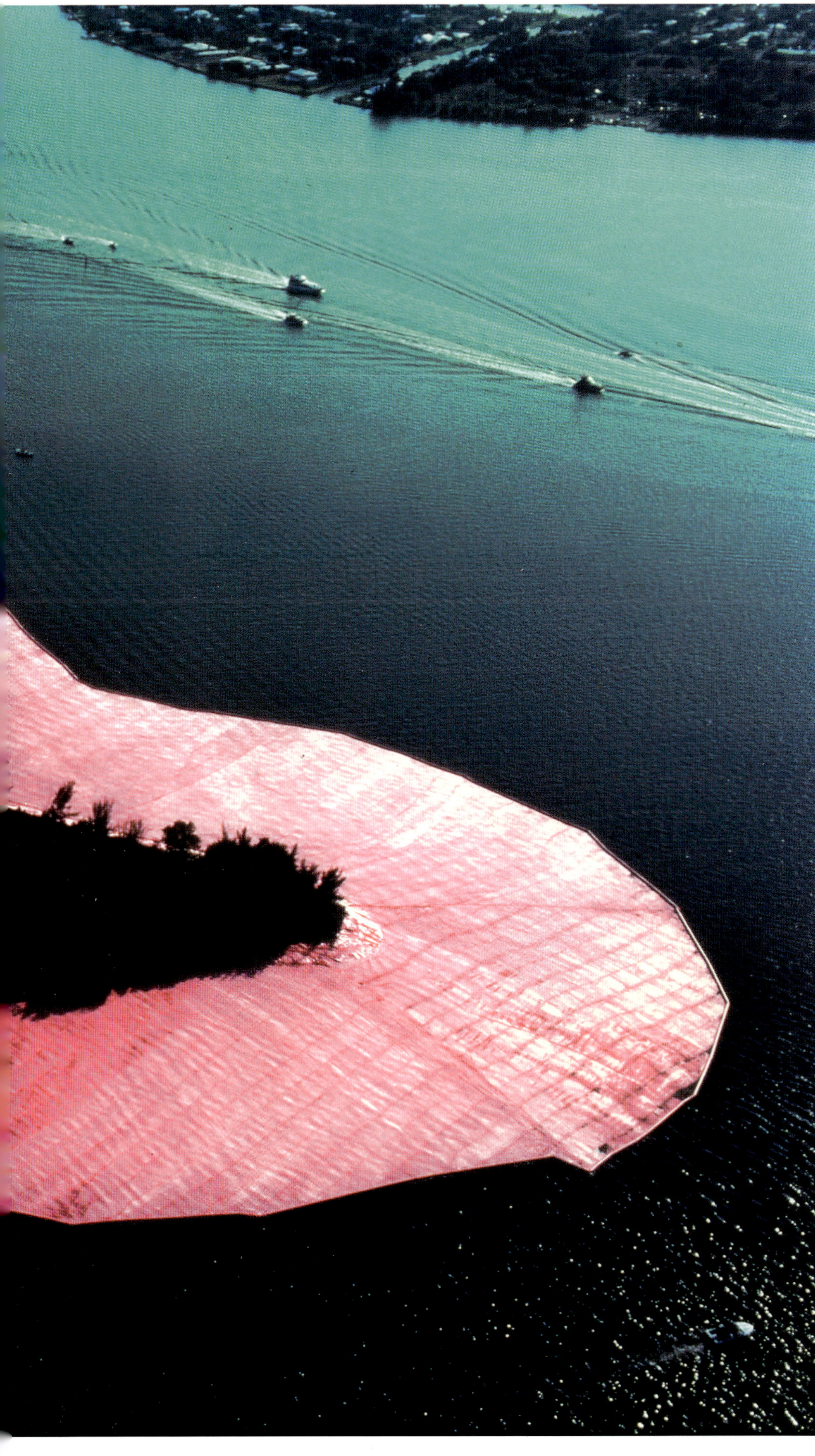

CHRISTO AND JEANNE-CLAUDE
Surrounded Islands, Biscayne Bay,
Greater Miami, Florida
1980–1983, fabric floating around 11 islands
585,000 square metres
Copyright Christo, photo: Wolfgang Volz

MONIKA SOSNOWSKA

The Wind House (below)
2008, steel, wood, paint, installation view
Portavilion, The Wind House, Primrose Hill,
London, 465 x 330 x 945 cm
Courtesy The Modern Institute

1:1 (opposite above)
2007, steel, installation view Polish Pavilion,
Venice Biennale, 700 x 1400 x 600 cm
Courtesy The Modern Institute

Corridor (opposite below)
2008, MDF, carpet, fluorescent lights,
739 x 826 x 1059 cm, installation view
Schaulager Musuem, Basel (with Andrea Zittel)
Courtesy The Modern Institute

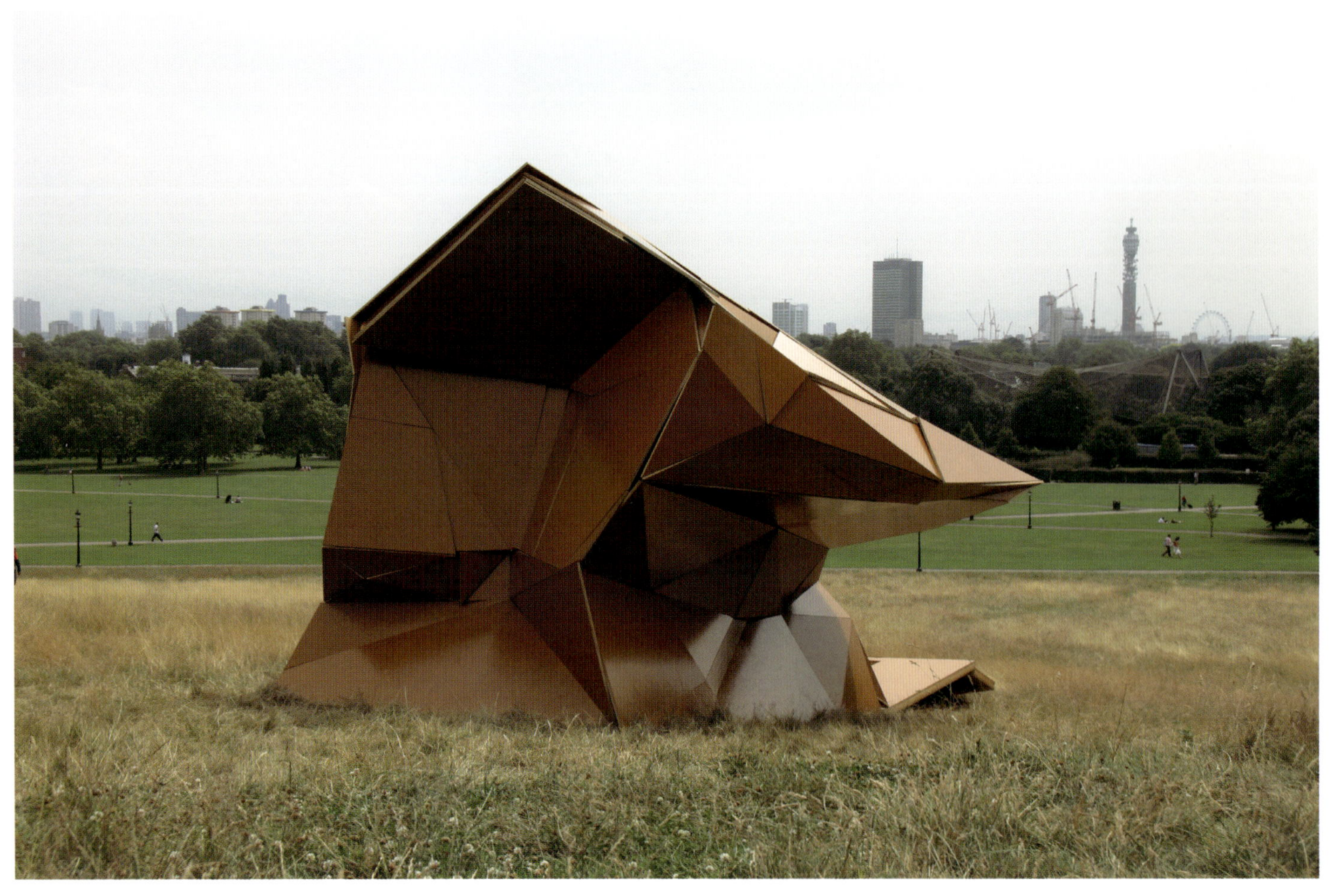

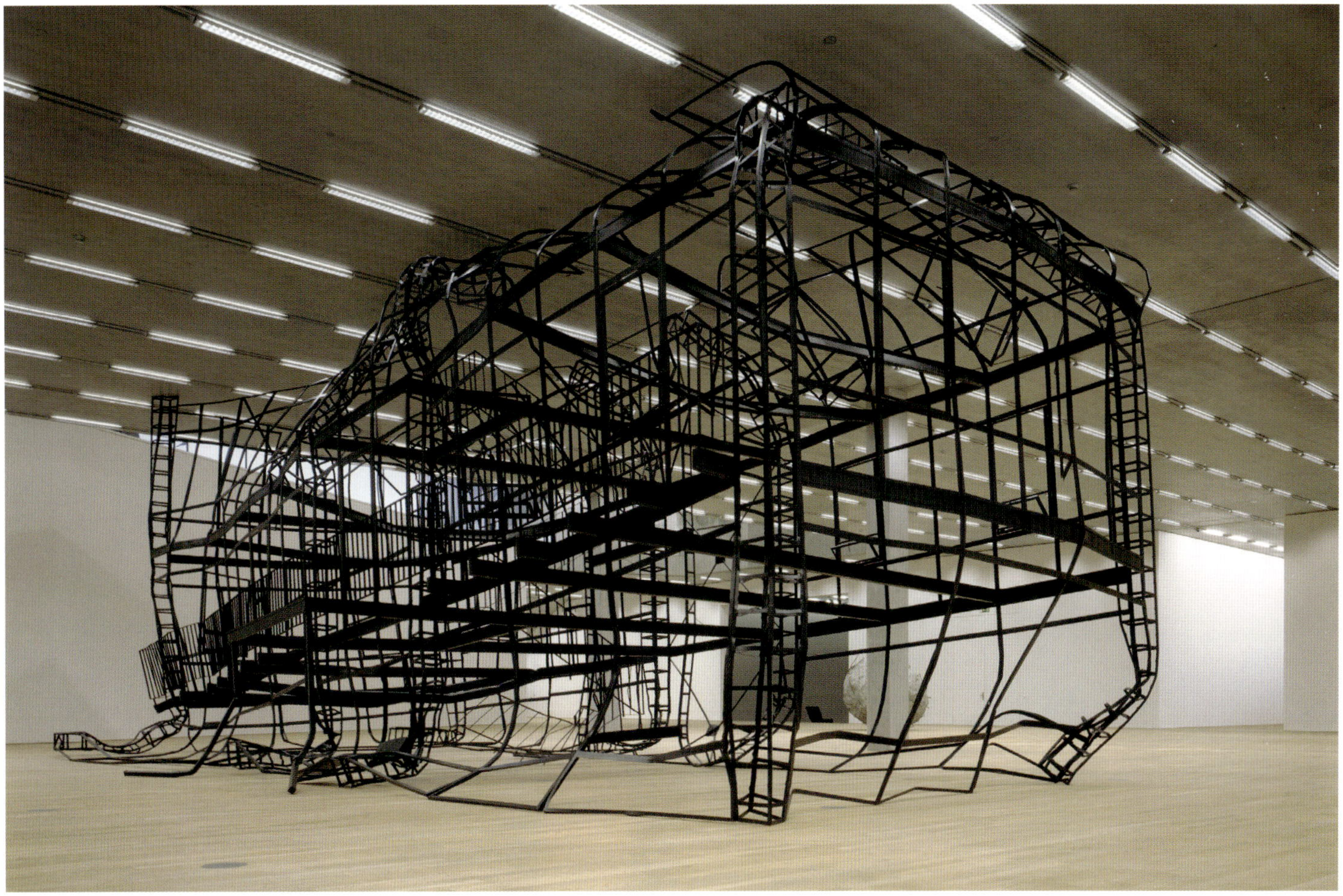

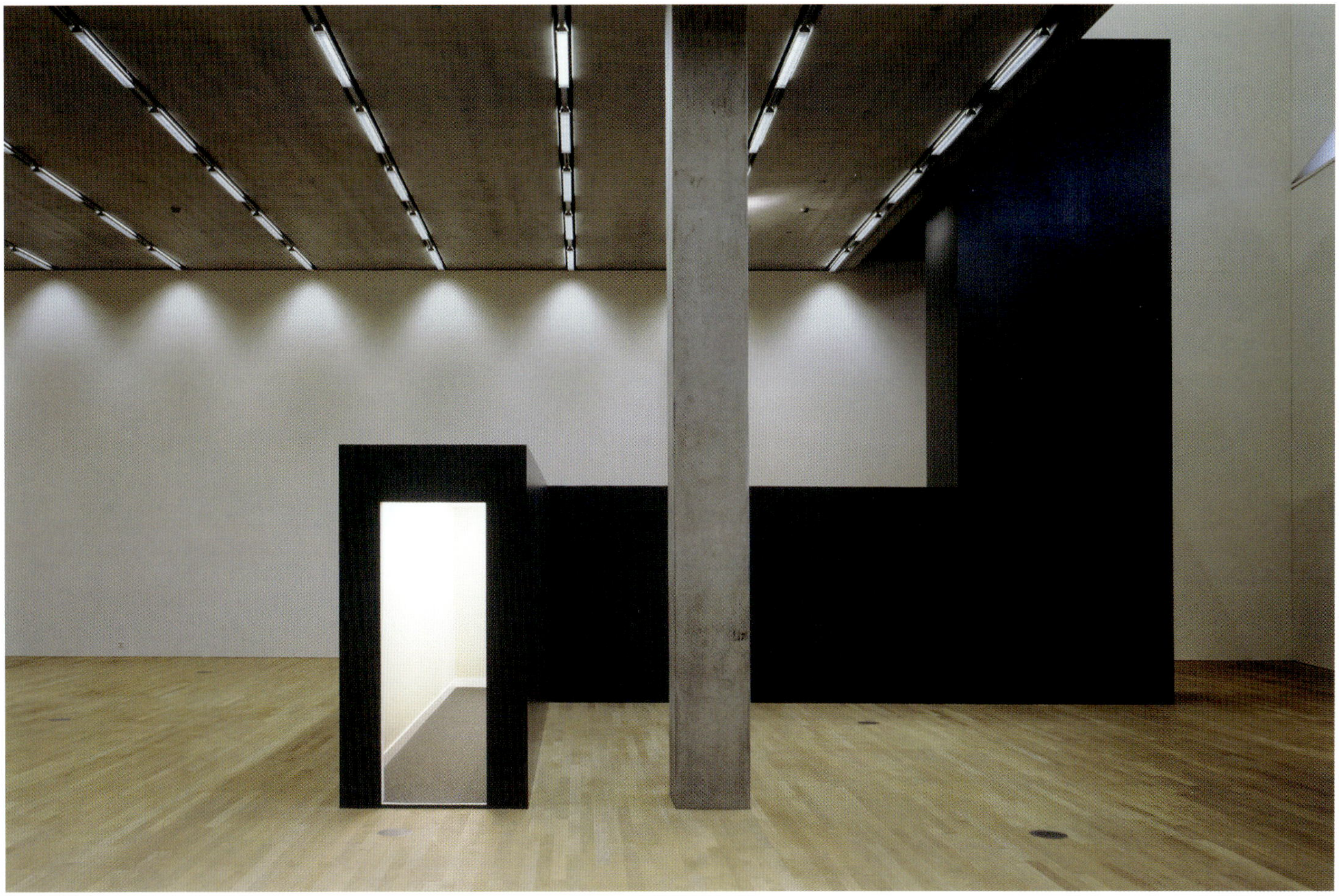

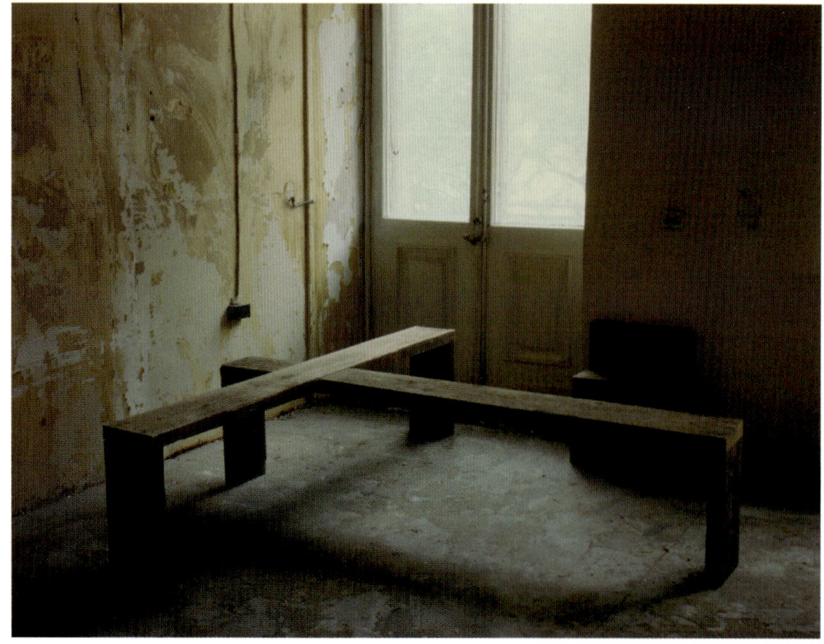

190 x 190 x 47, 2 x (55 x 25 x 20) (right)
1992, wood, steel and wax
Copyright the artist, courtesy White Cube

51 x 49 x 3723 x 15 x 11 (opposite)
2000, steel, glass and, felt
Copyright the artist, courtesy White Cube
photo: Steve White

MIROSŁAW BAŁKA

Mirosław Bałka, best known for *How It Is*—the ominous black box which filled Tate Modern's Turbine Hall from October 2009–April 2010—is one of Poland's best known contemporary artists. His work, tinged with a sense of nostalgia, is consciously informed by his country's fractured history, interpreted through both personal and collective memory.

Working primarily in sculpture, Bałka's practice is as much about the carefully placed objects he uses as the space between them. It is this acute spatial awareness and the heightened emotions these scenes seem to evoke that distinguish Bałka's artistic practice, alongside a strong sense of historical referential reliance. *190 x 190 x 47, 2 x (55 x 25 x 20)* and *51 x 49 x 3723 x 15 x 11* both exemplify the precise nature of his work, combining minimalist form and a subtle use of colour—reflected within each of the accurately defined titles. The range of materials explored by the artist pertains to his humanistic interest, particularly with reference to Poland's recent history; for example, the peeling paint and awkward simplicity of the wooden bench in *51 x 49 x 3723 x 15 x 11,* and more directly in his use of hair, soap and ash in other pieces.

The Crossroad in A is a series of four colour photographs—an unusual medium for Bałka—that highlights a number of discussions arising throughout his work, most notably the Holocaust and Nazi occupation in Poland, with the crossroads in the lithographs depicting the crossroads at Auschwitz from four different perspectives. Any identifying features in the photographs have been carefully erased beneath a wash of white paint —this idea of erasure of both place and person remaining omnipresent throughout Bałka's work.

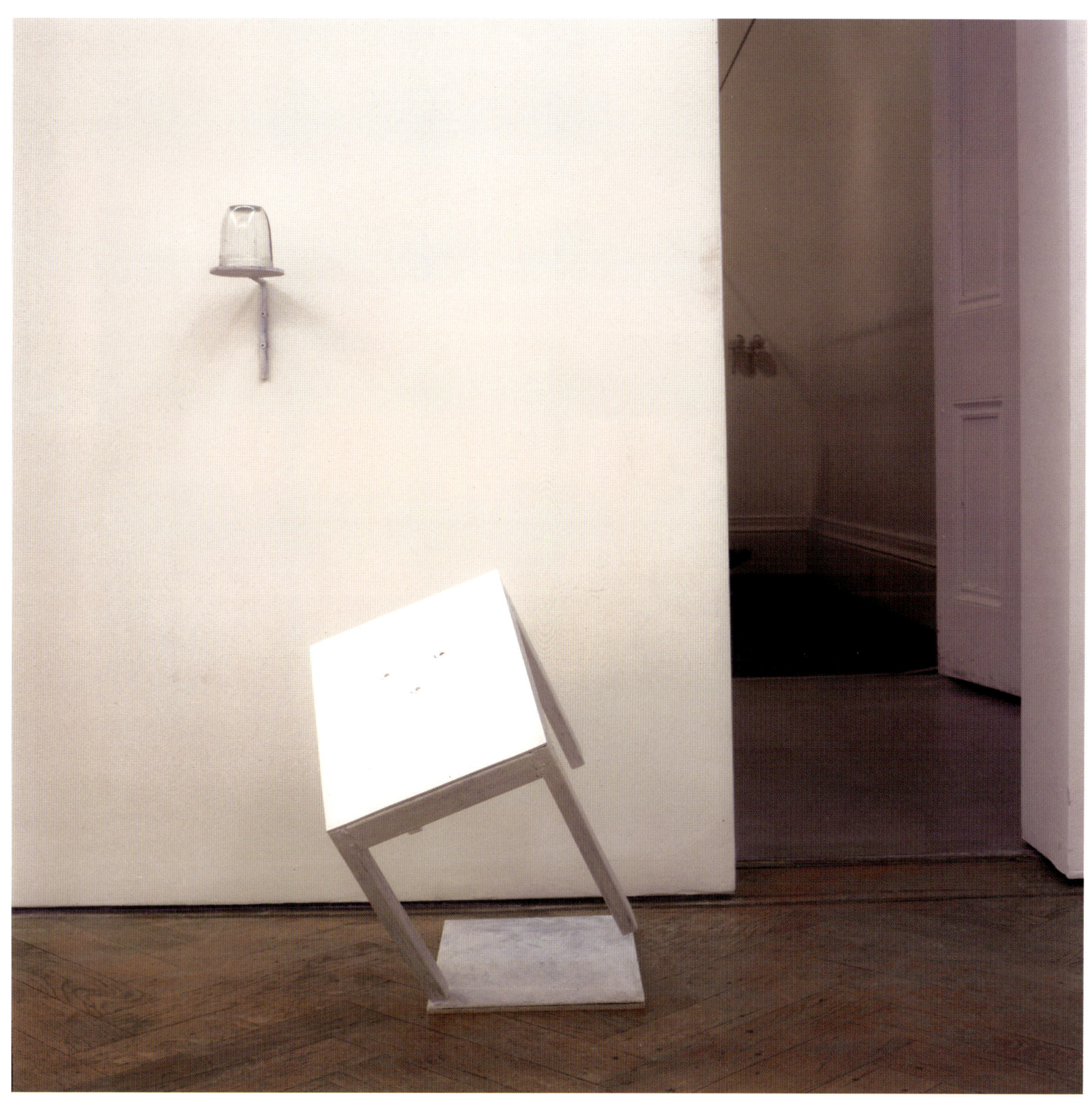

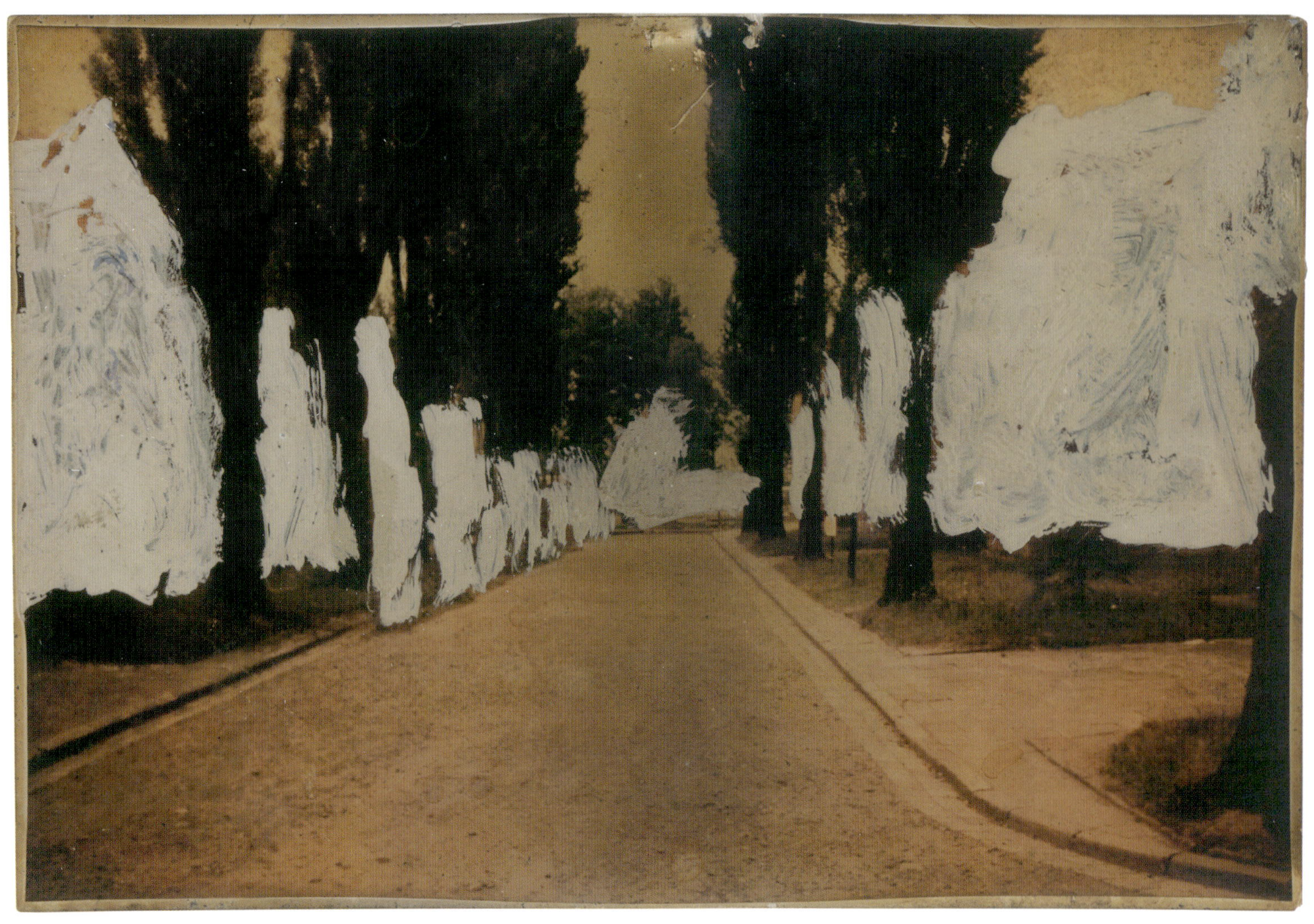

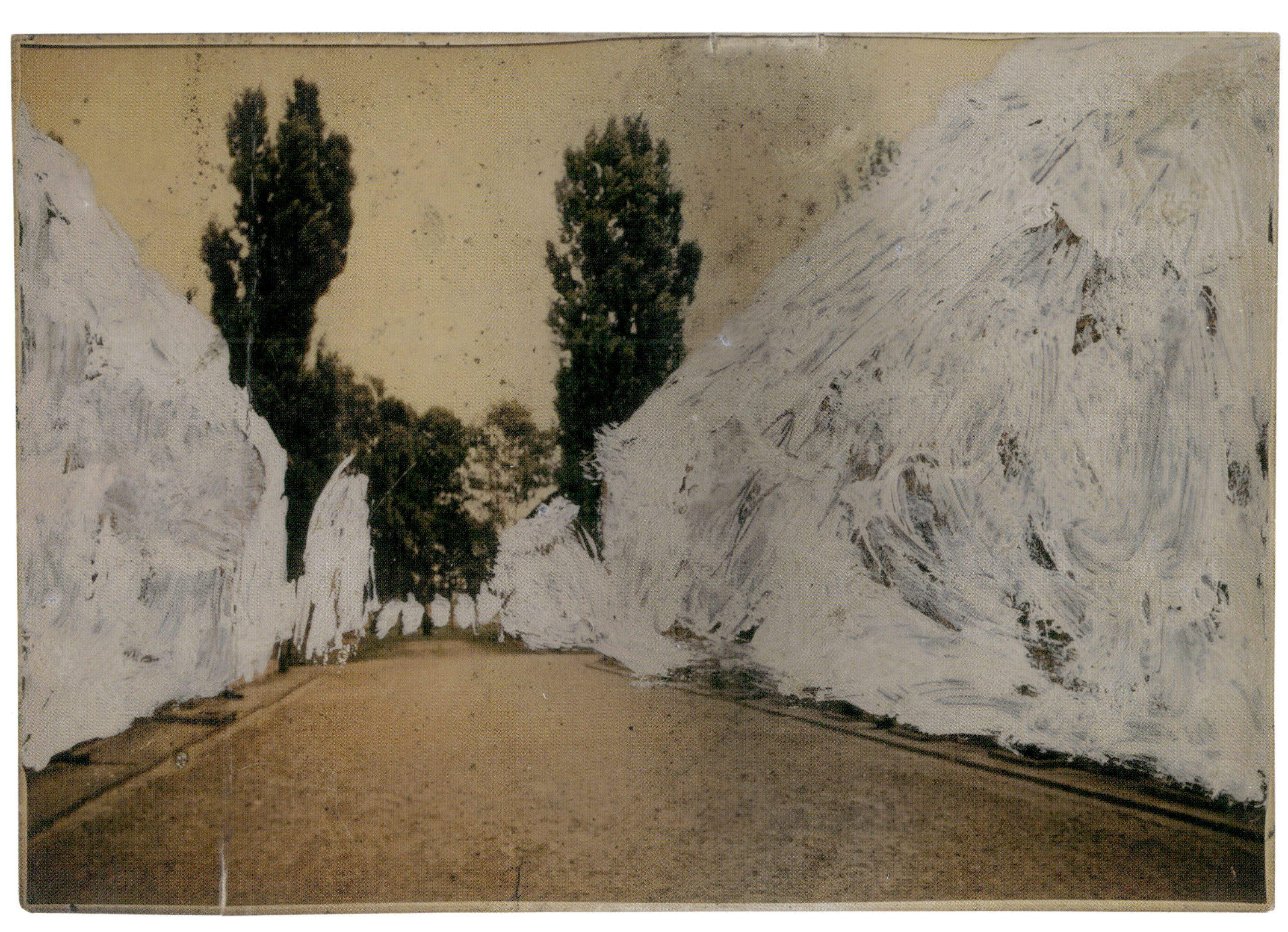

EDWARD KRASINSKI

Paper Clips (below)
1985, mixed media, 99 x 200 x 79 cm
Courtesy Anton Kern Gallery, New York

Intervention (opposite)
1981, acrylic paint, collage, blue tape
on board, 72 x 71 cm
Courtesy Anton Kern Gallery, New York

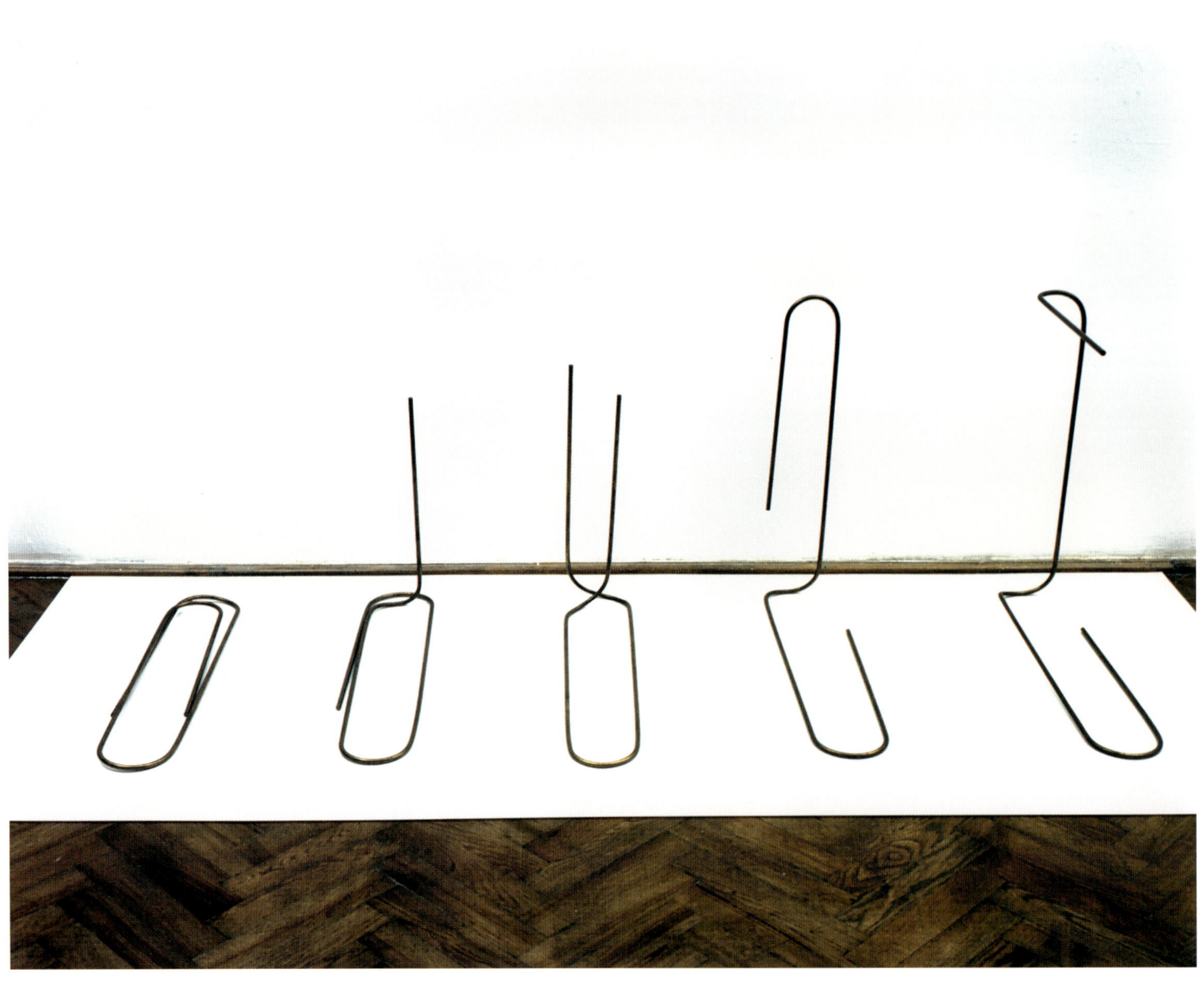

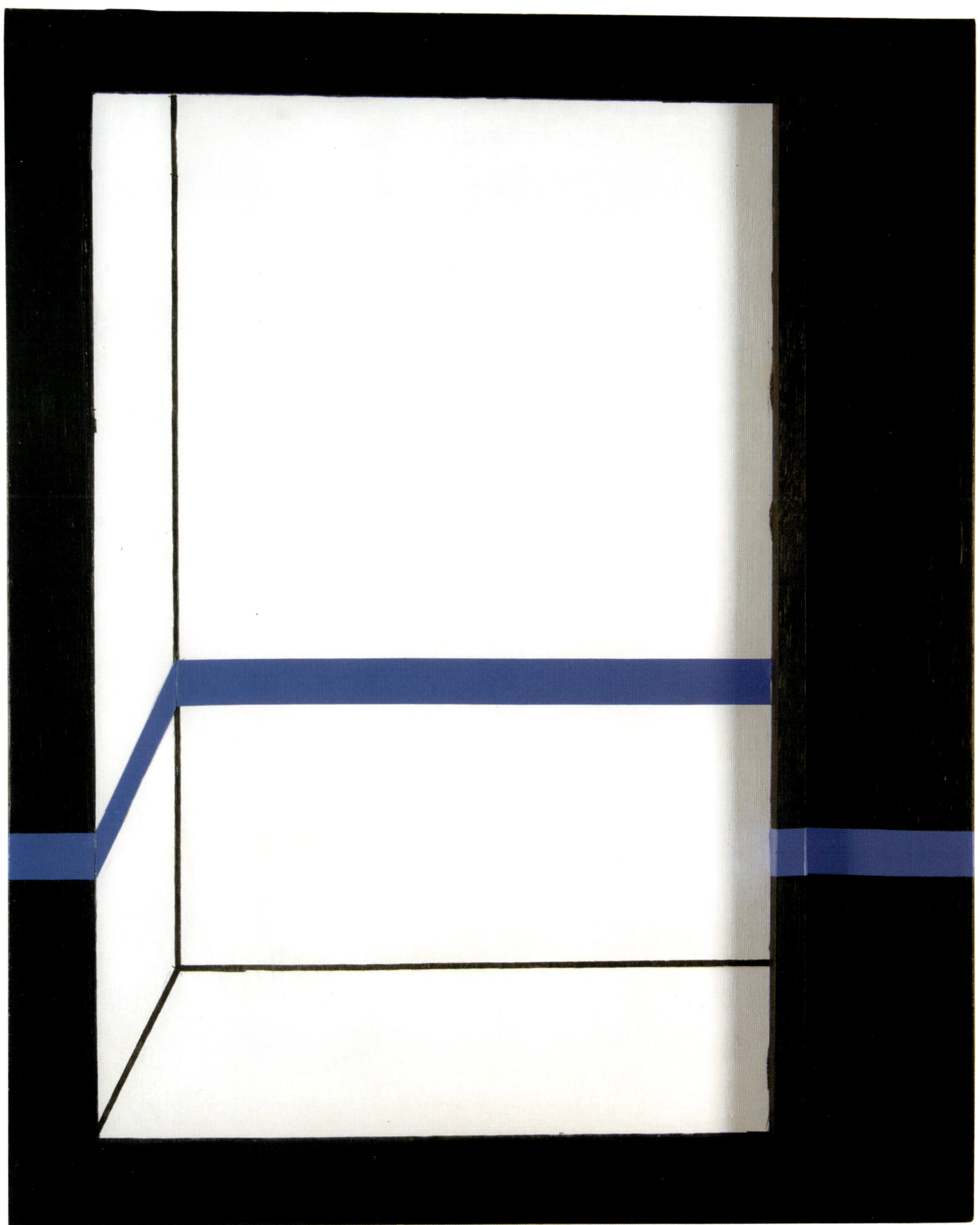

ALEXANDER BRODSKY

Sardine Can (open) (below)
1999, unfired clay, 7 x 18 x 8 cm
Courtesy Ronald Feldman Fine Arts, New York
photo: John Lamka

Untitled (street) (opposite)
2008, ink on paper, 61 x 91 cm
Courtesy Ronald Feldman Fine Arts, New York
photo: Hermann Feldhaus

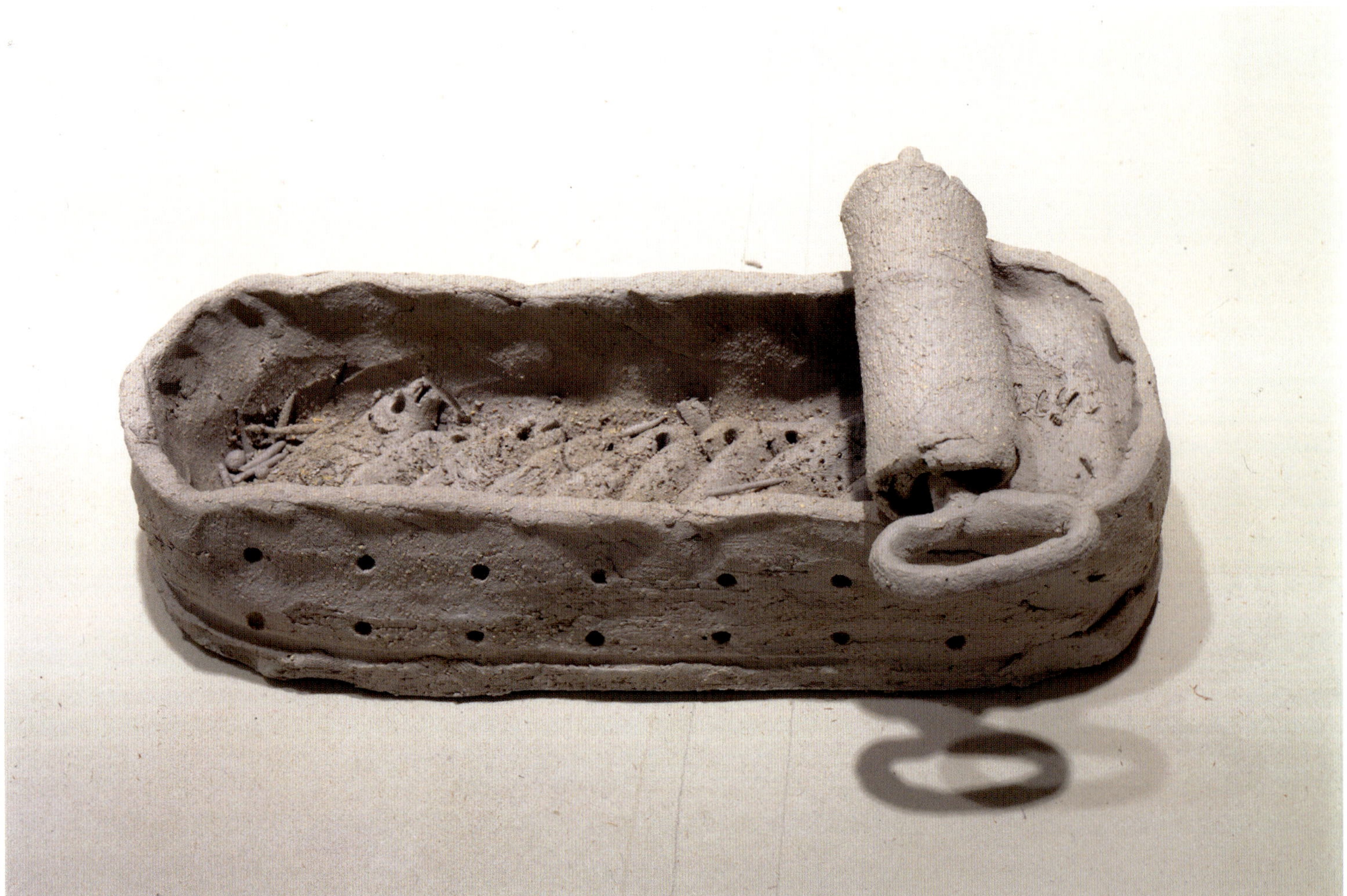

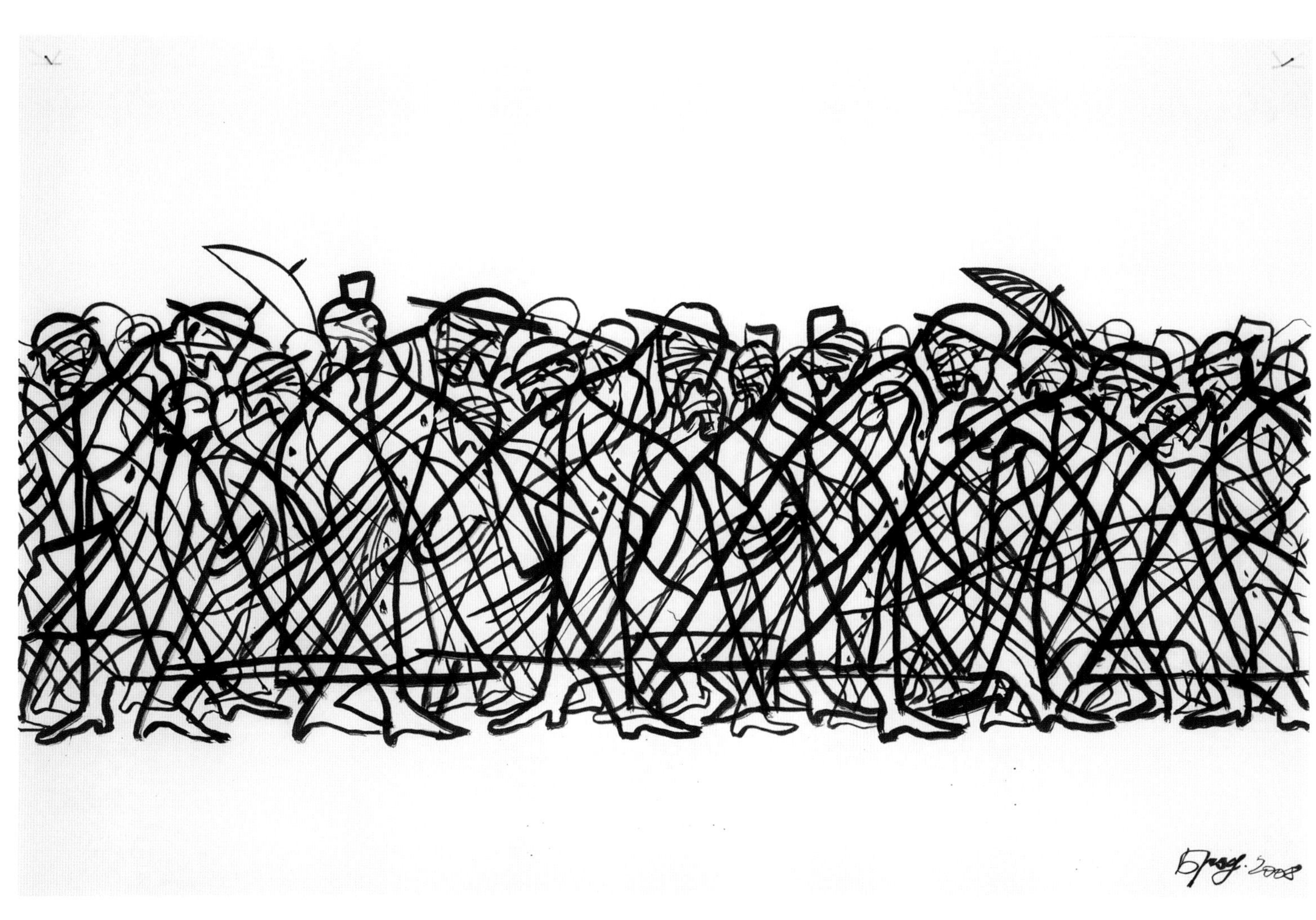

ALEXANDER KOSOLAPOV
Gorby (below)
1989, silkscreen print
Courtesy the artist

Mini and Mickey, Worker and Farmgirl (opposite)
2004, bronze
Courtesy the artist

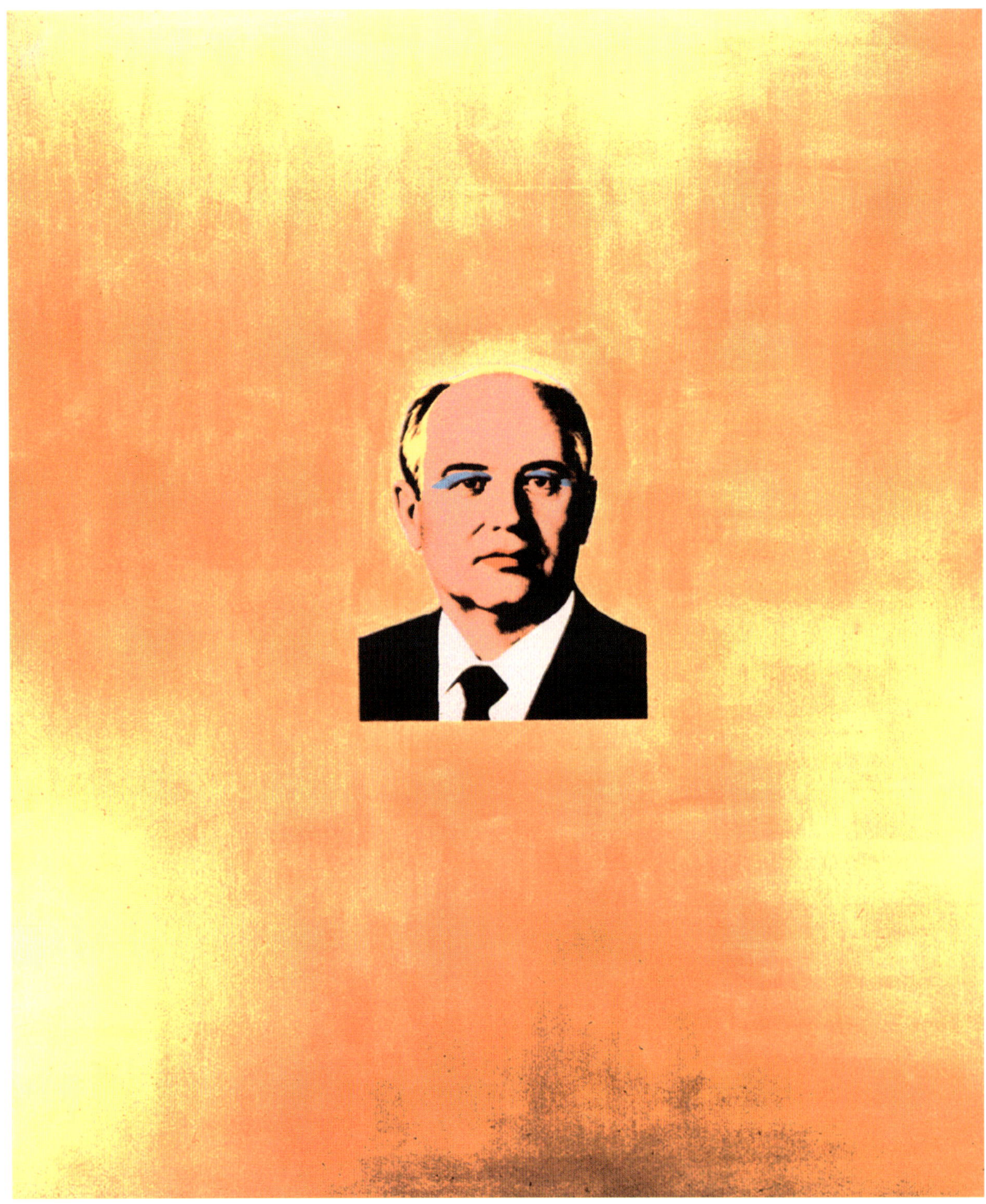

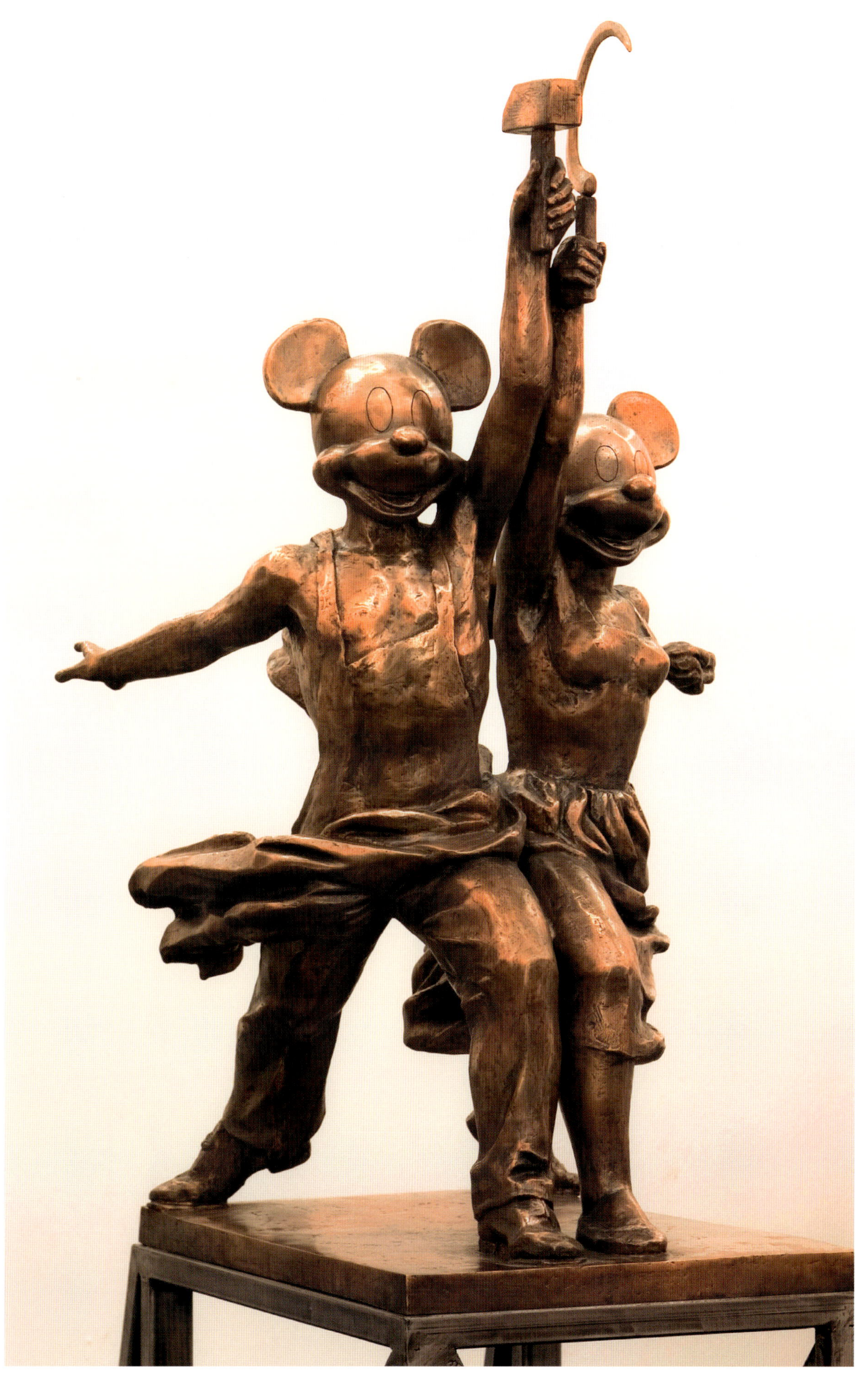

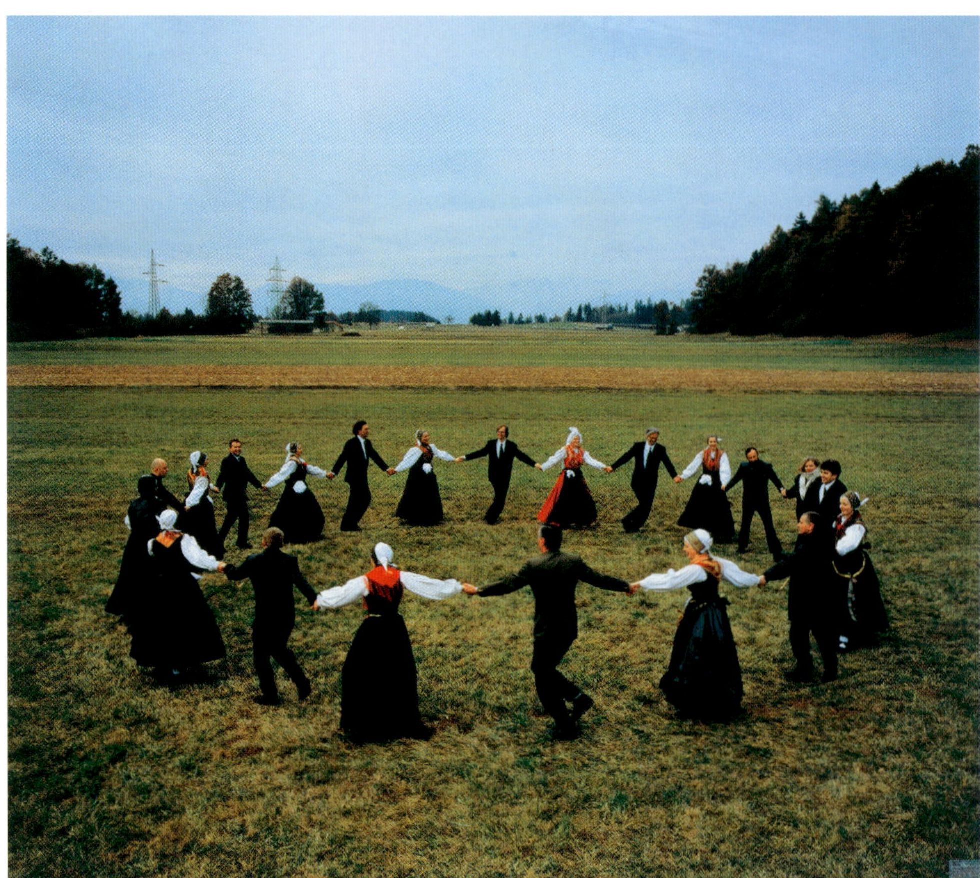

NSK

Formed in the Slovenian capital of Ljubljana in 1984, at a time when the former Yugoslavia was steadily approaching its moment of fracture, NSK—or Neue Slownische Kunst, a German Phrase meaning "New Slovenian Art"—is an artist collective whose significance to the political and cultural history of Eastern Europe is widely acknowledged. Their output over the past three decades can be characterised by a provocative approach and style of expression inextricably bound to the social and political struggles of their native Slovenia, and shared by the groups it comprises: the rock band Laibach, the visual arts group Irwin, the 'retro-garde' theatre group Noordung, the design group New Collectivism and the Department of Pure and Applied Philosophy. By utilising and appropriating iconographic and symbolic elements from the country's history, NSK has sought to challenge, critique and deconstruct representational models and 'natural' cultural values and rituals, an agenda that contributed to the disintegration of the aesthetics and ethics of Communist and post-Communist culture and identity.

In 1987, via the design group New Collectivism, NSK succeeded in exposing and critiquing the underlying, hidden power structures of Yugoslavian Communism with a poster they produced for the Yugoslavian 'Day of Youth', a holiday commemorating the birthday of the late President Josip Broz Tito. Originally accepted by Yugoslavian authorities—who agreed and identified with the posters visual ideology—and winning public acclaim for its 'politically' appropriate design, the poster eventually caused controversy and drew censorship when it became clear that it was in fact an appropriation of a Nazi painting entitled *The Third Reich*, produced by the artist Richard Klein in 1936. New Collectivism had simply replaced the Nazi symbols with socialist ones.

In 1992, in the aftermath of Slovenian independence, NSK formed the NSK State, a 'micro nation' conceived as an abstract social body that does not identify with any existing national state. Issuing passports to its members and with an all-inclusive citizenship policy, the NSK State has carried out 'Embassy' and 'Consulate' events around Europe. It now has several thousand citizens across all continents and forms a dynamic, collective cultural network that embodies NSK's founding principles.

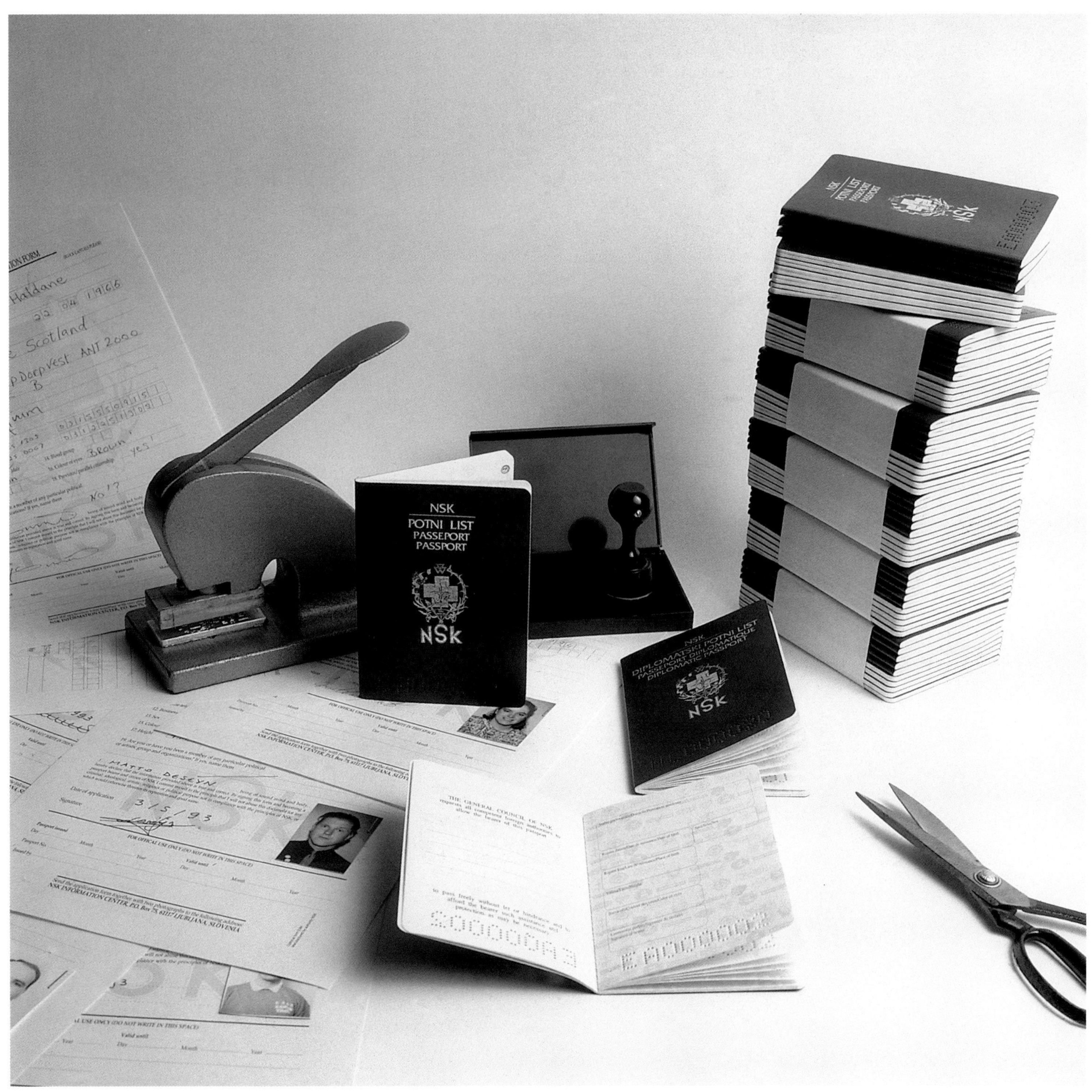

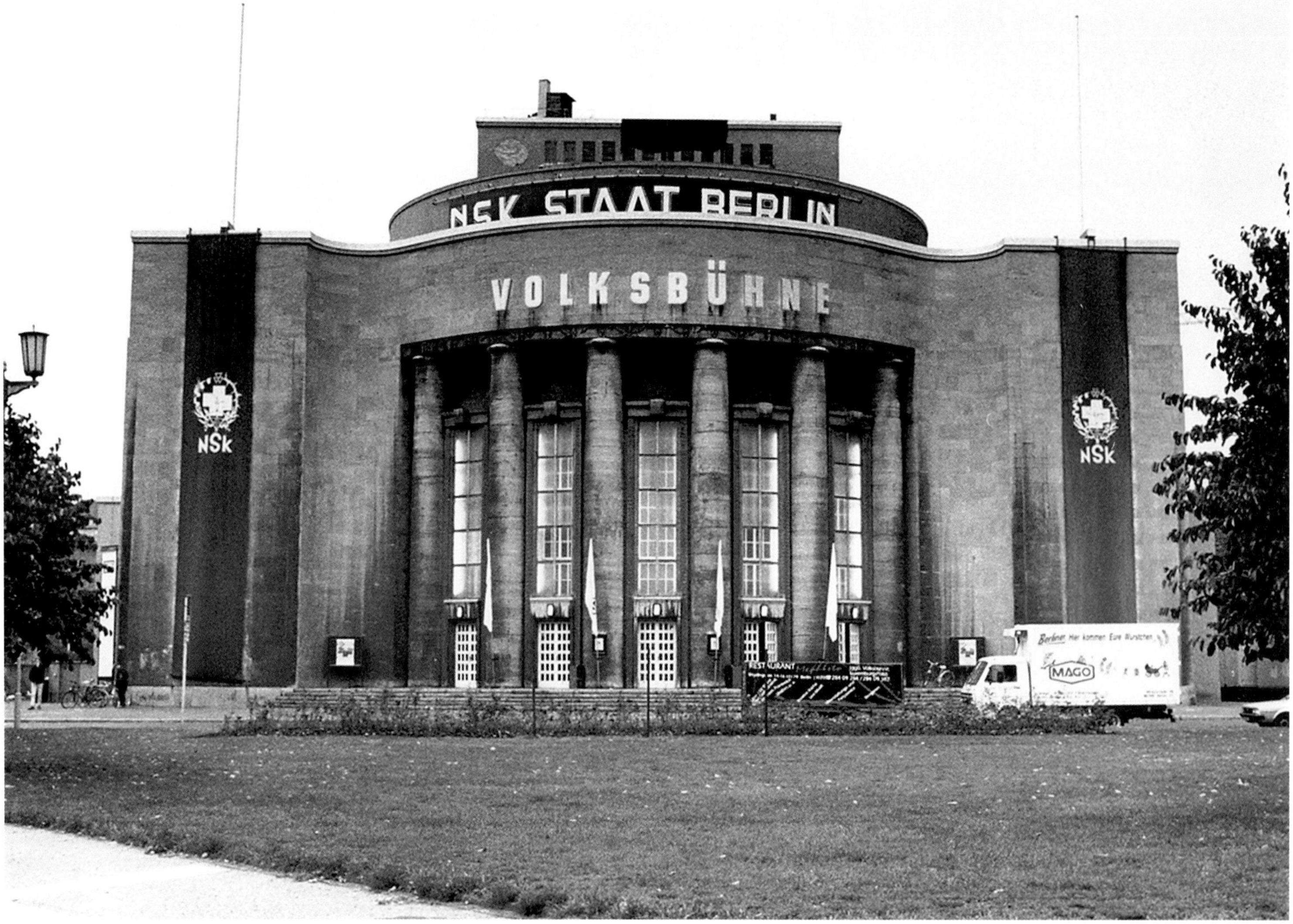

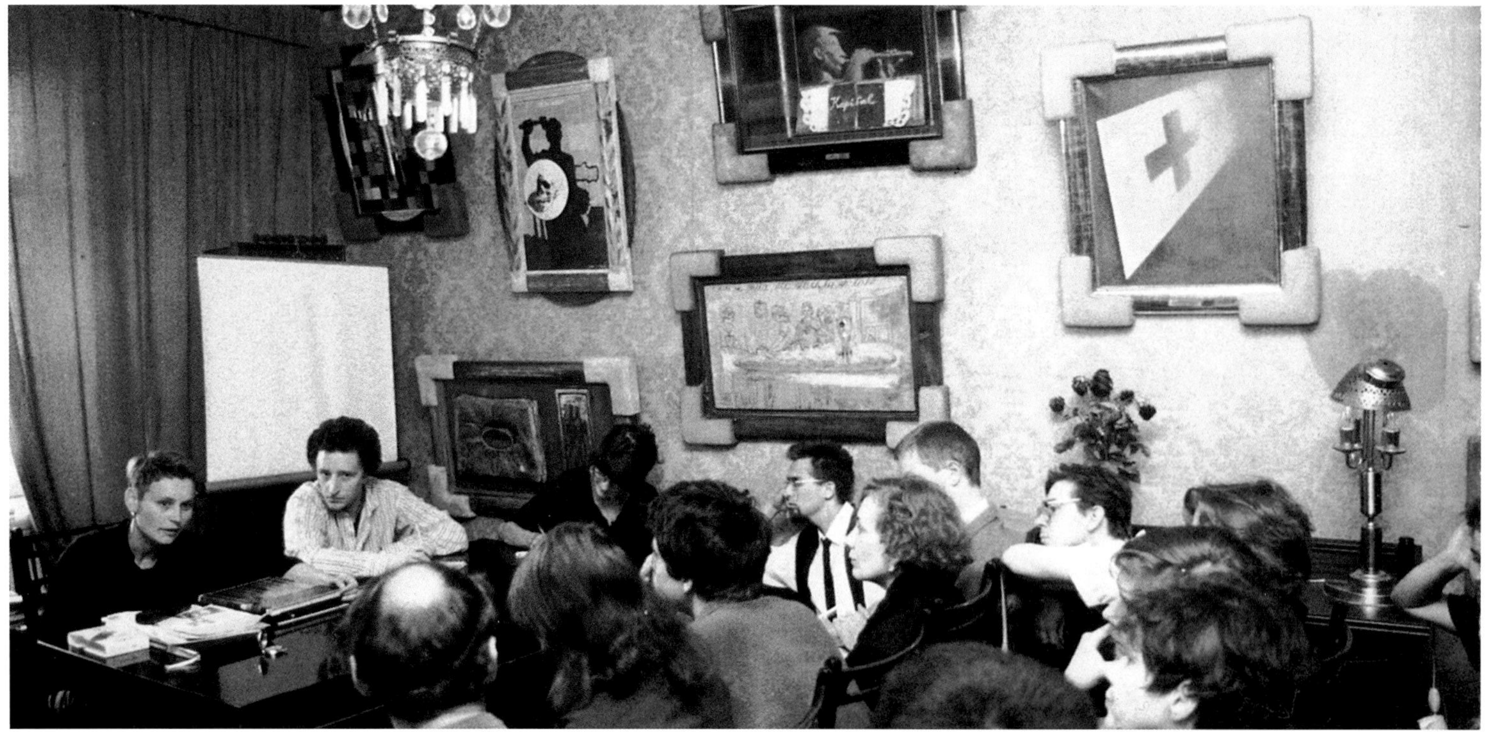

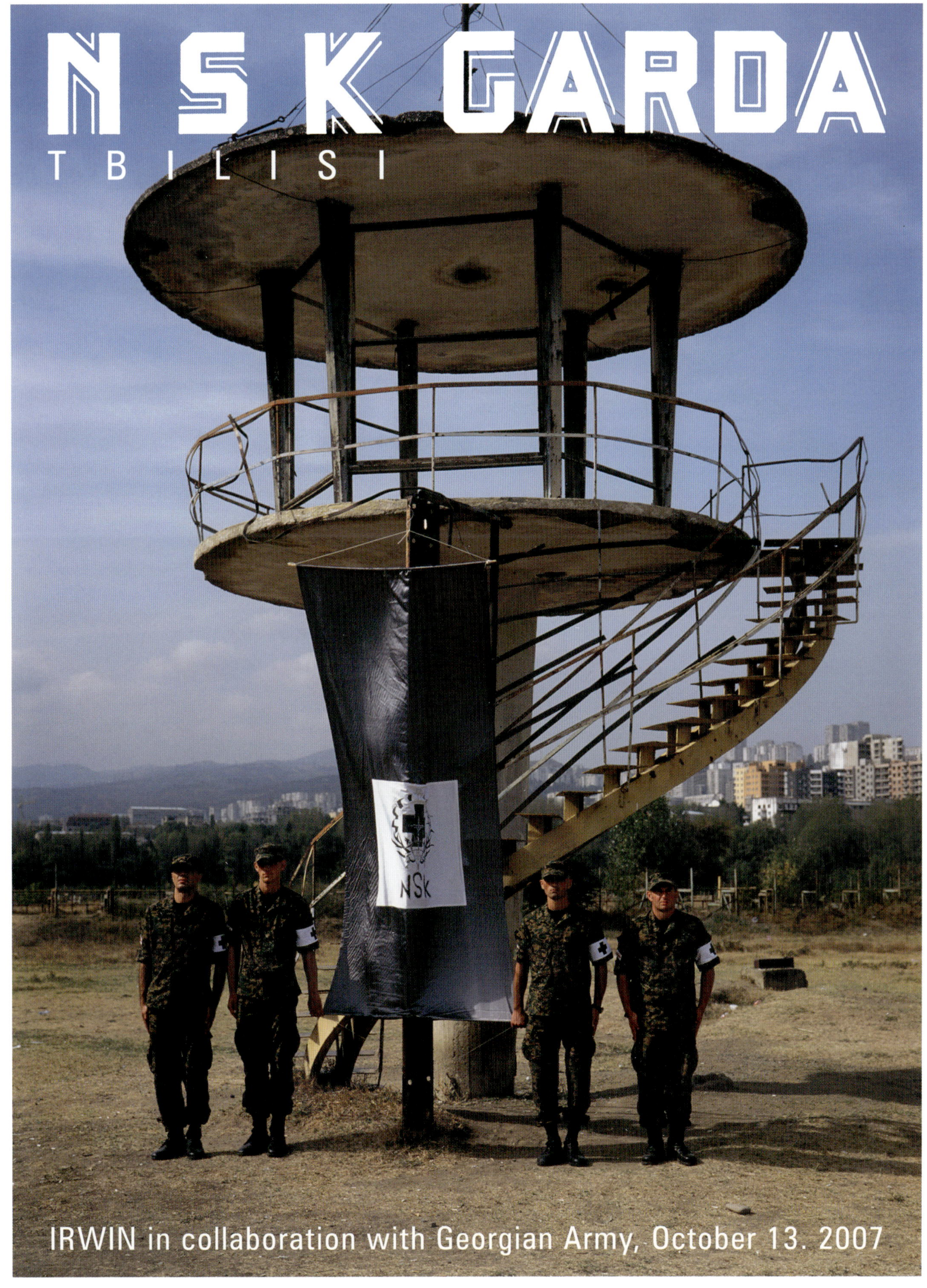

NSK GARDA
TBILISI
NSk
IRWIN in collaboration with Georgian Army, October 13. 2007

MARKO PEHLJHAN

Makrolab markIIex, Island of Campalto
Operations, Venice Lagoon (below)
2003, Venice Biennale
Courtesy Projekt Atol archive, photo: Ars Electronica, Rubra

Rhythmical Scenic Structure ATOL (opposite)
1994, Moderna Galerija, Ljubljana
Courtesy Projekt Atol archive, photo: Ars Electronica, Rubra

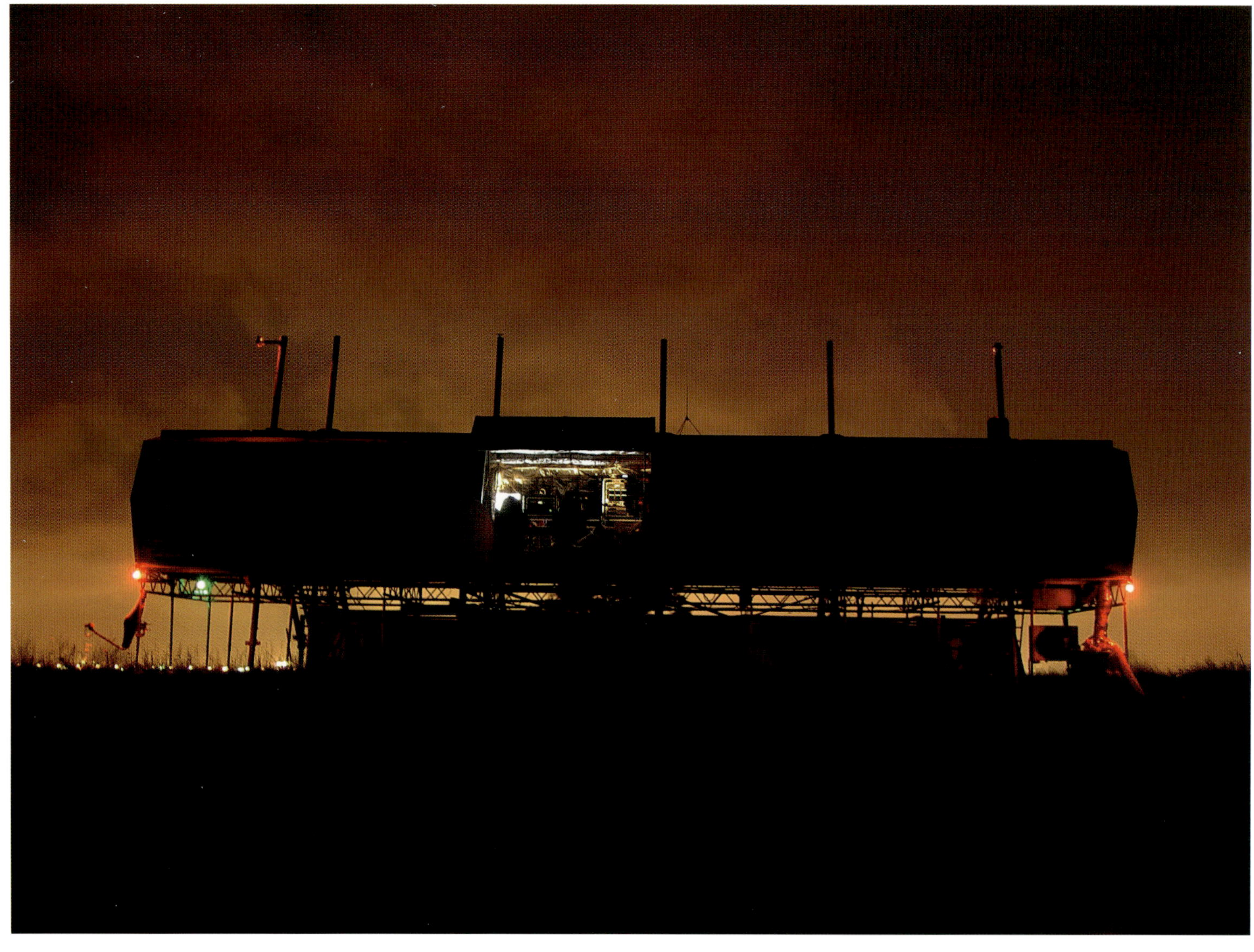

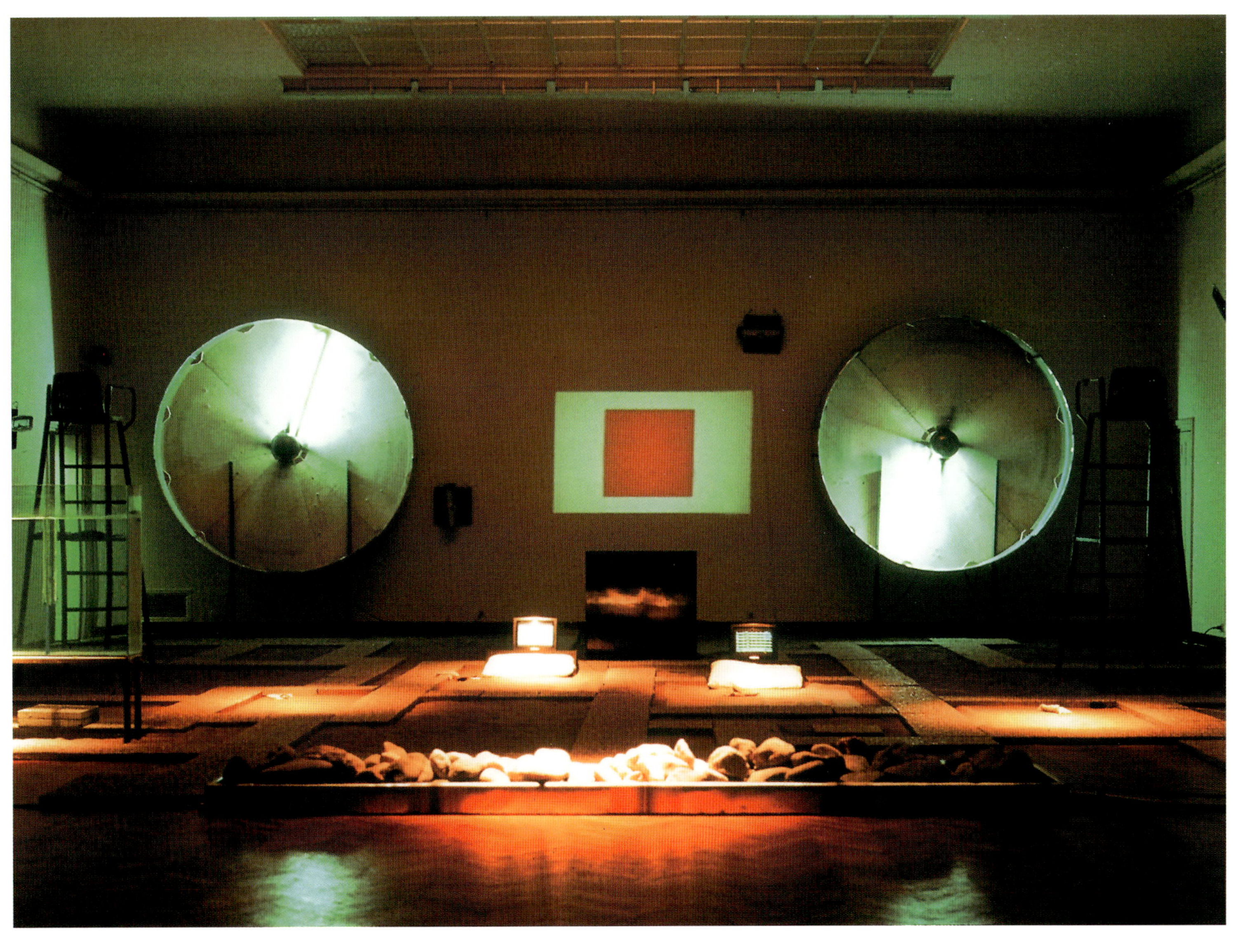

MARJETICA POTRČ

Dry Toilet

**2003, building materials and sanitation infrastructure
La Fila, La Vega barrio, Caracas**

Courtesy of Liyat Esakov and Marjetica Potrč, supported by La
Vega community, Caracas; Caracas Case Project and Federal
Cultural Foundation of Germany; Ministry of Environment,
Venezuela, photo: Andre Cyprian

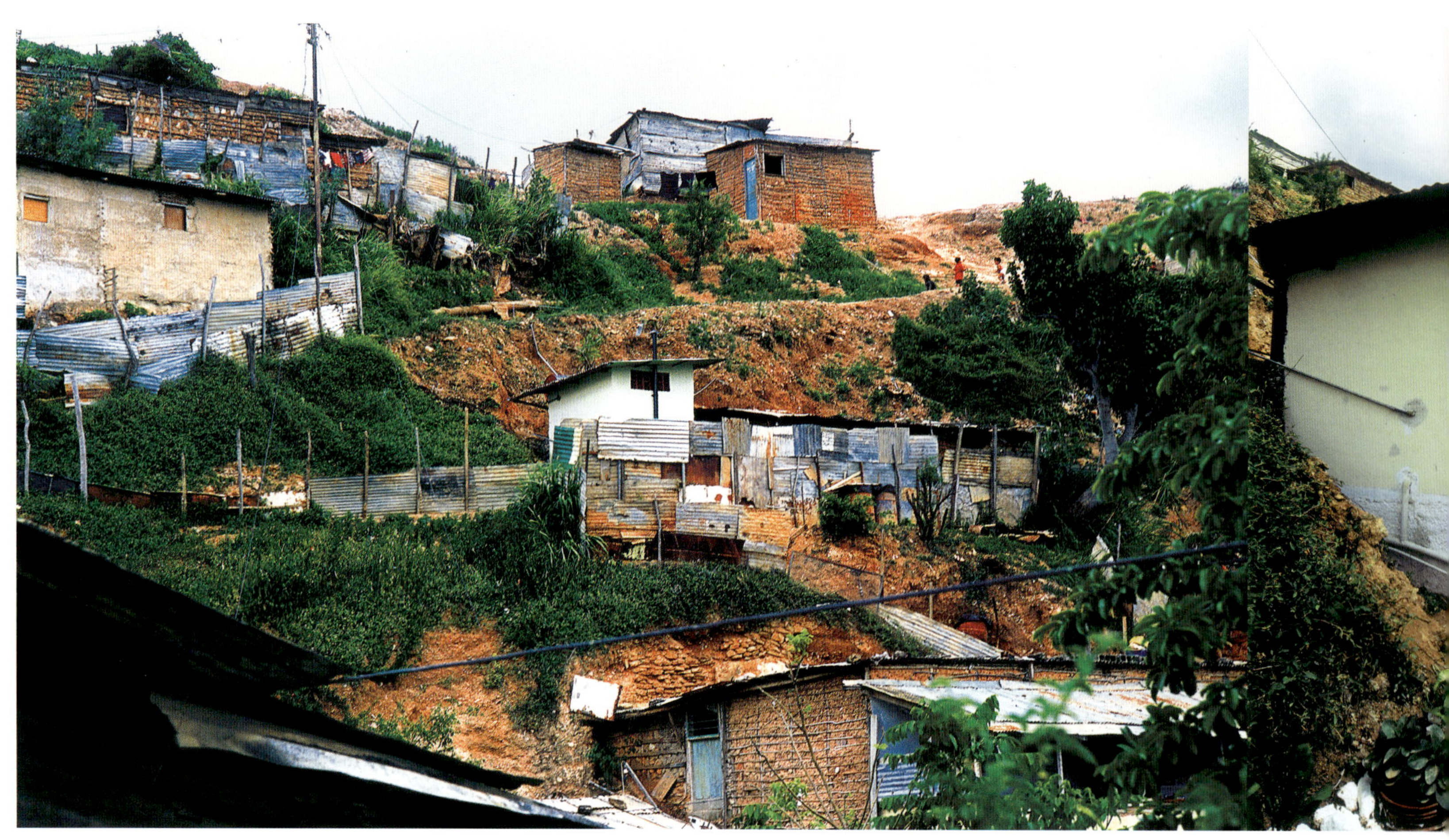

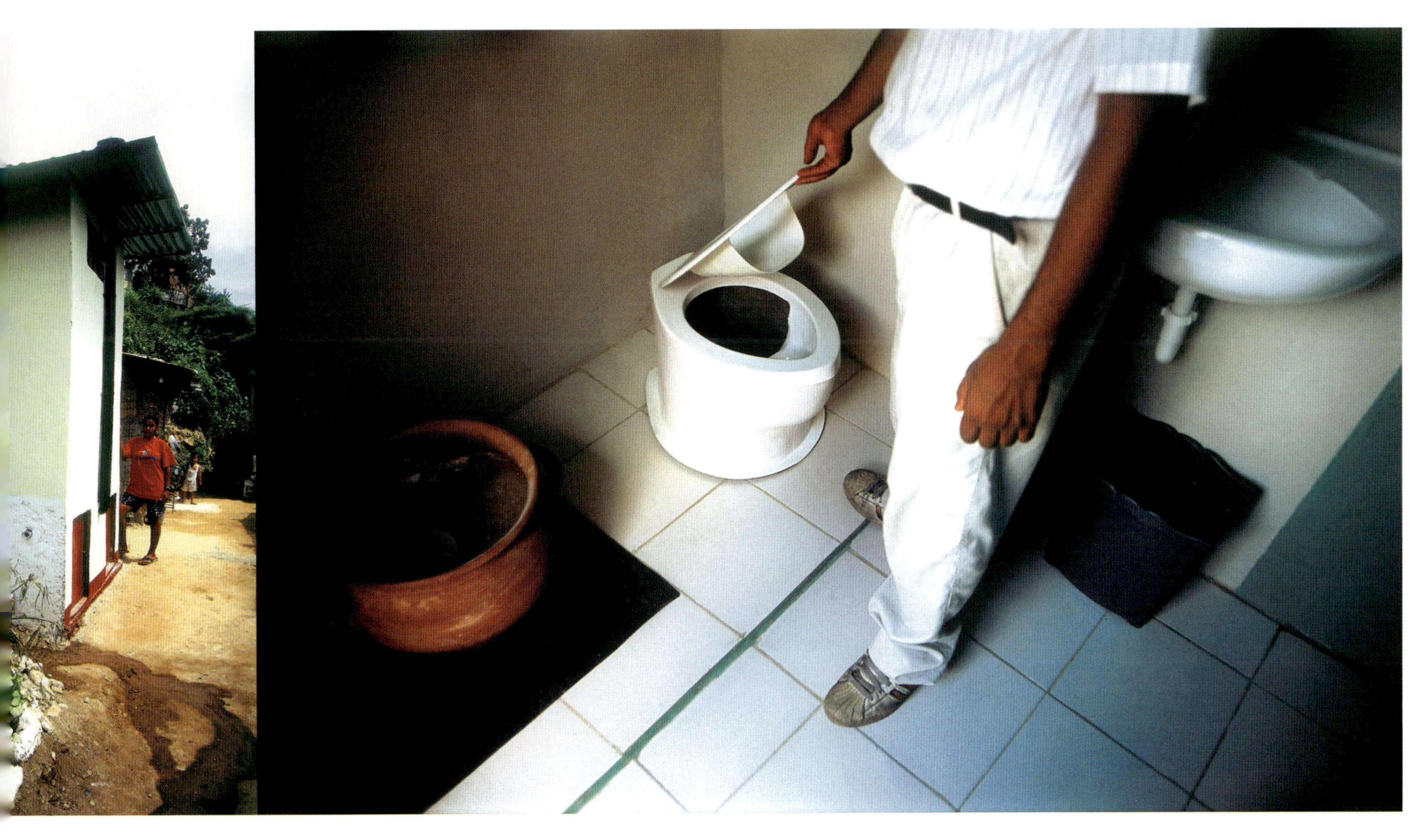

It Doesn't Matter (right)
2005, video, drawings photos, interview,
table, tablecloth and chairs, video: 5 minutes,
photo: 31 x 41 cm
Courtesy Franco Soffiantino Gallery, Turin, Italy

For Every Dog A Different Master (opposite above)
2007, texts, graphs, shirts, photographs, drawings,
animation and documentation, 90 x 120 cm
Documenta 12, Kassel, Germany
Courtesy Franco Soffiantino Gallery, Turin, Italy

Over and Over (opposite below)
2008, mixed media, diameter 10 m, installation
view at the fifth Berlin Biennial for Contemporary
Art at Skulpturen Park, Berlin
Courtesy Franco Soffiantino Gallery, Turin, Italy

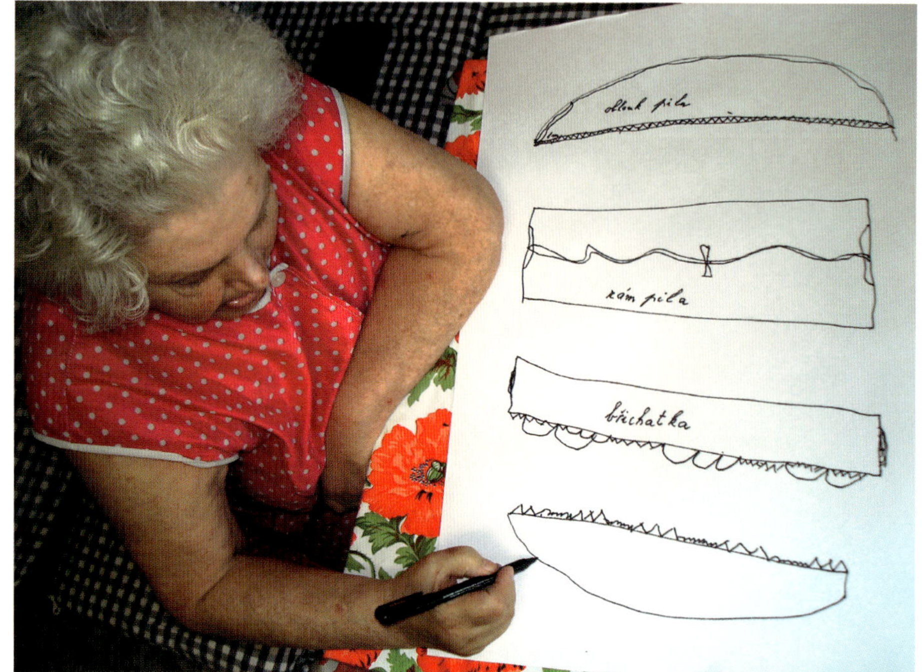

KATERINA ŠEDÁ

Katerina Šedá's sociologically driven work
follows a trend amongst artists in the Czech
Republic for 'intervention' art. Šedá uses
her everyday experiences—"normality"
in the artist's own words—as a canvas;
and her family, friends and fellow citizens
of her hometown of Brno as her subjects.

A reflection on everyday life, Šedá's work
is navigated by a narrative discourse
that explores ideas of familial bonds,
intergenerational interaction, and
communication, that differentiates her
from many of her contemporaries more
concerned with existential ideas. The
ordinariness of her chosen subject matters,

such as the items her grandmother sold
at a local hardware store in Brno over a 33
year period, recollected in hundreds of
sketches in *It Doesn't Matter*, distinguish
Šedá's work with an endearing eminence
that subtley proposes an underlying
artistic discourse.

Every Dog A Different Master is concerned
with ideas of familiarity and acknowledgement.
Šedá recollects her childhood when she
would travel from Brno into the recently
built Nova Lisen, and how gradually people
would stop greeting her—what she later
referred to as "social atomisation". Šedá
then printed a shirt with an image of the

multi-coloured Nova Lisen housing
project and posted these shirts between
households in both locations, mapping
the interactions that occurred.

Šedá's *Over and Over* can also be read
as an observation upon the loss of
familiarity within her community—and
other communities like it—as fences
and barriers are erected forcing people
apart. Šedá, along with a team of
volunteers, created an installation piece
that consisted of numerous different
fences, preceded by a collection of
sketches, both of which were exhibited
internationally.

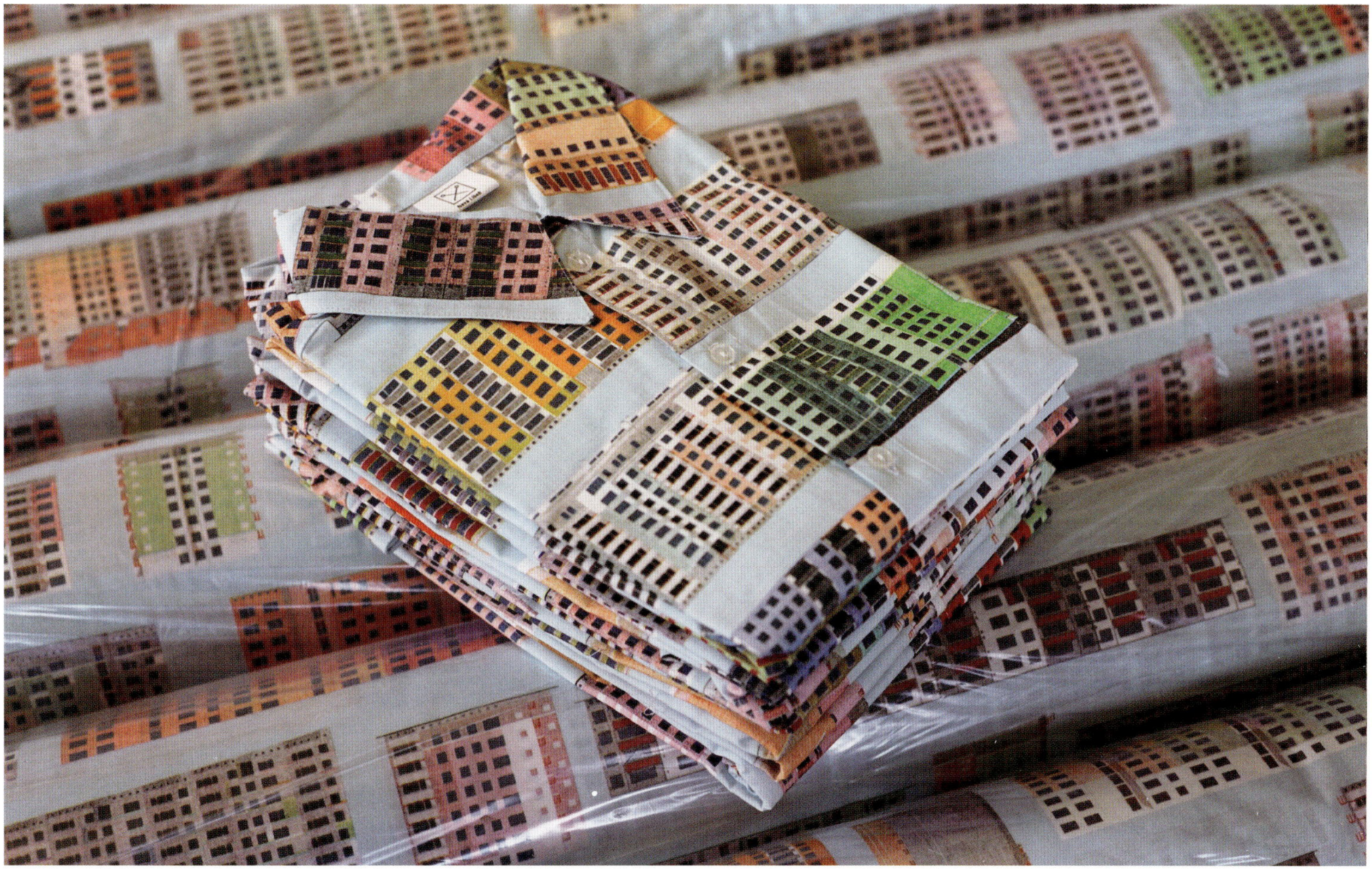

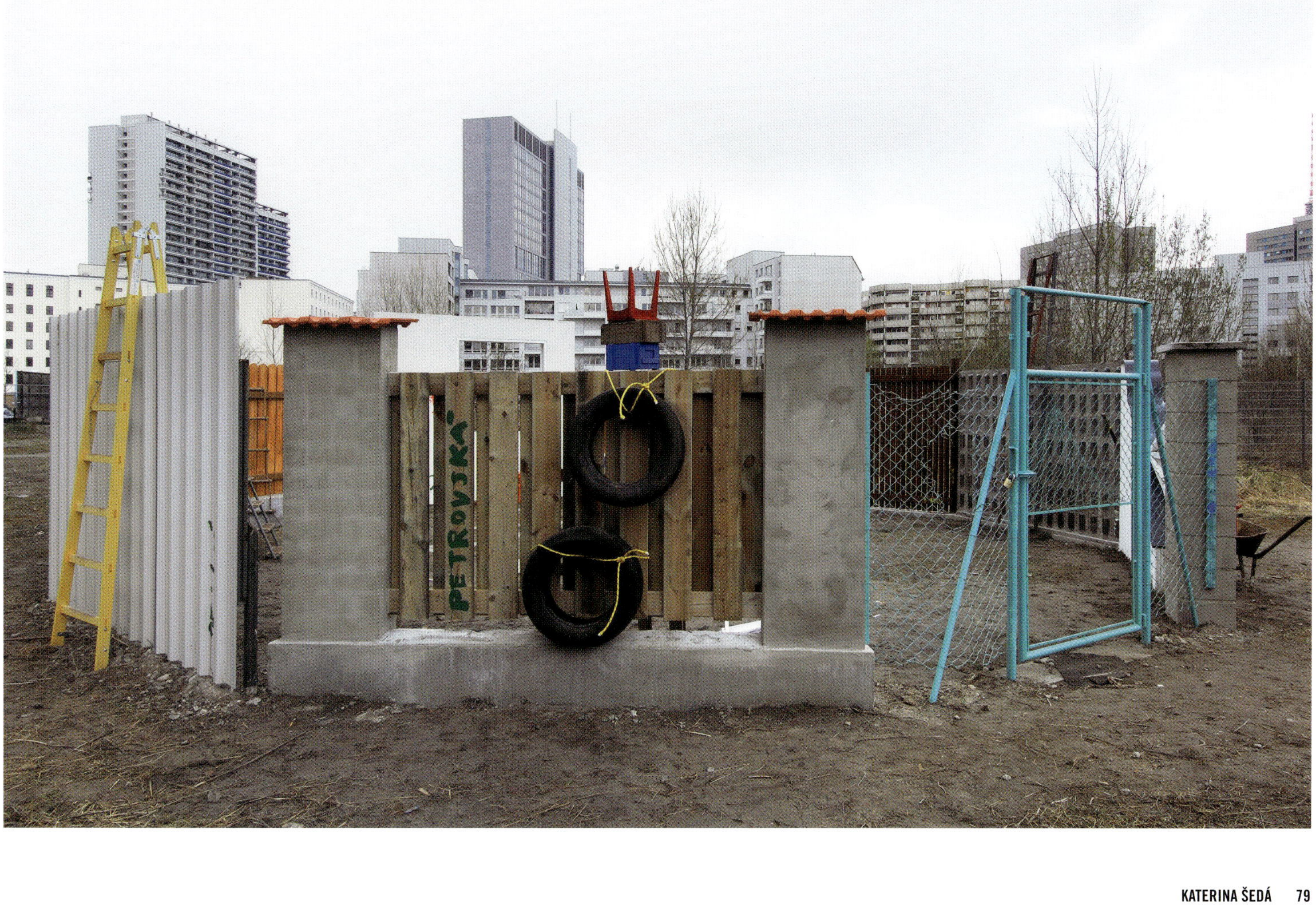

JOANNA MALINOWSKA
Boli (below)
2009, wood, plaster, clay
Courtesy the artist

String Quintet for Two Cellos, Two
Violas and a Corpse (opposite)
2009, performance
Courtesy the artist

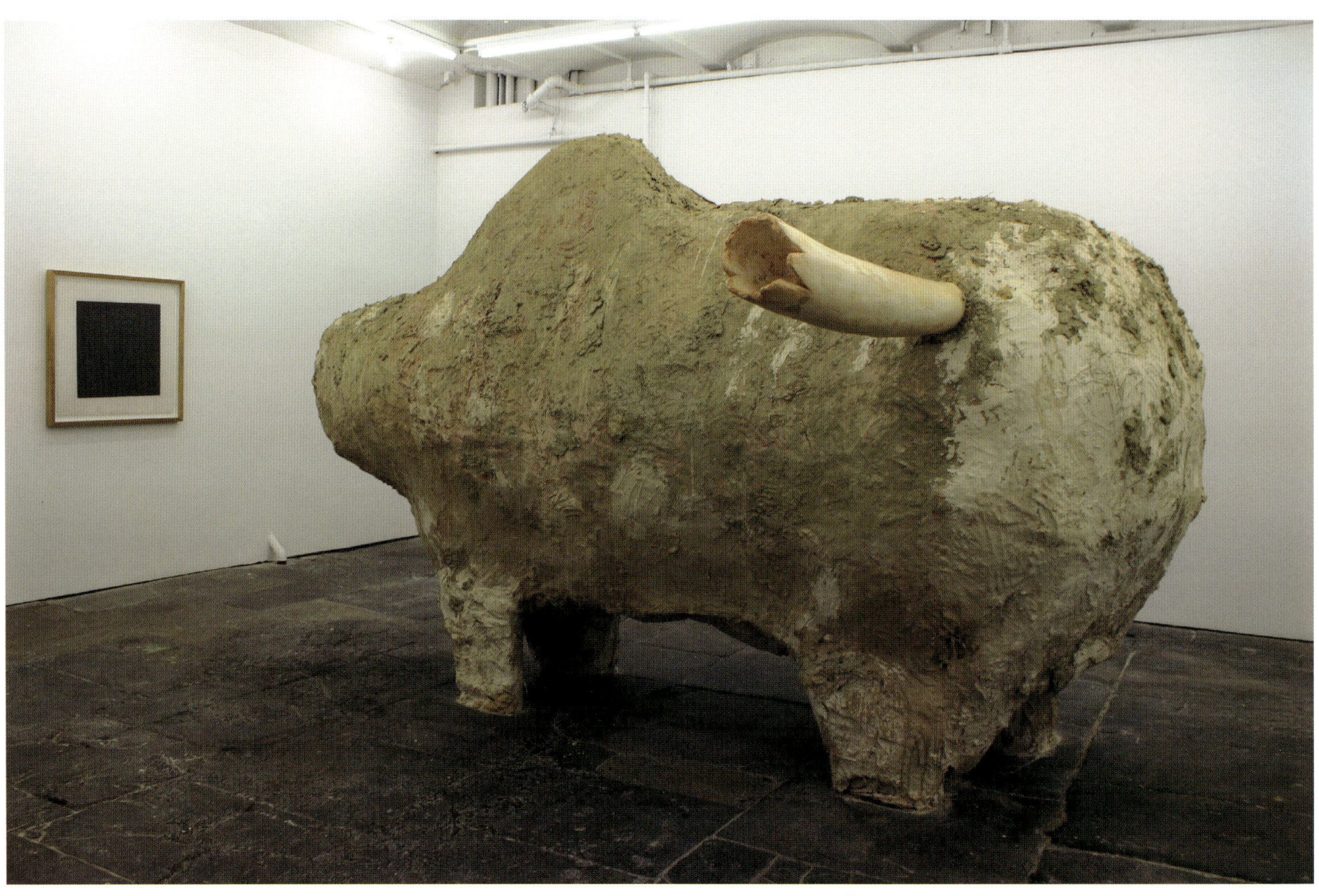

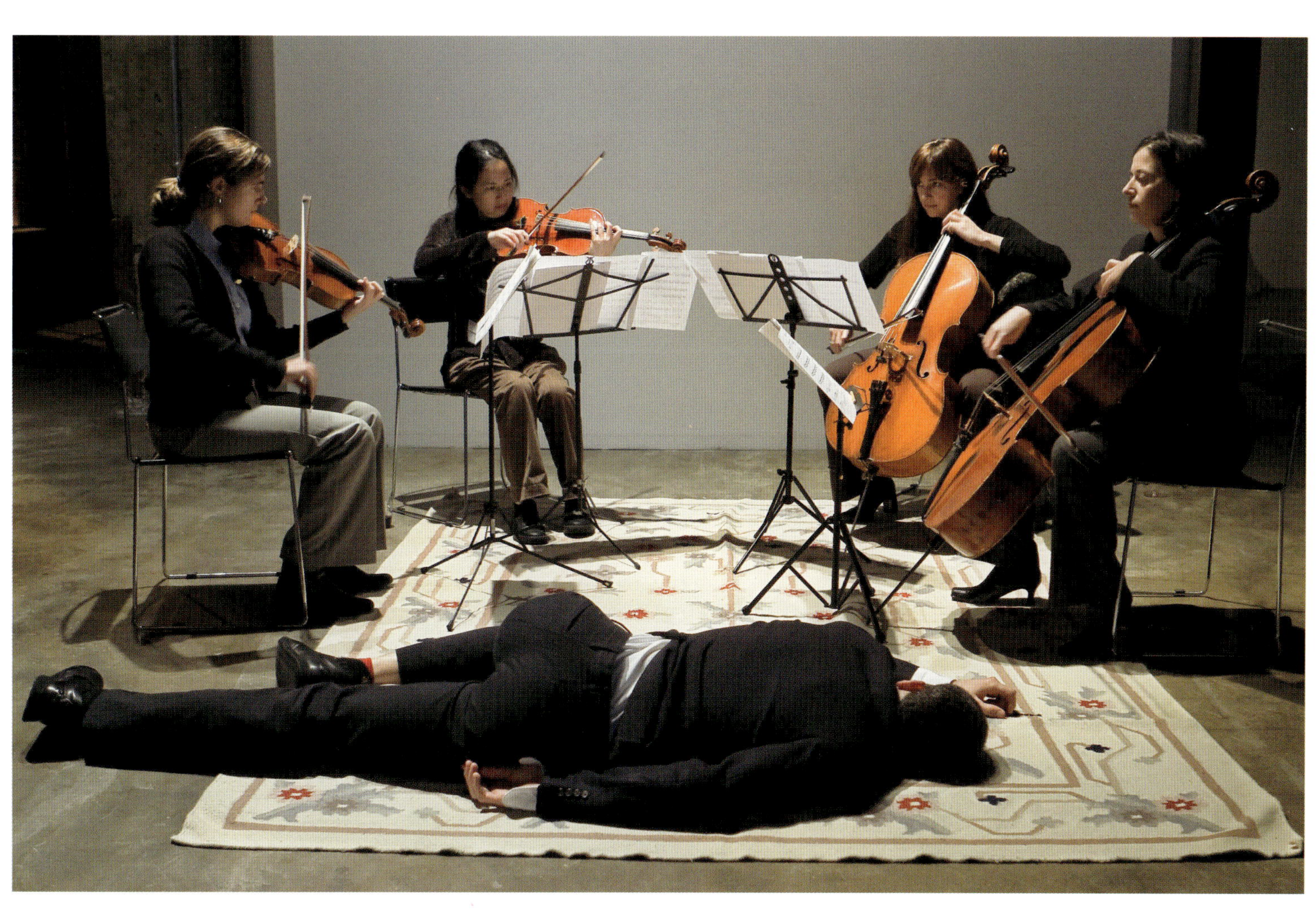

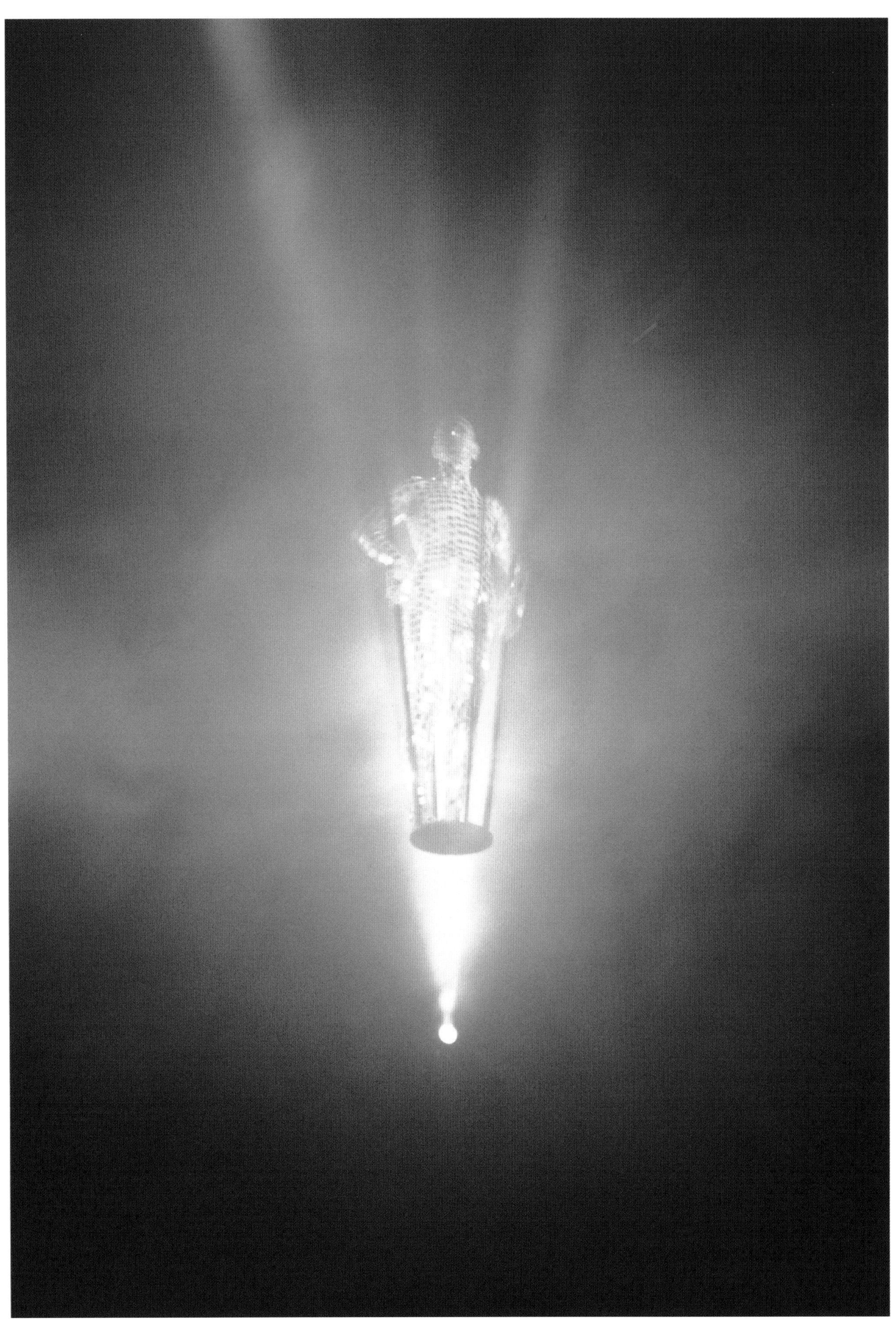

OLEG KULIK
Armadillo for your Show (opposite)
1999, performance
Courtesy the artist

I Love Europe (below)
1996, video 6:20 minutes
Courtesy the artist

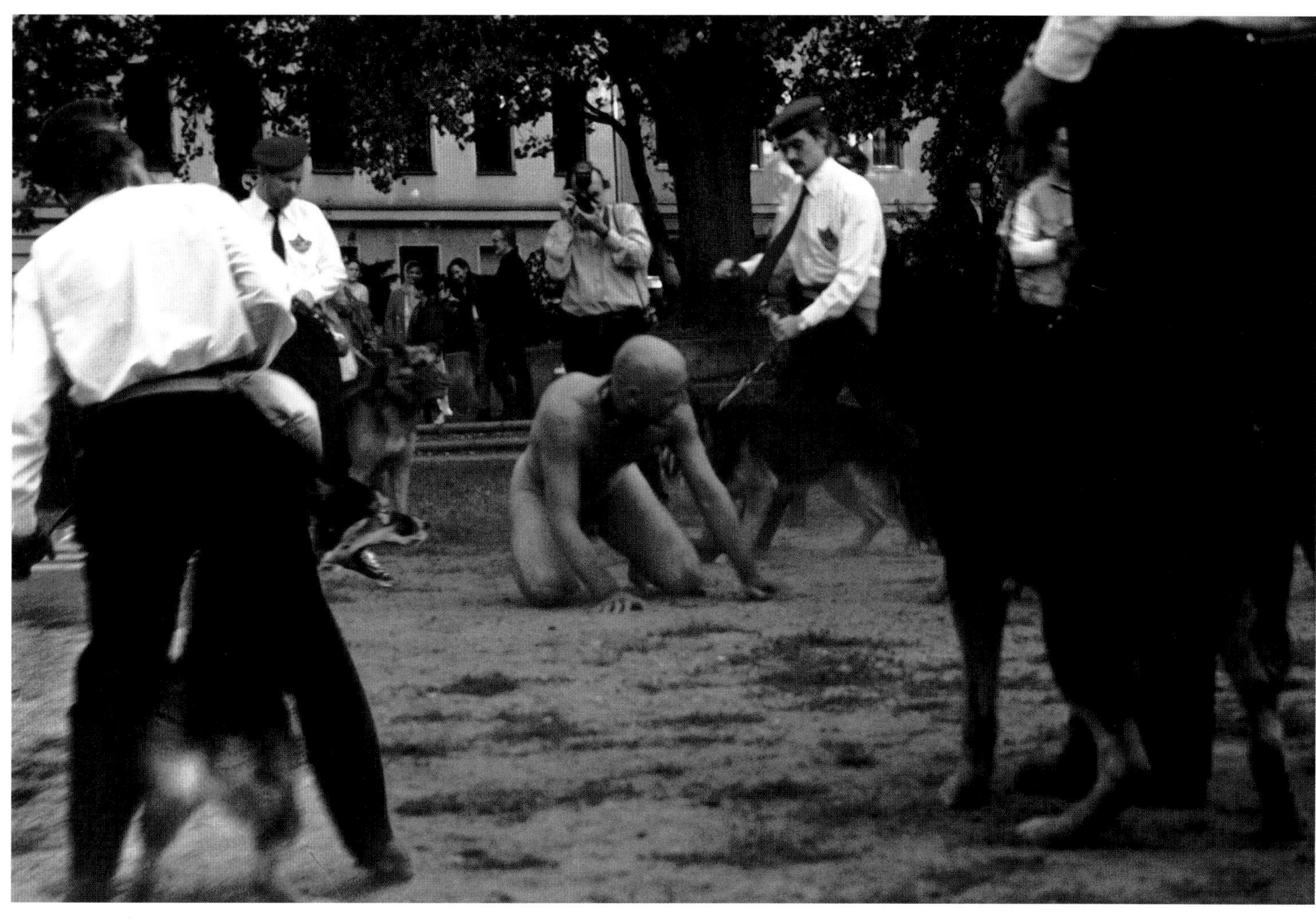

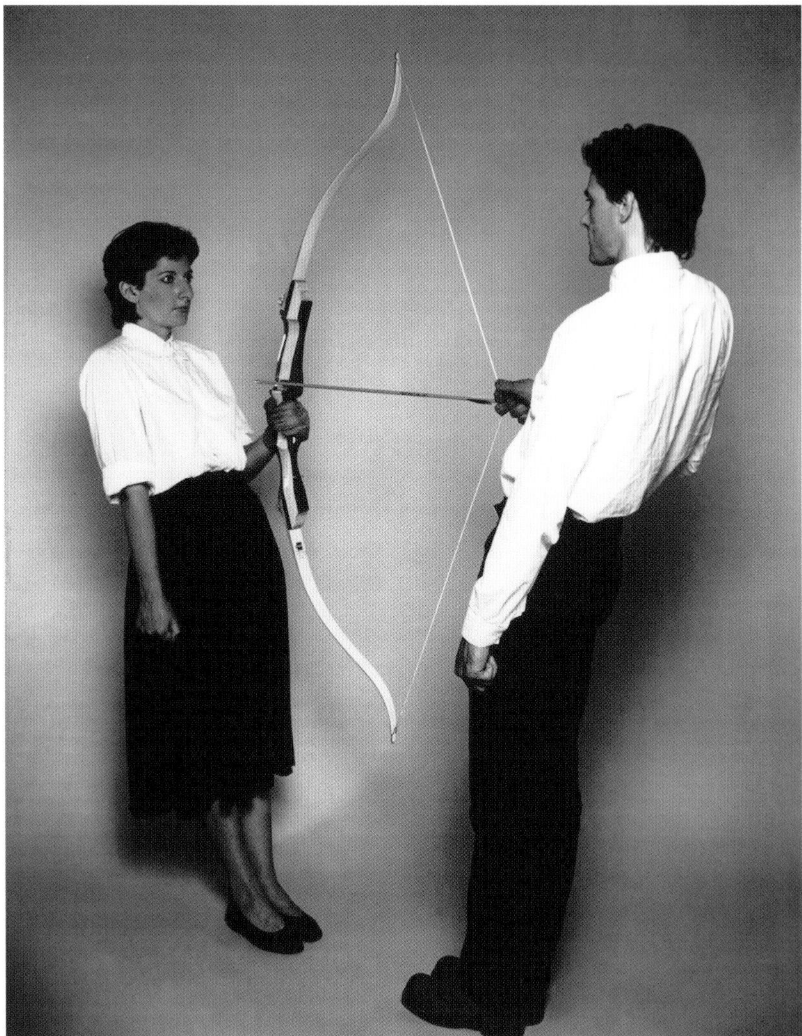

MARINA ABRAMOVIĆ

Born in Belgrade, Serbia, in 1946, Marina Abramović—the self-declared "grandmother of performance art"—is one of the most highly recognised international performance artists, her career recently being celebrated in a performance retrospective—The Artist is Present—at the Museum of Modern Art (MoMA), New York.

Using the body as her focus, Abramović explores the relationship between performer and audience within her work, pushing both the physical and mental limits of the body in a quest for emotional and spiritual transformation. In her recent retrospective at MoMA, Abramović remained silently seated in the museum's atrium, allowing visitors to participate in her performance by taking turns to sit opposite her; this performance, which lasted for 716 hours, became the longest solo piece performed by the artist.

After studying at the Academy of Fine Arts, Zagreb, Croatia, in 1972, Abramović moved to Amsterdam where she met German performance artist Uwe Laysiepen or 'Ulay', at which point they started to perform together, mainly exploring issues of spatial awareness and artistic identity. *Rest Energy*, 1980, is one of the pair's most recognised works—perhaps due to the powerful emotion the piece evokes. Abramović holds a bow at arm's length, with the arrow pointing towards her, whilst Ulay positions the arrow so that it is taut to the bowstrings as they both lean backwards. Microphones were attached to their chests, to capture the intensity of the piece.

In 1988, Abramović and Ulay decided to end their partnership, commemorating it with a highly poignant performance in which they walked across the Great Wall of China, each starting at different ends, until they eventually met in the middle, where they said goodbye.

Abramović's portfolio of work includes not only performance but also sound, photography, video and sculpture, with each piece pushing the body to its limits, in an attempt to transcend to a higher sense of self. *Carrying the Skeleton*, 2008—one of the artist's most revered pieces of recent years—shows Abramović dressed entirely in black, against a black background, carrying a skeleton upon her back.

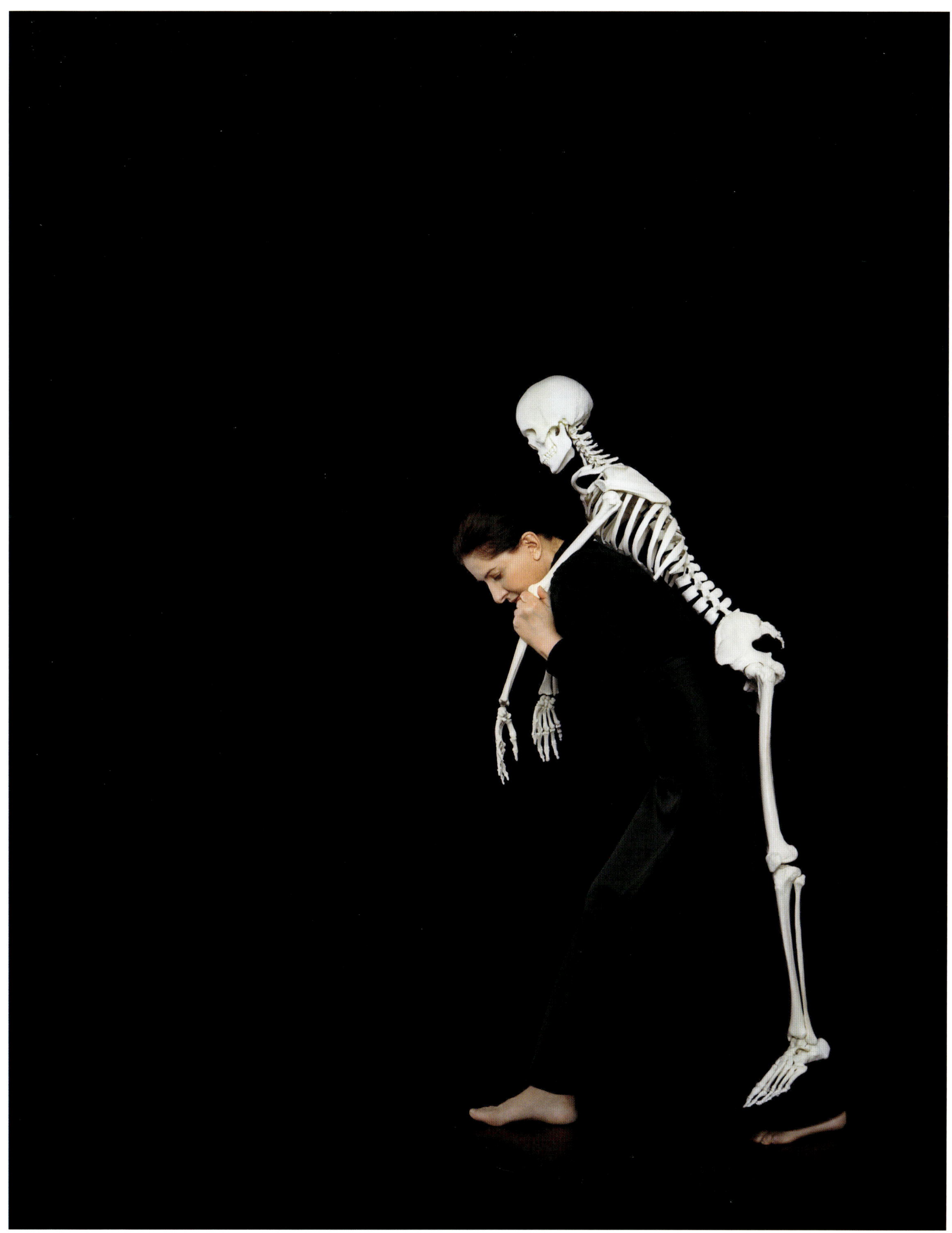

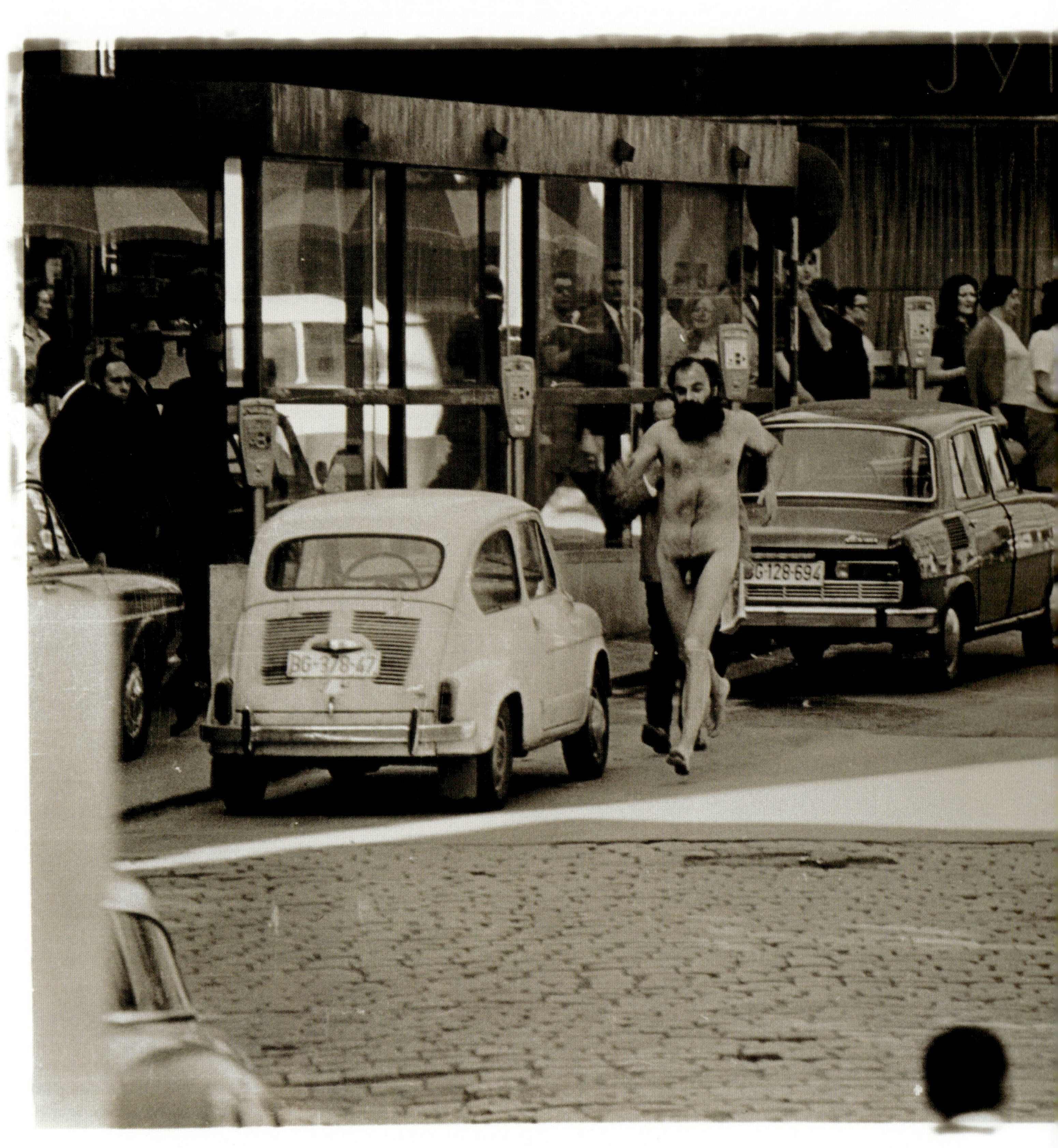

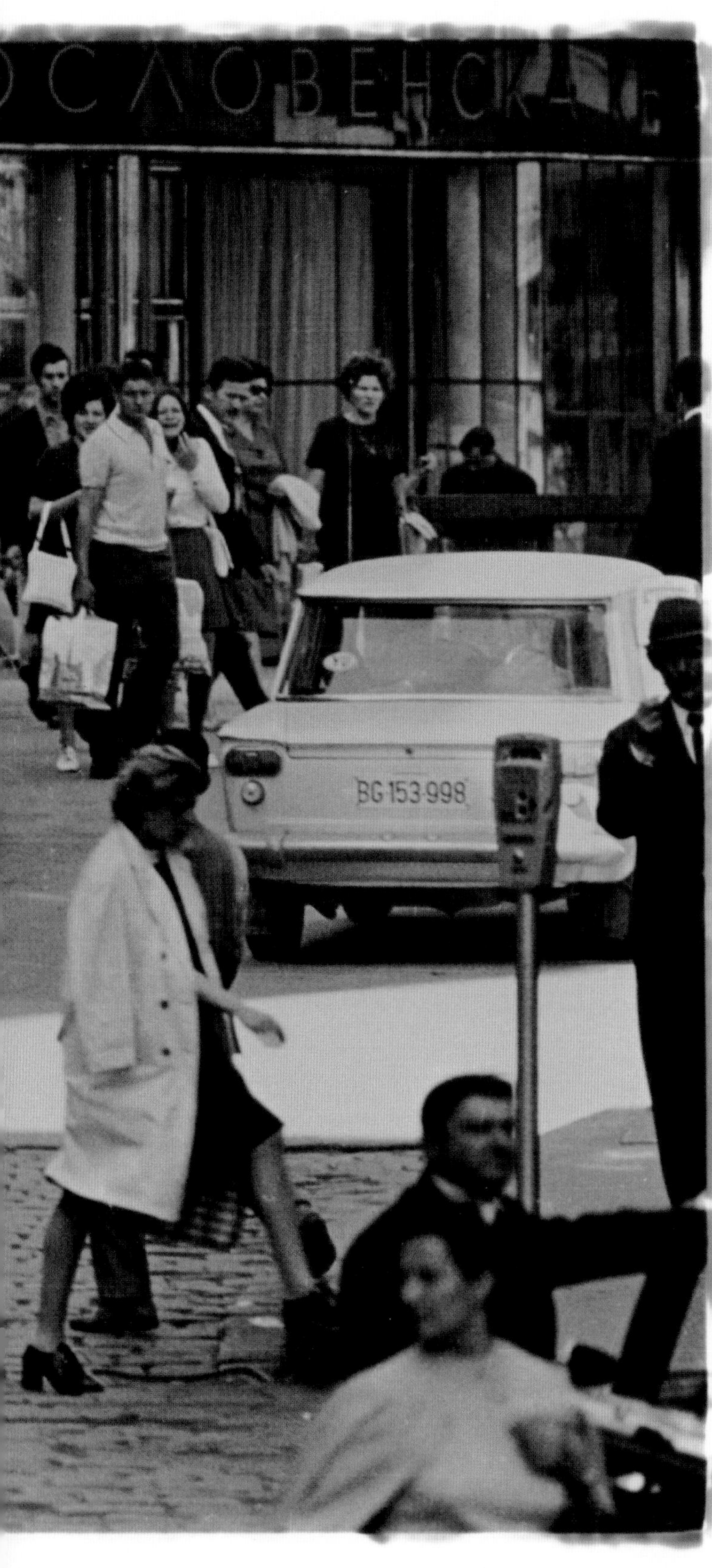

TOMISLAV GOTOVAC
Striking/Streaking (Action—Running Naked
in the Center of the City, Belgrade)
1971, three black and white photographs, 24 x 30 cm

I carry some water from the river in my cupped hands and release it a few meters downriver… (right)
May 19, 1977, Strelecky Ostrov, Prague black
and white photo
Courtesy gb agency, Paris

Two Little White Piles (opposite)
1980, Prague, black and white
photograph and text on paper
Courtesy gb agency, Paris

*On an escalator… turning around, I look into the
eyes of the person standing behind me…* (overleaf left)
3 September 1977, Vaclavské Namesti, Prague,
black and white photograph and text on paper
Courtesy gb agency, Paris

Sugar Tower (overleaf right)
Spring 1981, Vysehrad, Prague, black
and white photograph and text on paper
Courtesy gb agency, Paris

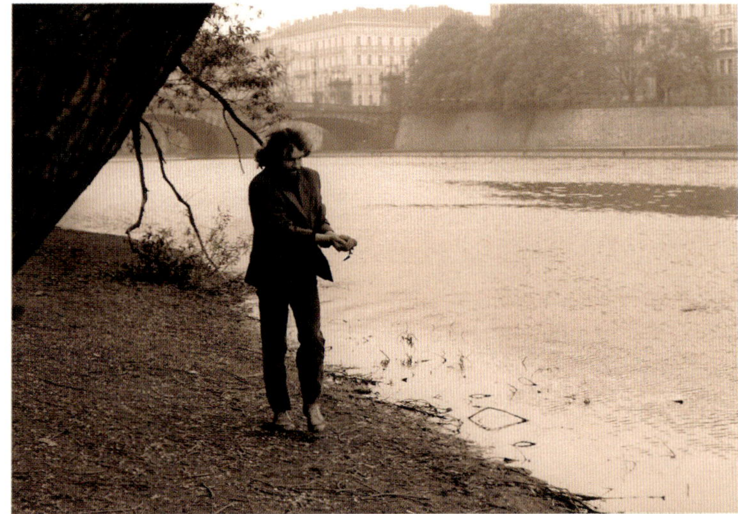

JIŘÍ KOVANDA

Self-taught Czech artist Jiří Kovanda is best known for his "action interventions" during a period of Czech Actionism, which he first began performing and recording during the 1970s. He is, however, just as well known for his penchant for consistently alternating between mediums and styles within his work—be it performance, installation or painting.

Kovanda's early "action and interventions" involved subtle use of performance, which were then documented in amateur photographs and annotated with descriptive texts, so that the artist could fulfil his intention of showing these performances in exhibitions. These pieces were so subtle that Kovanda's own presence often went unnoticed by members of the public who unintentionally and unknown to them were featured in these works.

In 1978, however, Kovanda ceased producing these performances in favour of installation work, within which the notion of leaving "traces" became a focal point to his practice. These installations were much like Kovanda's performance work in that they were documented in a similar fashion—photographed and referenced in much the same way— much like an instruction leaflet. These installations possessed a similar subtlety, achieved through the artist's preference for materials, of which organic remains, including dried flowers and leaves and foodstuffs such as tomatoes, salt, sugar cubes featured heavily; the latter of which were used in the ephemeral installation *Sugar Tower*, 1978.

Throughout the 1980s Kovanda's work began to incorporate collage and painting, for which he is lesser known, often being criticised as being overly conceptual. Recent years, however, have seen the artist return to the multi-faceted practice for which he is known, creating installations, paintings and performances once again—all of which possess the same poetic subtlety as his earlier work.

DVĚ BÍLÉ HROMÁDKY

podzim 1980
Praha

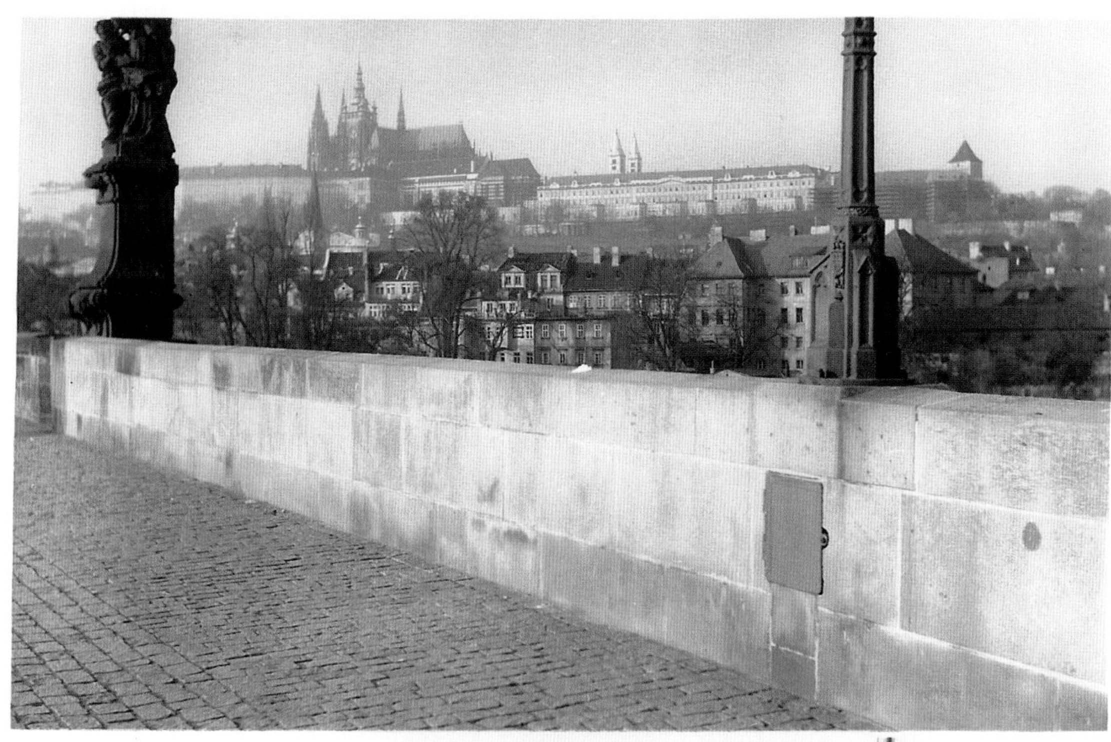

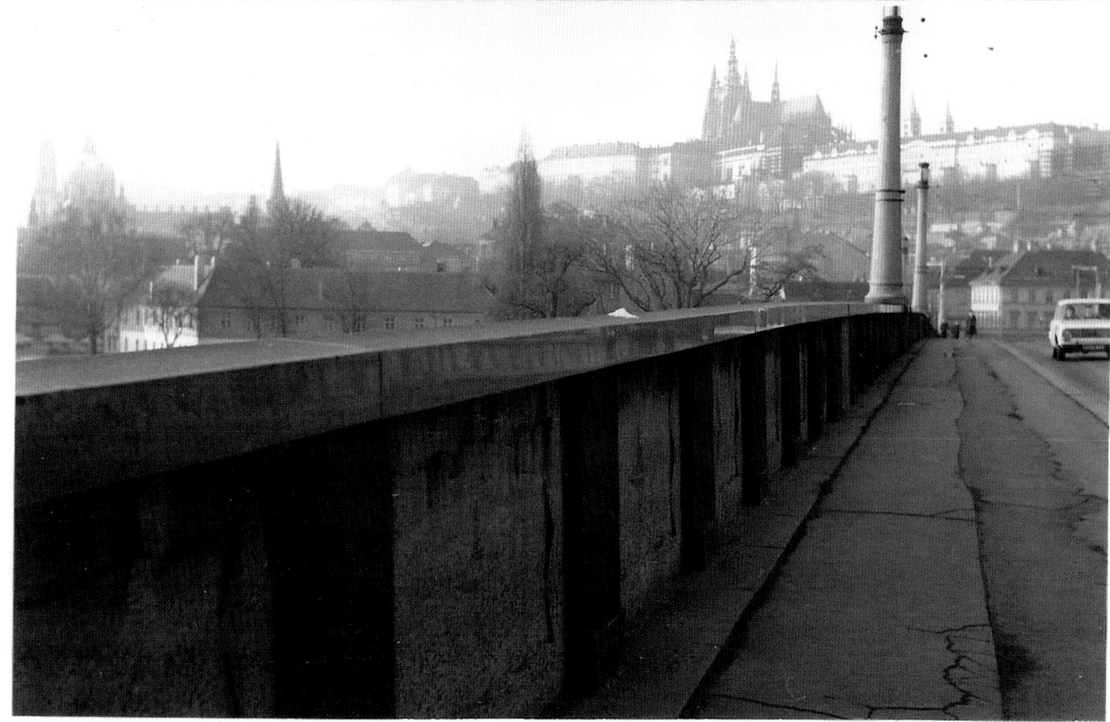

x x x

3. září 1977
Praha, Václavské náměstí

Na eskalátoru... otočen, hledím do očí člověku,
který stojí za mnou...

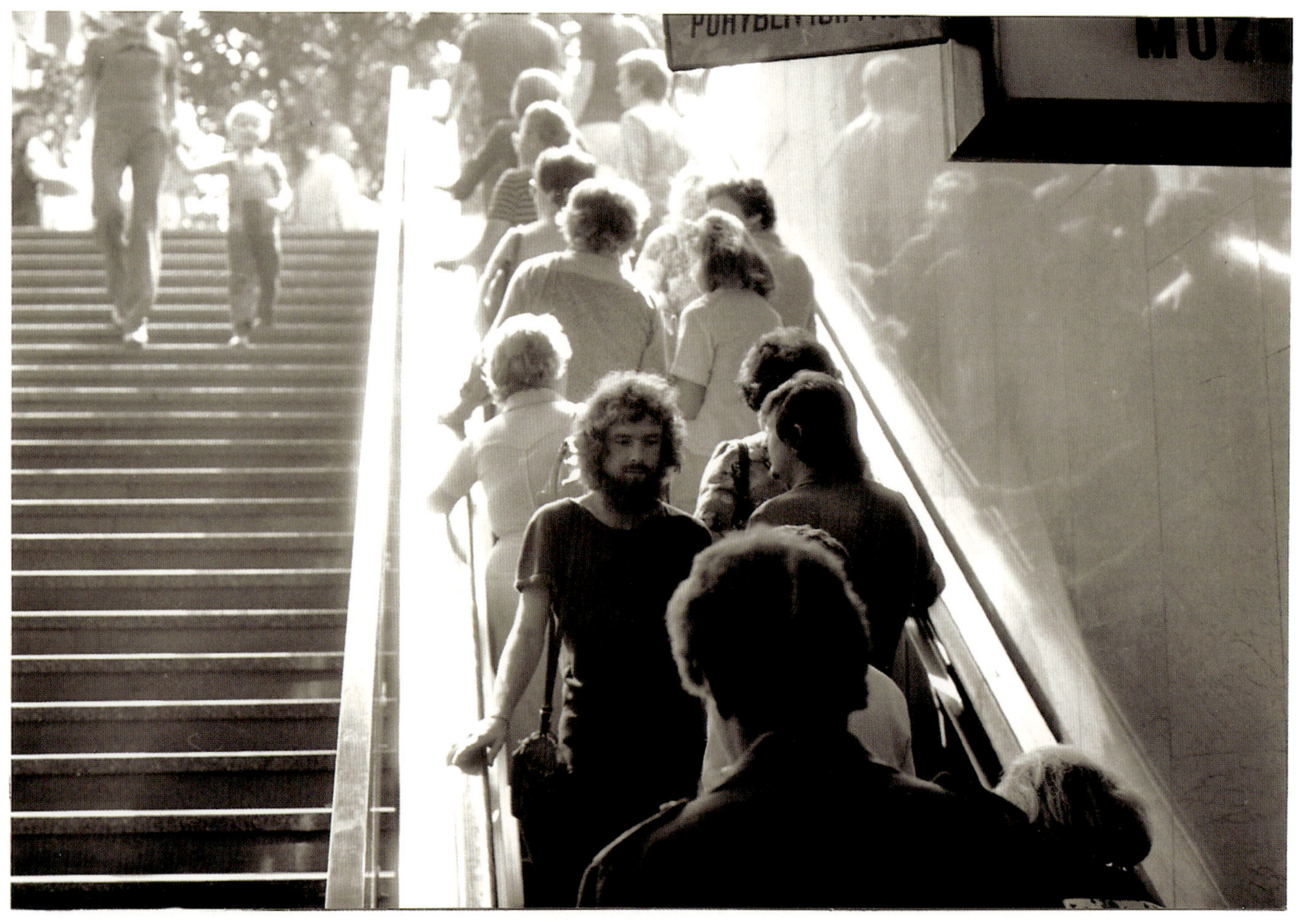

VĚŽ Z CUKRU

jaro 1981
Praha, Vyšehrad

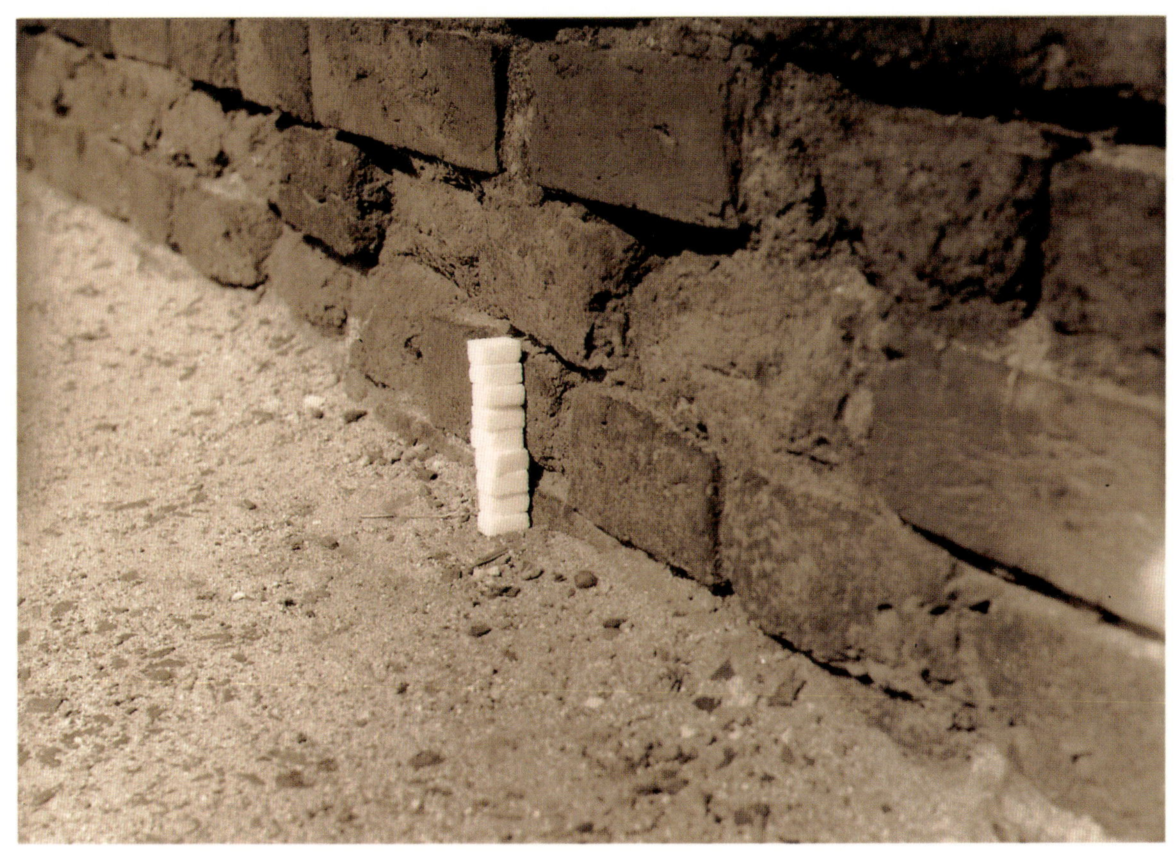

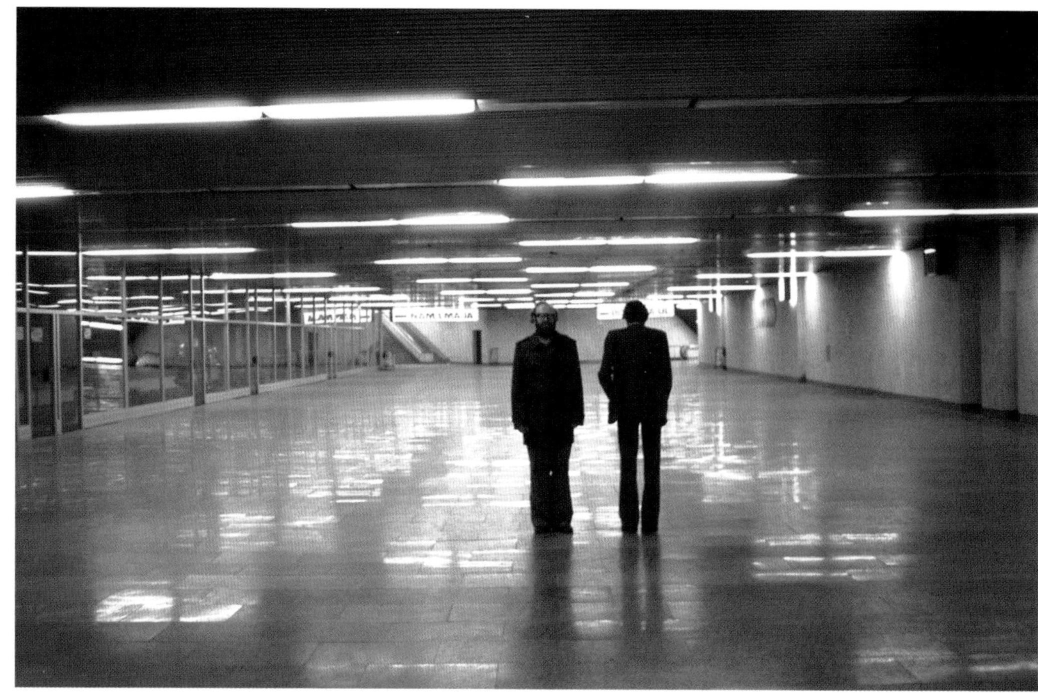

Underground (UFO) (right)
1981, black and white photograph
on paper, 40 x 60 cm, edition of 6
Courtesy gb agency, Paris

*Demonstrative Cultural Situation
1., 2. (UFO)* (opposite)
1989, diptych of black and white
photographs on paper, 30 x 40 cm
each, edition of 6
Courtesy gb agency, Paris

JÚLIUS KOLLER

Spanning five decades of immense political and cultural change in Slovakia, the work of the late Július Koller attests to an individual with a driven and singular temperament, responsive to his surroundings and committed to realising a practice of genuine consequence within the fabric of a social space.

A student at the Academy of Applied Arts and Design in Bratislava in the 1960s, Koller established the foundations for his practice within a climate of gathering hope and optimism, at a time of loosening strictures on civic freedom that culminated in the political reforms of the Prague Spring in 1968 and disintegrated with the Warsaw Pact intervention of the same year. During this period, and throughout the ensuing years of political and cultural 'normalisation', Koller remained committed to principles of free thought and intersubjective communication, and continued to develop methods for articulating the agency of social subjects in the face of institutional organisation and repressive force. His *Anti-Happenings*, originally formulated in response to the merican "Happenings" and what he perceived as their theatrical and artificial directing of reality, used everyday life as a given programme for artistic activity. Through the demonstration and sequential documentation of various cultural situations and everyday activities, such as tourism and popular sports events, Koller aimed to draw attention to the incremental shifts and possibilities for appropriation and divergence inherent to the practice of everyday life.

Much of Koller's work is underpinned by a questioning of forms of information and knowledge, together with a challenge to the position of the artist in society, with the purpose and efficacy of artistic activity called into question and the meaning of Koller's own artistic activity constantly displaced. From the 1970s onwards, he developed a number of projects under the adaptable acronym "UFO", extending and expanding upon the original formulation of the *Anti-Happenings*. In one particular work, *UFO-naut J.K.*, Koller depicted himself in a series of photographic self-portraits as a cultural alien. With humour and provocative wit, these photographs articulated a sense of marginality that Koller embraced throughout his work, and gave lyrical form to the independence, authority and critical space that belong to social subjects.

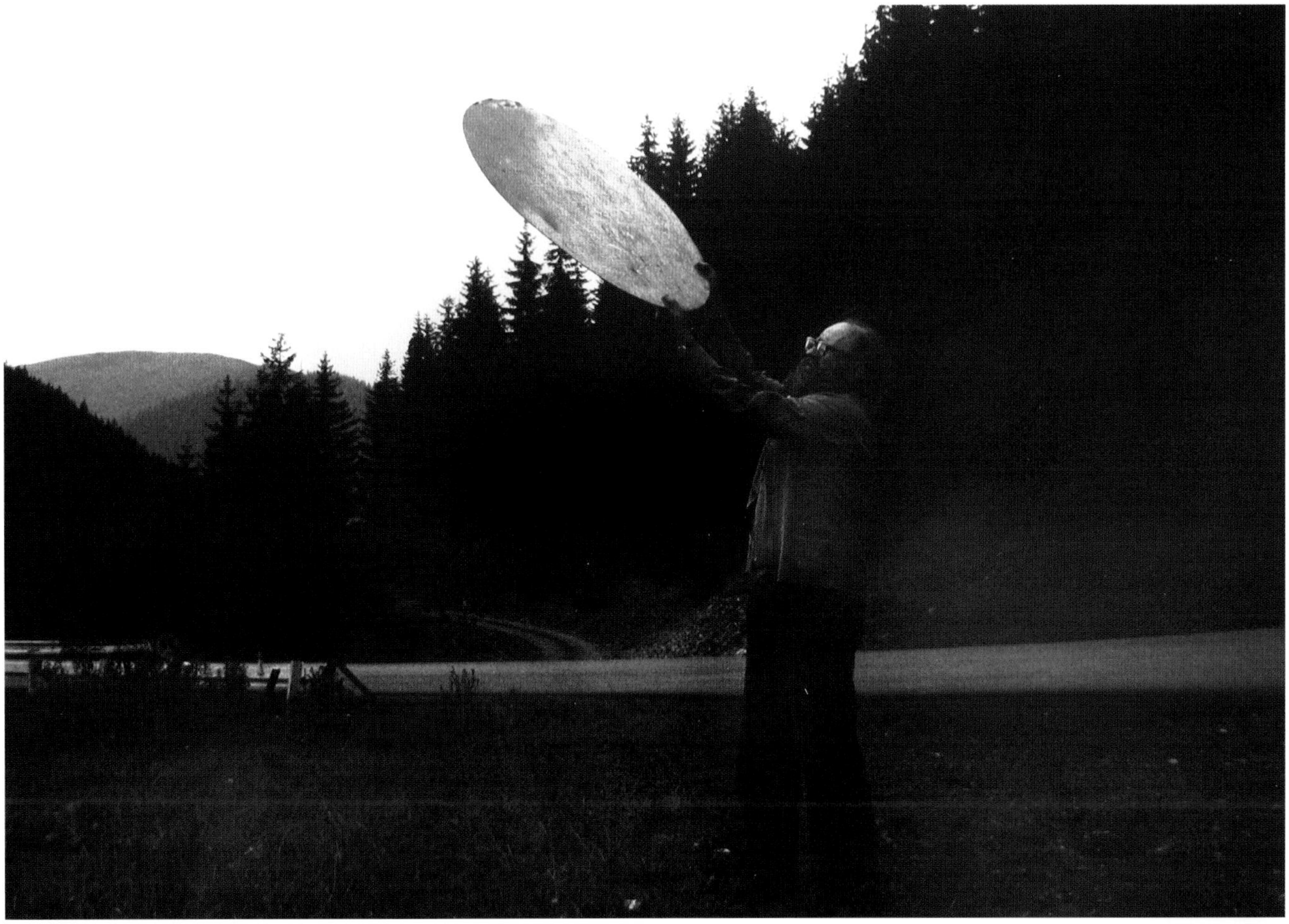

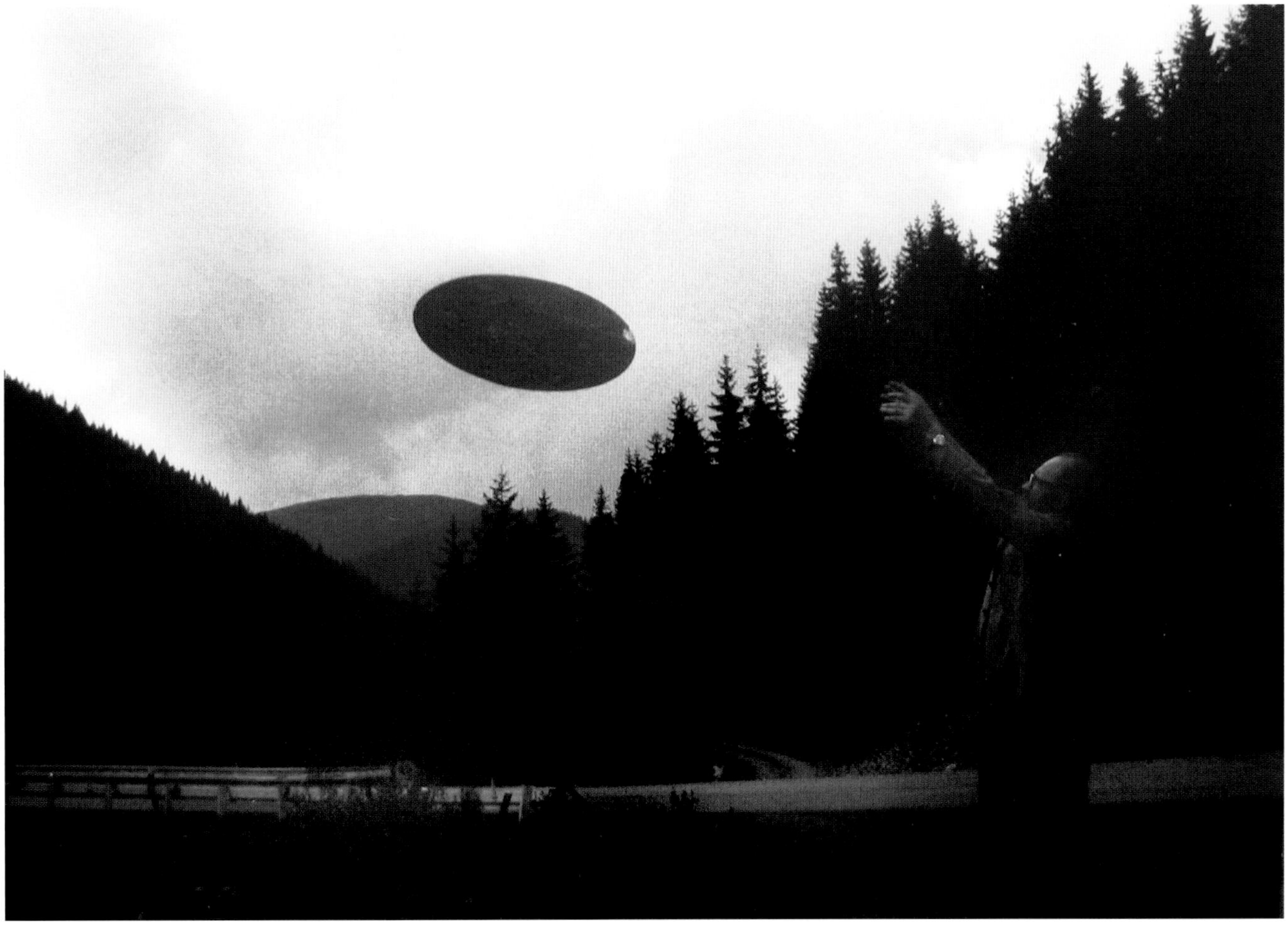

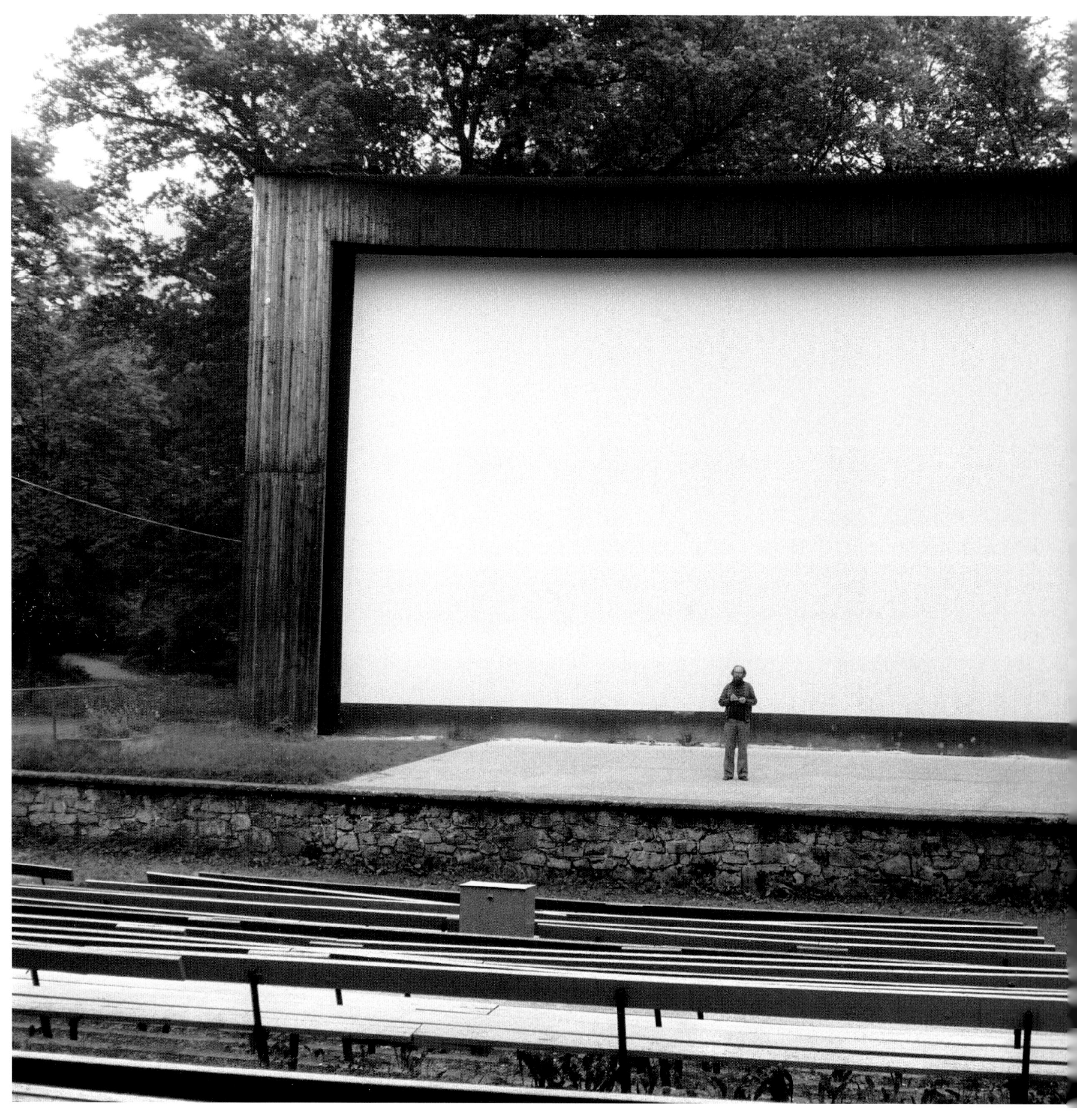

JÚLIUS KOLLER
Anti-Performance (UFO)
1980, black and white photograph
on paper, 40 x 60 cm, edition of six
Courtesy gb agency, Paris

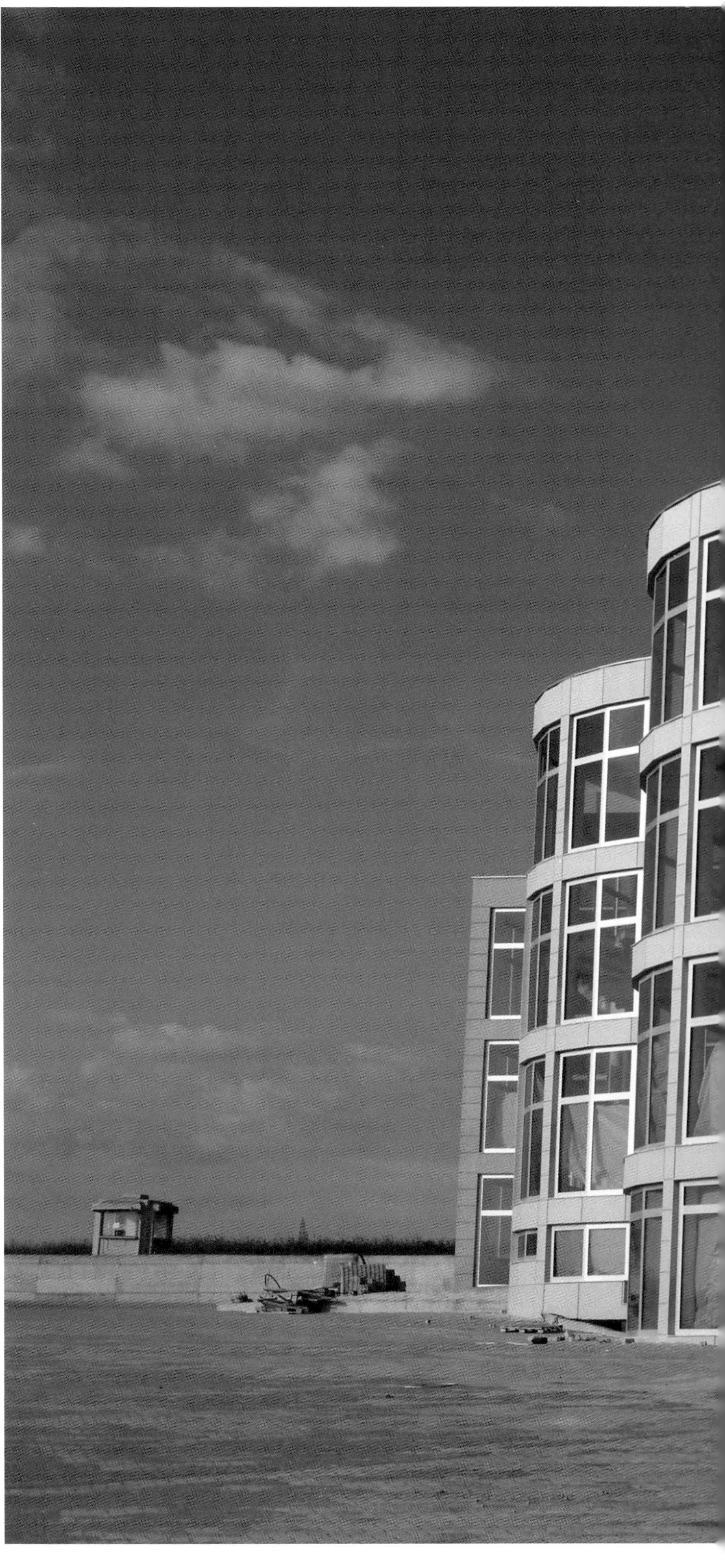

LALA MEREDITH-VULA
Shifting borders: Outskirts of Prishtina, Kosova
2007, photograph
Courtesy the artist

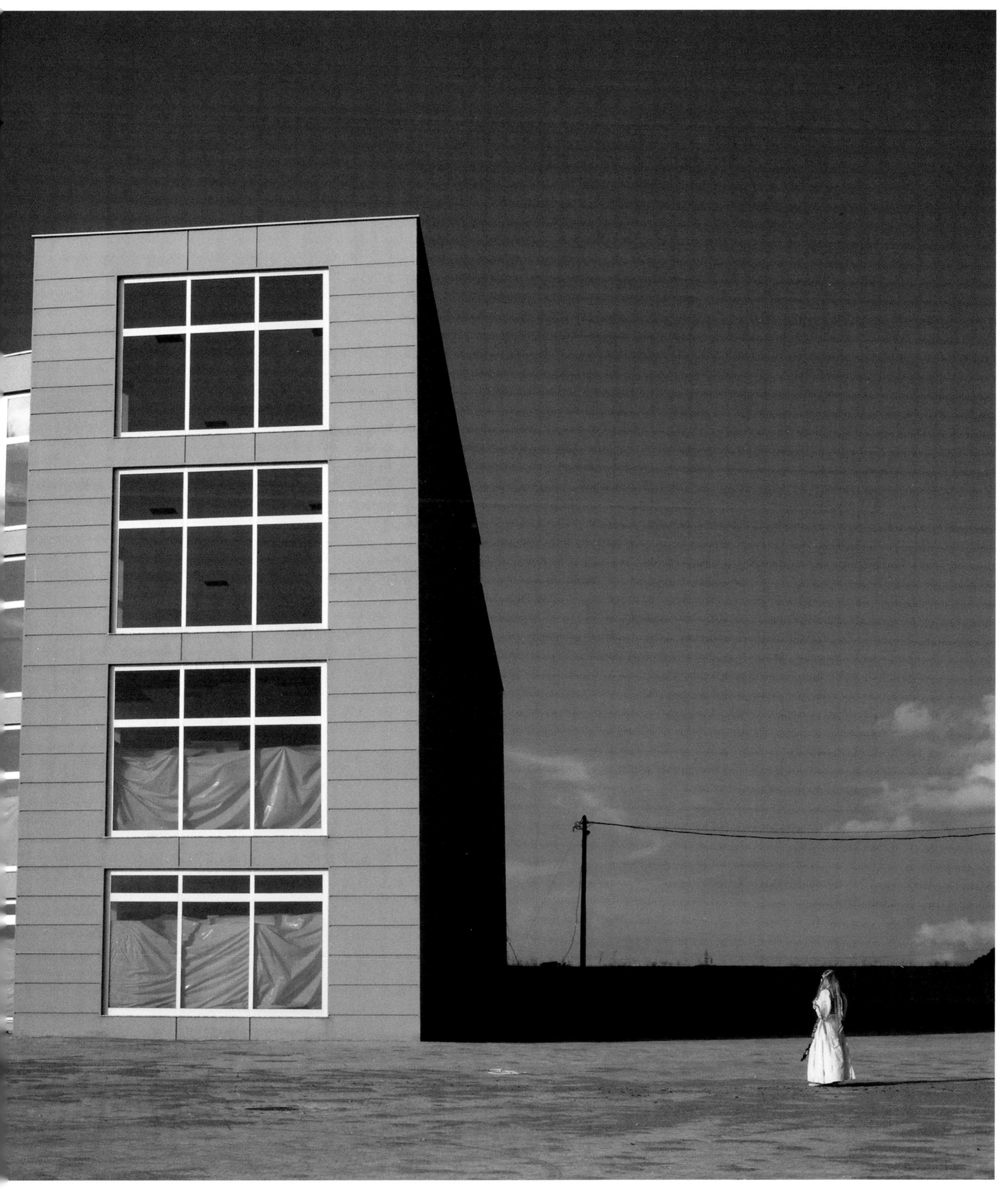

ANRI SALA

Albanian artist Anri Sala studied painting at the National Academy of Arts in his native Tirana before becoming acquainted with the mediums of film and photography at the Ecole Nationale Supérieure des Arts Décoratifs in Paris. A teenager when Communism came to an end, much of Sala's work is rooted in themes of loss and rupture; his practice emerges from the ruins of a collapsed power structure, and focuses on the human experience of a landscape of psychological, linguistic and architectural fractures where meaning is denied a means of legitimising itself.

Music features prominently in Sala's work. In particular, syncopation—the unusual occurrence of rhythmic stresses or accents—has functioned as an effective metaphor for words and ideas that are lost or hidden, and meaning that slips between the gaps of discourse. In the film *Answer Me,* a former Cold War listening station in Teufelsberg, Berlin, provides the setting for a couple playing out a final, absurd act in their failing relationship. A man is seen playing a drum kit, his beats resonating throughout the buildings architecture. At a distance, standing next to a snare drum with drumsticks resting on its skin, and with her back to an open window, a woman speaks in an attempt to end their relationship, and demands a response from the man. But this is refused: his drumming suffocates communication, and even when he ceases, the only answer the woman receives are the ghost notes that rattle out on the snare drum beside her.

The respective languages of film and photography are often pushed to their limits in Sala's work, and while he recognises the artistic possibilities offered by each, he is careful not to conflate the two. Perhaps his best-known photographic works, *No Barragan No Cry* and its companion piece *Fuera del Carrusel* present a horse perched in bizarre fashion on a rooftop overlooking the city of Guadalajara, Mexico. Made after a visit to the house of the late Luis Barragan, Mexico's most important modernist architect, the photographs demonstrate Sala's ability to respond intuitively to his environment, and furthermore confirm that, while his output is immensely varied, incorporating a range of subject matter and styles, it nonetheless remains highly distinctive.

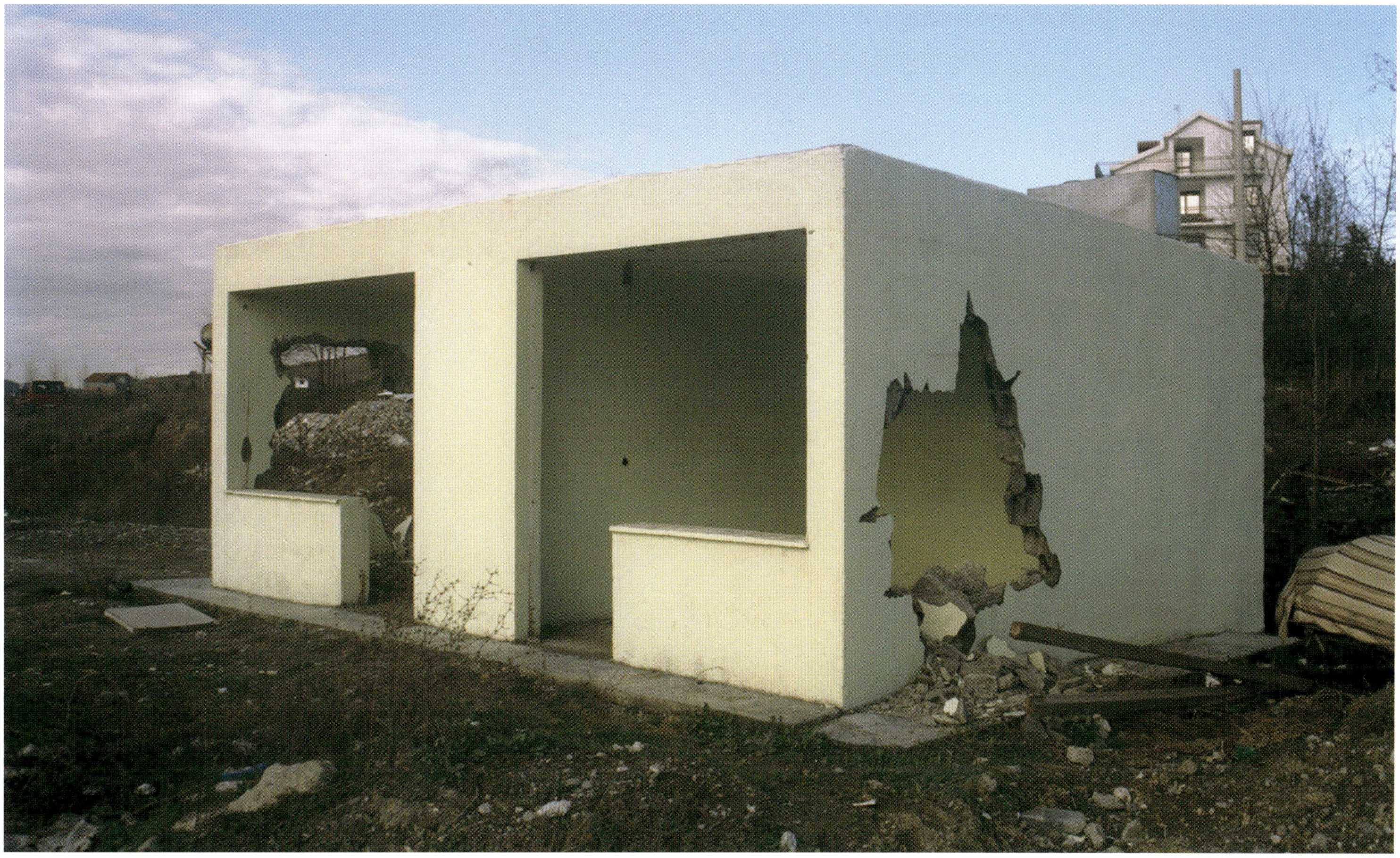

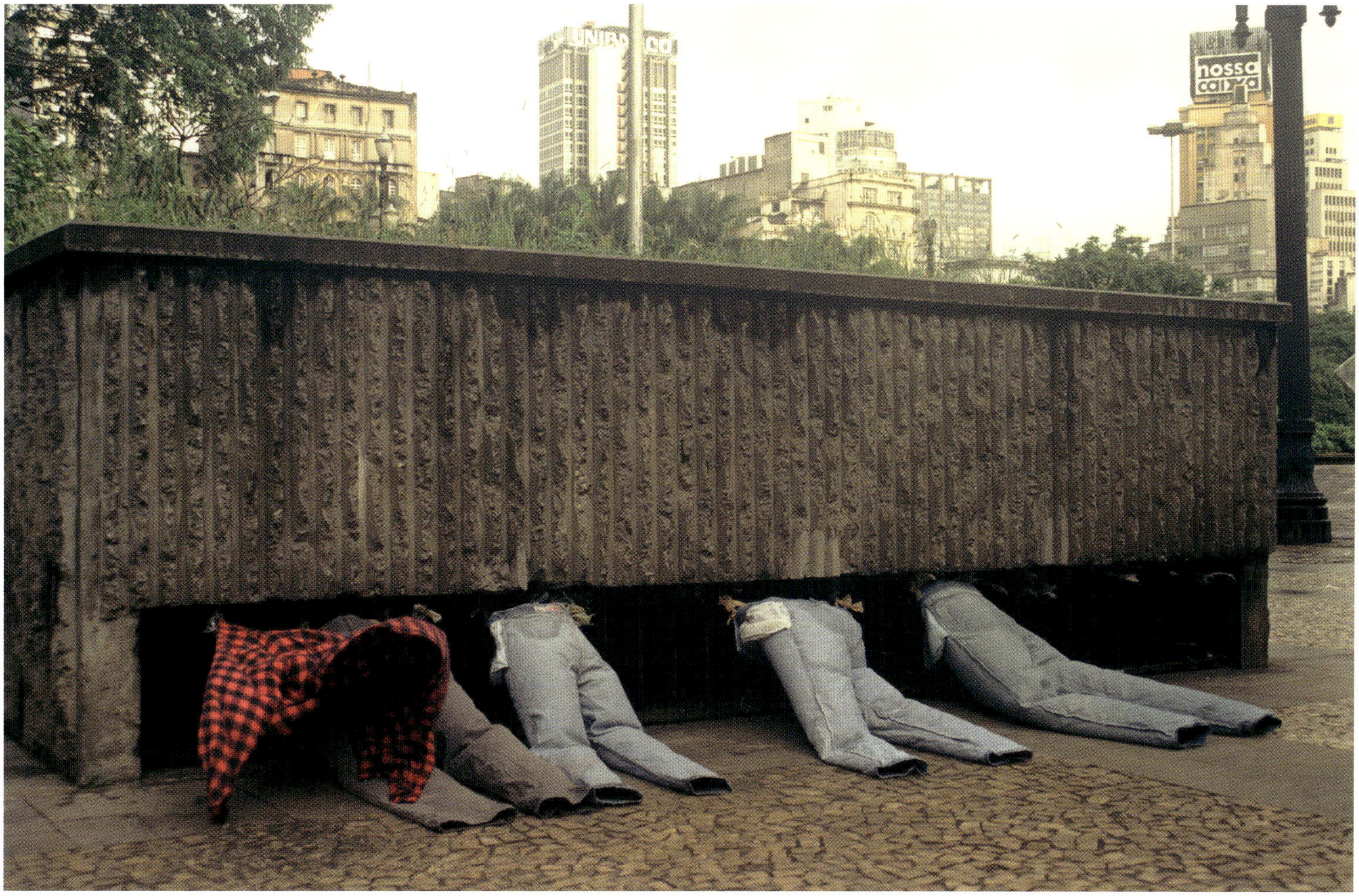

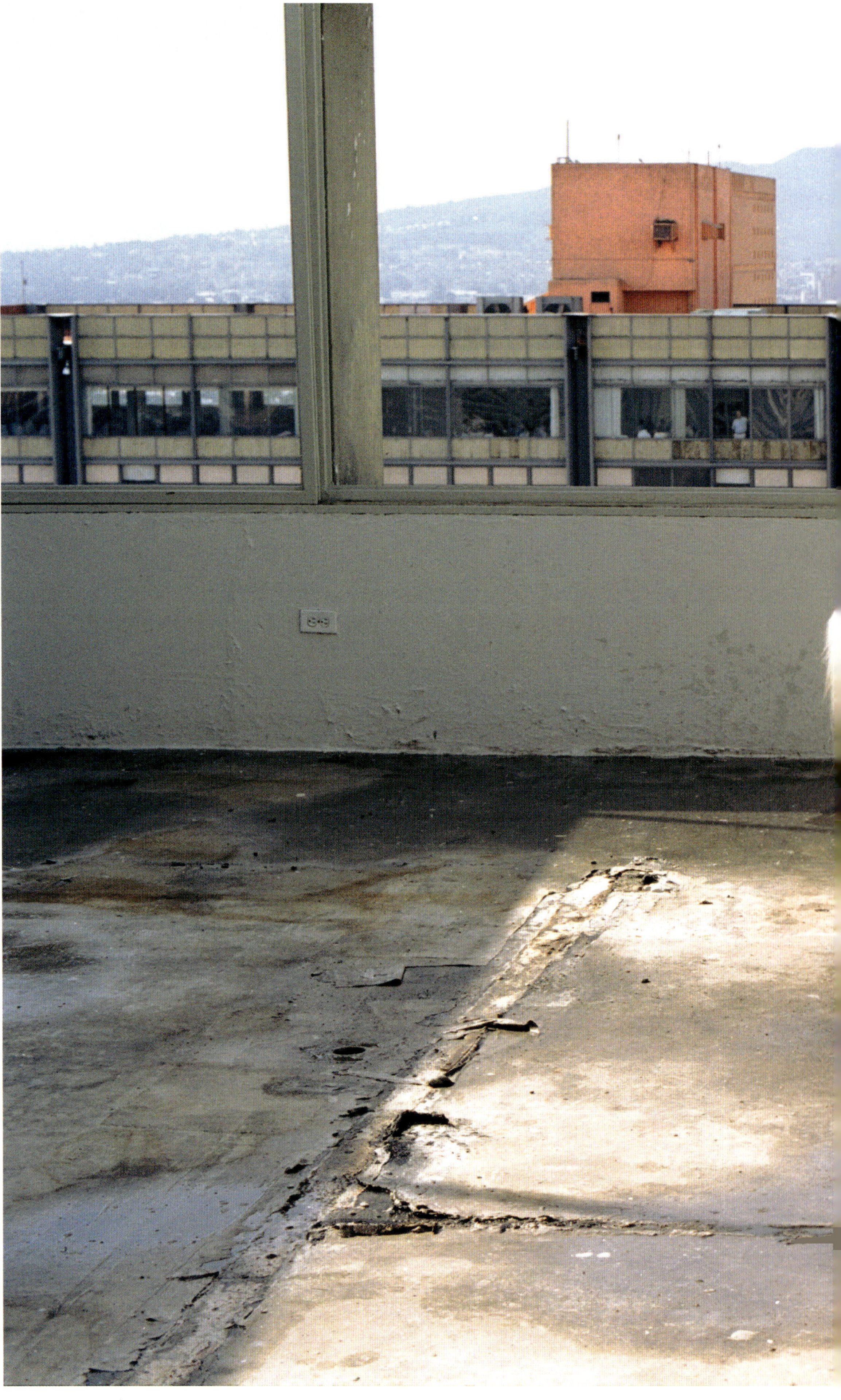

ANRI SALA
Fuera del Carrusel
2002, colour photograph, 82 x 112 x 4 cm

Copyright Anri Sala, courtesy the artist; Johnen Galerie,
Berlin; Marian Goodman Gallery, New York; Galerie
Chantal Crousel, Paris and Hauser & Wirth

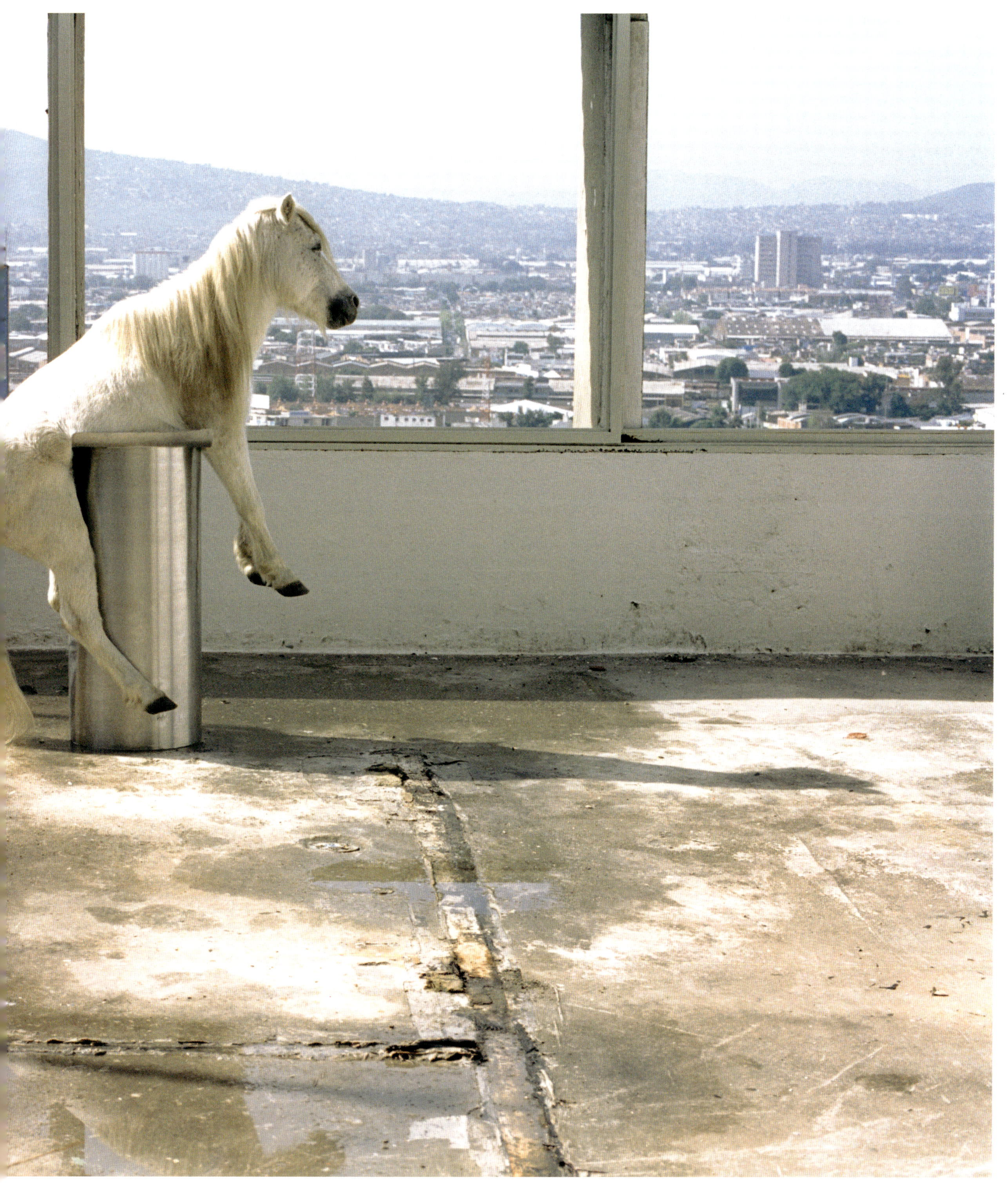

BRACO DIMITRIJEVIĆ

Braco Dimitrijević's humourous take on conceptual art has earned him an international reputation within the contemporary art world. Born in Sarajevo, Bosnia Herzegovina in 1948, Dimitrijević showed an eager enthusiasm for art at a young age, hosting his first one-man show at just ten years old.

As a reaction to the personality cult that consumed Yugoslavian society, Dimitrijević began to work on the idea that he would replace the portraits of dignitaries that covered billboards everywhere with portraits of street pedestrians chosen at random. This idea gradually evolved into the *Casual Passer-By* series for which Dimitrijević earned his name—developing it further when he moved to London to attend Central Saint Martins School of Art in 1971.

The *Casual Passer-By* series saw Dimitrijević create these large-scale photo portraits in various different cities internationally, including his first: *The Casual Passer-By I met at 11.40 am, Zagreb 1969*; alongside works in Venice, London and Paris—all of which follow the same premise, in which they feature portraits of unknown people on billboards and building facades. *Casual Passers-By I Met at 3.41 pm and 3.47 pm, Paris,* 1999 shows a landscape view of the Champs-Élysées, with banners depicting the faces of an unknown man and woman framing the ascent of traffic leading up to the Arc de Triomphe.

Triptychos Post Historicus is a series of installations in which Dimitrijević used original master paintings from various museum collections, combining them with everyday objects and fruit. This series epitomises the artist's statement: "Louvre is my studio, street is my museum." In *Triptychos Post Historicus: Part Two: Shovel used by Mihail Vilich*, 2005, the artist combines an apple, a shovel and Kazamir Malevich's painting *Red Square*. Whilst the masterpiece in the installation is Malevich's painting, Dimitrijević draws attention to the "shovel" in the title, and its unknown user "Mihail Vilich"—continuing the artist's interest in the rise of the stranger.

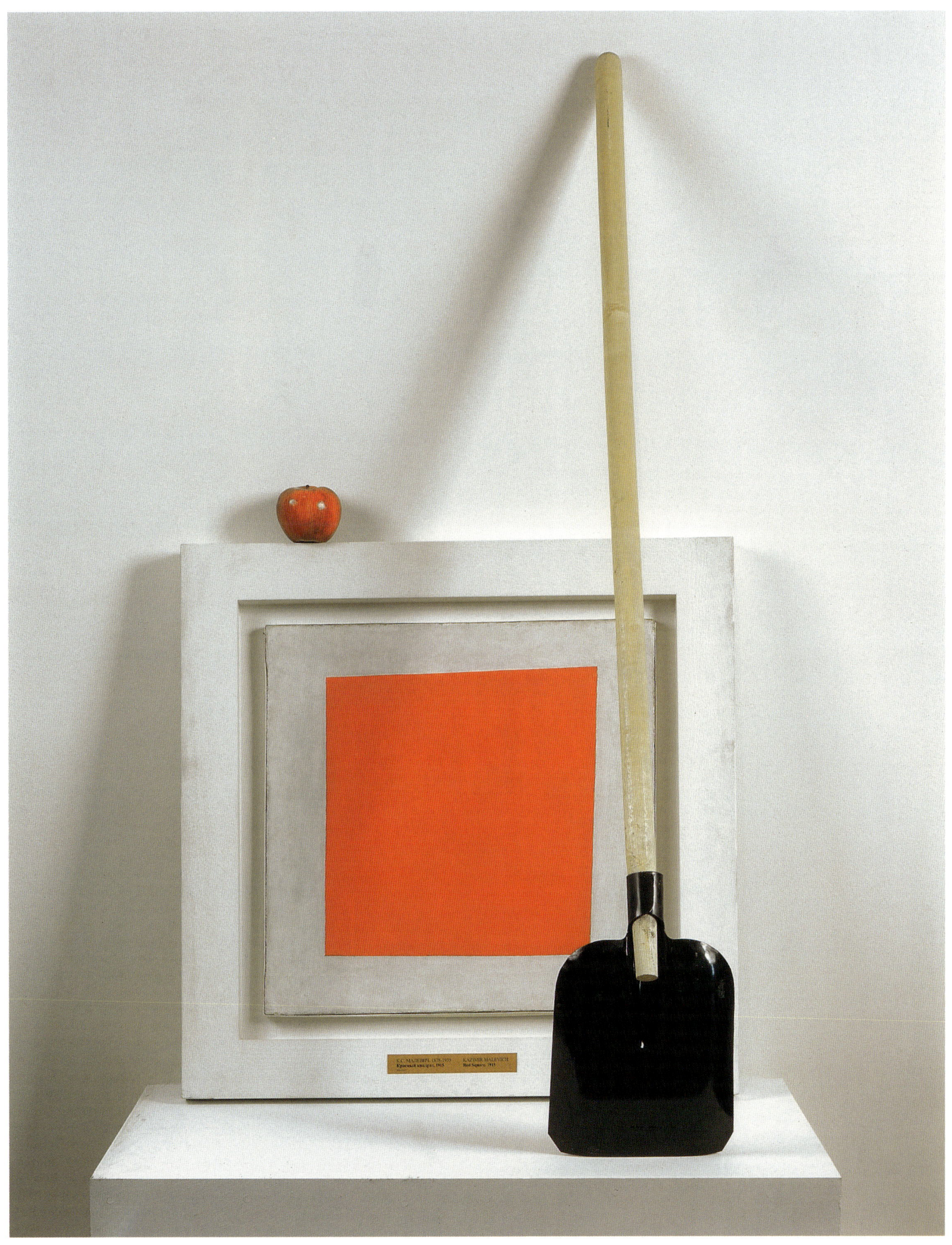

К.С. МАЛЕВИЧ, 1878-1935
Красный квадрат, 1915
KAZIMIR MALEVICH
Red Square, 1915

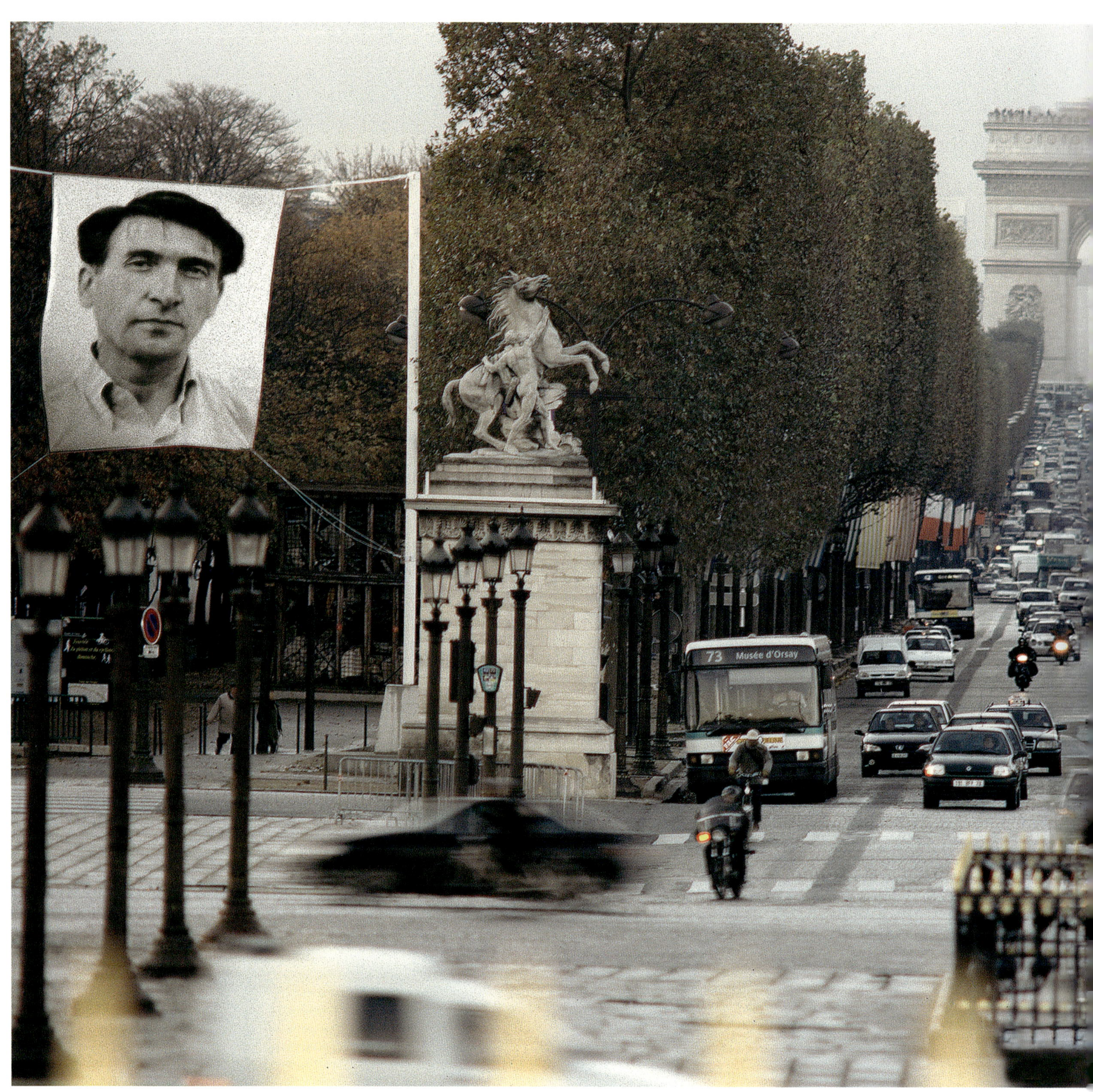

73 Musée d'Orsay

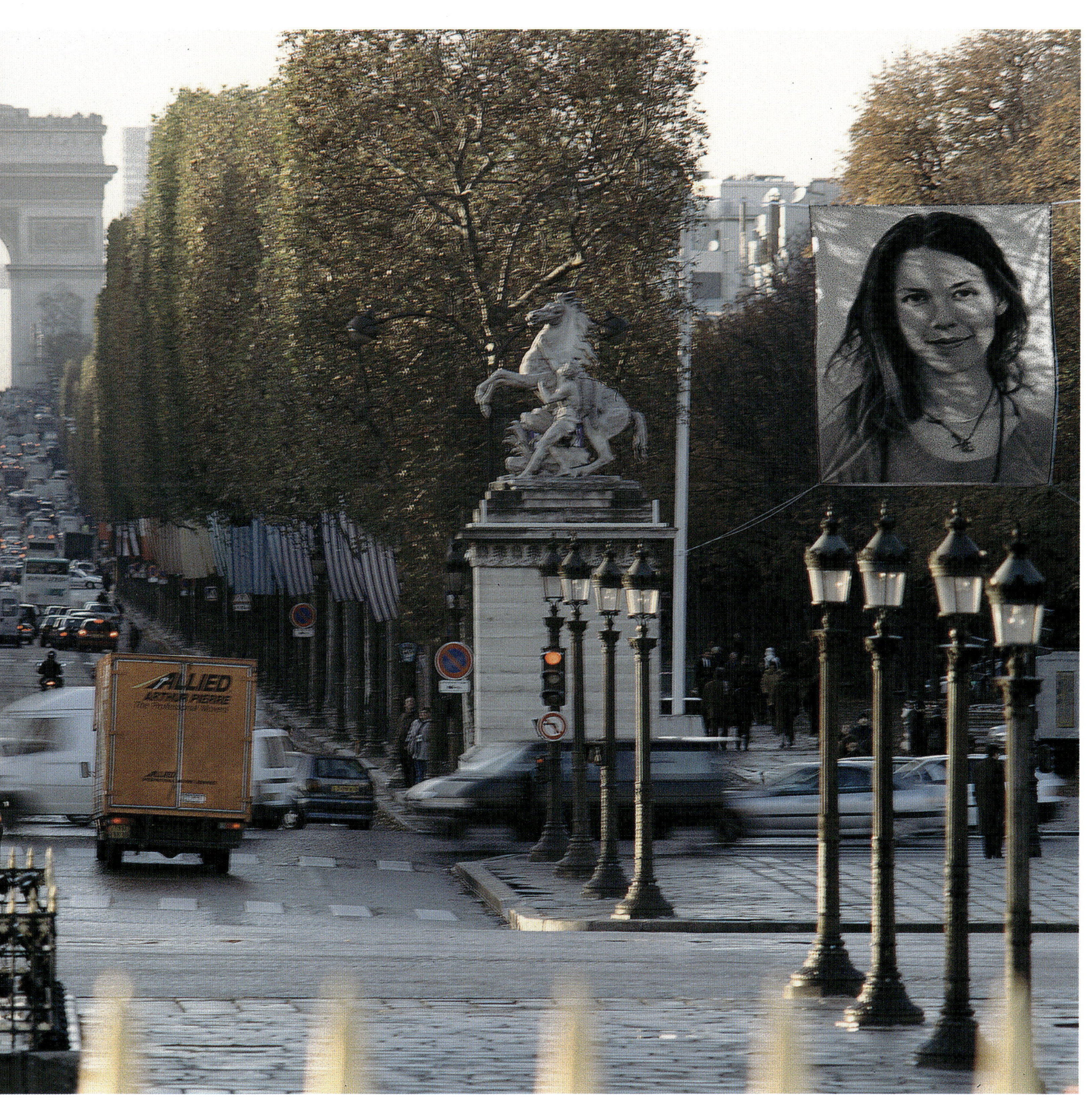

ALLIED
ARTHUR PIERRE

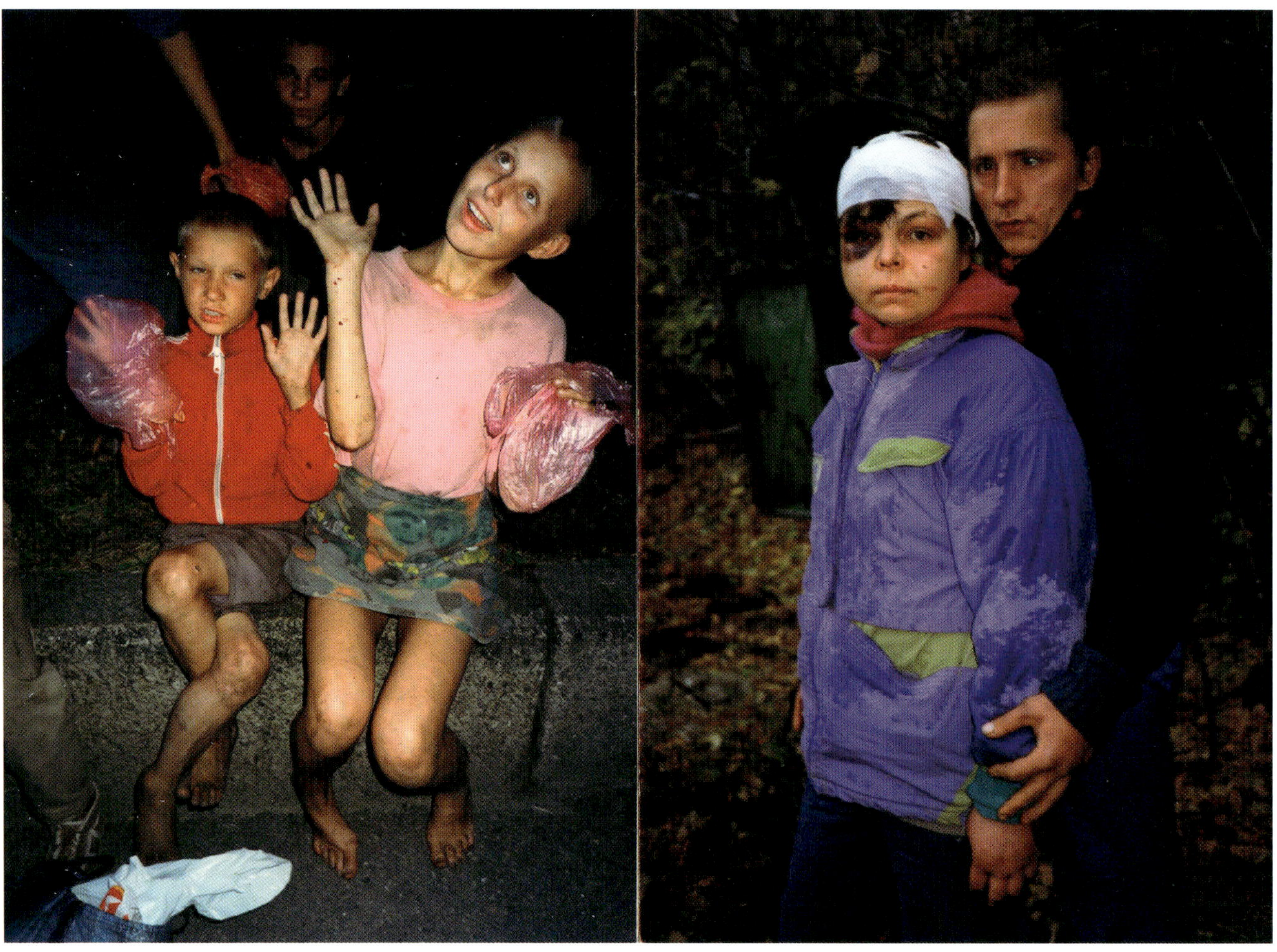

BORIS MIKHAILOV

Photographer Boris Mikhailov's work provides a candid interpretation of the years since the collapse of the Soviet Union. Born in 1938 in Kharkov, Ukraine, Mikhailov has spent the latter half of his career focusing on the humanistic after-effects of this social collapse, using society's most vulnerable as his subjects.

Originally specialising in satirical criticism of the Soviet regime, Mikhailov's work eventually evolved into his own brand of social documentation—before the collapse the photographer was closely watched by the Russian secret police, and was only able to use a camera as a forbidden hobby. Post-collapse his work excelled in rebelling against that which was forbidden. Never being formally trained as a photographer,

Mikhailov instead saw the medium as a forum for free exchange, using it as a platform from which to present a controversial subject matter that allowed for discussion and interpretation.

Case History, 1997–1998, is a series of almost 500 photographs that focuses upon the homeless and poverty stricken of Mikhailov's home town of Kharkov, Ukraine. Paying his subjects to pose for him, the photographer was heavily criticised for the harsh realism of his work that depicted the ravaged bodies of the homeless—at times crude and animalistic. The poverty of these people's existence is also heightened by Mikhailov's preference for photographing them nude—exposing their scars, tattoos,

breasts and genitals—a technique with which he proposed would show them as "people", removing them of their torn and battered clothes, which immediately revealed their social positioning.

In answering his critics, Mikhailov defends his work as being merely a reflection of the general post-Soviet condition and that by taking these photographs he is highlighting society's ills: "It is a disgraceful world, populated by some creatures that were once humans, but now these living beings are degraded, ghastly, appalling. This 'fauna' is specific especially to the period of quasi-general diffidence, specific for most of the post-Communist world."

Case History
1997–1998, from a series of 500
photographs, dimensions variable
Courtesy the artist

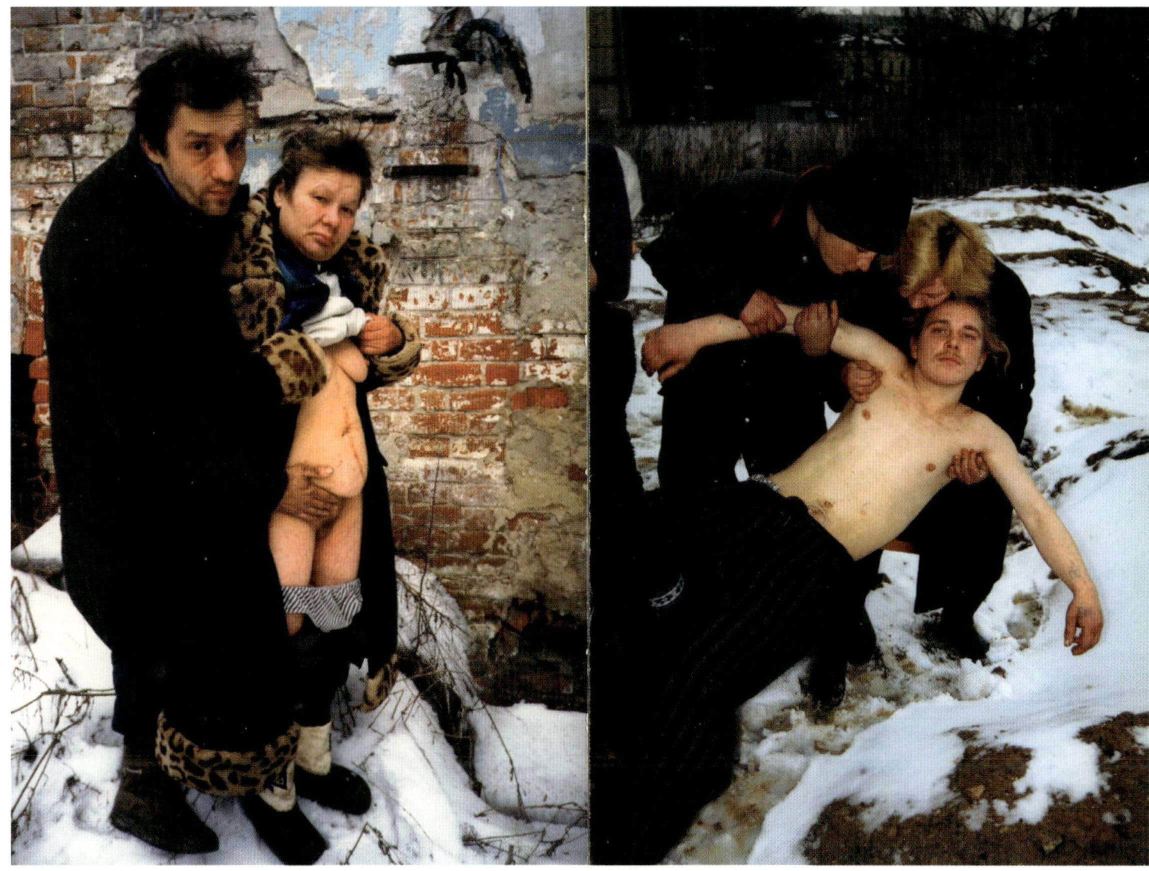

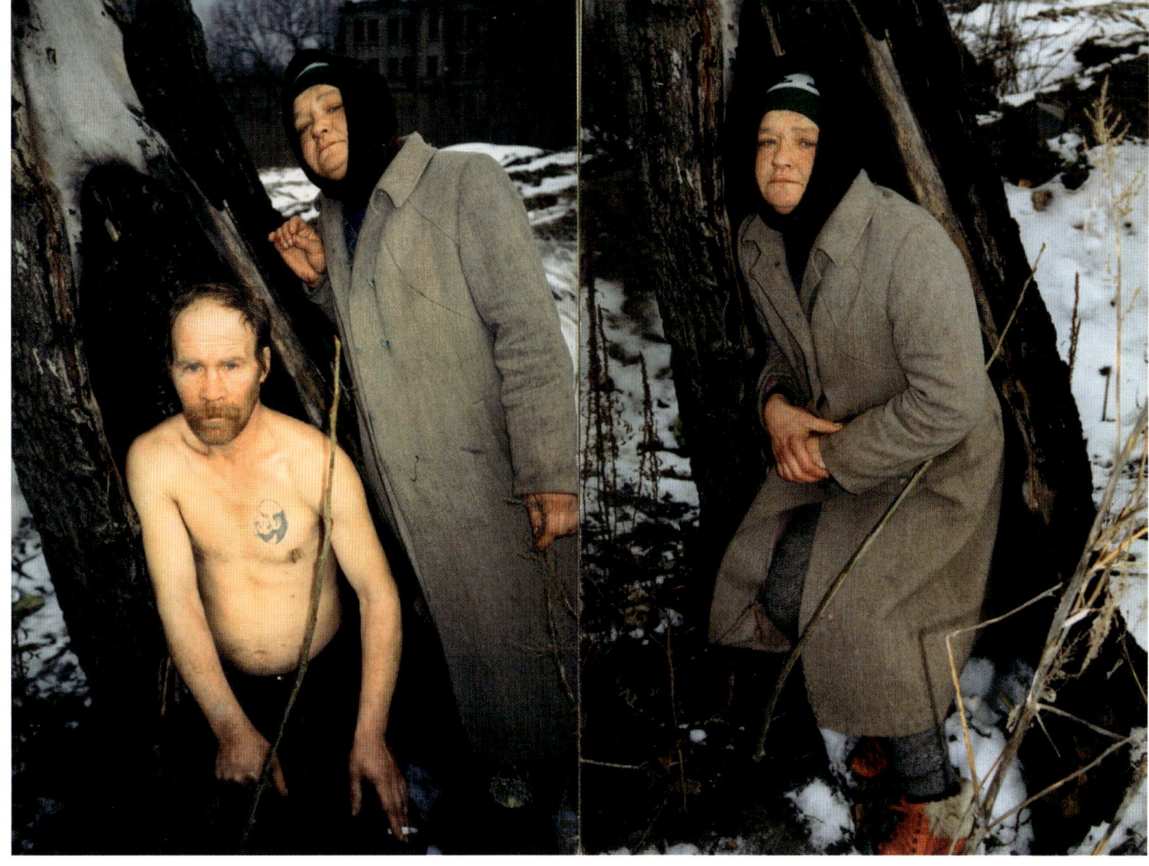

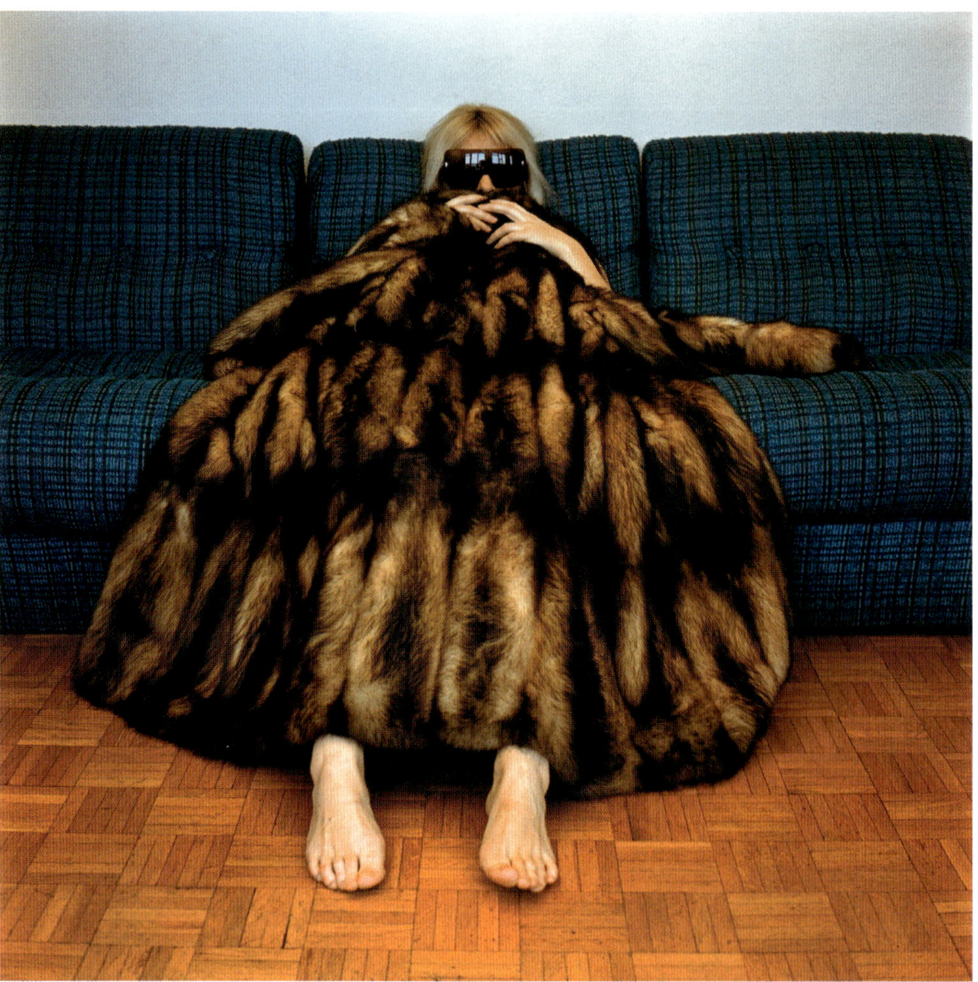

NATALIA LL

Since the work first emerged in 1972, Natalia LL's *Consumer Art* has come to occupy a position of prominence in Eastern European art history, helping establish the artist's reputation as an important figure amongst the first generation of Polish conceptual artists. Despite this, and as the art critic Agata Jakubowska has described, it remains "a very interesting example of an art work which, in a way, has become canonical, but has not seen its canonical interpretation yet".

Realised as a series of photographs, the work presents women—including the artist herself—eating bananas, sausages and puddings. The images are confrontational and provocative in their erotic allusions, clearly evidencing the artist's early concerns with the feminine body and the sensual. At the same time, the form of these works—the repetitive photographic record that structures and objectifies these otherwise banal events, subjecting them to rationalisation and formal discipline—is representative of the ideas Natalia LL developed within the Polish conceptual art movement of the 1970s. Originally shaped by a desire to explore the morphological potentials of a sign within a medium such as photography, the female subject of the work, together with its inevitably sexual content, has subsequently rendered *Consumer Art* an increasingly potent site for developing feminist, social, and cultural discourses in art history and criticism.

In her more recent work, narcissism and a focus on bodily pleasures have been subsumed by a fear of death and affecting portrayals of ugliness and suffering. The artist's body remains a central element, but it is subjected to visceral and challenging explorations that often render it unrecognisable.

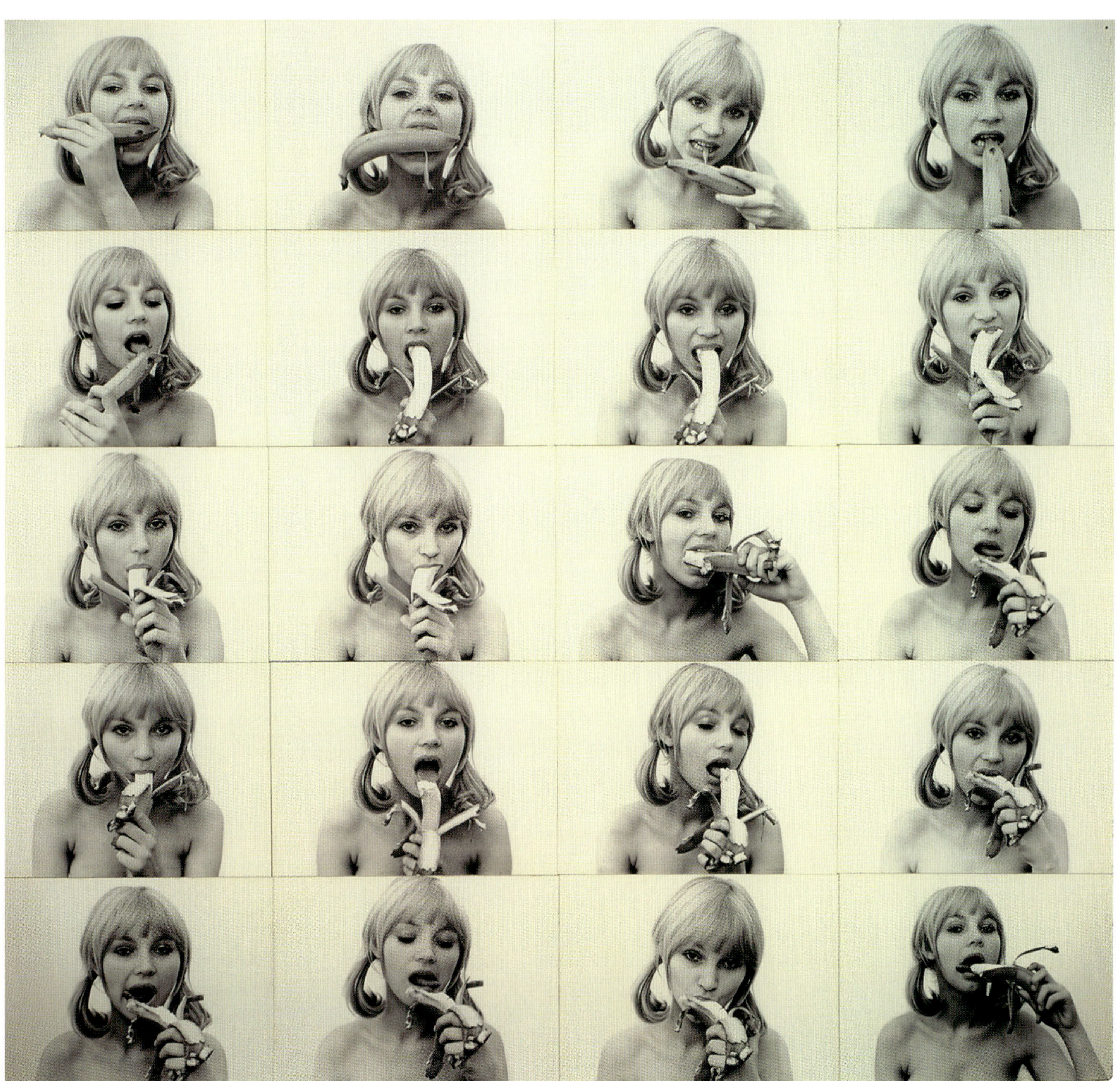

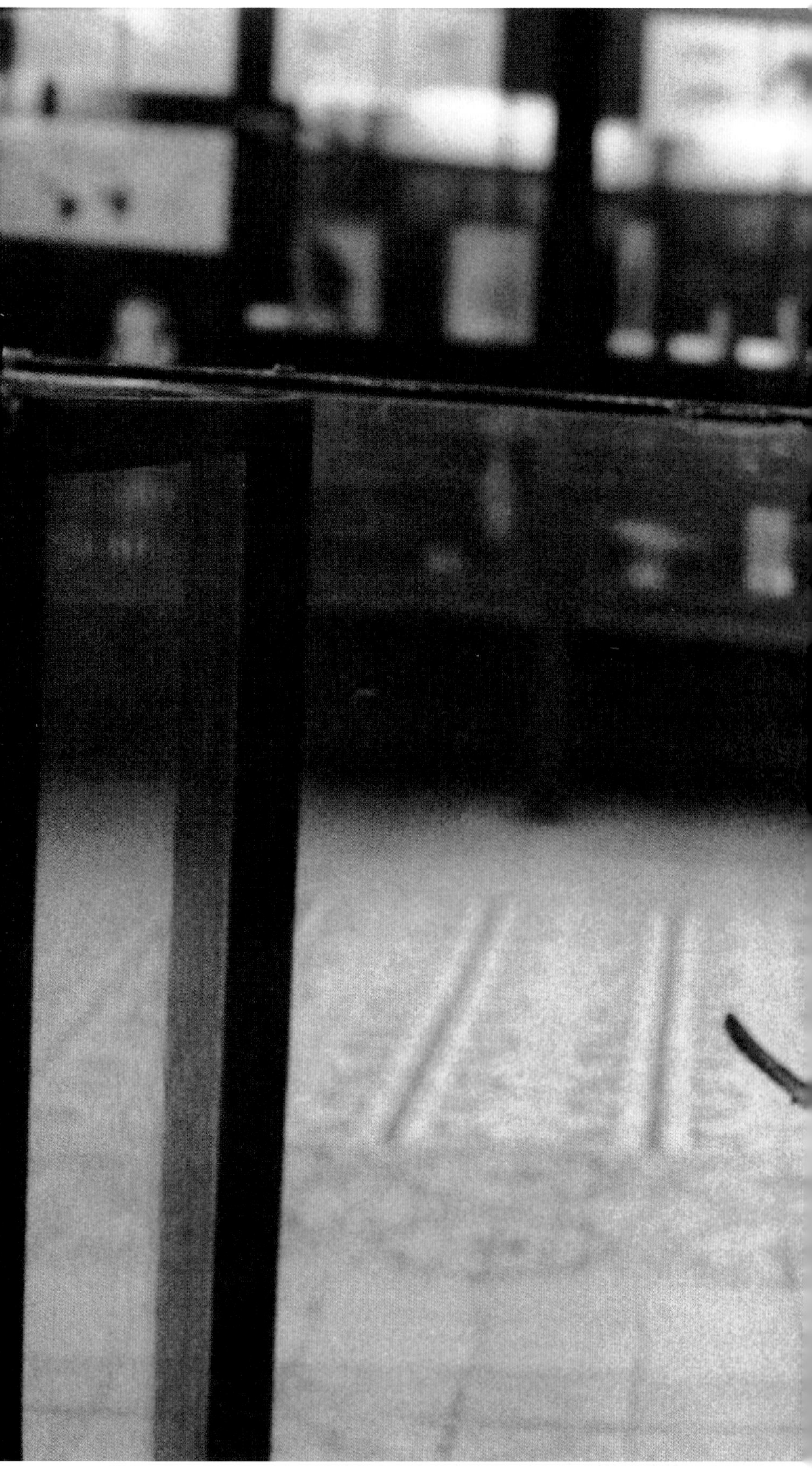

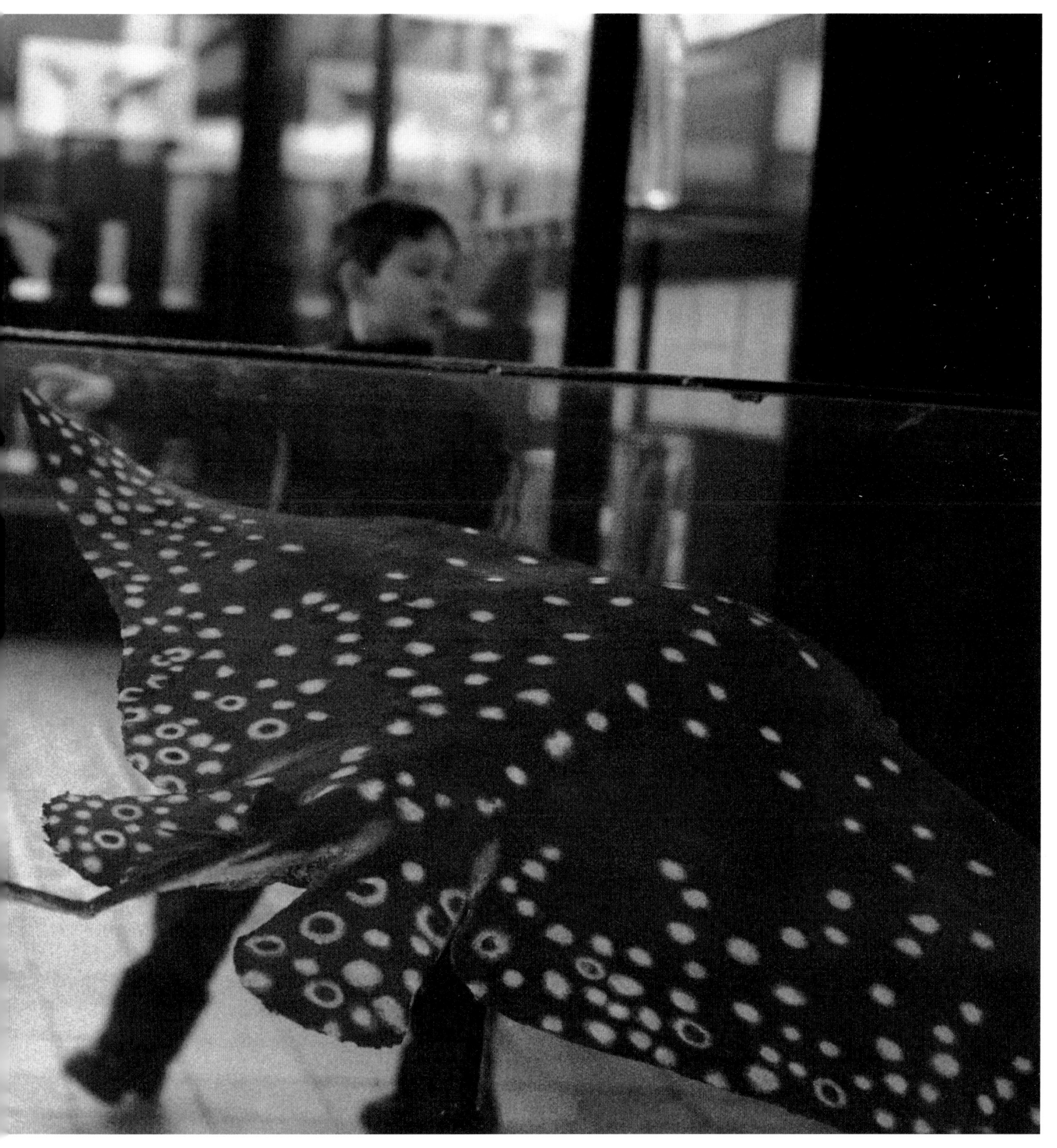

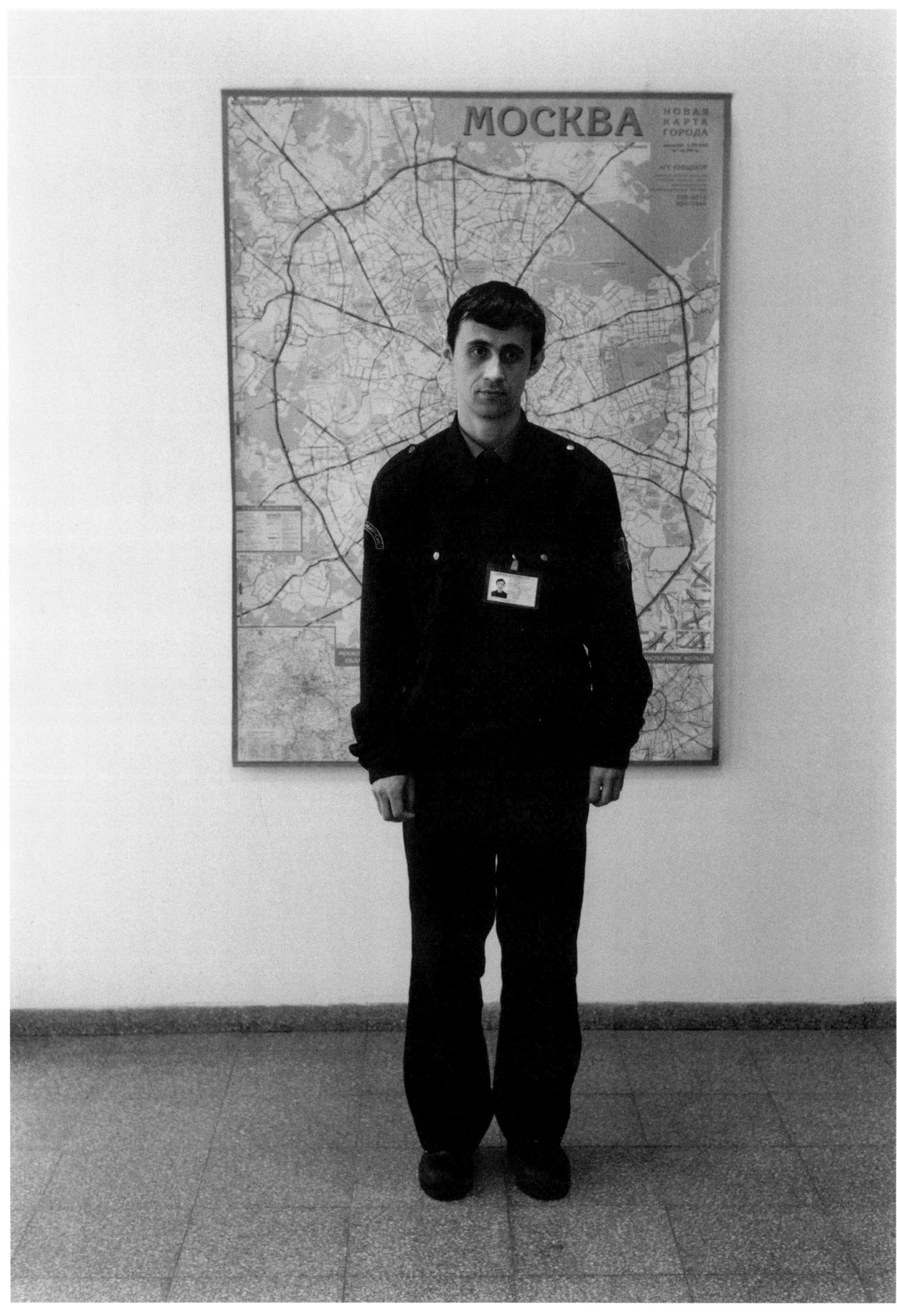

МОСКВА
НОВАЯ
КАРТА
ГОРОДА

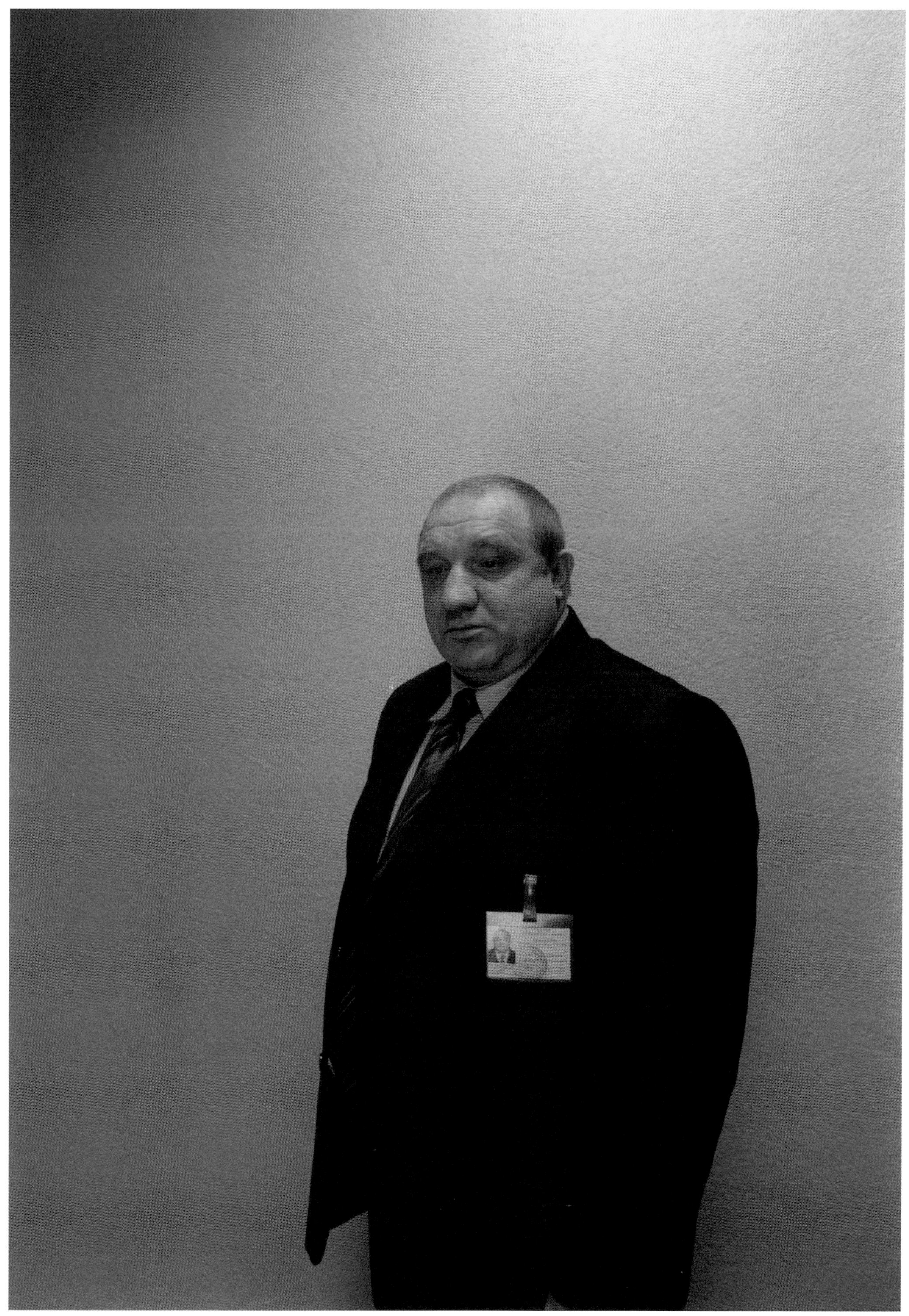

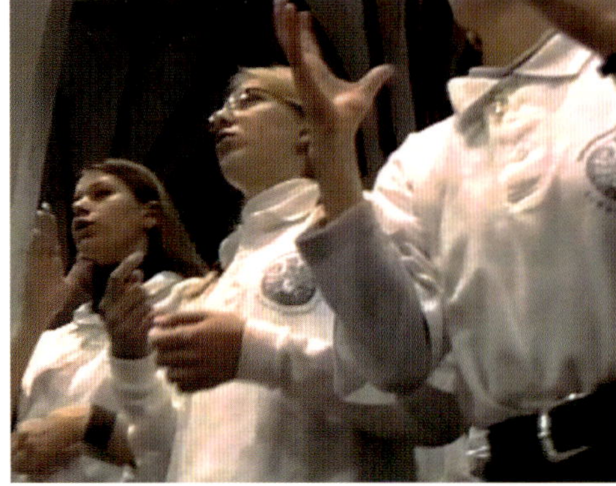
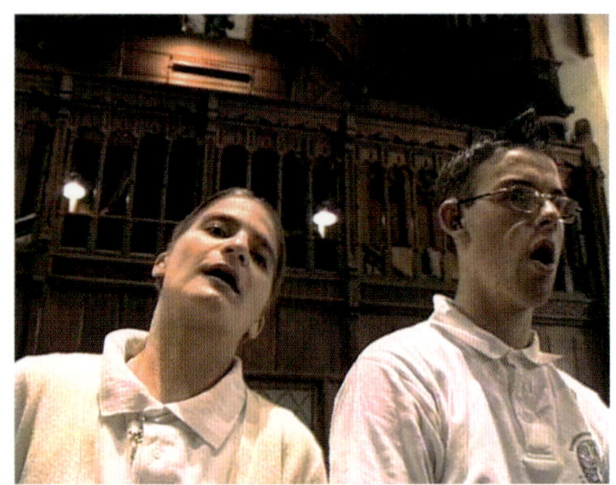
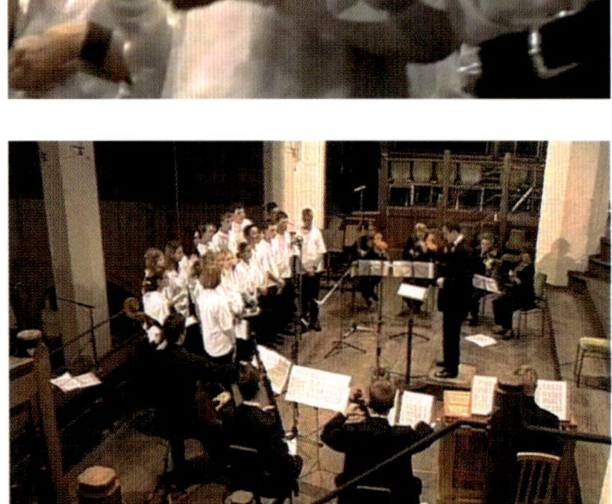
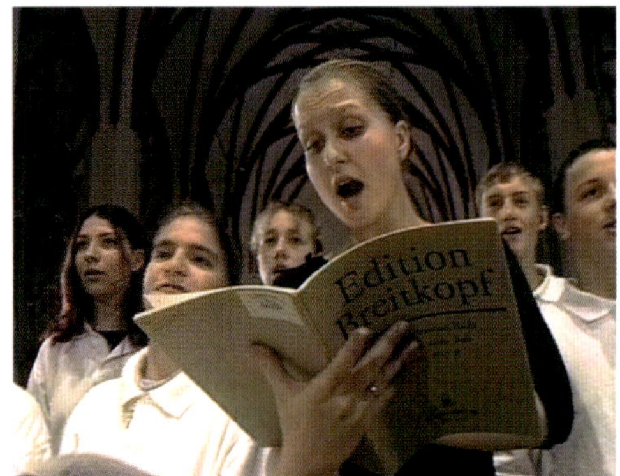

Singing Lesson 2 (right)
2003, video stills
Courtesy Foksal Gallery Foundation

Them (opposite above and below)
2007, video still
Courtesy Foksal Gallery Foundation

ARTUR ŻMIJEWSKI

Central to Artur Żmijewski's practice is an understanding that, through a language of images, art is in possession of effective means of influencing the consciousness of individuals and the way we perceive our environment; it is thus equipped for presenting a constructive challenge to established social and cultural institutions —i.e. science and politics—that claim to offer authoritative and exclusively credible systems of thought and knowledge. Żmijewski's practice therefore proceeds upon a conception of art as a powerful, autonomous discipline, which nonetheless forms a piece with existent discourses that constitute the epistemological fabric of a social space.

At the same time, Żmijewski strives to integrate his practice within the everyday reality of social life. Working predominantly with film and photography, he employs a strategy of "directed documentaries", introducing a group of people into a situation, which he has devised, and observing how they behave. The result is a reflexive space for human activity to occur, where ideological currents and normative societal values become exposed and come under scrutiny.

Many of Żmijewski's films feature individuals with some kind of physical impairment who consequently occupy a position that is excluded from a locus of cultural normality. In the film *Singing Lesson 2,* Żmijewski recreates the format of the first *Singing Lesson*, with a group of hearing-impaired teenagers assembled as a choir of singers. This time, the choir attempt a cantata by Johann Sebastian Bach, and are joined by a professional opera singer for the final performance. This latter inclusion produces an audible conflict between the experienced vocals of the opera singer and the vocal attempts of the teenagers, who respond to the task with enthusiasm, while a conductor struggles and manoeuvres against the inexorable wave of noise. In an affecting way, the young choir enacts a transgression of an impossible boundary, with pressure placed on the binary opposition between the 'normal' and the 'Other'.

Following a trip to Israel in 2003, Żmijewski produced a series of films that dealt specifically with the complicated Polish—Jewish relationship that arose from the events of the Holocaust. For *Our Songbook,* filmed in Tel Aviv, Żmijewski sought out Israelis with Polish roots that had left for Israel during The Second World War, and asked if they were able to recall any Polish songs from that time. Amidst fragments of pre-war hits, traditional cavalry songs and the Polish national anthem, the work puts forward a discussion of a receding, stigmatised past and a collective historical memory that is gradually fading.

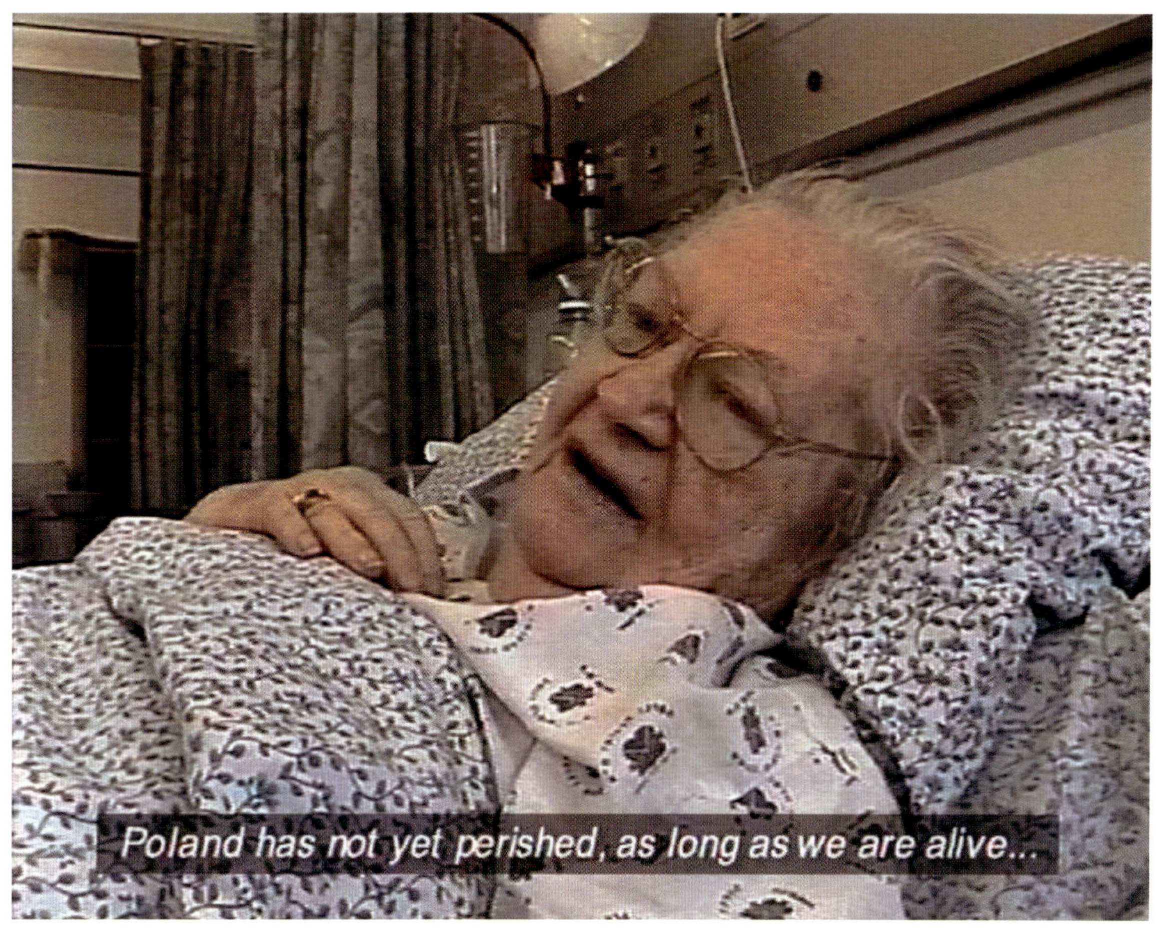

Poland has not yet perished, as long as we are alive...

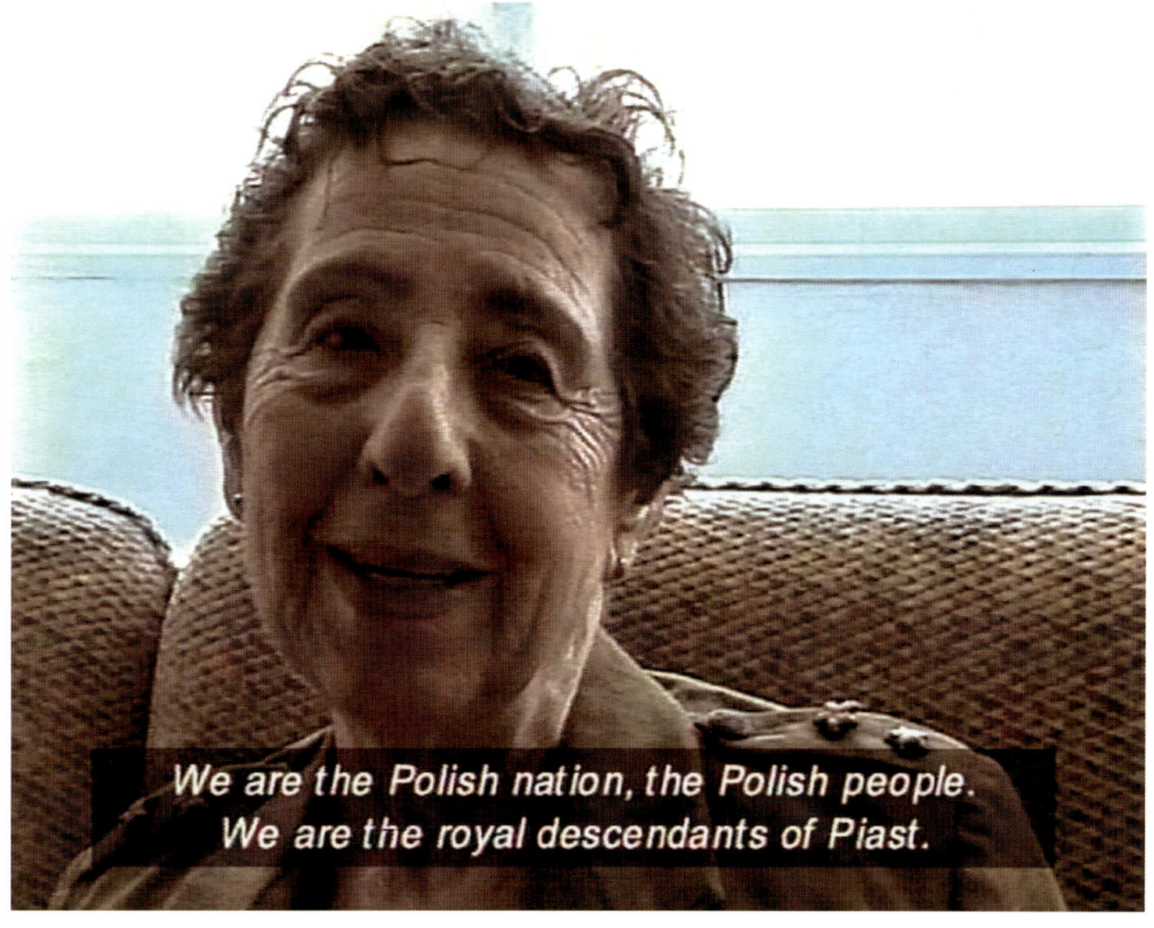

We are the Polish nation, the Polish people.
We are the royal descendants of Piast.

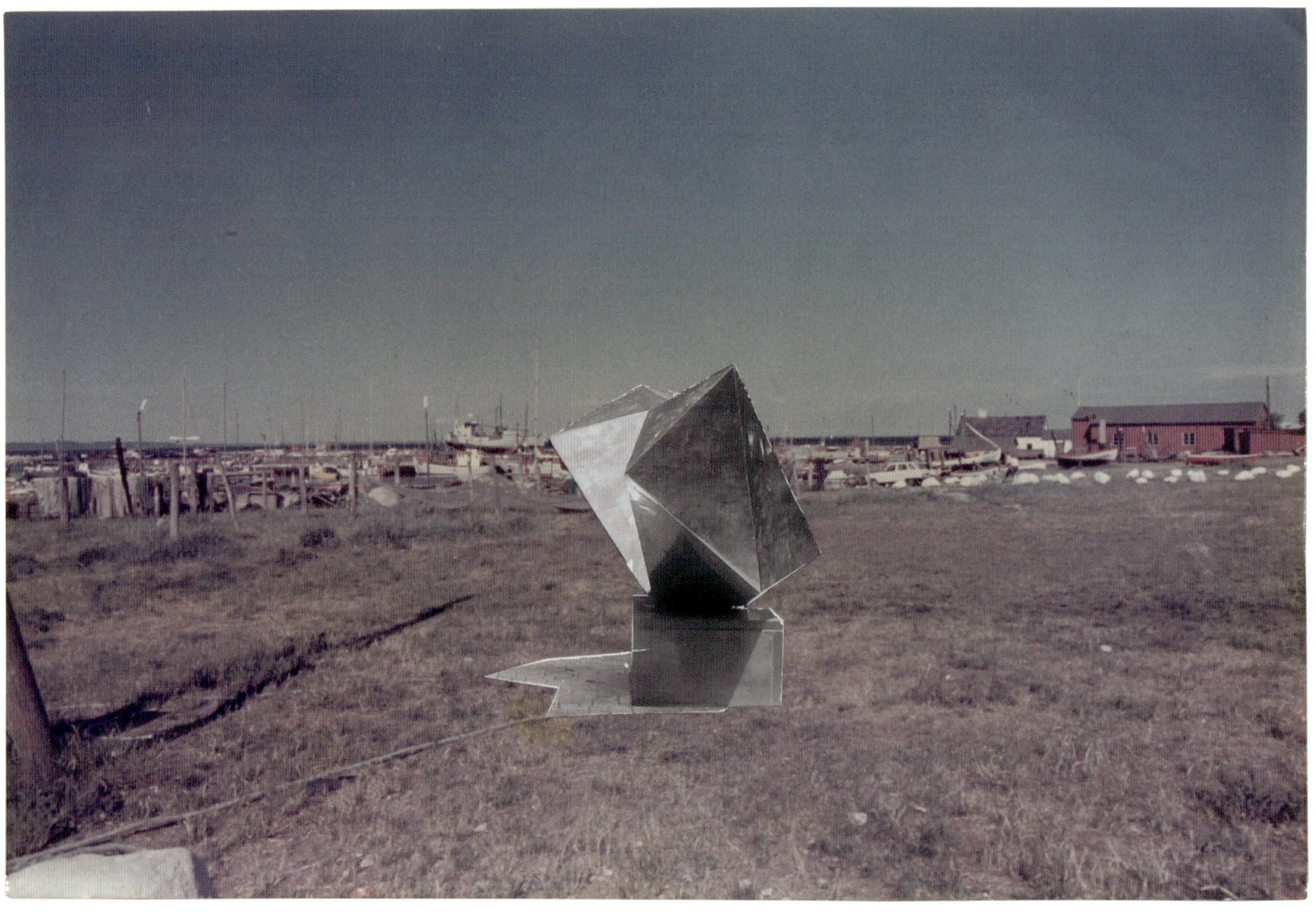

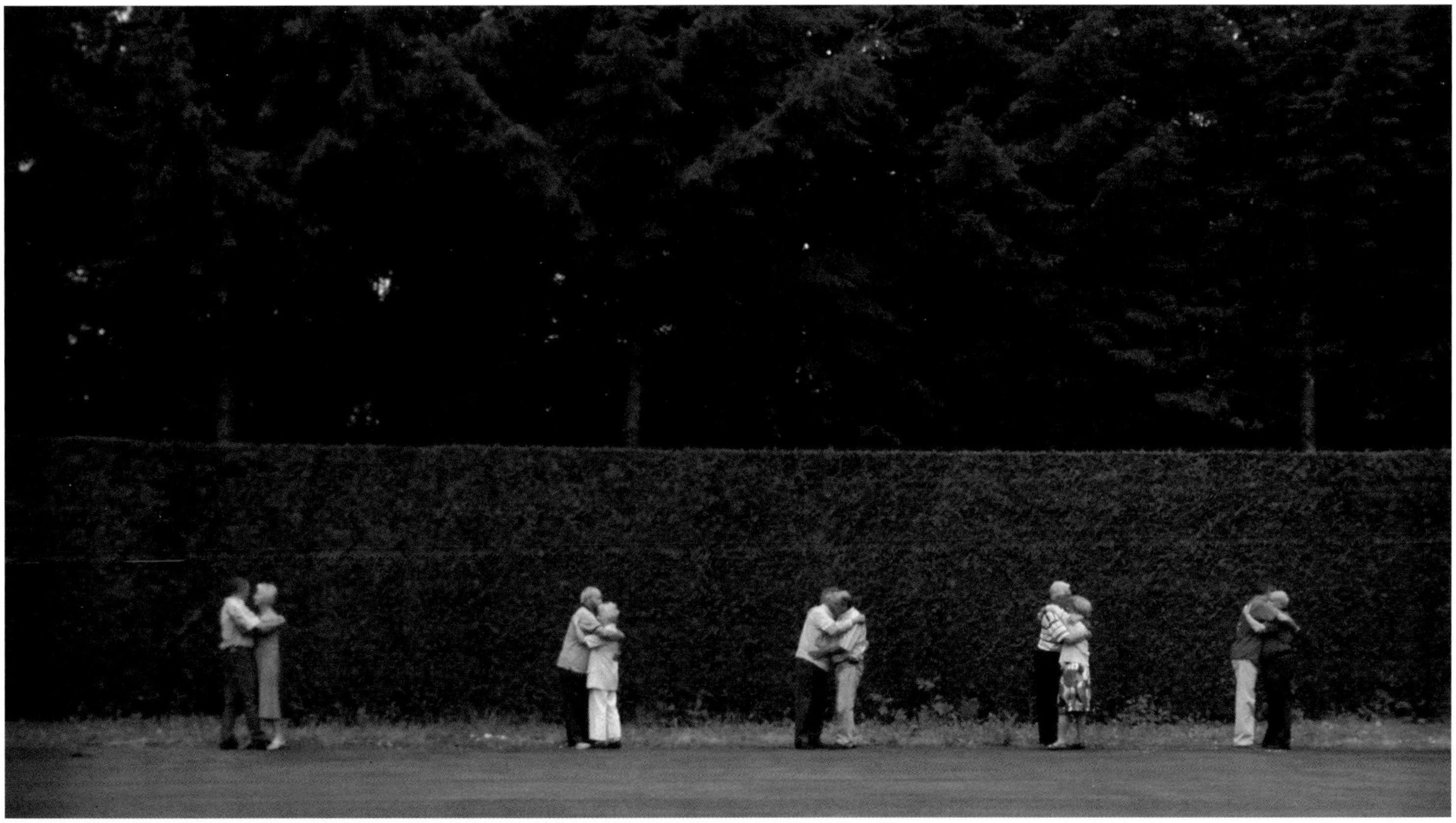

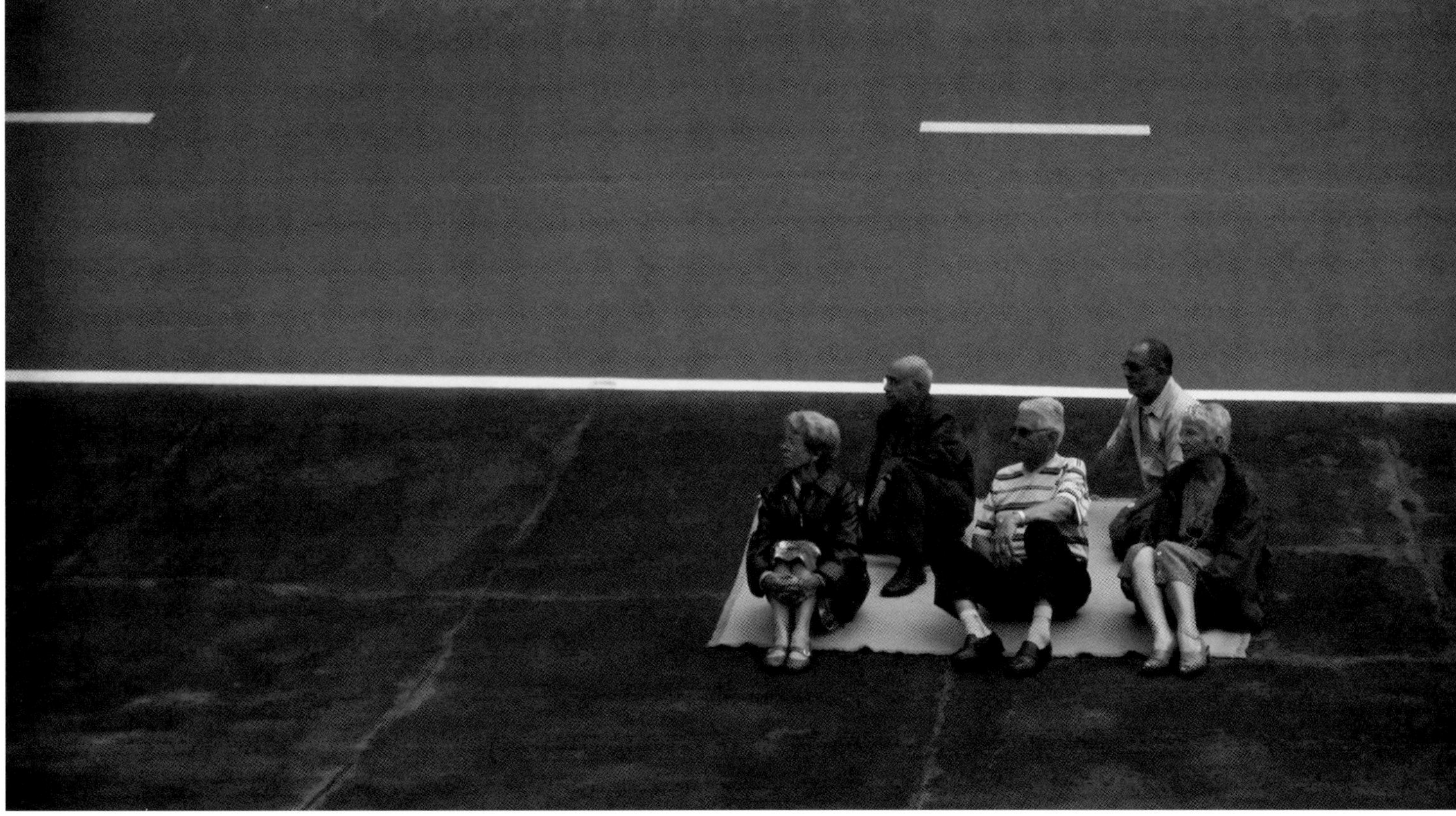

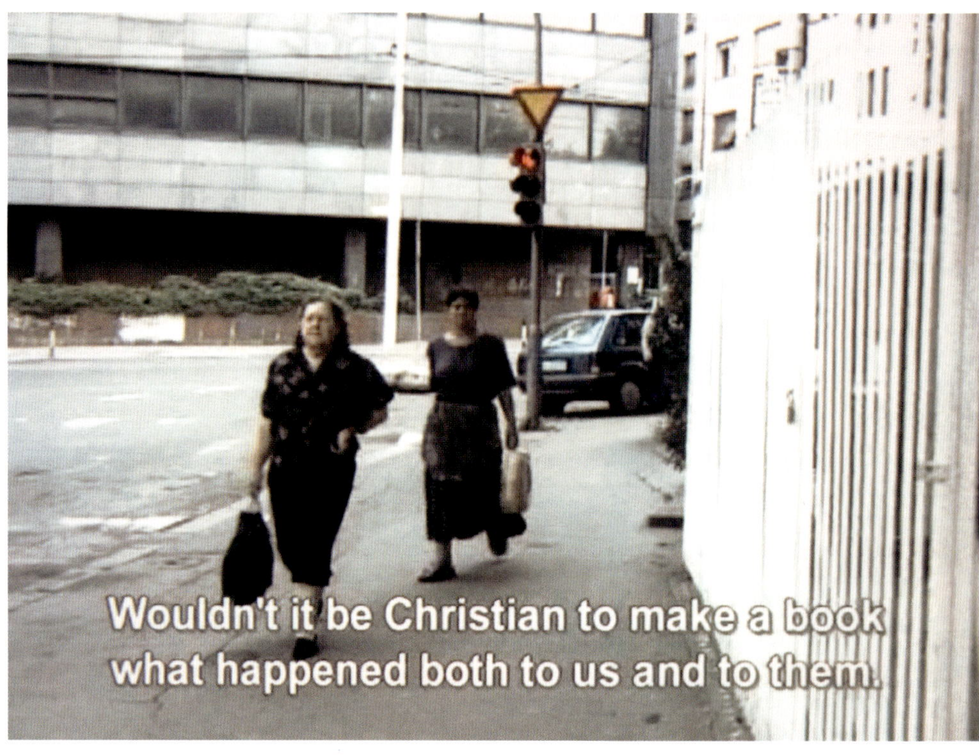

Portrait of my Mother (right and opposite)
1999, DVD, 64 minutes

MILICA TOMIĆ

The complex and fractious history of the former Yugoslav territories occupies a significant position within the practice of Serbian artist Milica Tomić. Through her video, photographic and performance works, Tomić attempts to place the raw materials of identity, nationality and ethnicity under critical scrutiny, so as to make sense of a legacy of political violence, confront the trauma of past events and engage with the present-day realities that exist to give shape to her native Serbia.

Underpinning Tomić's project is an understanding of the epistemological violence inherent to forms of language and social activity and the ways in which linguistic experience can govern the consciousness of individuals. In the video/installation work *I am Milica Tomić,* the artist herself stands before us. Calm and composed, she proceeds to declare her name and nationality 64 times. With each declaration, however, the stated nationality changes, and each time it does, a fresh, gaping wound appears somewhere on Tomić's body. Unfazed but increasingly bloodied, the artist proceeds with her recital and brings it to its conclusion, at which point the process begins afresh. In a provocative manner, Tomić manages to frame the declaration of identity as a performative utterance that in itself works to produce identity, and furthermore draws attention to the political consequences this identification carries.

Tomić's video and slide-projection installation *Portrait of my Mother* was made soon after the 1999 NATO bombing campaign in Belgrade. The work presents an intimate conversation between the artist and her mother, Marija Milutinovic, interspersed with footage describing the journey Tomić takes to arrive at her mother's apartment. As we venture into a satellite town on the periphery of the city, past Muslim housing blocks constructed at the turn of the century and neighbourhoods devastated by NATO bombs, we learn of the biography of Milutinovic, a theatre and television actress who retired in the late 1970s as a result of a personal and professional crisis.

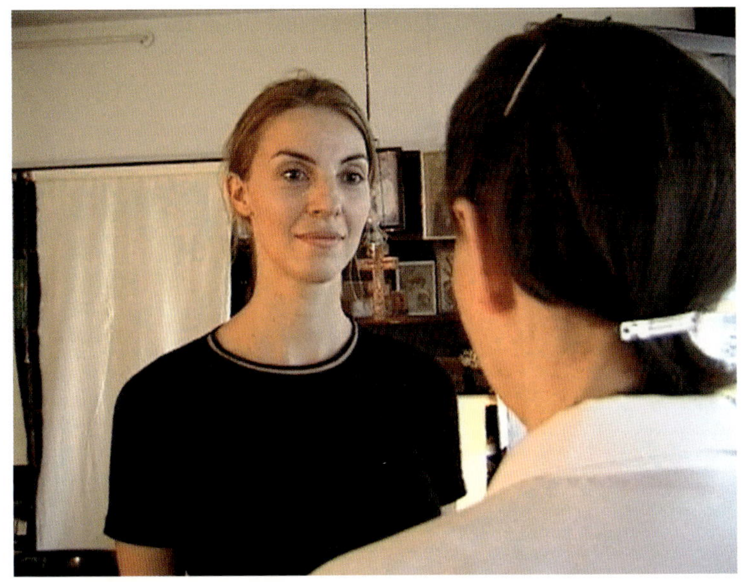 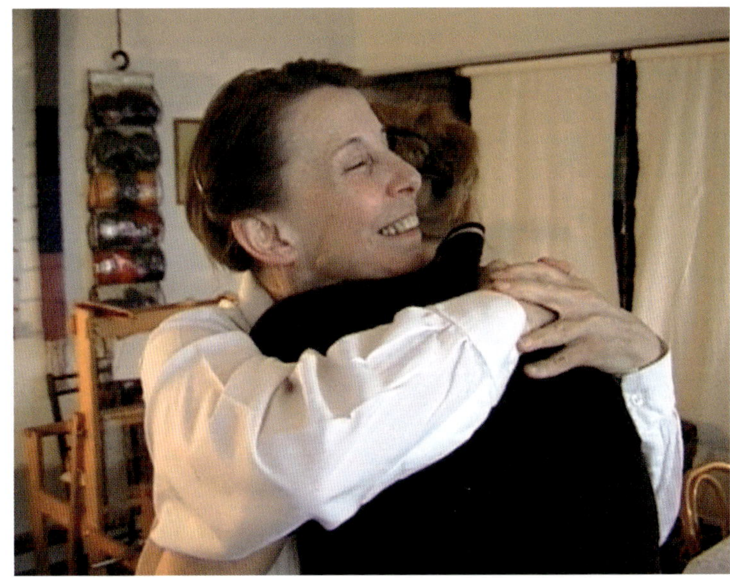

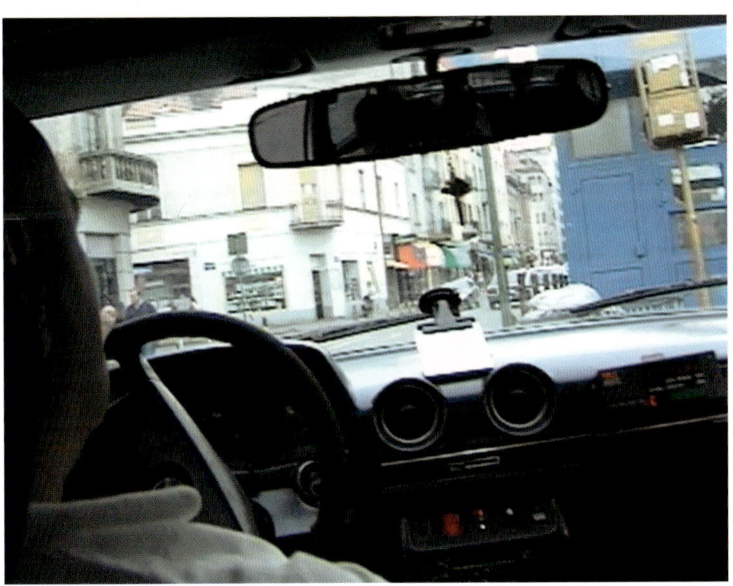 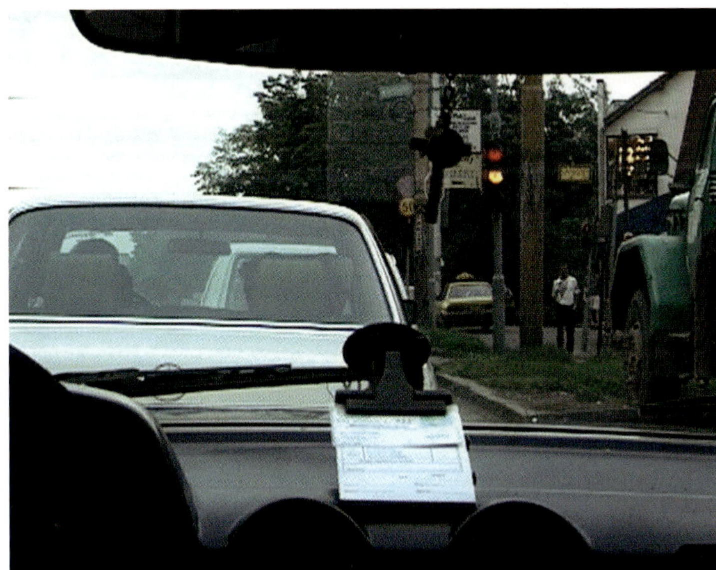

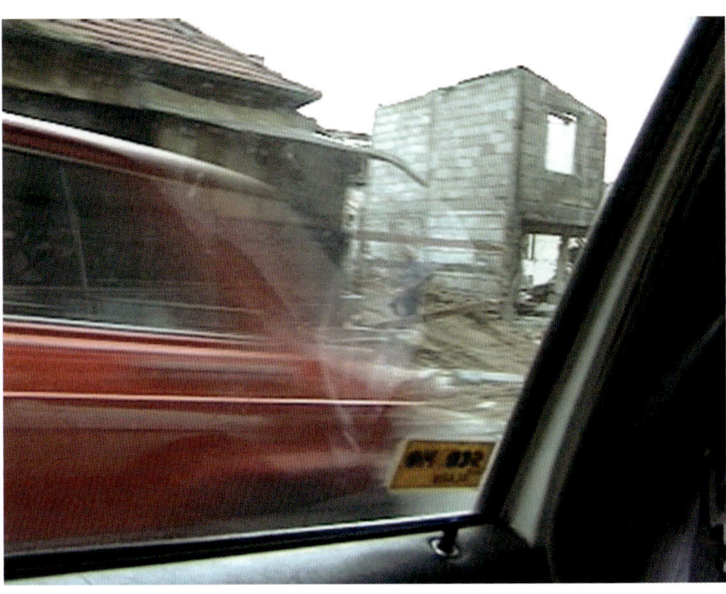 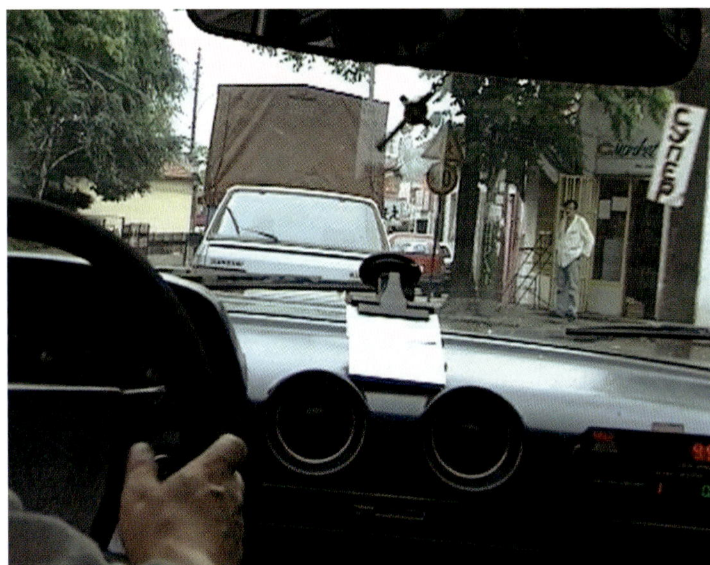

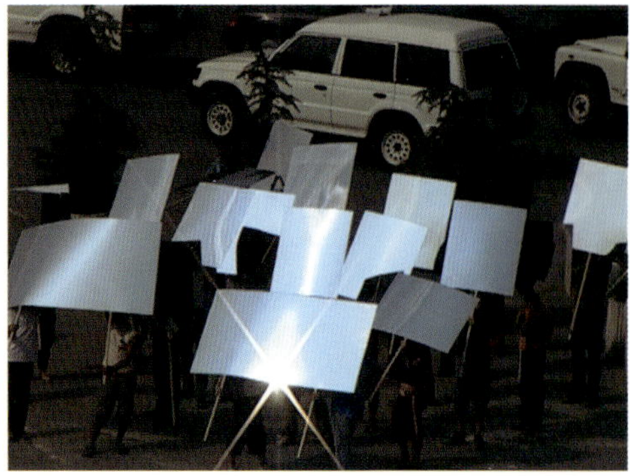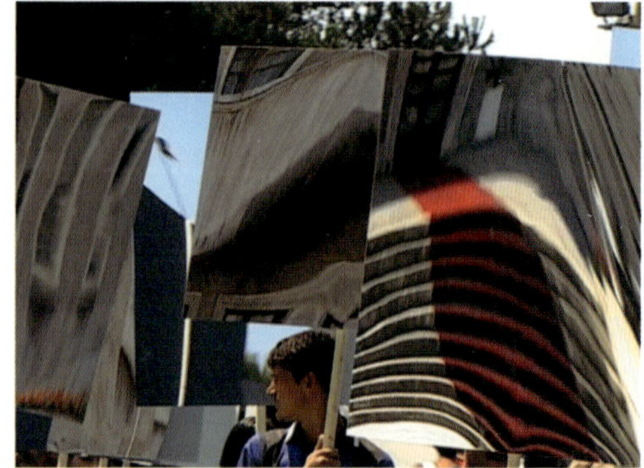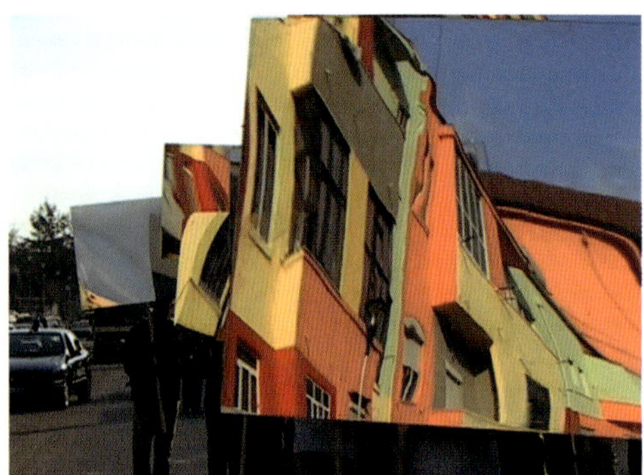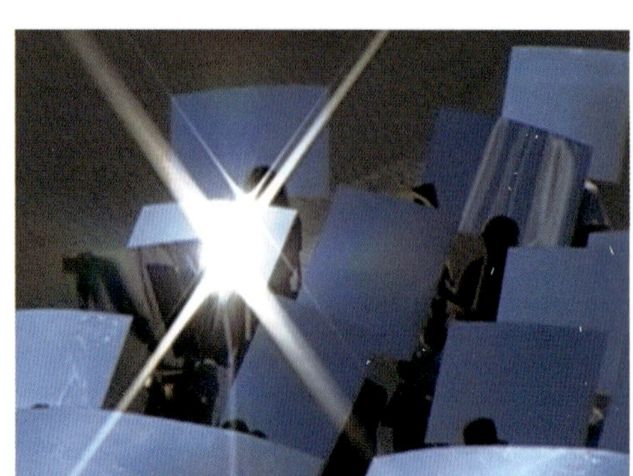

MIRCEA CANTOR

Mircea Cantor, a Romanian-born artist who at 22 uprooted from his home country to hitchhike Europe before settling in France, creates multidisciplined works that feature film, animation, painting, drawing, sculpture and installation. Closely examining the overlapping of cultural, natural and ideological boundaries, Cantor often chooses to delineate his ideas through delicate metaphors. While he has expressed an aversion to work that is self-referential, Romanian folk traditions—particularly labour—remain a continual point of allusion. Cantor's art often concerns itself with strange encounters and displacement: worlds made to coexist in often-deadpan pairings, together appearing incongruous —but mutually inquisitive rather than problematic. *Hiatus* sees the insertion of a geometric sculpture—loosely based on a structure made by shepherds to spin wool—into a woodland setting; its very title eliciting the expectation about what is to come from nature's acquisition of a foreign body that is normally in permanent vibration.

This preoccupation with adjusted realities is expanded on in *The Landscape is Changing*, a 22 minute video that sees protestors marching through the streets of Tirane, Albania, brandishing placards—a surface on which we are normally accustomed to impactful slogans being articulated. Instead, they are mirrored, and only reflect back the urban journey of a rally that is apparently meaningless. The city is recomposed within the moving mirrors, possible to make out at one moment, distorted and unrecognisable the next. If a mirror reveals a world that we understand to be truthful and stable, Cantor's placards seem like a fairground hall of mirrors—visually reconfiguring a country such as Albania, which suffered under the political rigidity of a Stalinist government, as a place that is altogether more unstable and incomprehensible.

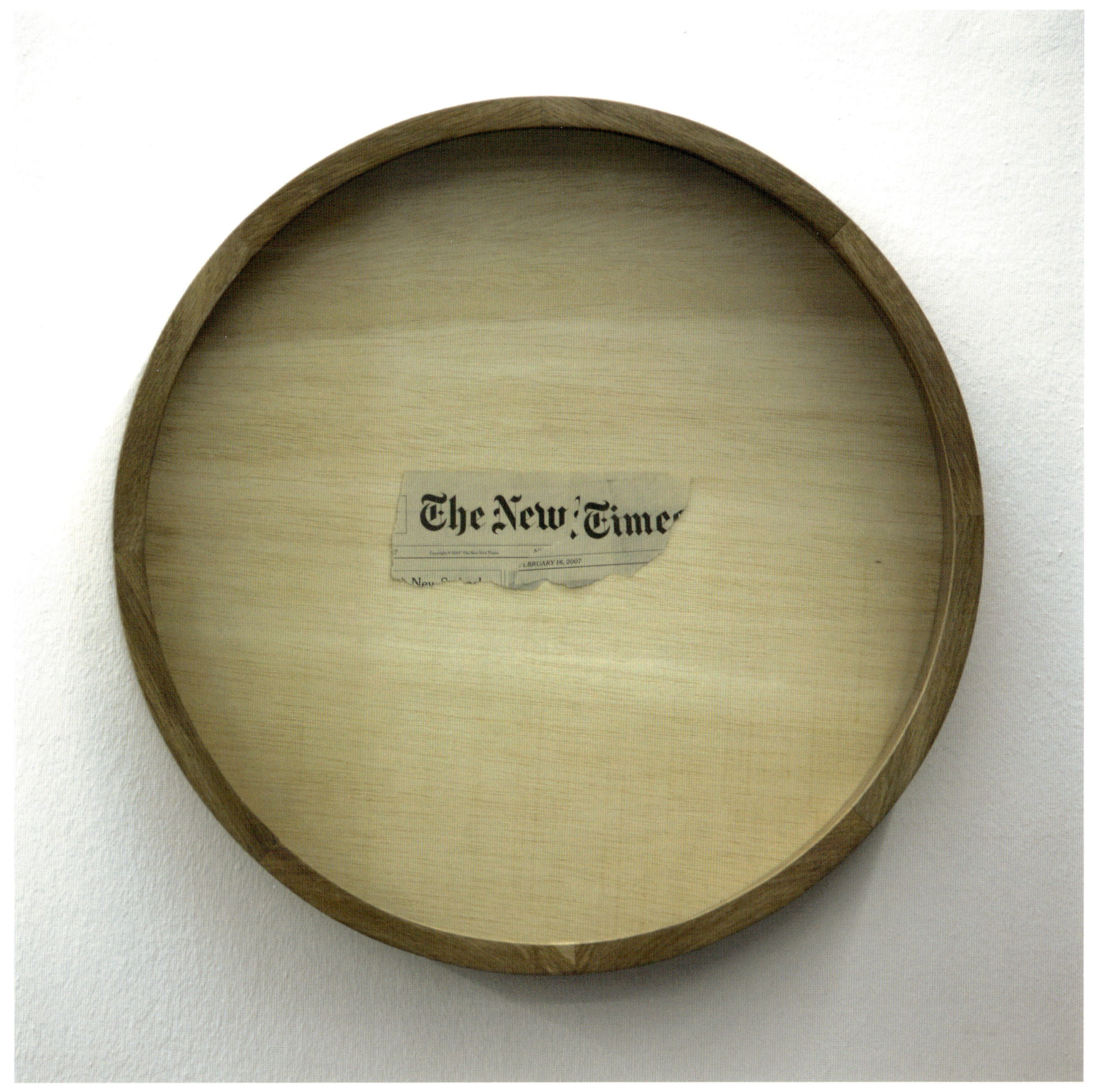

The New Times
FEBRUARY 16, 2007

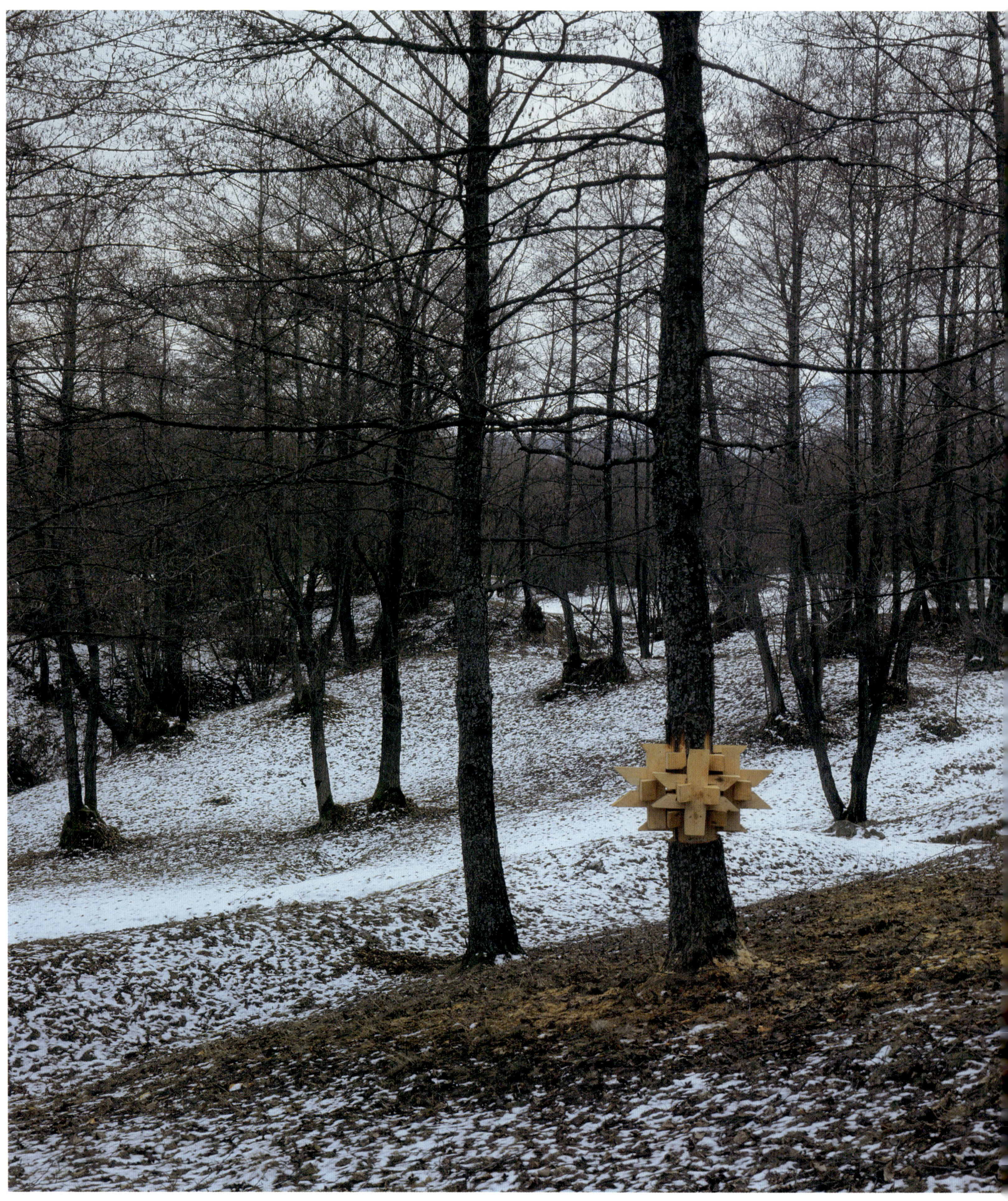

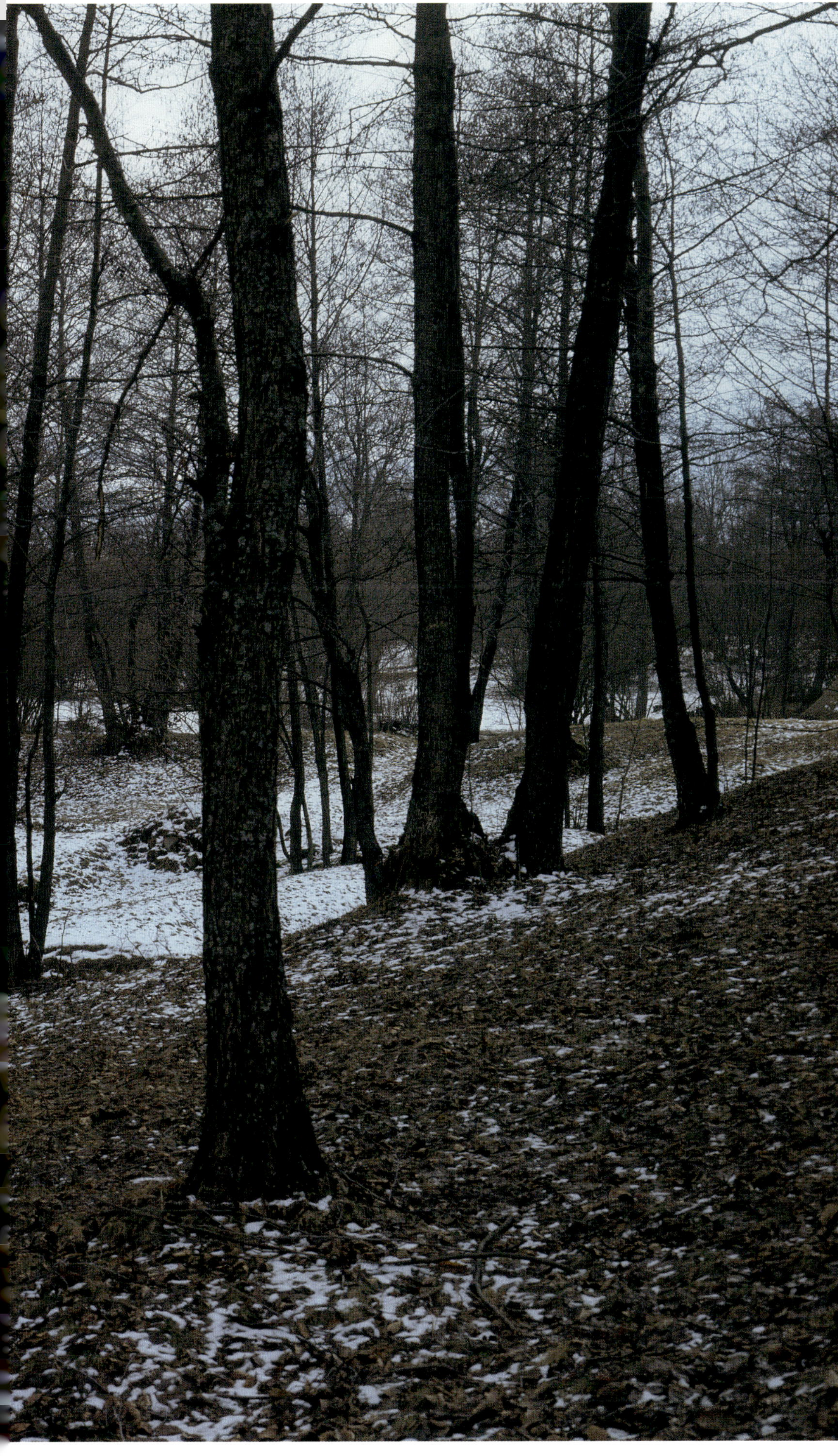

MIRCEA CANTOR
Hiatus
2008, colour photograph, 100 x 161 cm
Courtesy the artist

Homeless Vehicle (right)
1988–1999, New York City
Courtesy the artist and Galerie Lelong

Lenin Monument Projection (opposite)
1990, East Berlin
Courtesy the artist and Galerie Lelong

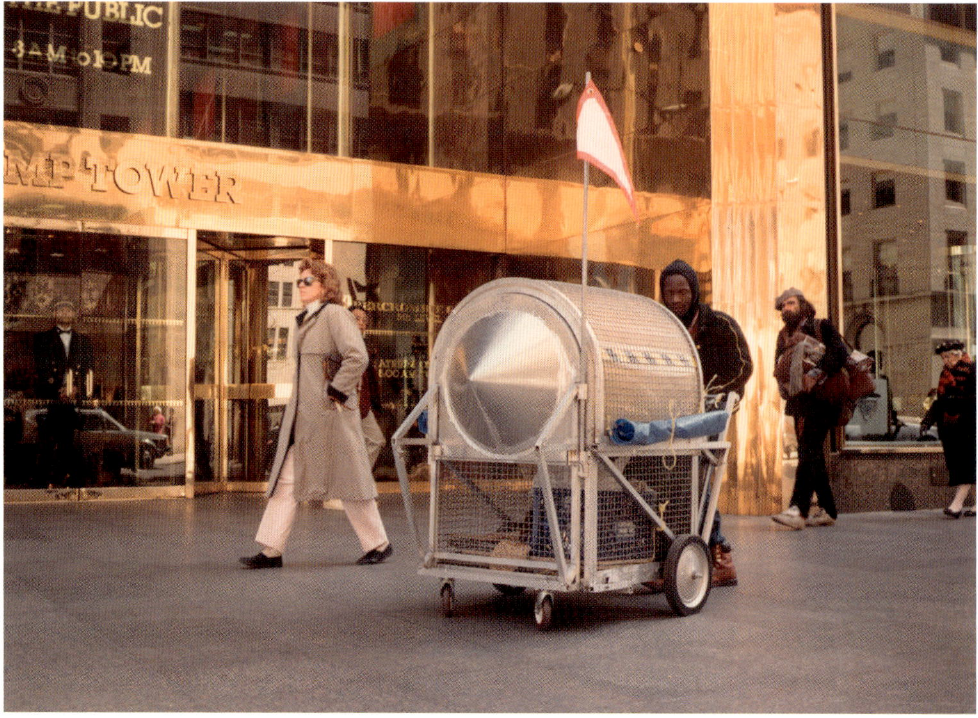

KRZYSZTOF WODICZKO

Krzysztof Wodiczko can be considered one of the most significant Polish artists of the past 50 years. His so-called "public-art" is firmly rooted within socially conscious ideas that have been informed by his politically turbulent upbringing in Eastern Europe, reflected in both the form and content of each of his works. Wodiczko has lectured widely on his practice—he is currently engaged in a professorship at Harvard—through which he came up with the term "Monument Therapy": a kind-of social healing process, in which he engages with the subject of each piece (memorial) through various methods that articulate topical issues of social and political awareness (therapy), most notably in his slide and video projections. Wodiczko's work has gained him international recognition and in 1998 the artist received

the 4th Hiroshima Art Prize "for his contribution as an artist to world peace".

The subjects of Wodiczko's large-scale projections, for which he has created more than 80 worldwide since the late 1980s, are highly recognised building facades and monuments, including Nelson's Column, London; The Lenin Monument, Berlin; and Arco del la Victoria, Madrid. The artist views these structures as iconic symbols of a nation's collective memory, through which he seeks to challenge people's perceptions of history, with a focus upon those on the periphery. In 1996, Wodiczko began to add sound and motion to his projections, the first of which was projected onto Kraków's City Hall Tower, Poland.

Alongside his projections, Wodiczko's portfolio also includes his 'Vehicles': *First Vehicle*, *Vehicle Podium*, *Homeless Vehicle*, *Poliscar* and *War Veteran Vehicle*. These works can be considered as heavily influenced by his time spent at the Academy of Fine Arts, Warsaw, where he graduated in Industrial Design in 1968; their purpose being imagined by the artist as therapeutic 'instruments' that aid human beings in different ways, from survival for the homeless to physical enablement for those with disabilities. Wodiczko's work in recent years continues along a similar thematic vein to his previous projects, engaging with issues of society, communication, authority and disability.

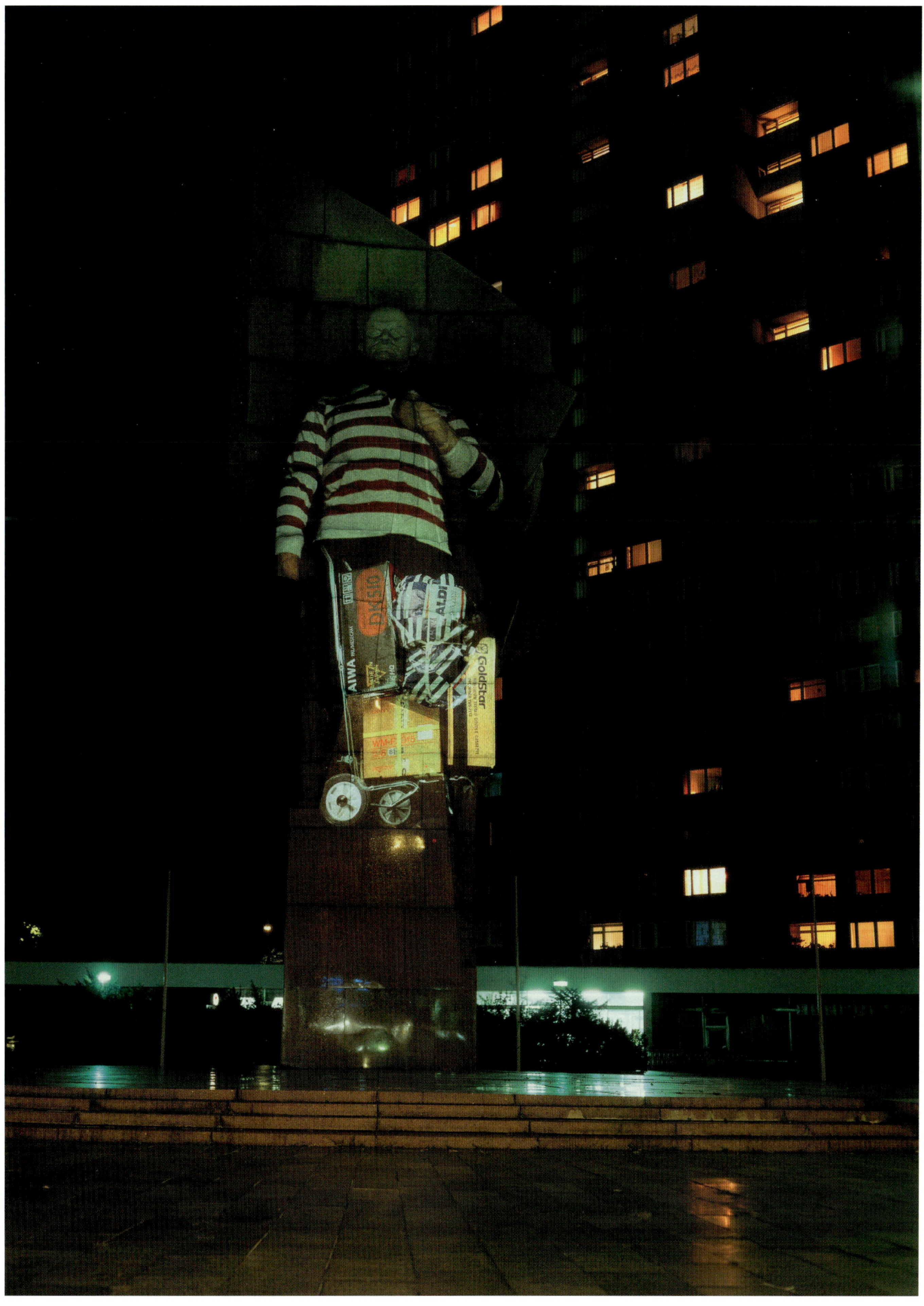

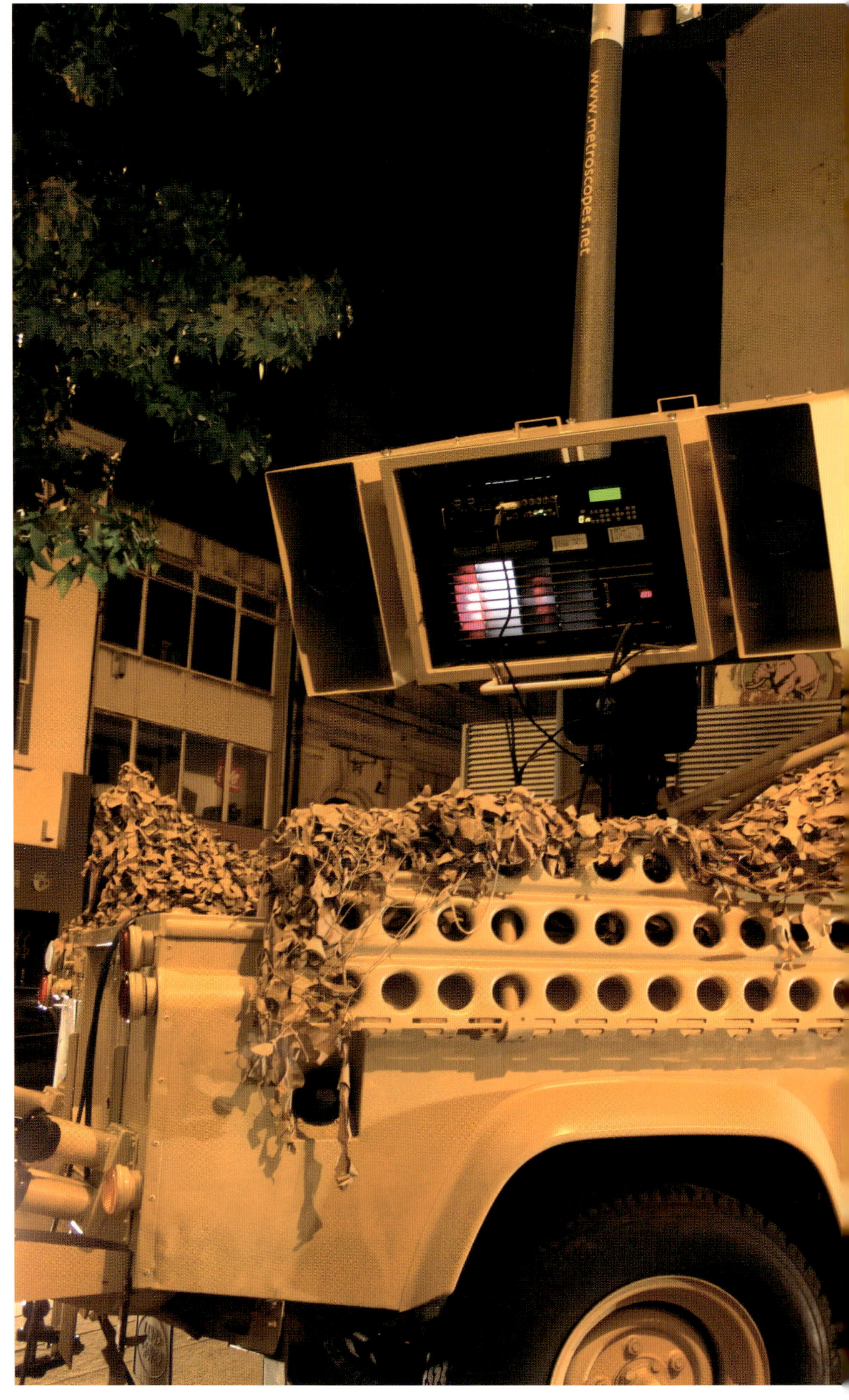

KRZYSZTOF WODICZKO
War Veteran Vehicle
2008–2010, Denver/Liverpool
Courtesy the artist and Galerie Lelong

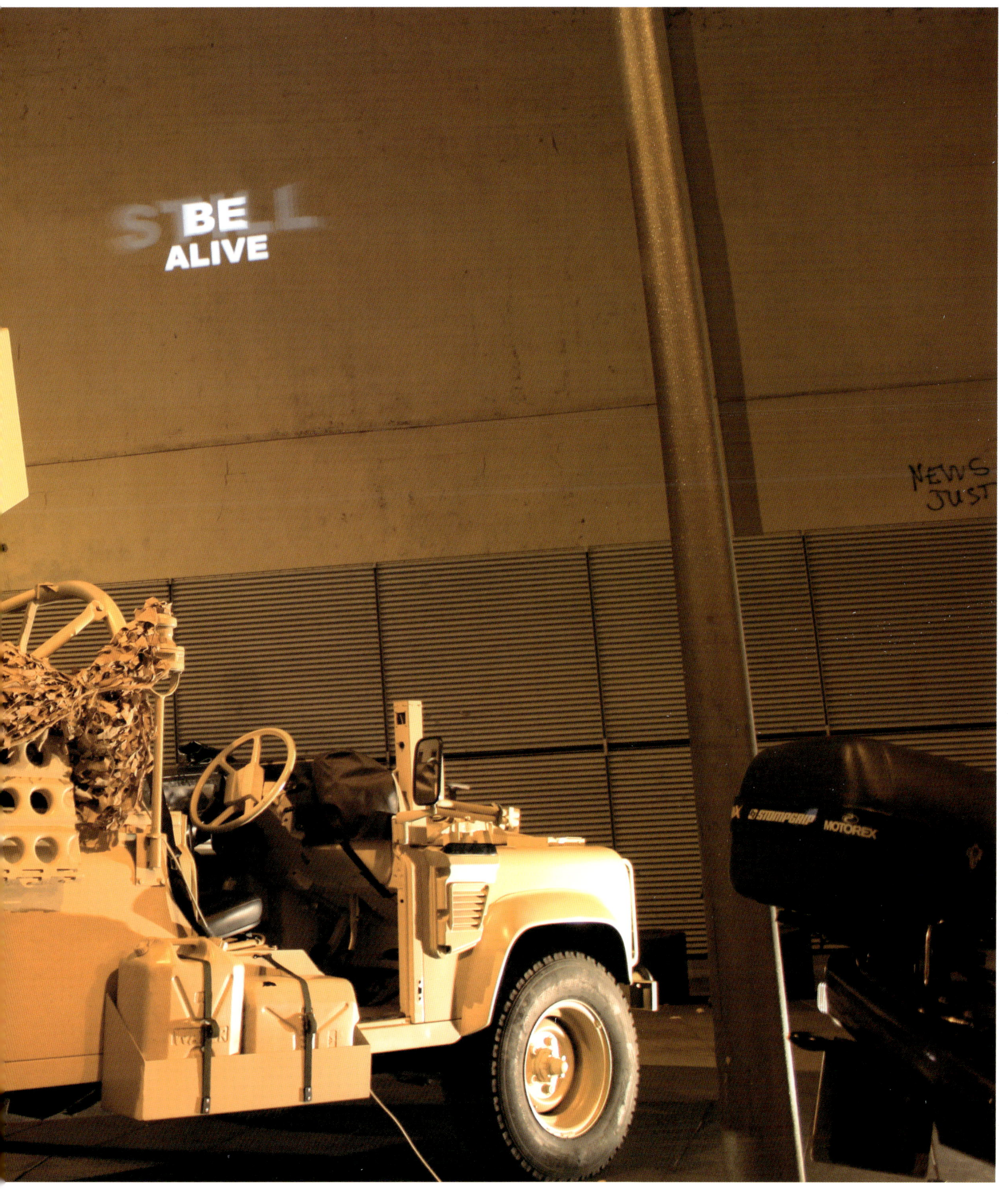
S BE L
ALIVE
NEWS
JUST
STOMPGRIP
MOTOREX

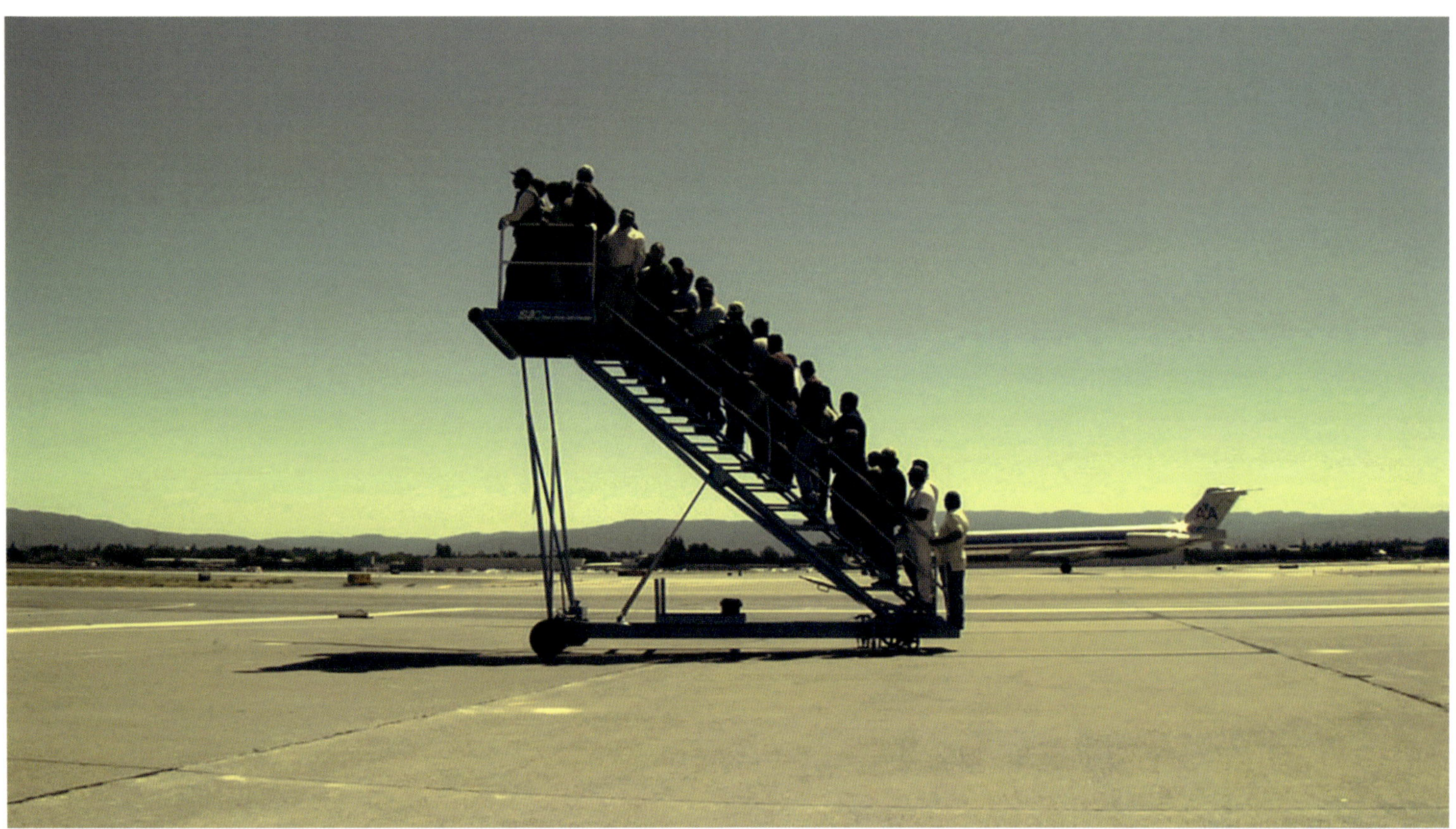

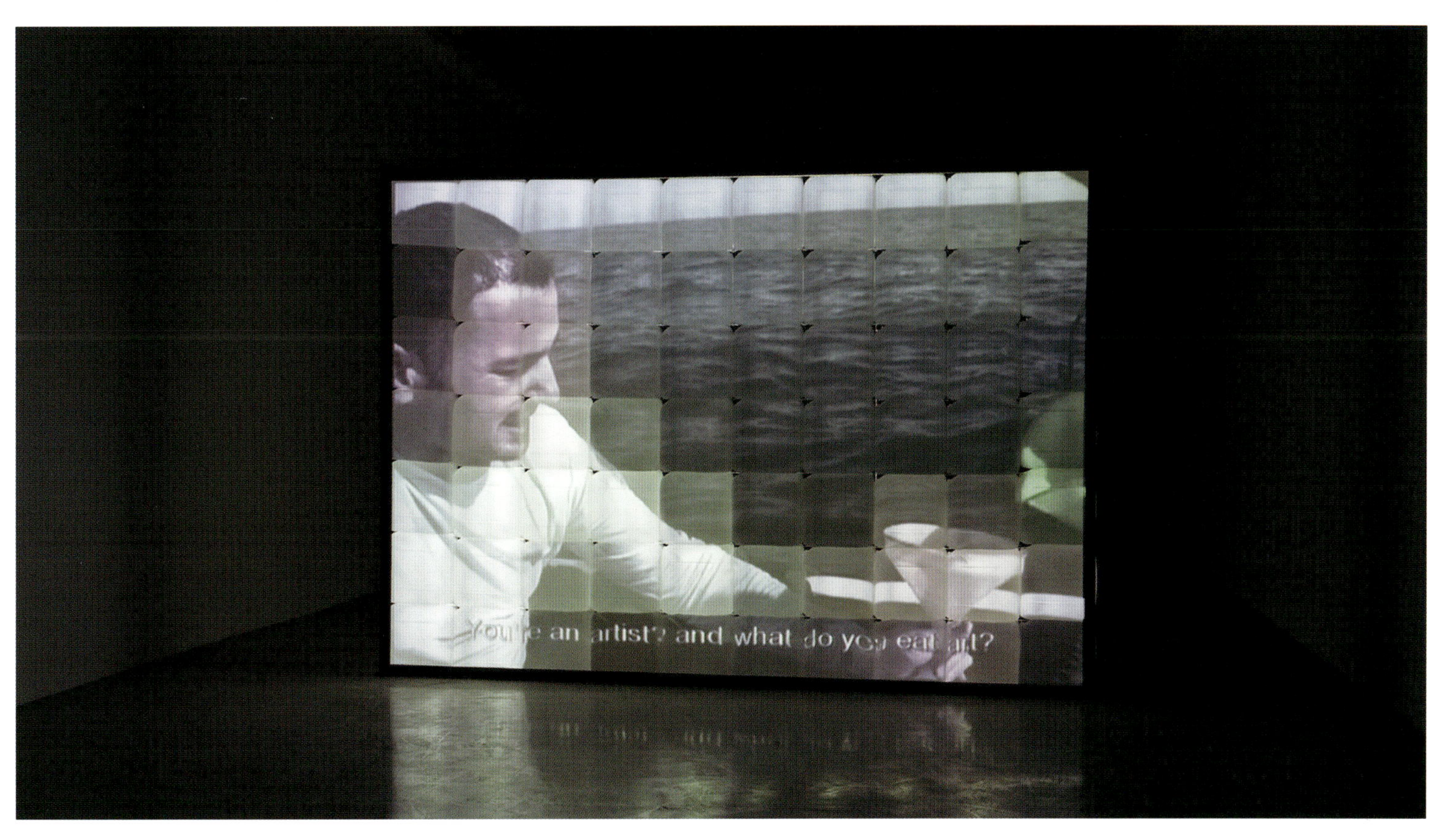
You're an artist? and what do you eat art?

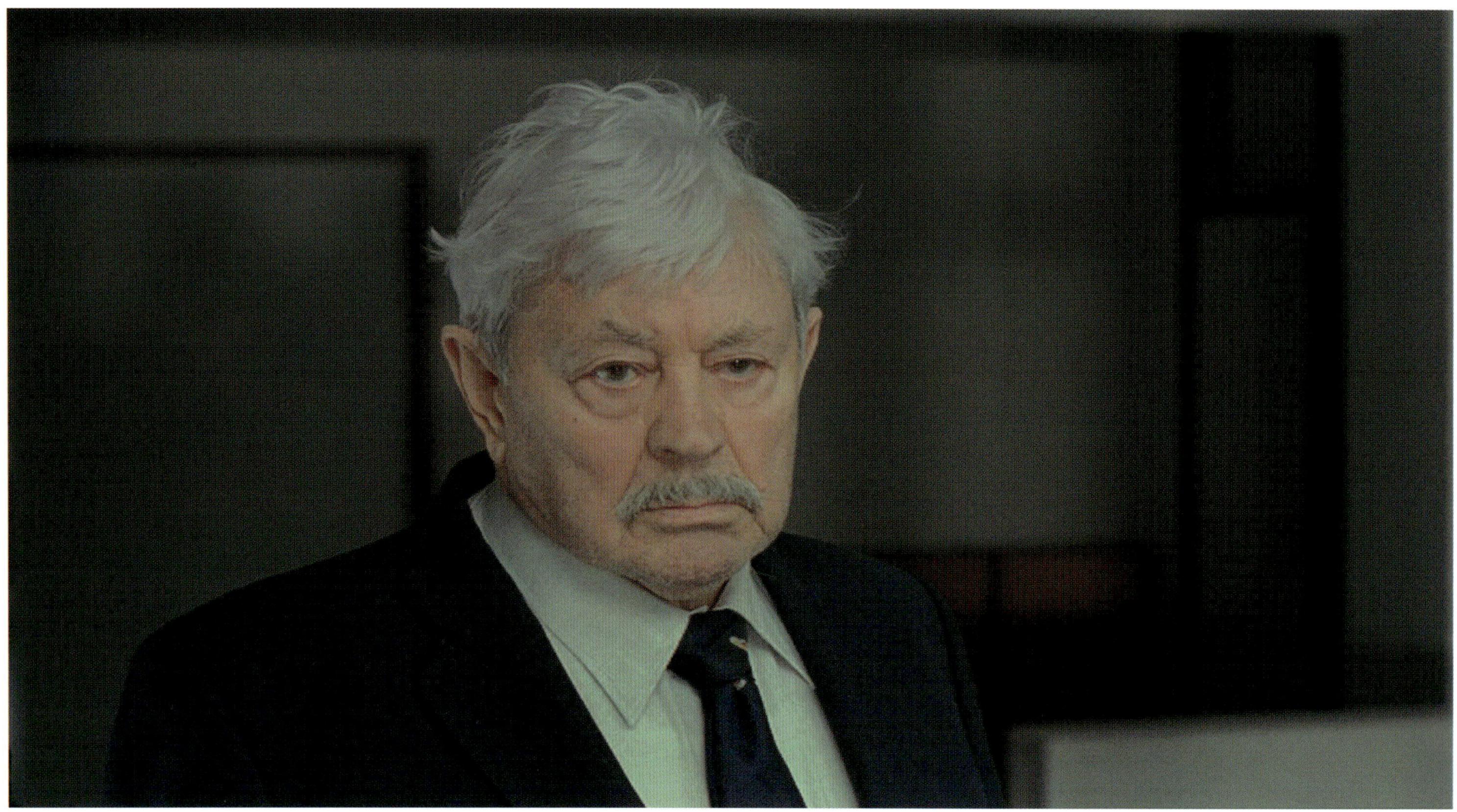

DEIMANTAS NARKEVIČIUS

Working primarily from a socially historic point of view, internationally recognised Lithuanian video artist Deimantas Narkevičius' work is heavily influenced by the politically turbulent era into which he emerged as an artist. Originally trained as a sculptor, Narkevičius' interest in filmmaking fast became apparent, as an emphasis upon a narrative structure became the focal point of his proceeding work, historical in subject, yet stressing the humanistic impact of this period.

Similar themes and discussions arise throughout Narkevičius' films, such as collective memory, personal recollection, time and experience. These are then interpreted through a range of Soviet-era filmmaking traditions including the use of found footage from Soviet films. One of his most highly recognised films, *Once in the XXth Century*, 2004, features re-edited footage of the infamous Lenin Monument in Vilnius being dismantled during the 1990s. In actual fact, Narkevičius presents a "reversal of images" so that it appears that the monument is actually being erected to celebrations from the crowd. Within this film, Narkevičius explores the idea of a disruption of linear time, in relation to contemporary history, and in doing so highlights a society's collective memory and projections of themselves in the future.

Revisiting Solaris, 2007, is inspired by Andrei Tarkovsky's cult film *Solaris*, 1972, originally based on Stanislav Lem's science fiction novel of the same name. *Revisiting Solaris* articulates similar ideas as his previous films—in particular time and memory—by using the main protaginist of the original film, only 40 years later. Based on the last chapter of the book—the chapter which Tarkovsky omitted from *Solaris*—Narkevičius' brooding interpretation combines film with a series of photographs taken by the Lithuanian symbolist painter and composer Mykalojus Konstantinas Čiurlionis, used to represent the futuristic space landscape of the planet Solaris. Narkevičius saw Čiurlionis' work as representative of the meanings he himself was trying to convey of "infinite expanse and limitless time".

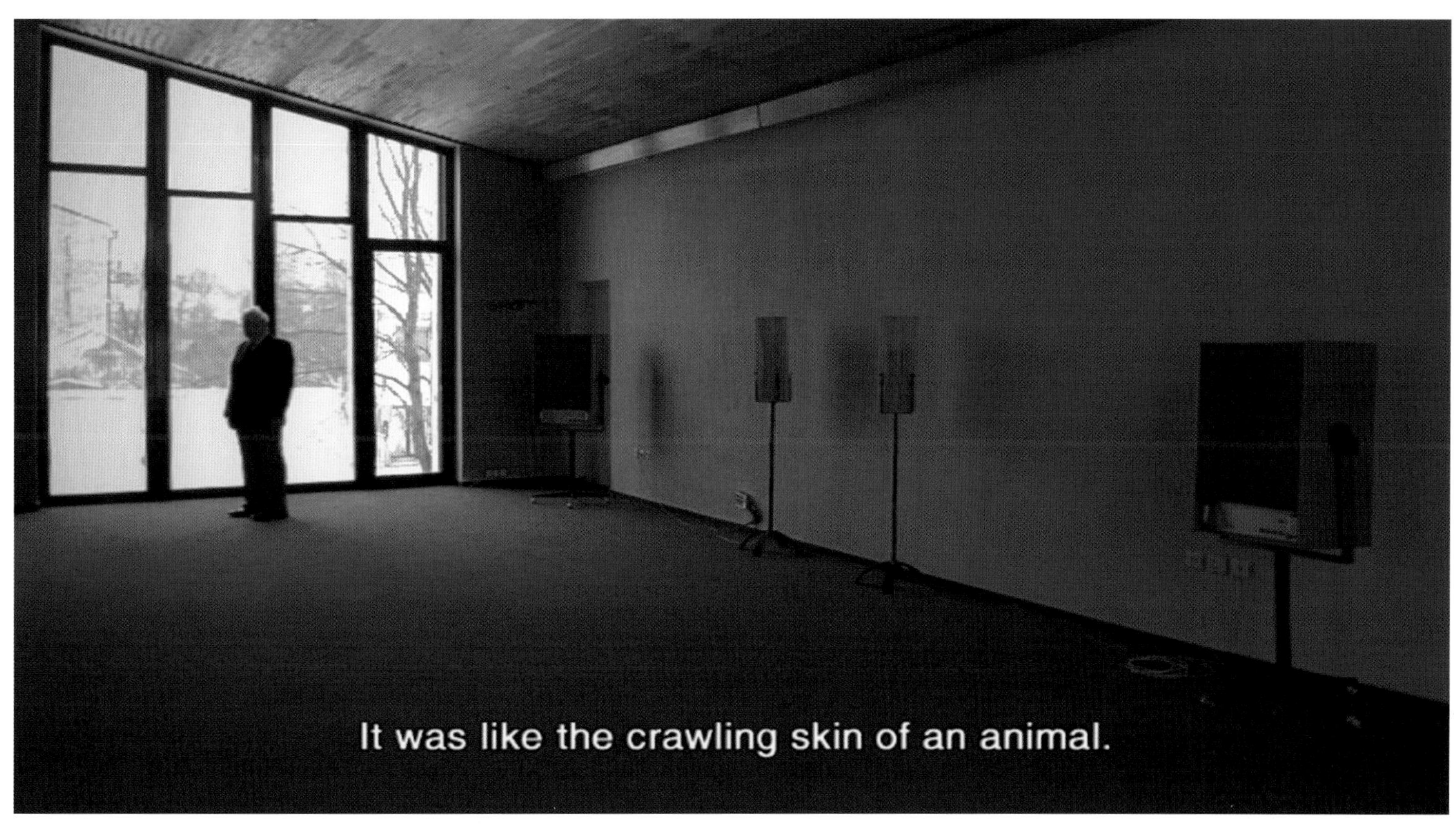

It was like the crawling skin of an animal.

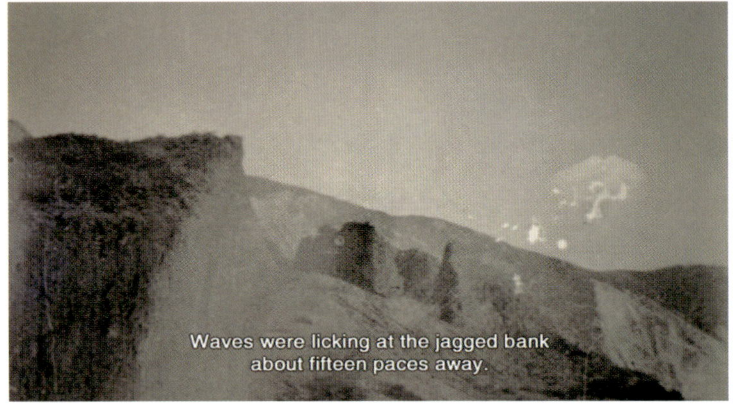
Waves were licking at the jagged bank
about fifteen paces away.

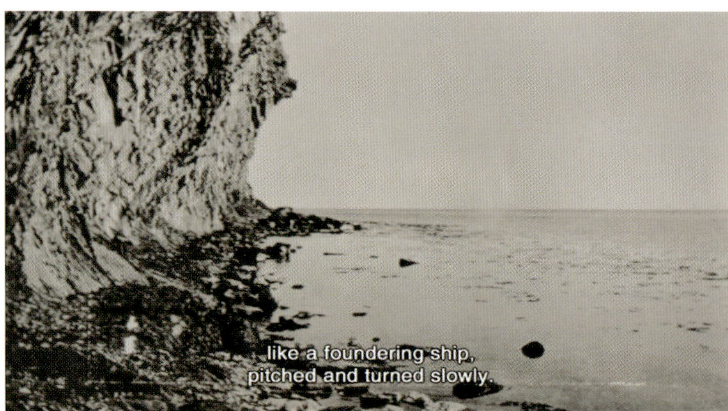
like a foundering ship,
pitched and turned slowly.

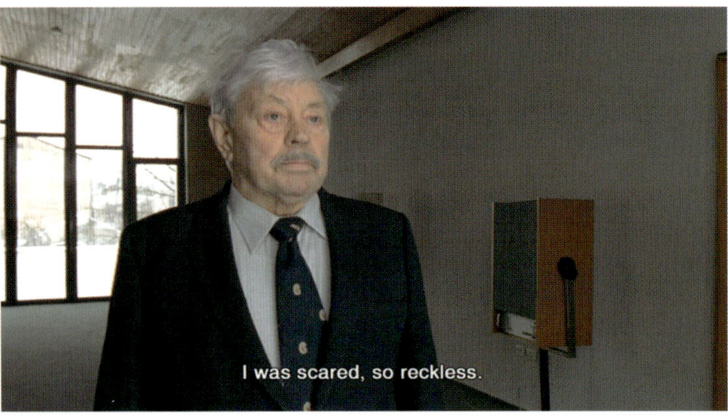
I was scared, so reckless.

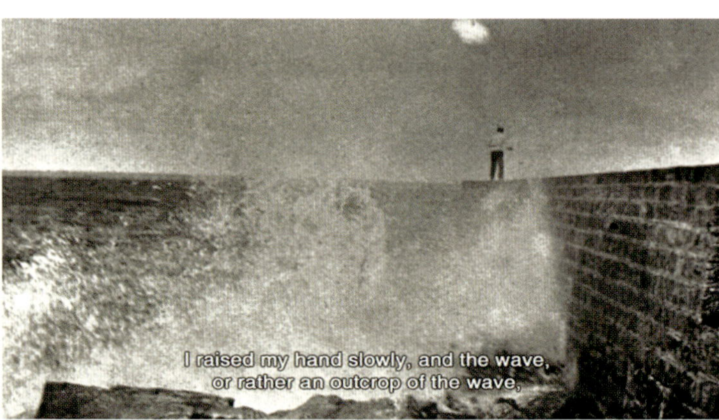
I raised my hand slowly, and the wave,
or rather an outcrop of the wave,

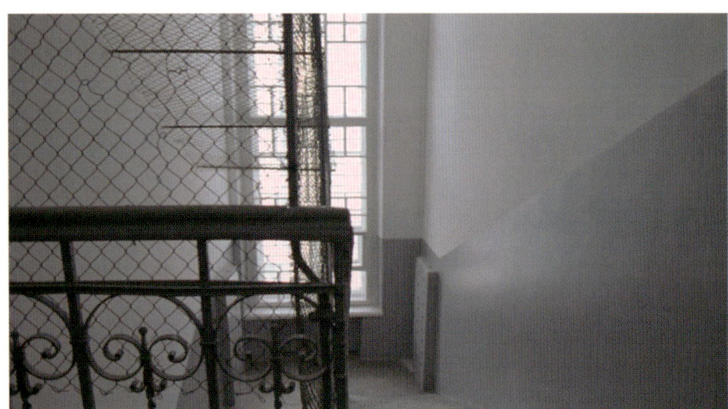

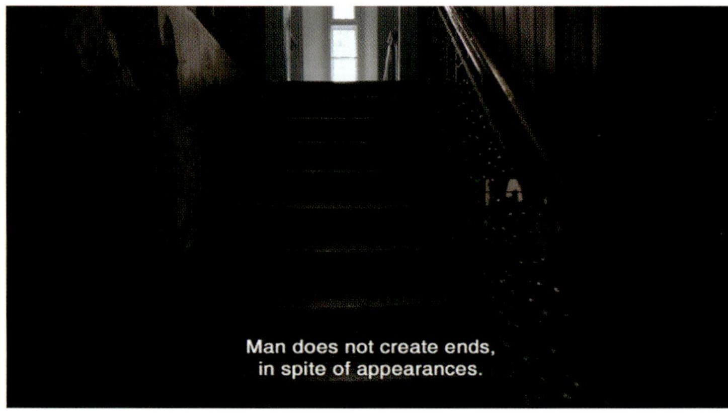
Man does not create ends,
in spite of appearances.

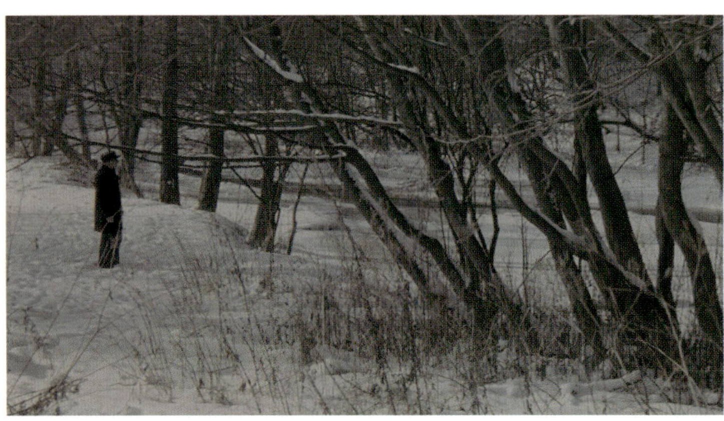

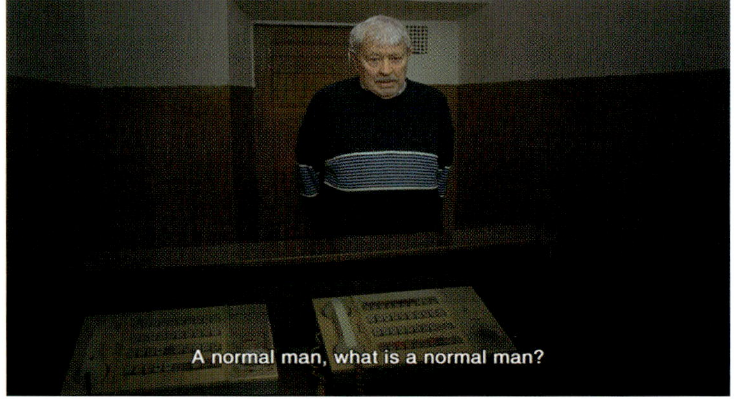
A normal man, what is a normal man?

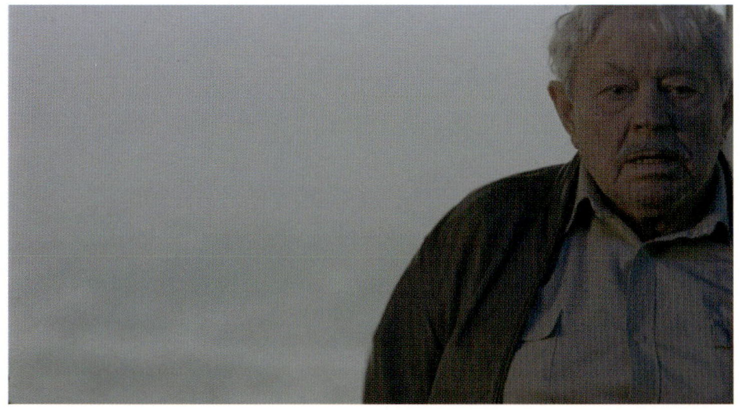

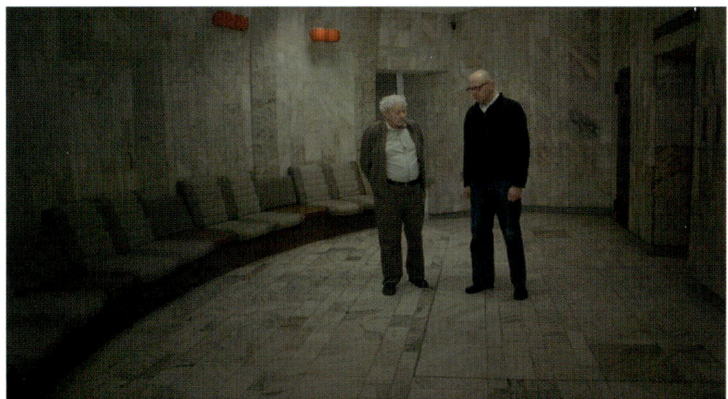

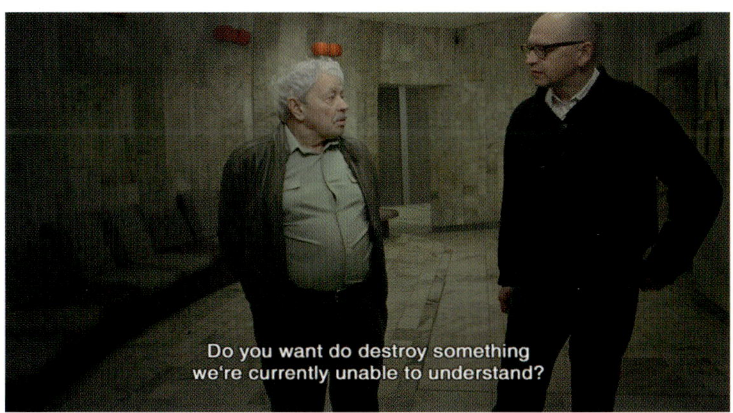
Do you want do destroy something
we're currently unable to understand?

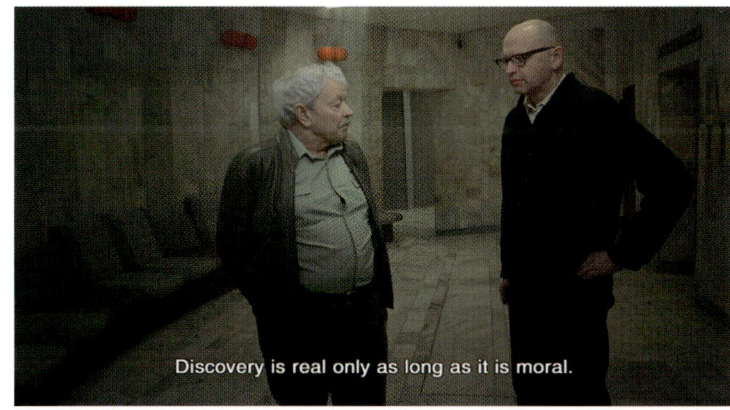
Discovery is real only as long as it is moral.

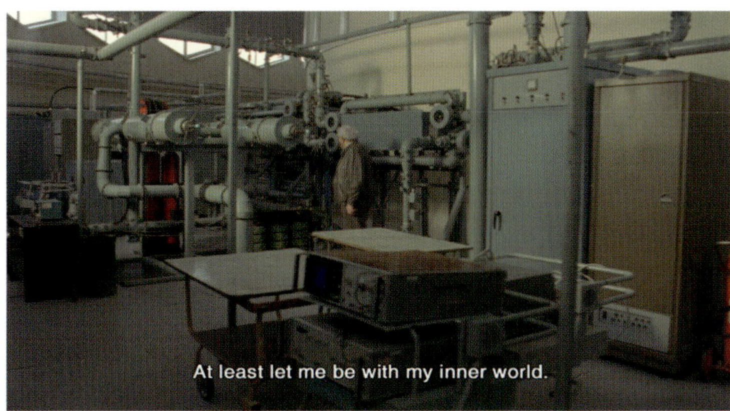
At least let me be with my inner world.

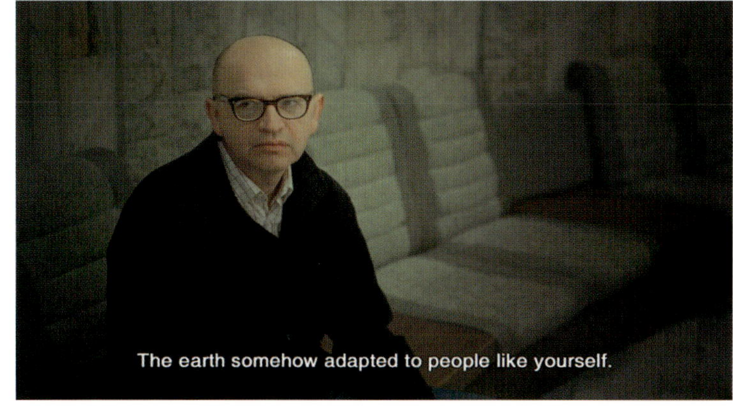
The earth somehow adapted to people like yourself.

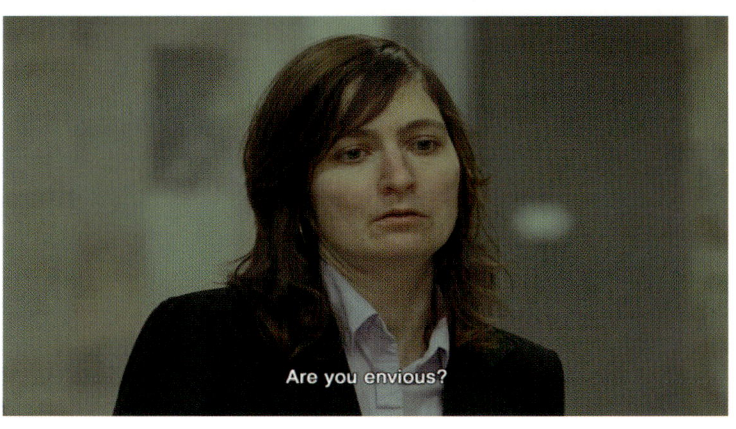
Are you envious?

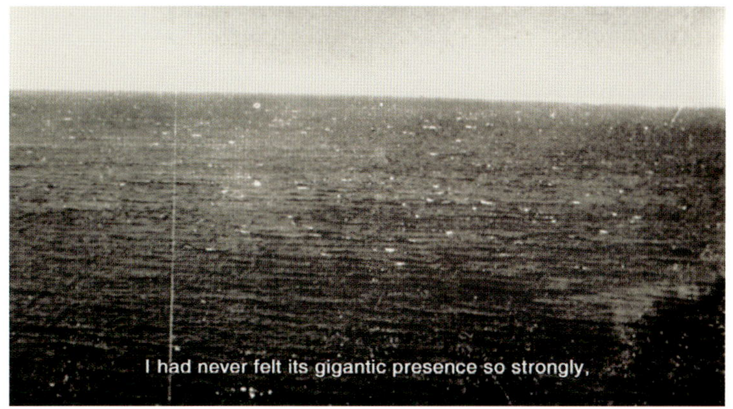
I had never felt its gigantic presence so strongly,

ANDREI MONASTYRSKI
Cycle (below)
1979, collage, paper, 40 x 42 cm
Courtesy the artist and Regina Gallery, Moscow

Perserverance or Breath (opposite)
1977, plywood, 32 x 20 x 12 cm
Courtesy the artist and Regina Gallery, Moscow

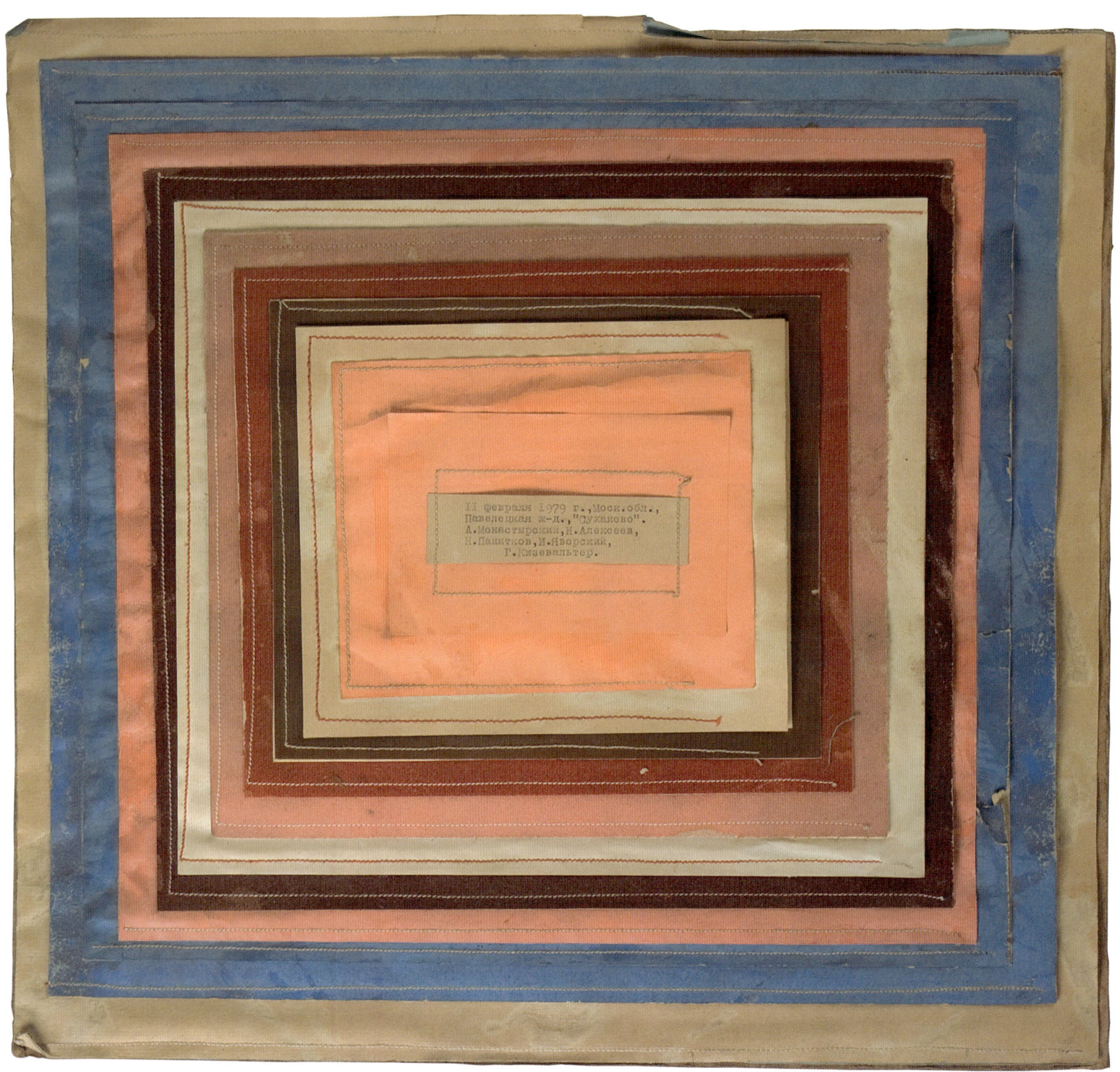

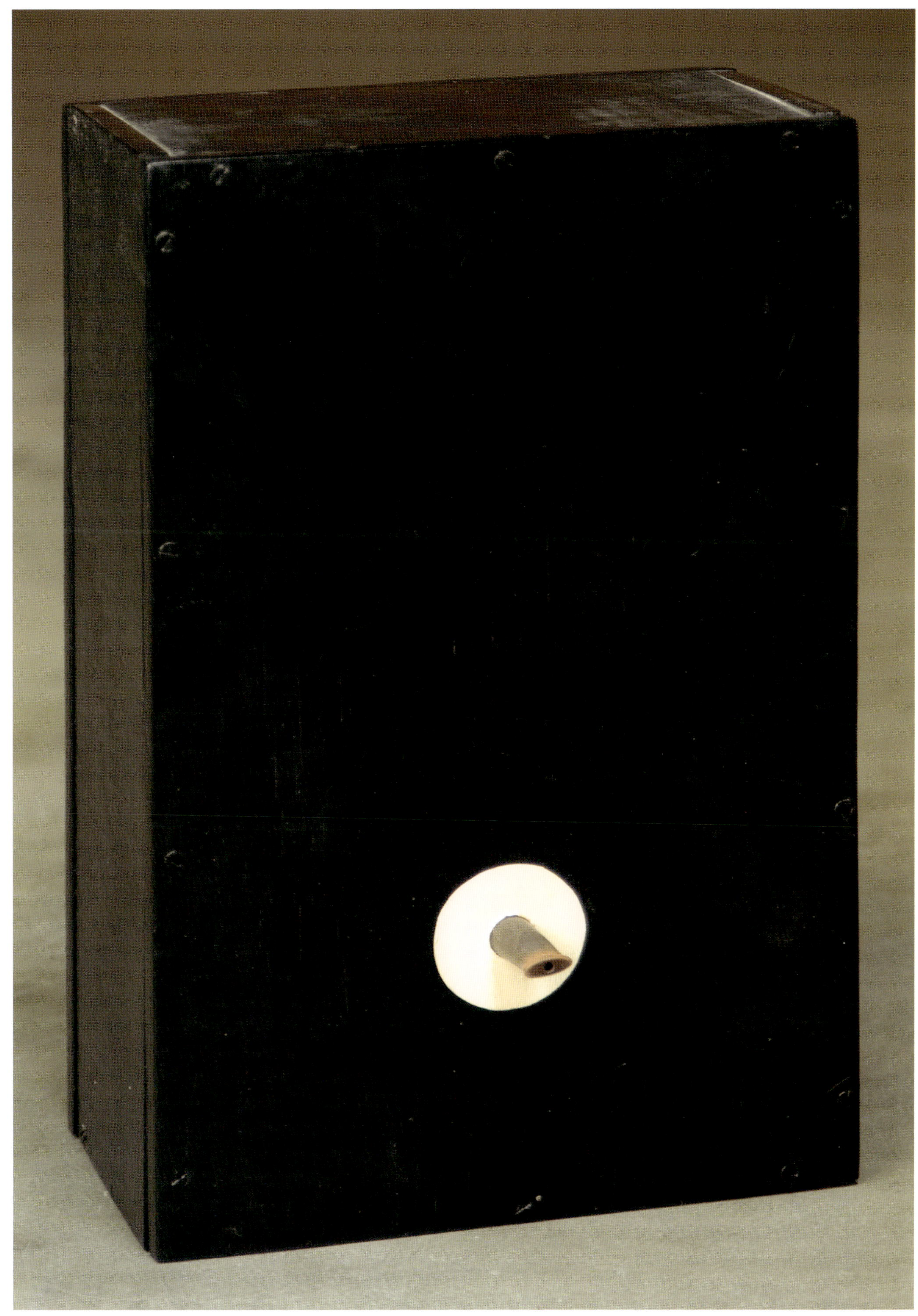

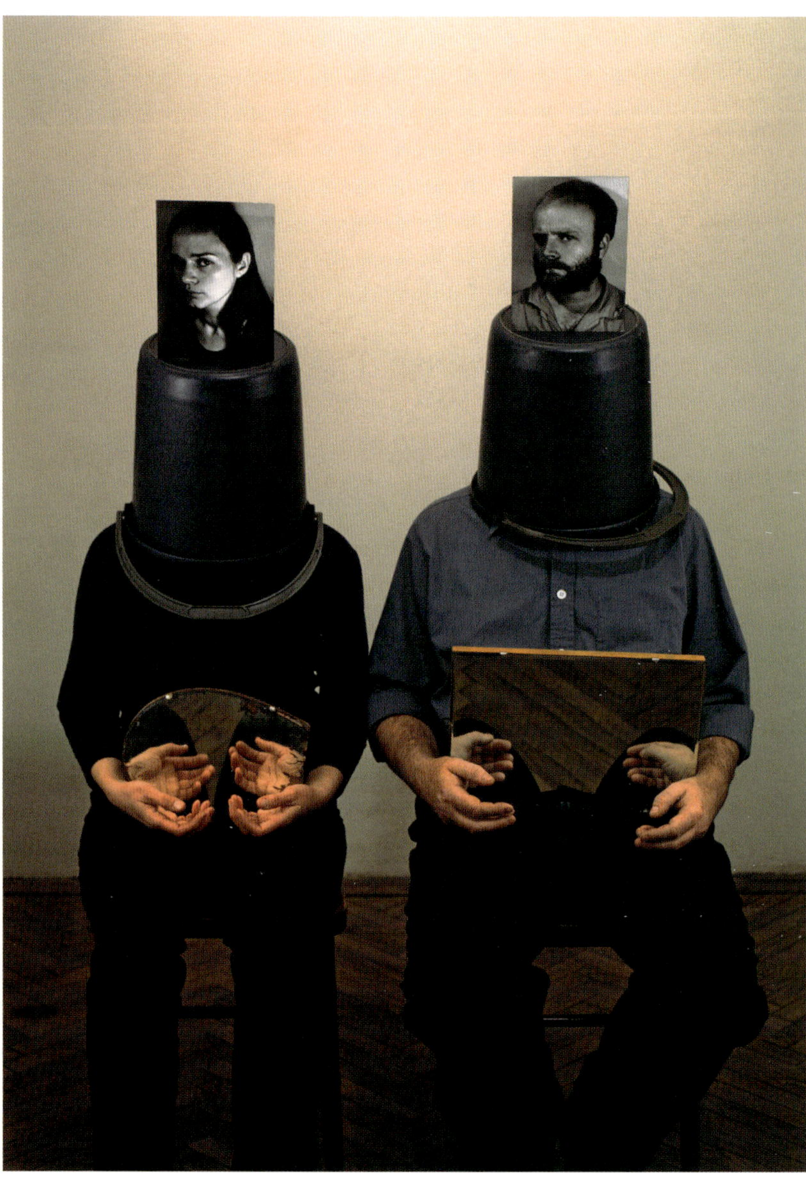

ZOFIA KULIK

Known for both her solo work, for which she has exhibited internationally, and her work as part of the artistic duo KwieKulik, which she co-founded with her then partner, Przemyslaw Kwiek in the 1970s, Zofia Kulik's work remains prominent on the Polish contemporary art scene.

Through the introduction of performances, social actions and artistic situations, KwieKulik pioneered a conceptual investigation of language and power structures. Following the birth of their son Dobromierz in 1972, the artists spent the following two years basing a huge portfolio of work upon him, with their installations, actions, and photographic work revolving around the everyday actions of the boy—in an attempt to engage in theoretical discussions that investigated the applicability of art to mathematical logic, cybernetics and the linguistic theory of signs.

In 1987, Kulik pursued a solo career thus working and individually exhibiting within a realm of her private photographic archive. Characterised by her use of black and white photography, Kulik favours large-format work, often composed in a collage format, as seen in *All the Missiles Are One Missile*, 1993. For this piece, as in numerous other pieces from the same period, Kulik used the artist Zbigniew Libera as her model. Kulik describes this piece as:

"an attempt at an analysis of the language of persuasion and propaganda; an attempt at answering the question, 'what kind of language builds the relationship between an individual and authority, how are media used in this process?'"

In more recent years, Kulik has begun to work increasingly with colour. In *The Garden (Libera and Flowers)*, Kulik returns once again to use Libera as her model—his naked figure dressed in plants and flowers.

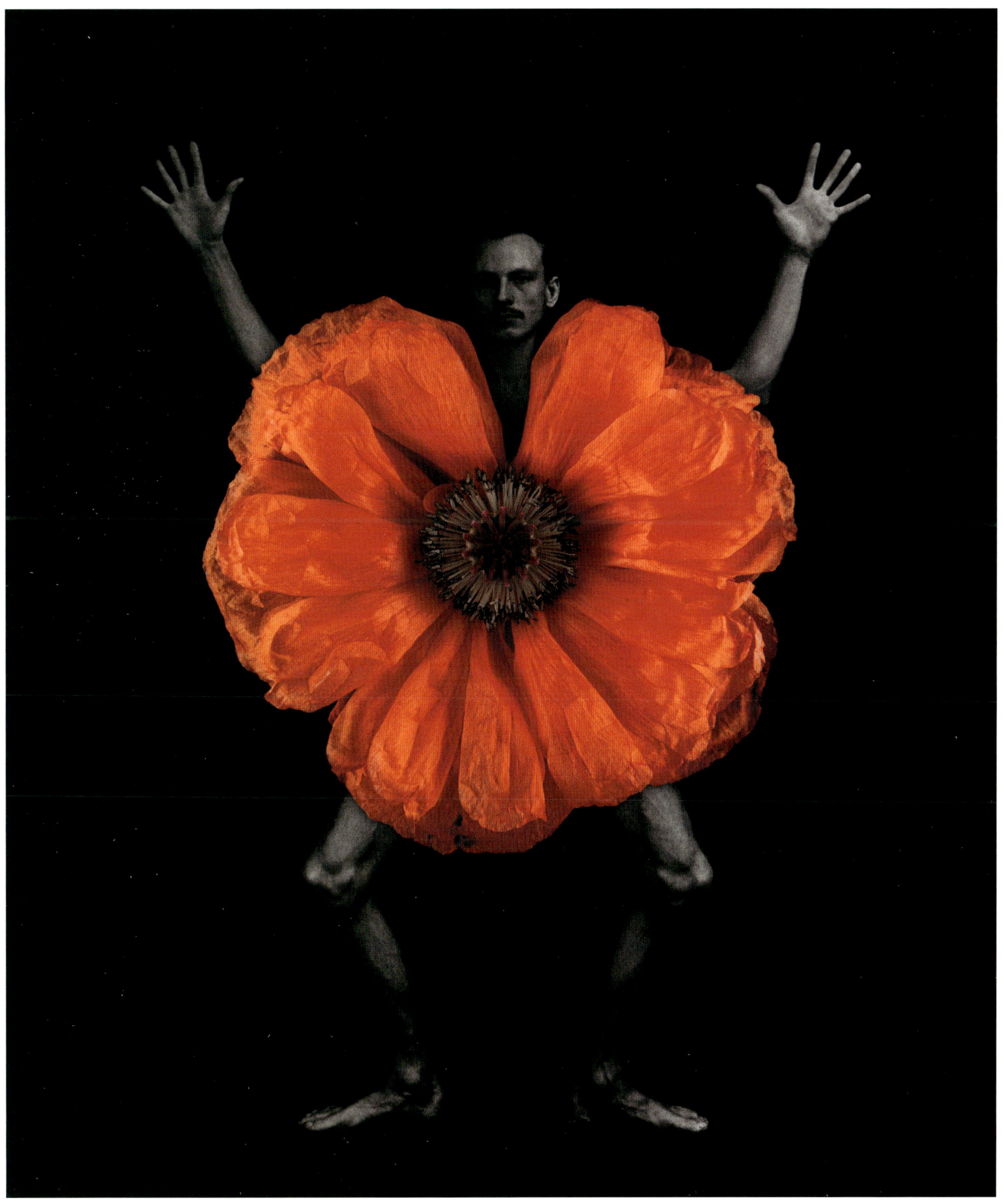

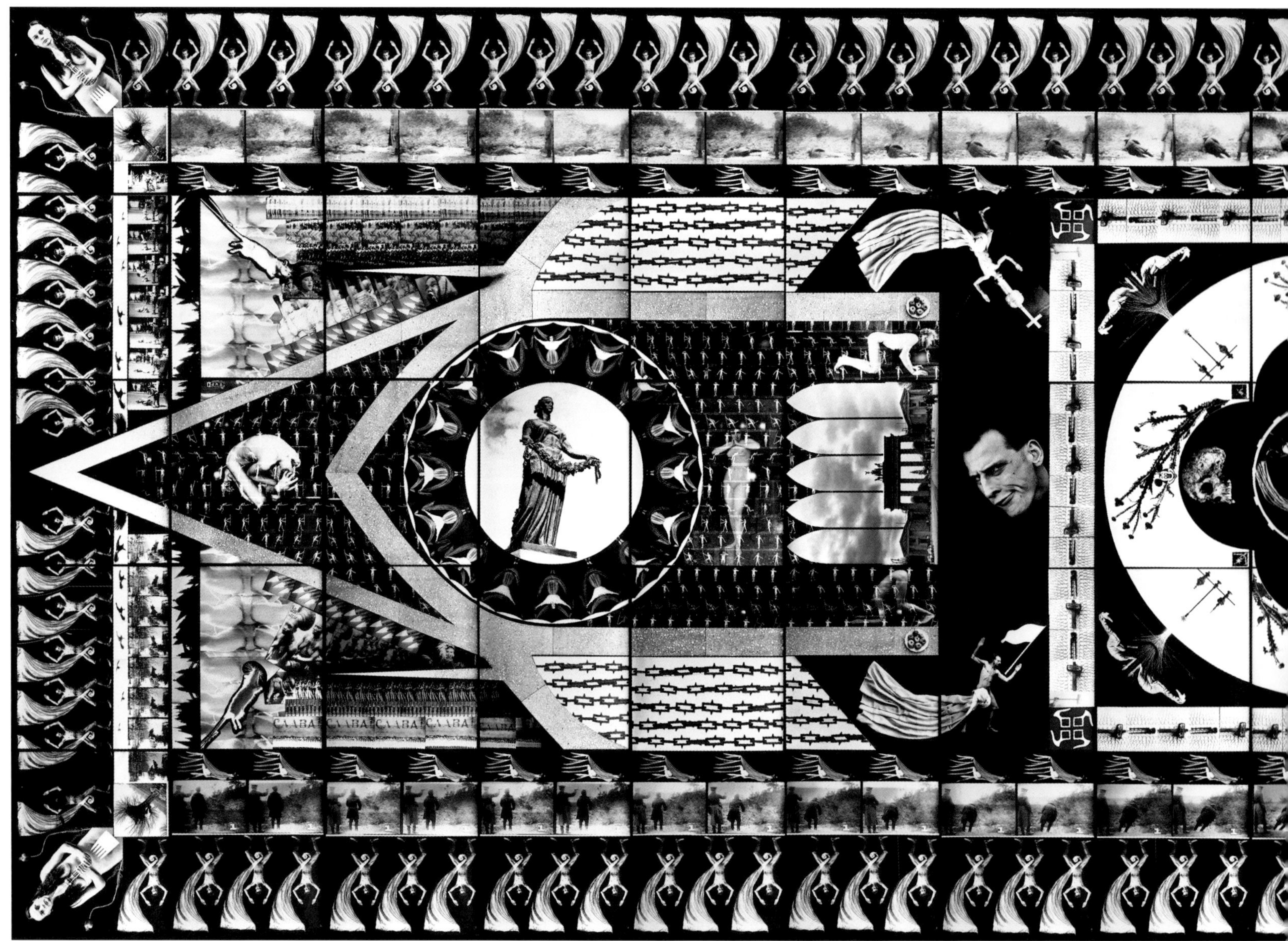

ZOFIA KULIK
All the Missiles Are One Missile
1993, photo-collage, 300 x 850 cm
Courtesy the artist

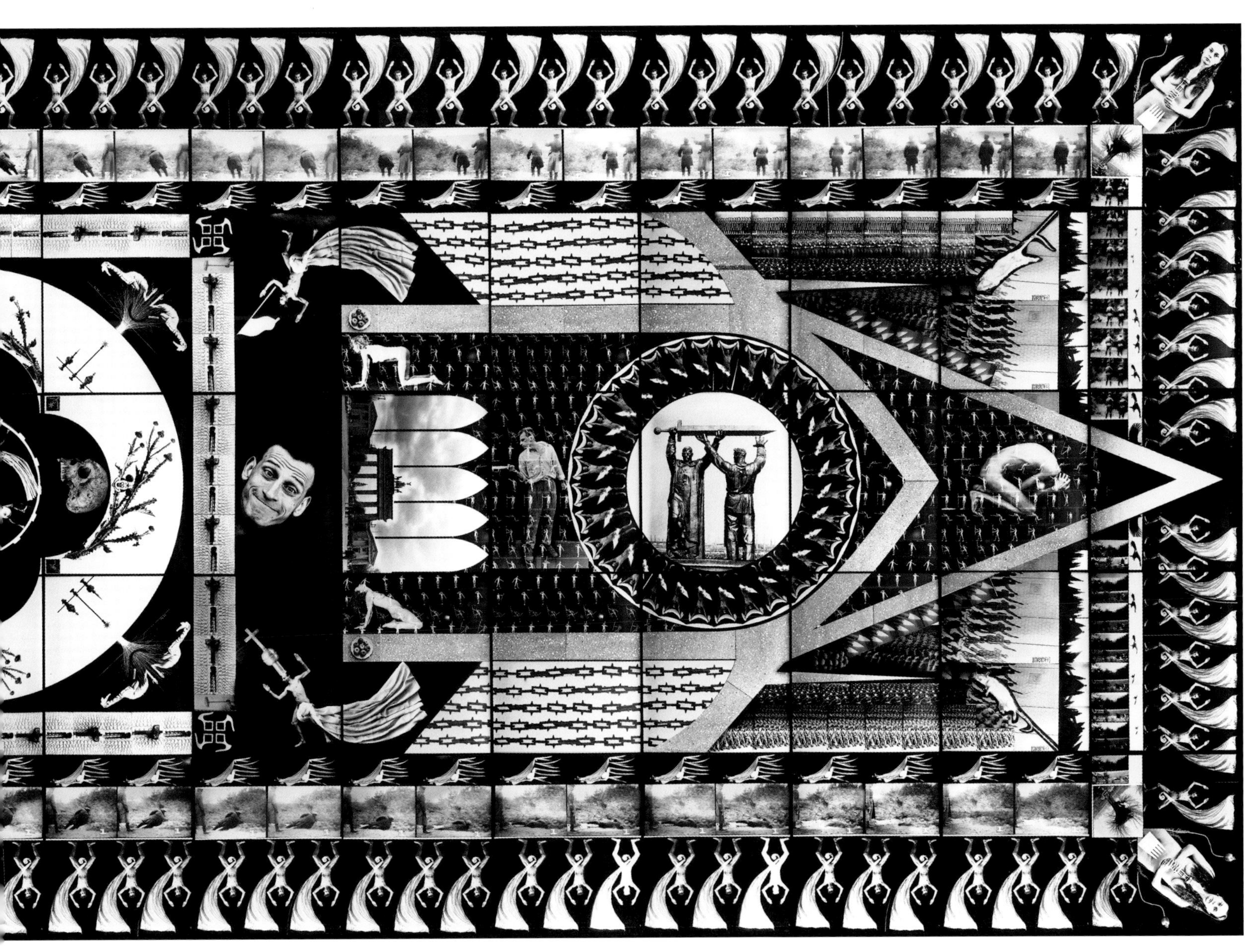

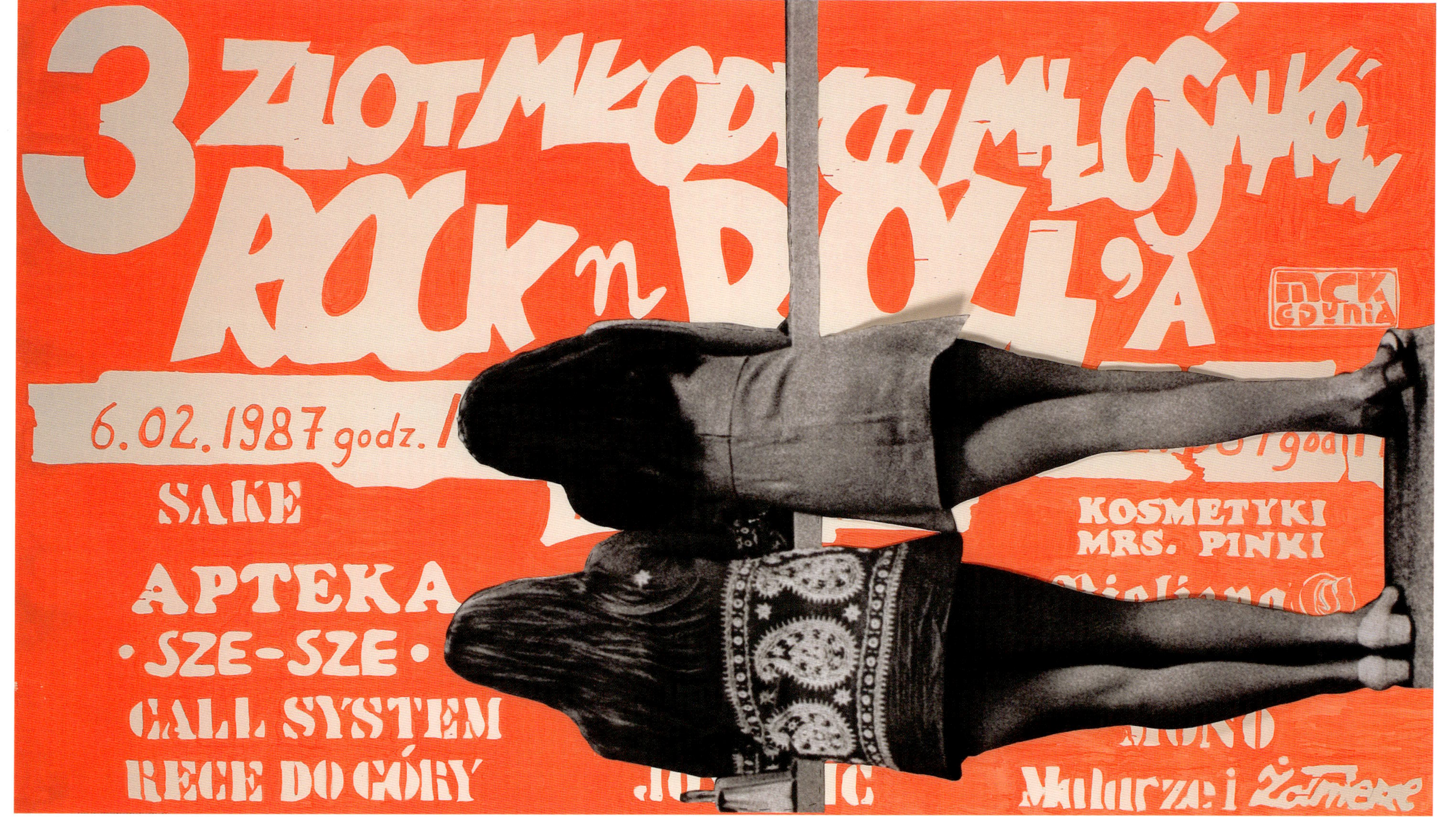

3 ZŁOT MŁODYCH MIŁOŚNIKÓW
ROCK'n ROLL'A
DCK GDYNIA
6.02.1987 godz.
SAKE
KOSMETYKI
MRS. PINKI
APTEKA
·SZE-SZE·
CALL SYSTEM
RĘCE DO GÓRY
MONO
Malarze i Żmierek

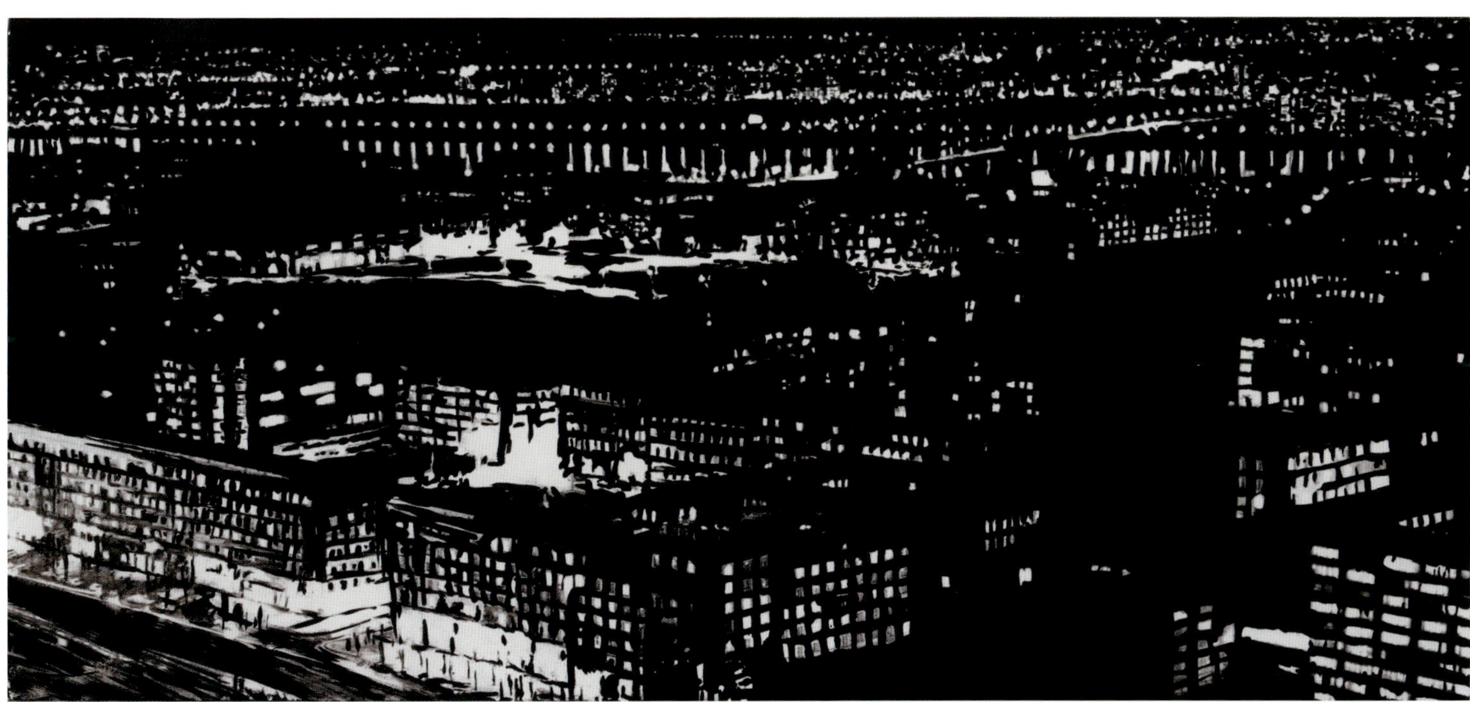

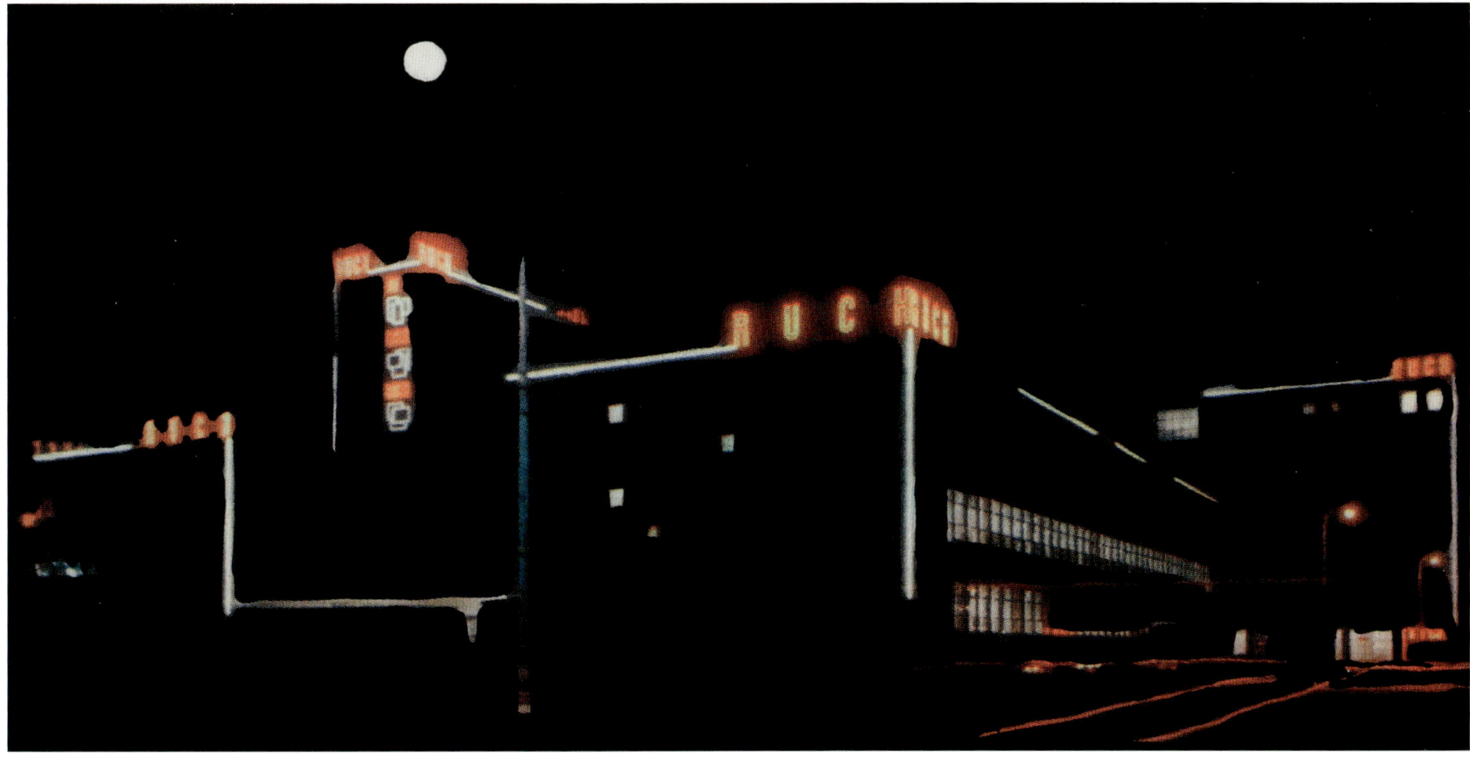

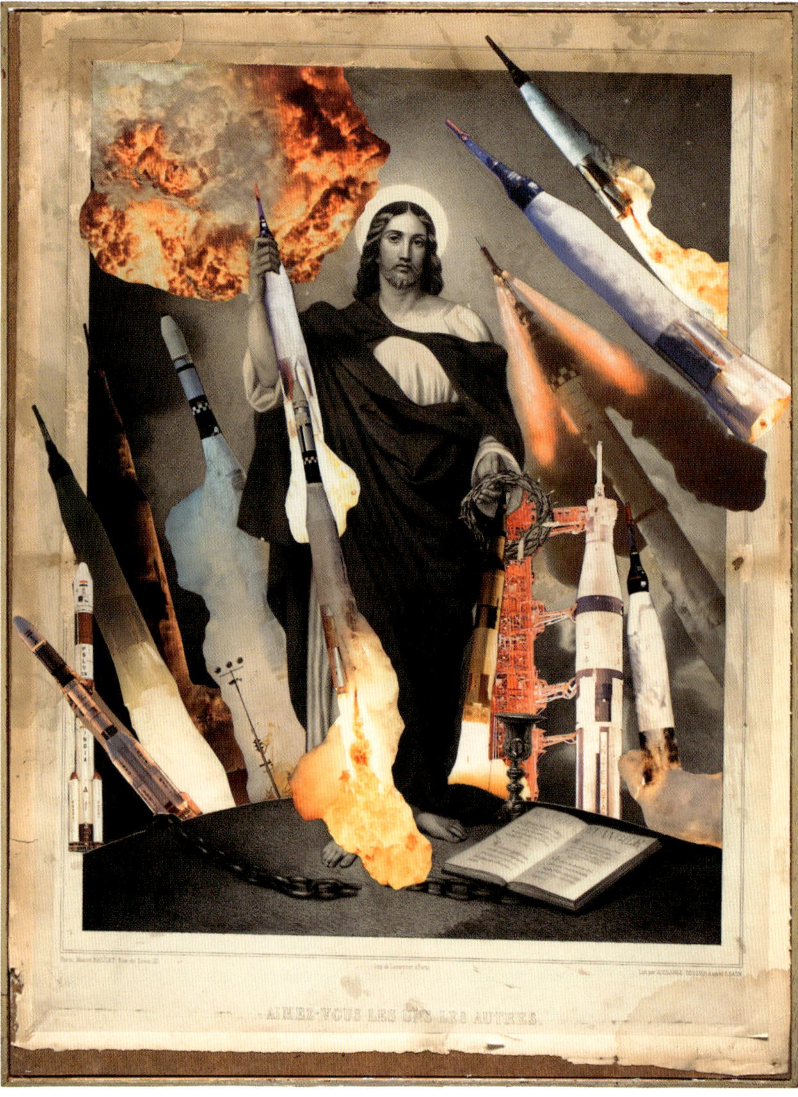

The Dream and The Promise (Aimez-vous) (right)
2008, collage on board with gold leaf frame
59 x 44 cm including frame
Courtesy the artist, Joan Prats, Barcelona

World Map of Natural Hazards (opposite above)
2009, marker on paper, 250 x 385 cm
Courtesy the artist

World Map of Social Networks (opposite below)
2009, marker on paper, 250 x 385 cm
Courtesy the artist

ALEKSANDRA MIR

Aleksandra Mir's work demonstrates an admirable facility when it comes to encouraging the involvement and active contribution of the public. There is a strong humanistic current, as well as a refreshing sense of optimism, prominent in many of her ambitious site-specific projects, which often materialise as social processes whose precise form and meaning is achieved through the interaction of individuals.

At the same time, it is clear that the purposeful direction of Mir's practice owes much to her academic background in Cultural Anthropology. Her material of choice is the substance of everyday life and human experience, and with her dynamic and considered approach to initiating her socially inclusive projects— "I use whatever is inherent to the subject matter I am working with that day…" —Mir is able to present a critique of the authoritative superstructures, traditions and norms that serve to organise a social space. In this way, her work attempts to stimulate our consciousness directly and resensitise us to the connective fibres of social existence—an area of Mir's work that is explicitly explored within *World Map of Social Networks* and *World Map of Natural Hazards*.

Plane Landing attests to the artist's wonder at seeing a plane land, back-lit by the sun, making it appear as if it were standing still. Mir describes this as the inspiration behind the mammoth project, which involved building an inflatable helium jet plane. From here Mir photographed the model at various different locations around Paris, as well as exhibiting it at Zurich Airport and Compton Verney, UK. Mir imagined *Plane Landing* as an event encompassing the different stages of the plane's production, inflation, travel, and 'landing' —all of which constitute different parts of the artwork.

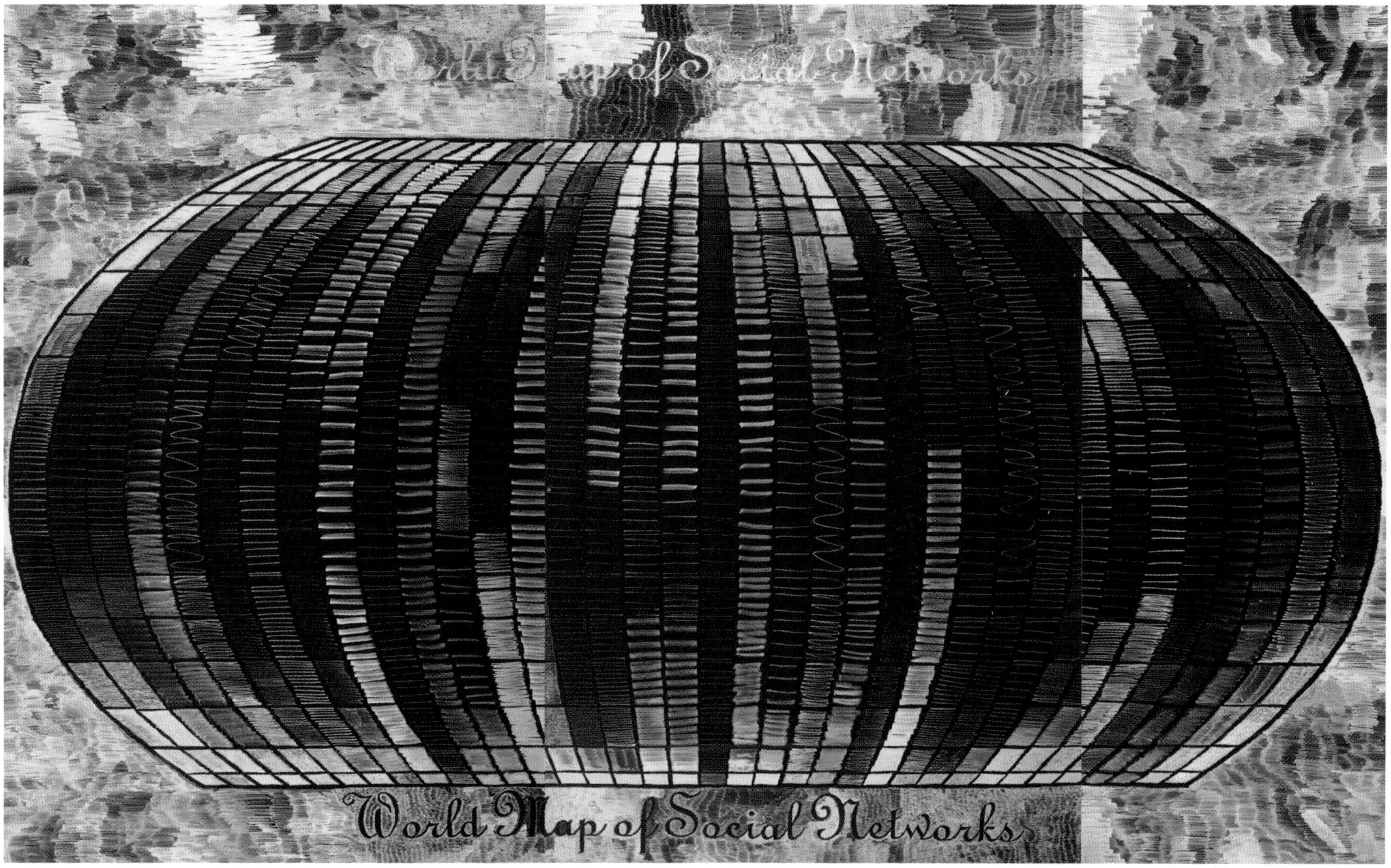

World Map of Social Networks

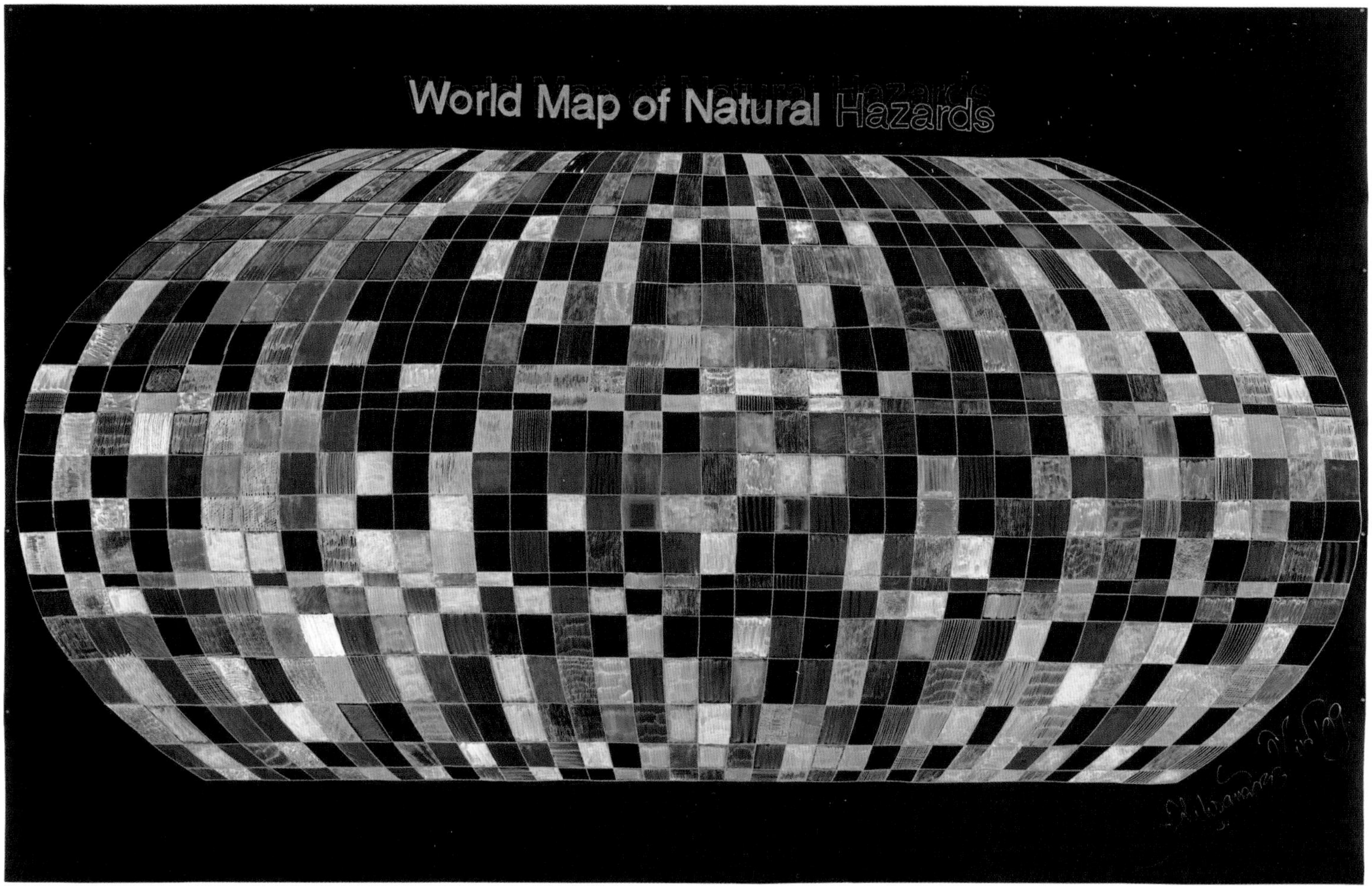

World Map of Natural Hazards

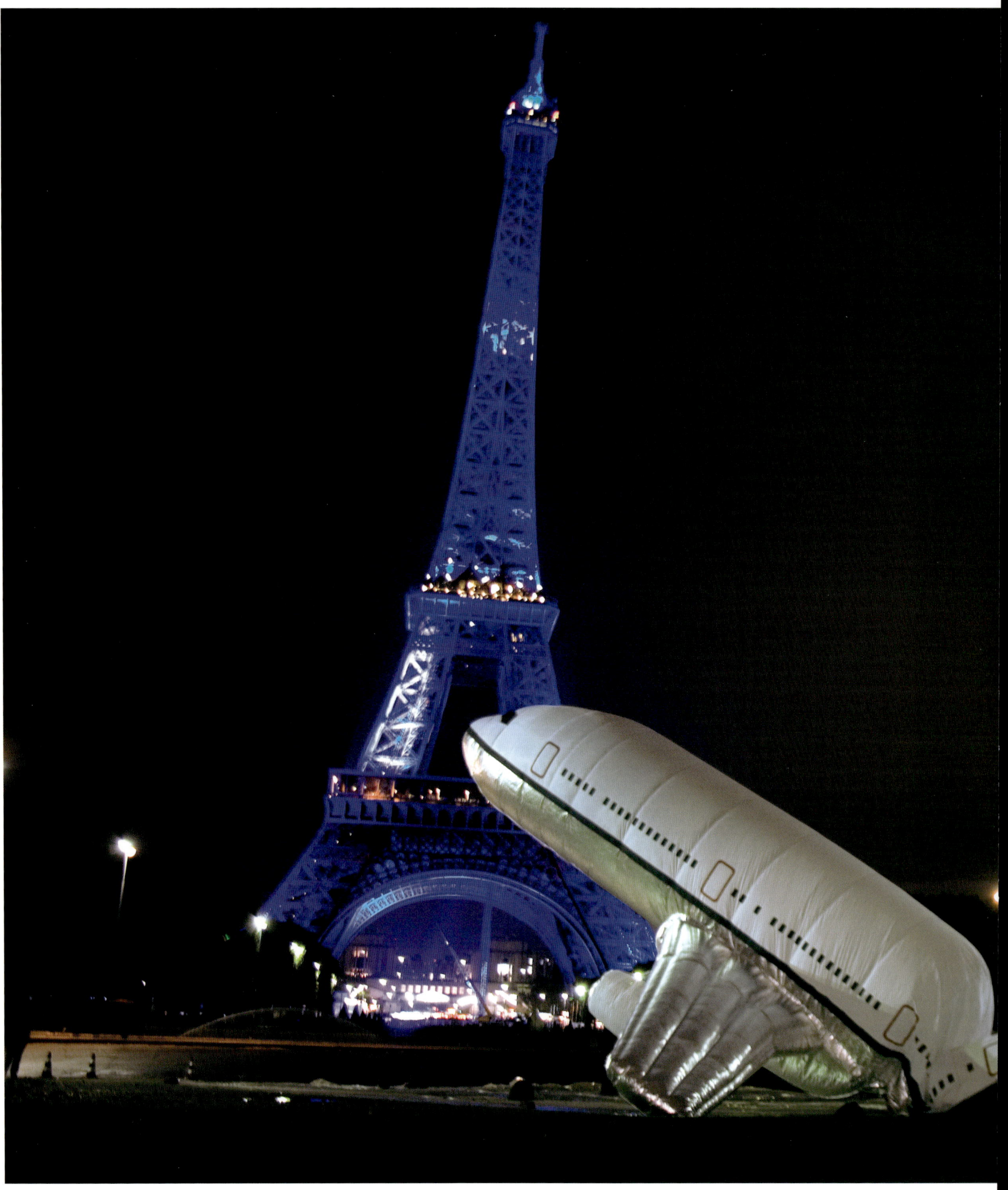

ALEKSANDRA MIR
Plane Landing
20–23 October 2008, C-print, diasec
Courtesy the artist and Laurent Godin Gallery, Paris

Untitled (opposite)
2010, wall drawing for the International
Theatre Festival in Sibiu, Romania
Courtesy the artist

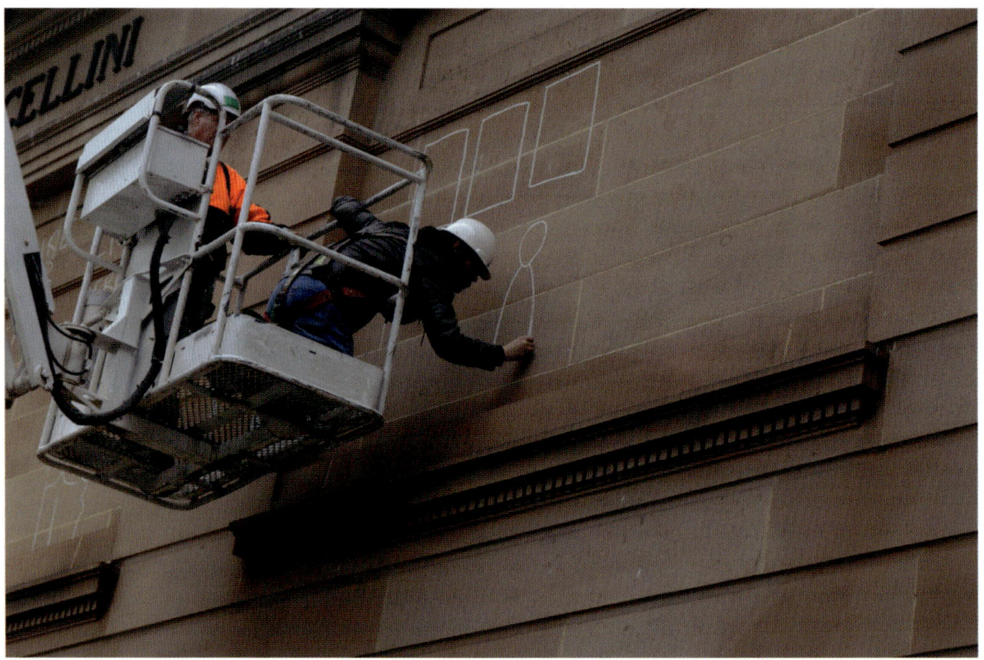

DAN PERJOVSCHI

The site-specific works of Romanian artist Dan Perjovschi present a commentary on contemporary social, cultural and political issues, in a manner that meshes together international and regional perspectives. Working from an extensive archive of material, ranging from intimate observations of everyday life—which reflect on the particular context of a work—to newspaper headlines, Perjovschi produces stark, rapidly executed drawings that scale walls, traverse floors and ceilings and scramble across glass, animating the architectural features of a space with irreverent humour and incisive wit. As evidenced by his exhibition at London's Bloomberg space, his work becomes a part of its environment, creating spaces that are primed but open. However, due to his materials of choice—

marker pen, pencil and chalk—it remains marked by its impermanence.

The medium of drawing, which lends itself to quick, instinctive activity, is in itself crucial to Perjovschi's practice: it is precisely this aspect that determines the medium as a concise form of communication, a way of formulating assertions that does not require a specialist knowledge of sophisticated materials and which subsequently facilitates a fluid and continuous exercising of free thought and ideas. This is in turn conducive to Perjovschi's artistic project. His intention is to impress upon his audience a sense of personal responsibility, to provoke the formulation of subjective positions in response to the issues raised by his work,

and to generate a dialogue that can then travel with consequence out into the world.

Since the Romanian Revolution of 1989 and the collapse of Nicolae Ceauşescu's autocratic regime, Perjovschi has played an active role in the development of civil society in his native country, most notably as art director and political cartoonist for the Bucharest-based newspaper *Revista 22*. Perjovschi does indeed demonstrate a sensibility informed by Romania's history and present development. Questions of geopolitics underpin his practice, and he has continued to address the tensions and conflicts regarding national identity that have arisen in Romania since the fall of Communism.

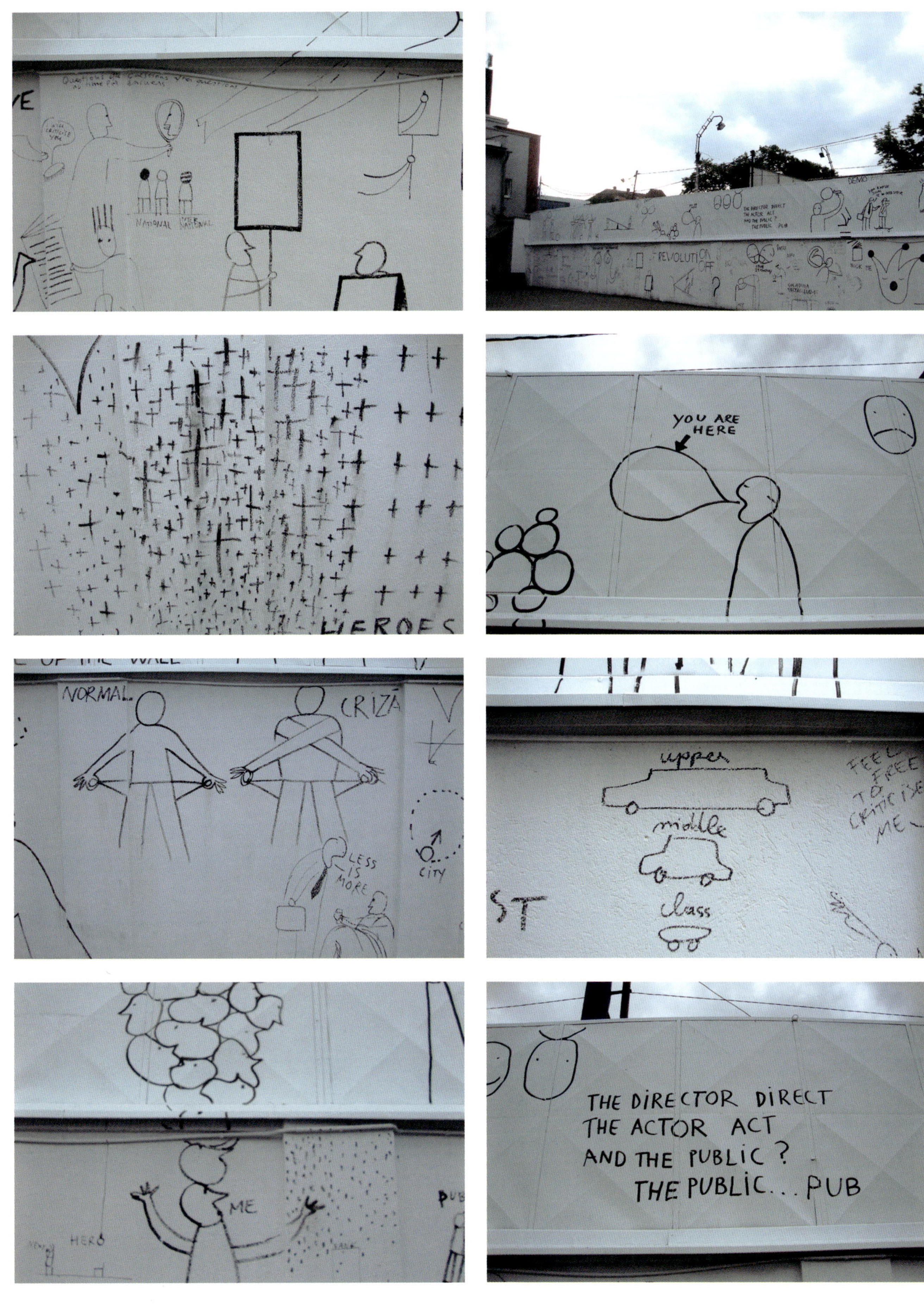
NATIONAL
YOU ARE HERE
HEROES
NORMAL
CRIZA
LESS IS MORE
CITY
upper
middle
class
THE DIRECTOR DIRECT
THE ACTOR ACT
AND THE PUBLIC ?
THE PUBLIC... PUB
ME
HERO
REVOLUTI
FEEL FREE TO CRITICIZE ME

CIPRIAN MUREŞAN

Incorrigible Believers (below)
2009, graphite on paper, 39 x 31 cm
Courtesy the artist and David Nolan Gallery, New York

Leap Into the Void-After Three Seconds (opposite)
2004, digital print mounted on aluminium,
170 x 120 cm, edition of seven AP
Courtesy the artist and David Nolan Gallery, New York

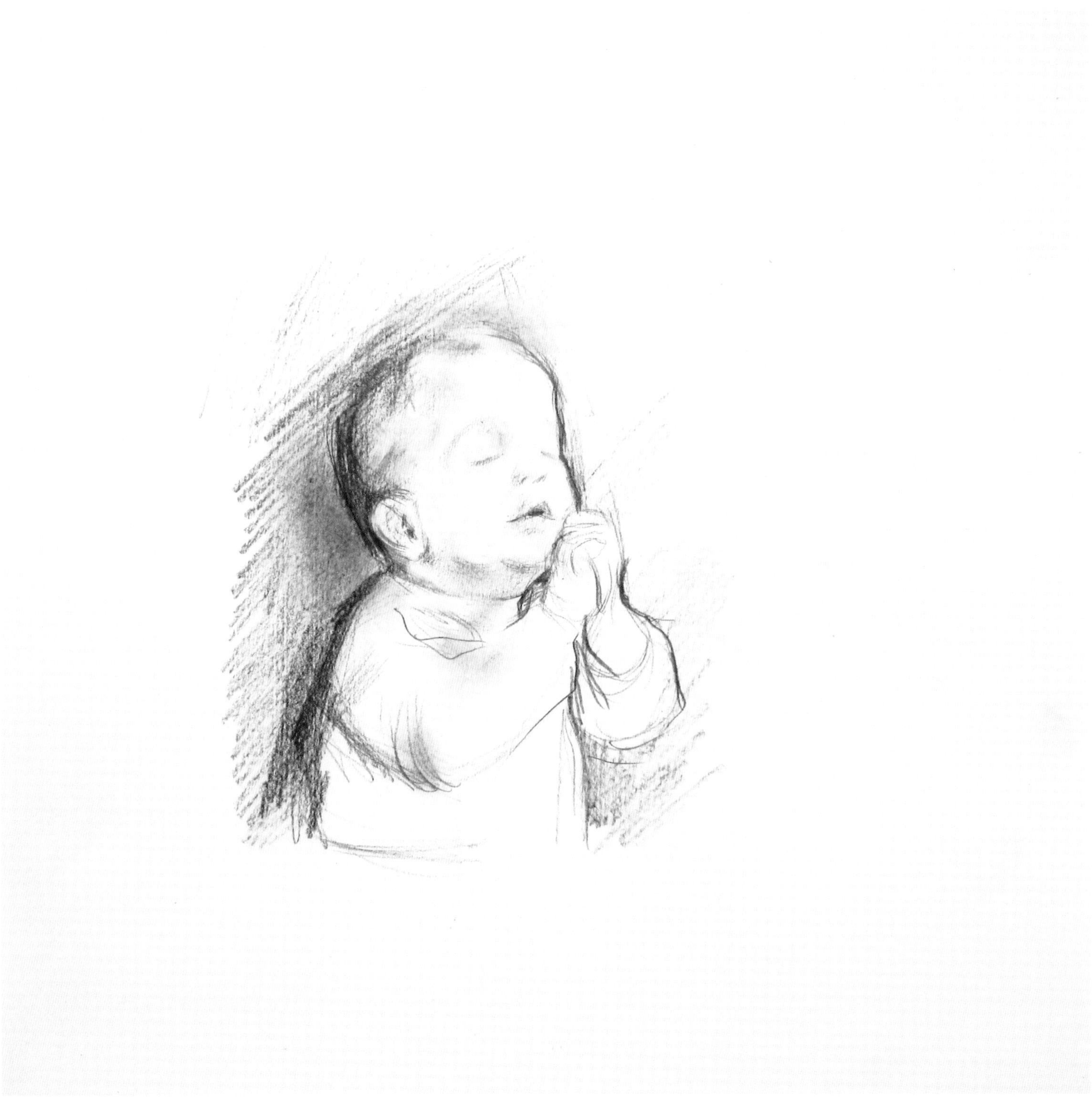

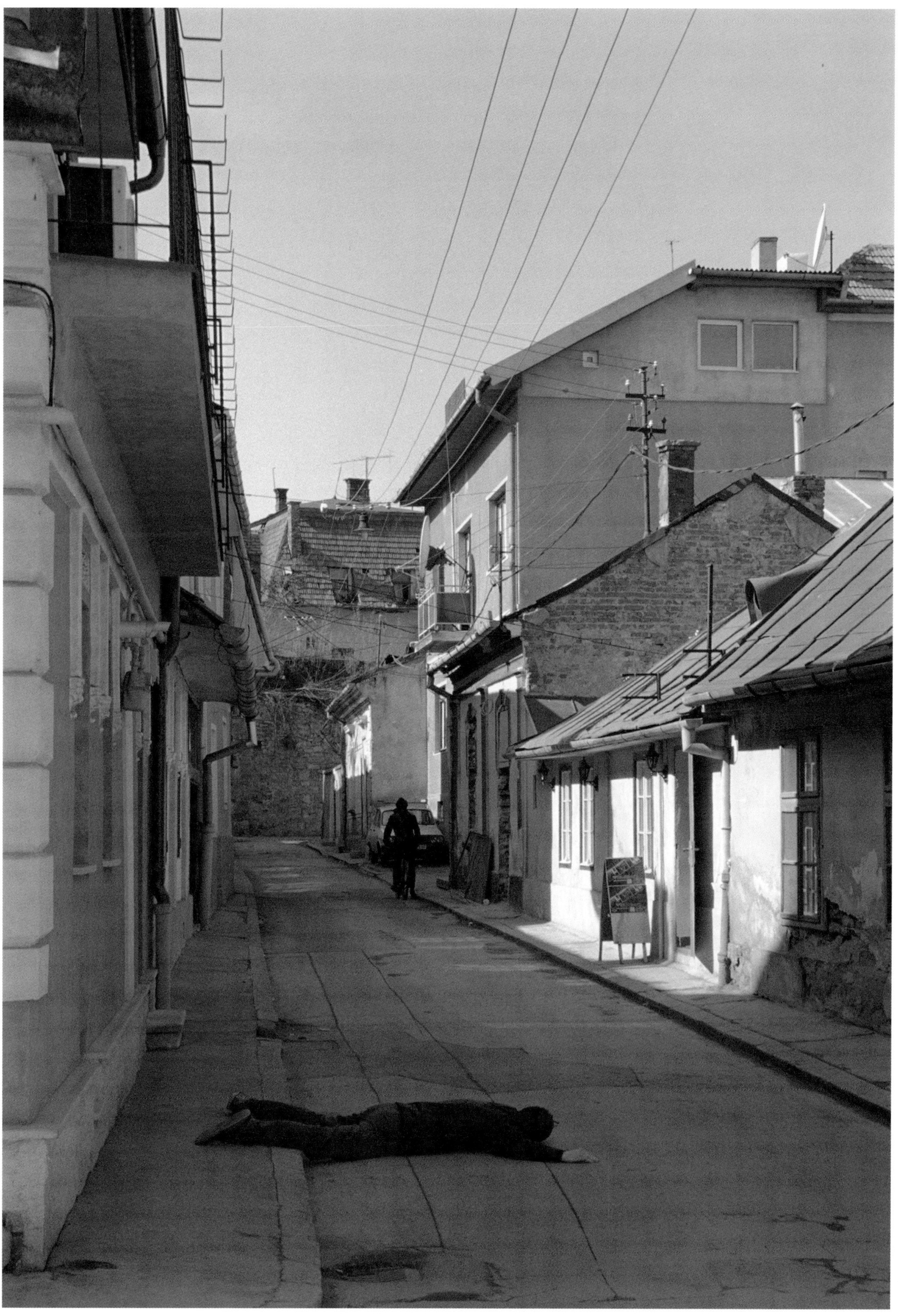

ILYA AND EMELIA KABAKOV

Ilya and Emilia Kabakov have been working in collaboration since 1988, fusing elements of literature, art, philosophy and history into complex and intelligently conceived "total installations": extensively detailed, wholly immersive environments that tactfully elicit the engagement of an audience. Drawing predominantly from narrative art forms, the Kabakovs' installations often manifest as interactive fictions that generate a flux of allegorical meanings. Everyday objects, strategically arranged around a space, resemble the evidence of some past event involving absent characters, with texts and sound pieces serving to explicate several often-contradictory narratives.

The spectre of the Soviet Union is discernable in the Kabakovs' practice, and much of their work belongs to a lineage that extends from Ilya Kabakov's early work with the underground Moscow conceptualist group NOMA, throughout the latter half of the last century. Drawing on the critical ideals of early Modernism, and exploring its limits and embracing its aesthetics, this loose association of artists sought to practice an art independent of the sanctions of the Soviet State, which could furthermore respond to the gulf between a utopian ideology and the oppression experienced by those living under the regime. Incorporating Soviet iconography, furniture, rubbish, and other fragments of everyday living, NOMA's project focused on creating a frame for reality that placed the human subject at its centre, and this has remained consistent in the Kabakovs' subsequent collaborative work.

The Man, Who Flew into Space from His Apartment, first produced in 1968, presents an apartment that must be viewed through the cracks in a boarded-up door. A cramped, claustrophobic living space is visible, scattered with objects and festooned with Soviet propaganda posters, powerfully evoking the repressive, overpopulated communal living conditions that characterised Soviet Russia. But this scene has been devastated: a wash of white light falls through a gaping hole in the roof onto a catapult-like contraption, apparently constructed by the apartment's tenant to launch himself into cosmic space. Technical drawings and blueprints have been tacked to the walls, and a text accompanying the installation provides us with a sense of whom this character was, through statements given by his neighbours. A fiction thus transforms the space, and a repressive environment becomes dramatically dominated by a sense of liberation, escape, and human ambition.

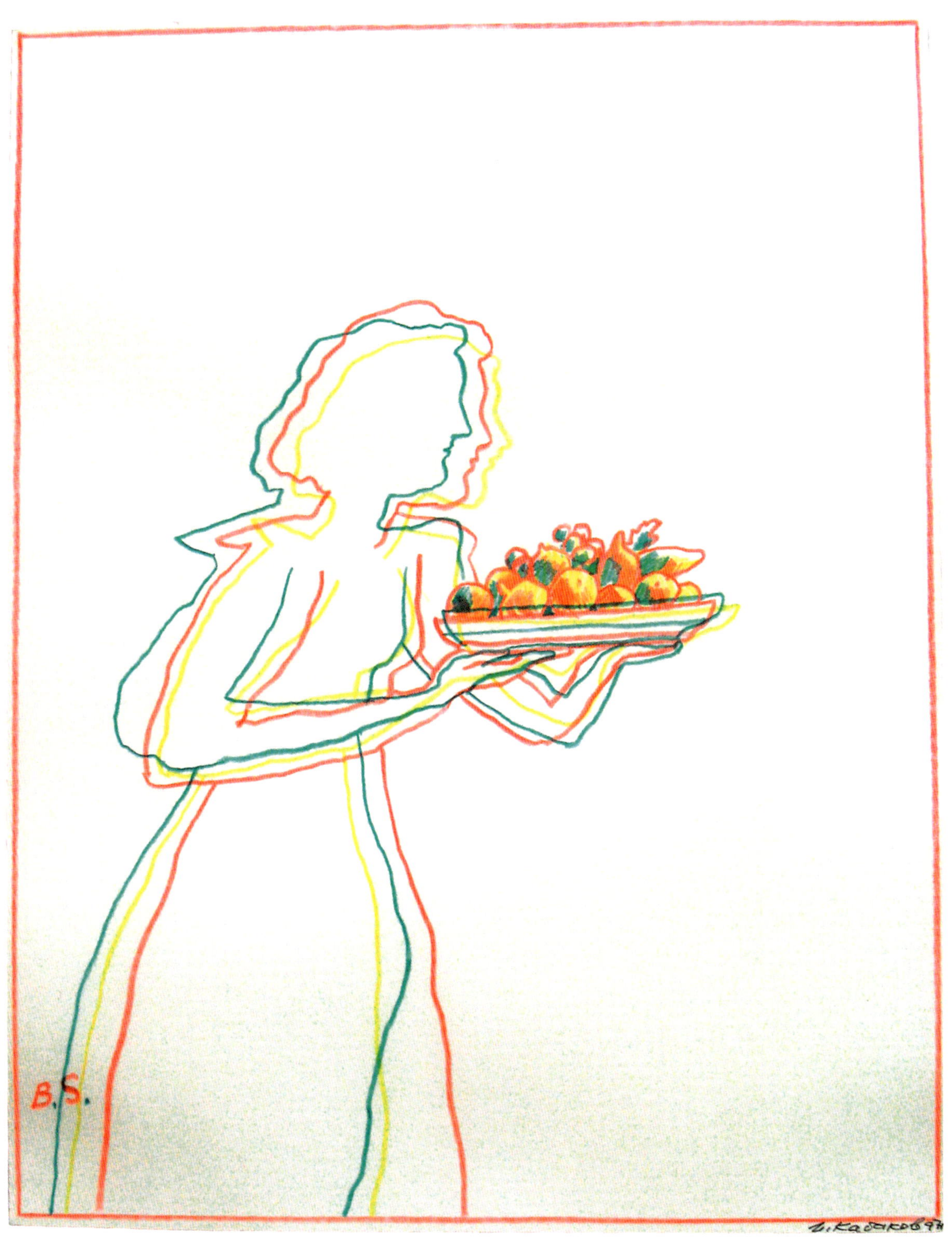

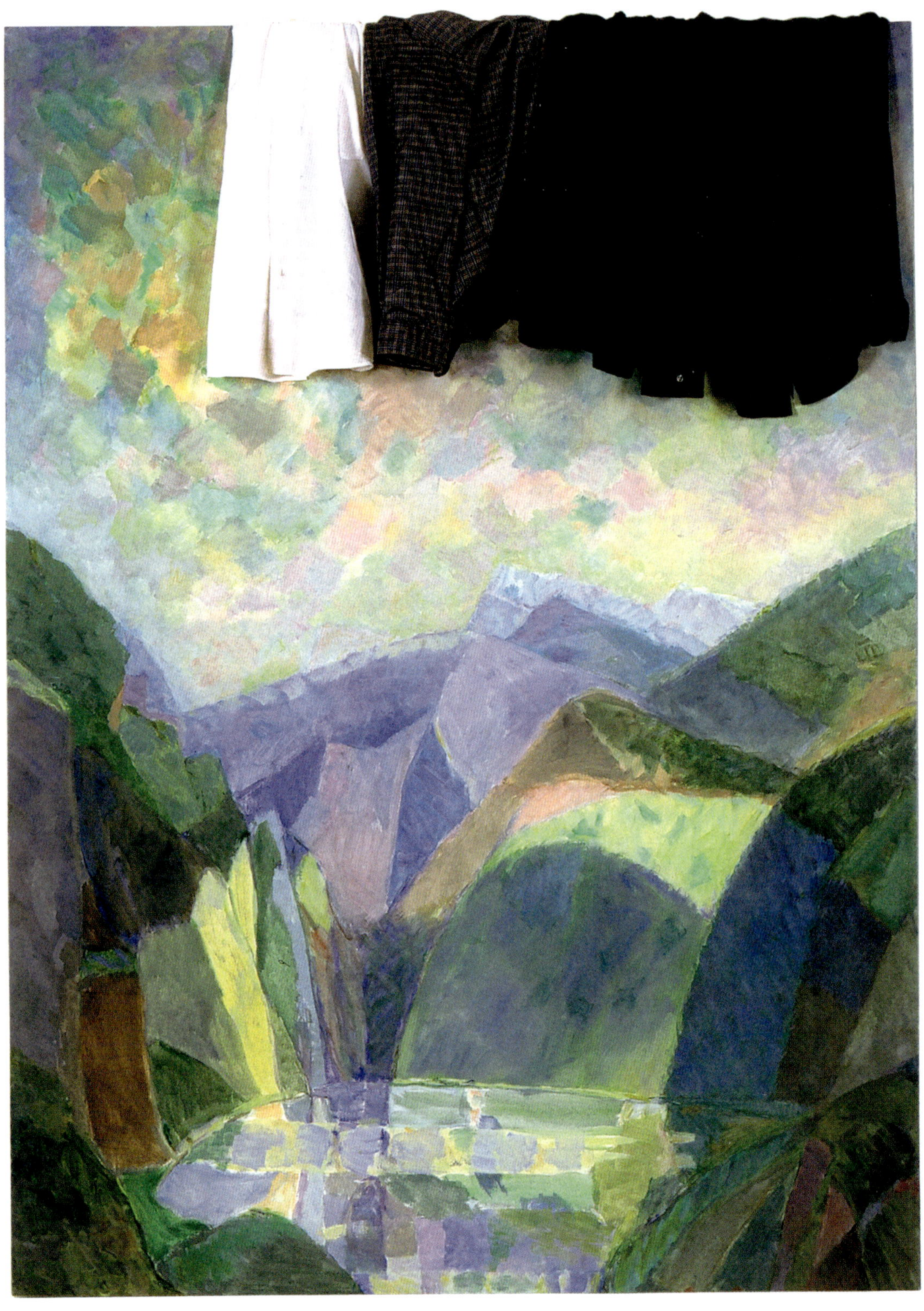

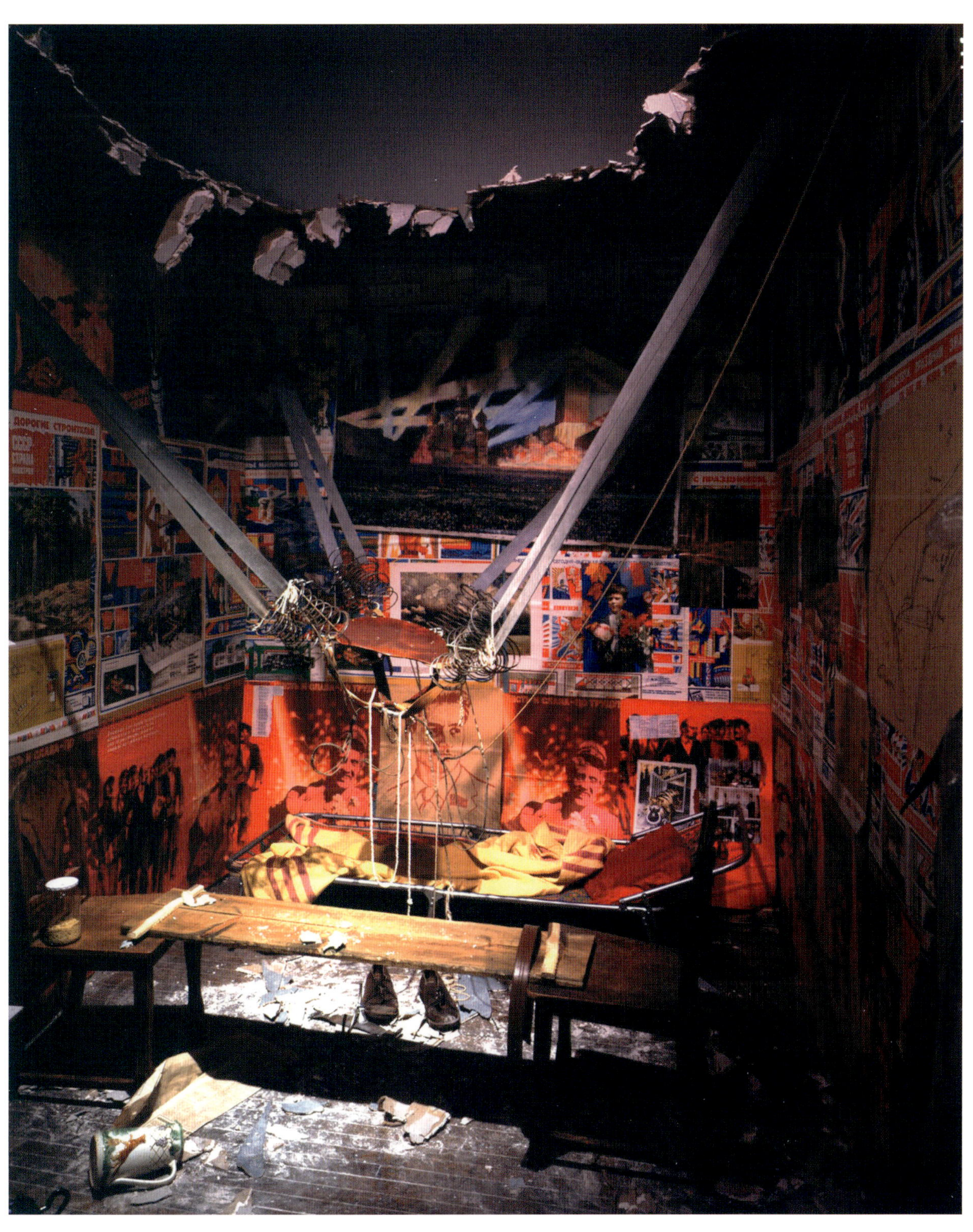

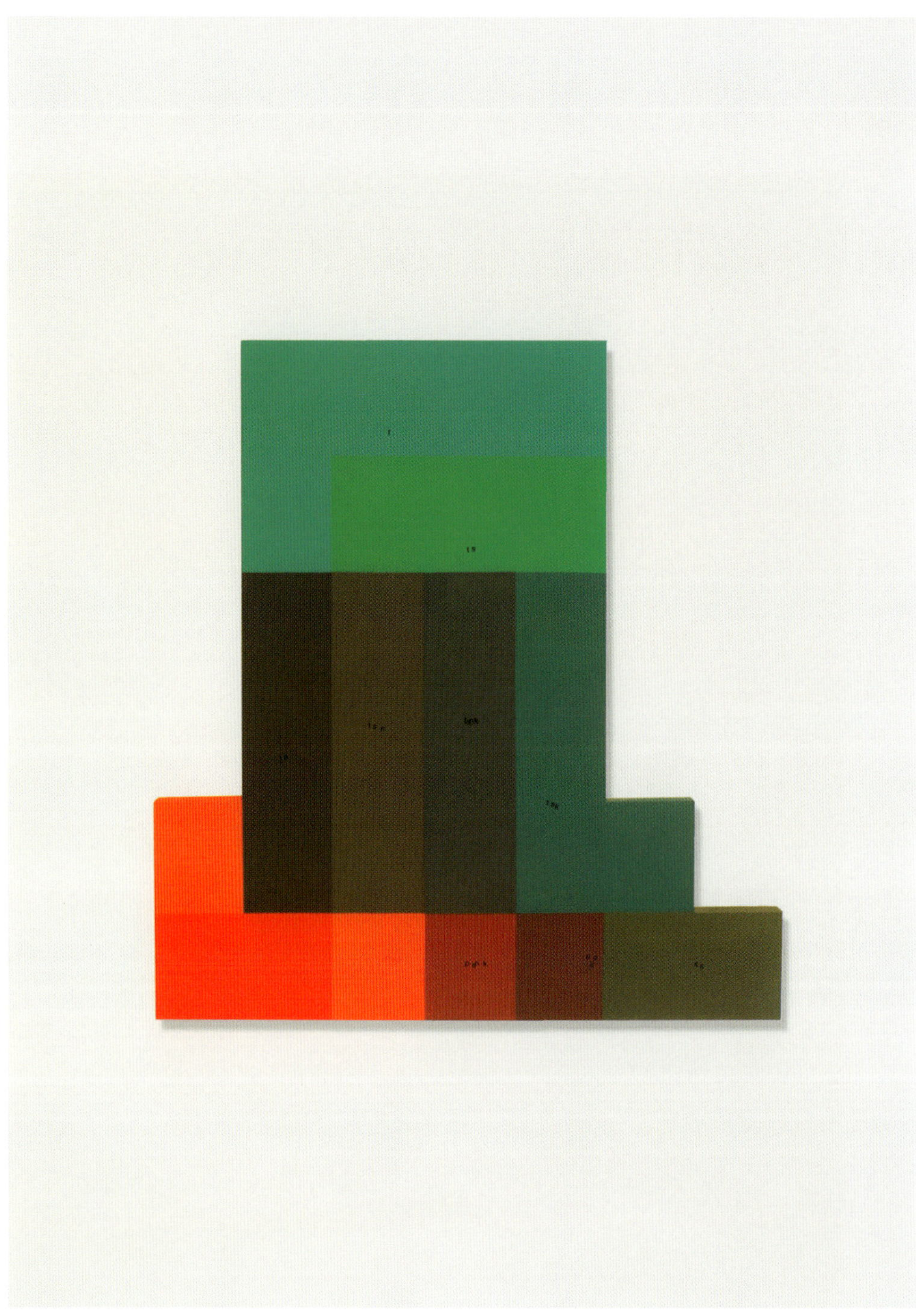

DÓRA MAURER

Since the 1970s, Dóra Maurer has been a significant figure on the Hungarian art scene, as both a lecturer and artist. Predominantly known for her early work with brightly coloured, geometrically composed printed works—such as *Regatta 1* and *Regatta 5*—Maurer's work shows a clear appreciation of colour and form. Whilst gaining recognition for these pieces, Maurer's work has also covered various other disciplines that include photography, film, painting and sculpture, as well as exploring action art and feminist body art.

There are several notable themes that have continuously run through Maurer's work, which mainly revolve around space, colour and perception. Her graphic pieces, for which she has gained much acclaim, explore ideas of shape and structure. Her series *Overlappings* sees brightly coloured forms fuse together and contort, transforming images of mathematical stature into playful characters. An interest in form plays a predominant part in Maurer's photographic work—both in style and content, as seen in *Reversible* and *Changeable Phases of Movement*, a series of black and white photos that depict a ball being thrown into the air at different stages. Each piece has been annotated to include mathematical sketches of charts and diagrams, along with textual references.

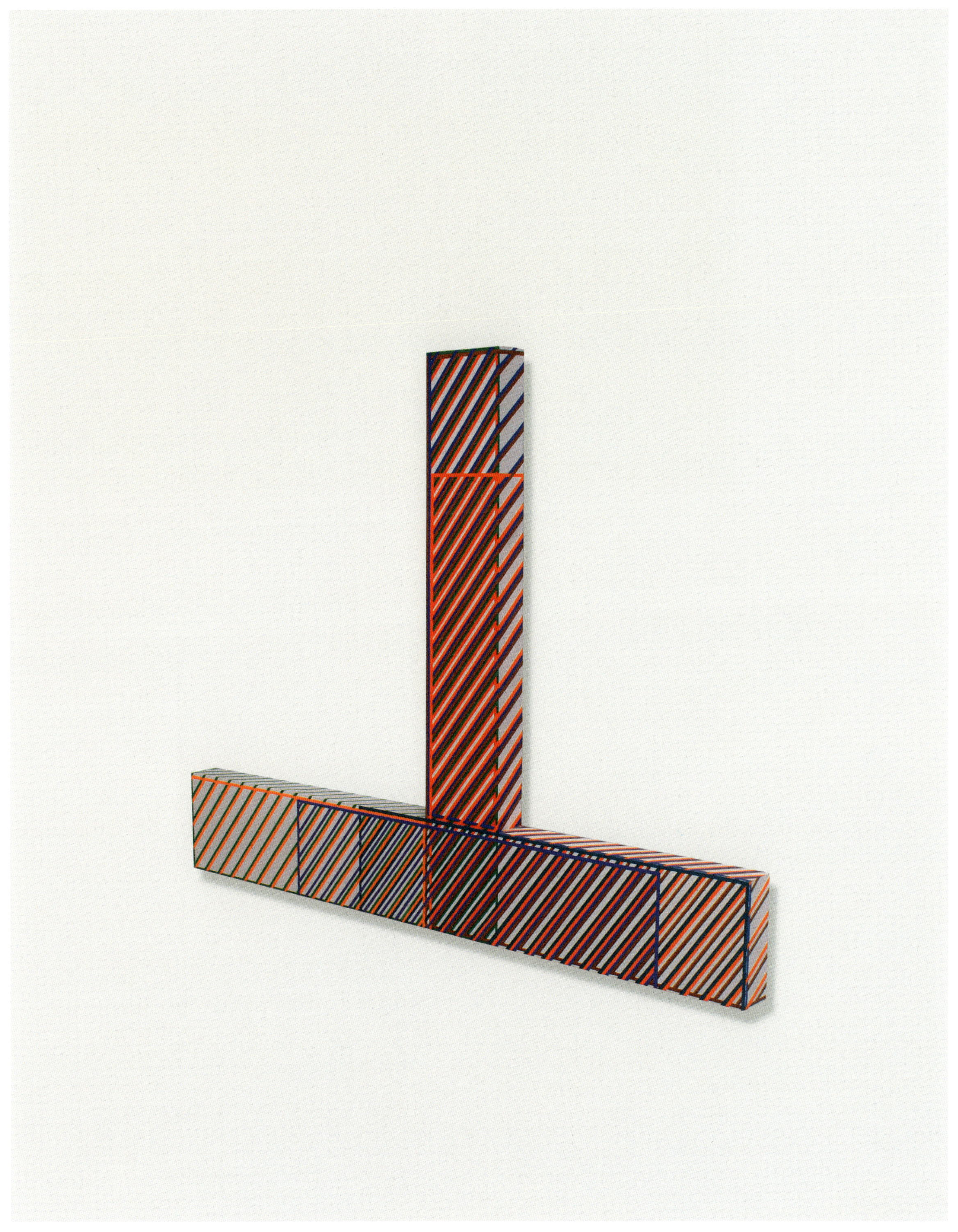

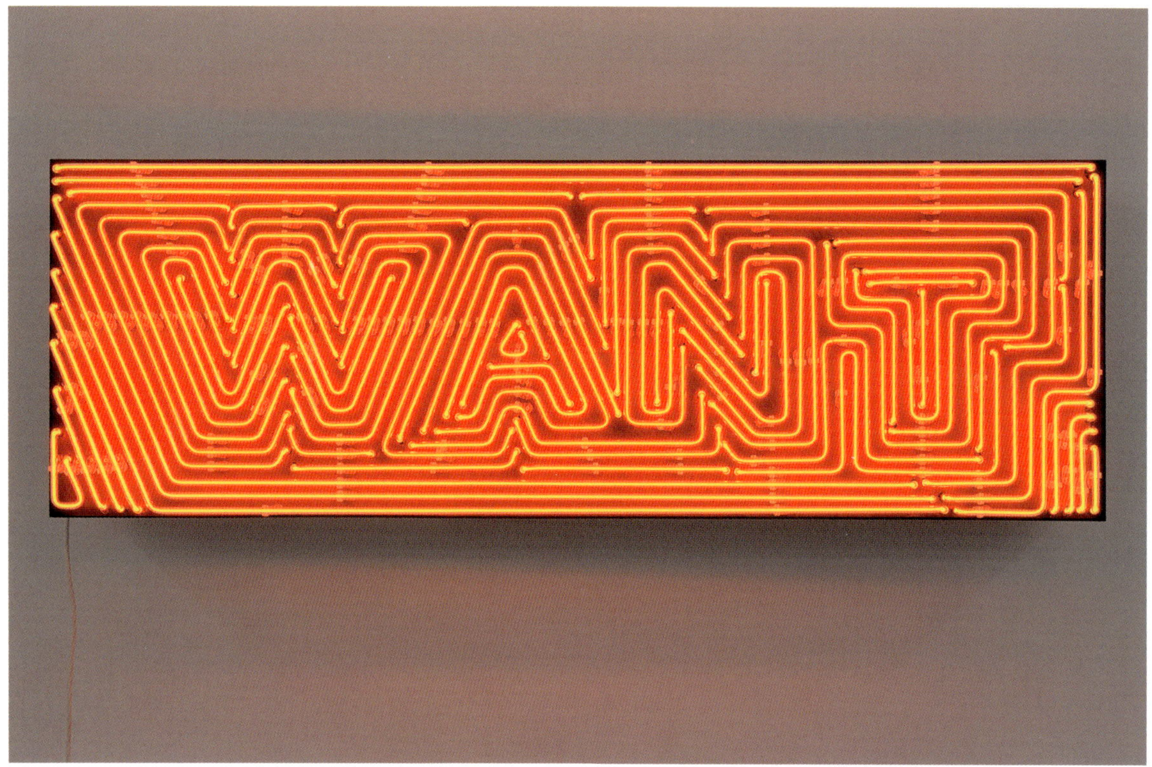

Want (right)
2008, 50 x 150 x 25 cm
Courtesy the artist

*Probably Moldova
doesn't exist* (opposite)
2002, poster, 90 x 60 cm
Courtesy the artist

PAVEL BRAILA

Emerging onto the Moldovan contemporary art scene off the back of the CarbonART3 event in 1996, Pavel Braila's preference for contemporary art methods more in favour of Western artists, distinguished him from the traditional styles of other Moldovan artists practicing at the time. Braila eventually went to study at the Jan van Eyck Academie in Maastricht, where he developed his artistic style further. His work is best described by his preference for highlighting the differences between the old Soviet generation and the new post-Socialist generation, which eventually led to his emersion within the international—largely Western—art scene. However, despite his appreciation and use of Western techniques, much of Braila's work remains topically rooted within a Moldovan context.

The artists work capitalises upon a diverse range of mediums and techniques, from minimalist performances to sculpture and video installation. His series of paintings *The Dreams of My Father About His Son (Me)*, 2008, from which *Winemaker* is taken, depicts various aspirations of Braila's father for his grown-up son's occupation. This series reflects the artist's position on the forefront of the Moldovan art scene by highlighting his somewhat less-than-traditional contemporary art style: "What kind of artist are you if you cannot even paint a portrait?" Braila commissioned a professional painter—clear in the disparity between styles of *The Winemaker* and *Want*—to produce this series, with each painting representing the various occupations his father would have liked his son to fulfil

during different stages throughout his youth; before university his father wanted Braila to study agronomy and become a winemaker.

Inspired by *The Dreams of My Father About His Son (Me)*, *Want*, 2008, directly references Braila's father's aspirations for his son. Whilst explaining the concept behind this previous series of work, Braila realised the repetition of the word "want" within his father's spoken desires for his son—"I want my son…" and chooses to encapsulate this within neon lighting. Each letter lights up in intervals of ten, from the centre out, gradually increasing the size of "want" and its impact—until virtually indecipherable. Then, in a complete reversal, the lights decrease step-by-step until it is impossible to grasp what is written.

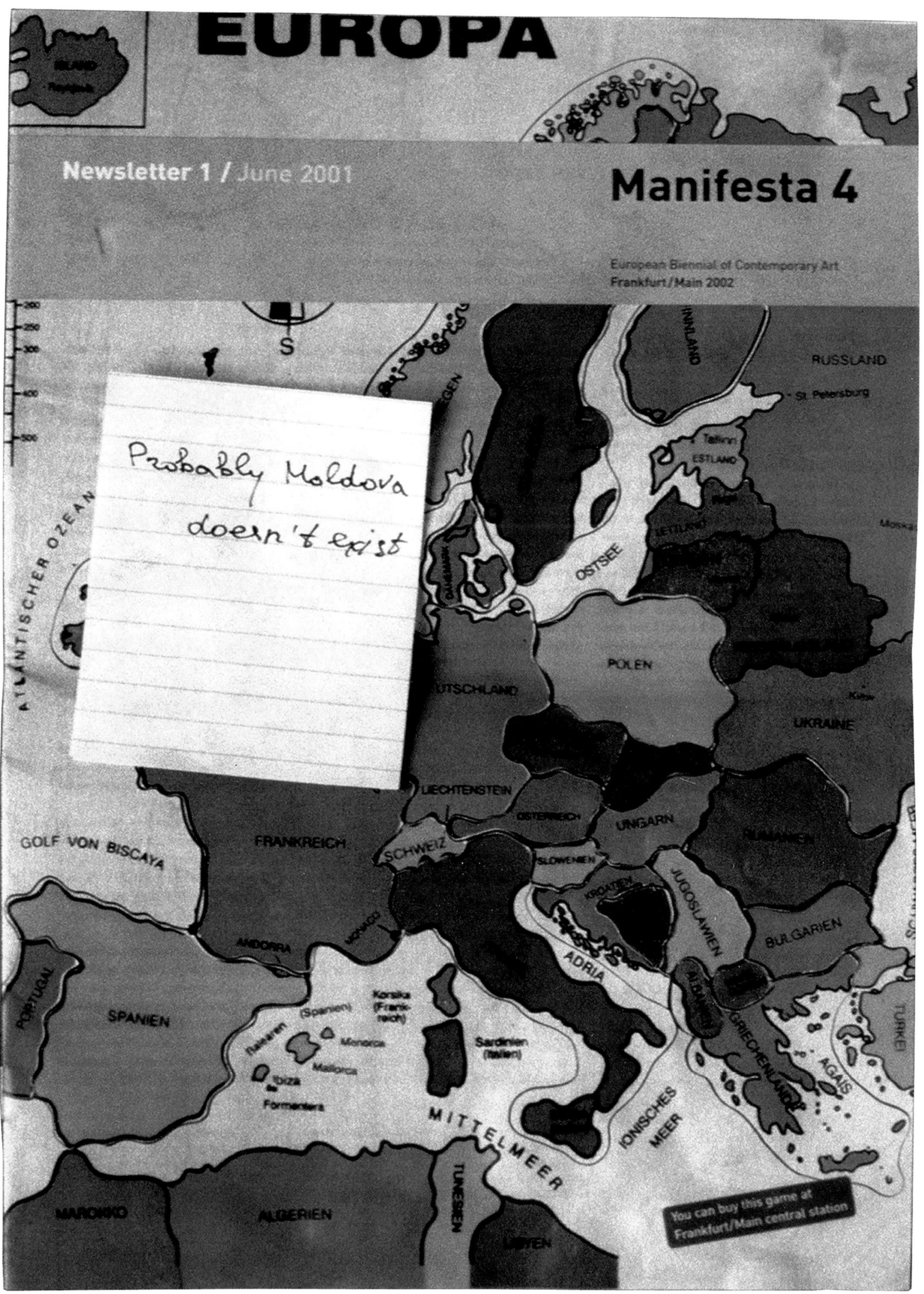
EUROPA
Newsletter 1 / June 2001
Manifesta 4
European Biennial of Contemporary Art
Frankfurt/Main 2002
Probably Moldova doesn't exist
ISLAND
RUSSLAND
St. Petersburg
FINNLAND
ESTLAND
Tallinn
LETTLAND
Moska
OSTSEE
POLEN
Kiew
DEUTSCHLAND
UKRAINE
ATLANTISCHER OZEAN
LIECHTENSTEIN
ÖSTERREICH
UNGARN
RUMÄNIEN
FRANKREICH
SCHWEIZ
SLOWENIEN
GOLF VON BISCAYA
KROATIEN
JUGOSLAWIEN
BULGARIEN
MONACO
ANDORRA
ADRIA
ALBANIEN
TÜRKEI
PORTUGAL
SPANIEN
Korsika (Frankreich)
Sardinien (Italien)
GRIECHENLAND
AGÄIS
Balearen (Spanien)
Menorca
Mallorca
Ibiza
Formentera
IONISCHES MEER
MITTELMEER
MAROKKO
ALGERIEN
TUNESIEN
LIBYEN
You can buy this game at Frankfurt/Main central station

PAVEL BRAILA
Winemaker
2008, oil on canvas, 160 x 200 cm
Courtesy the artist

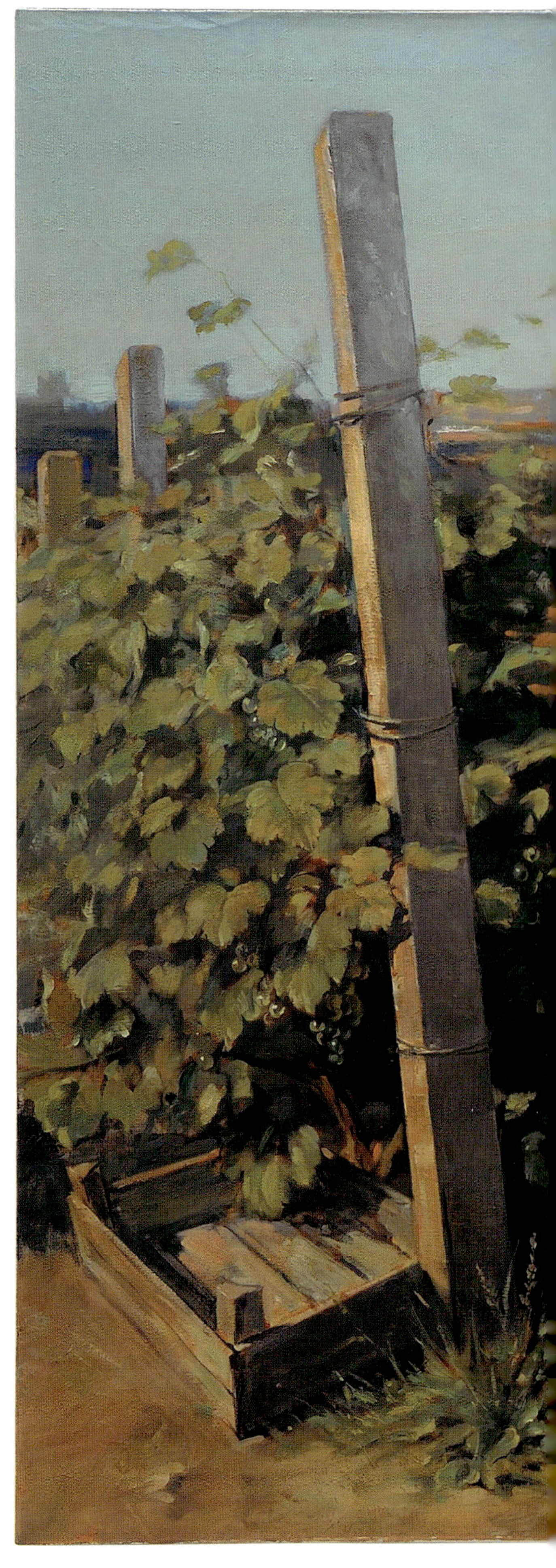

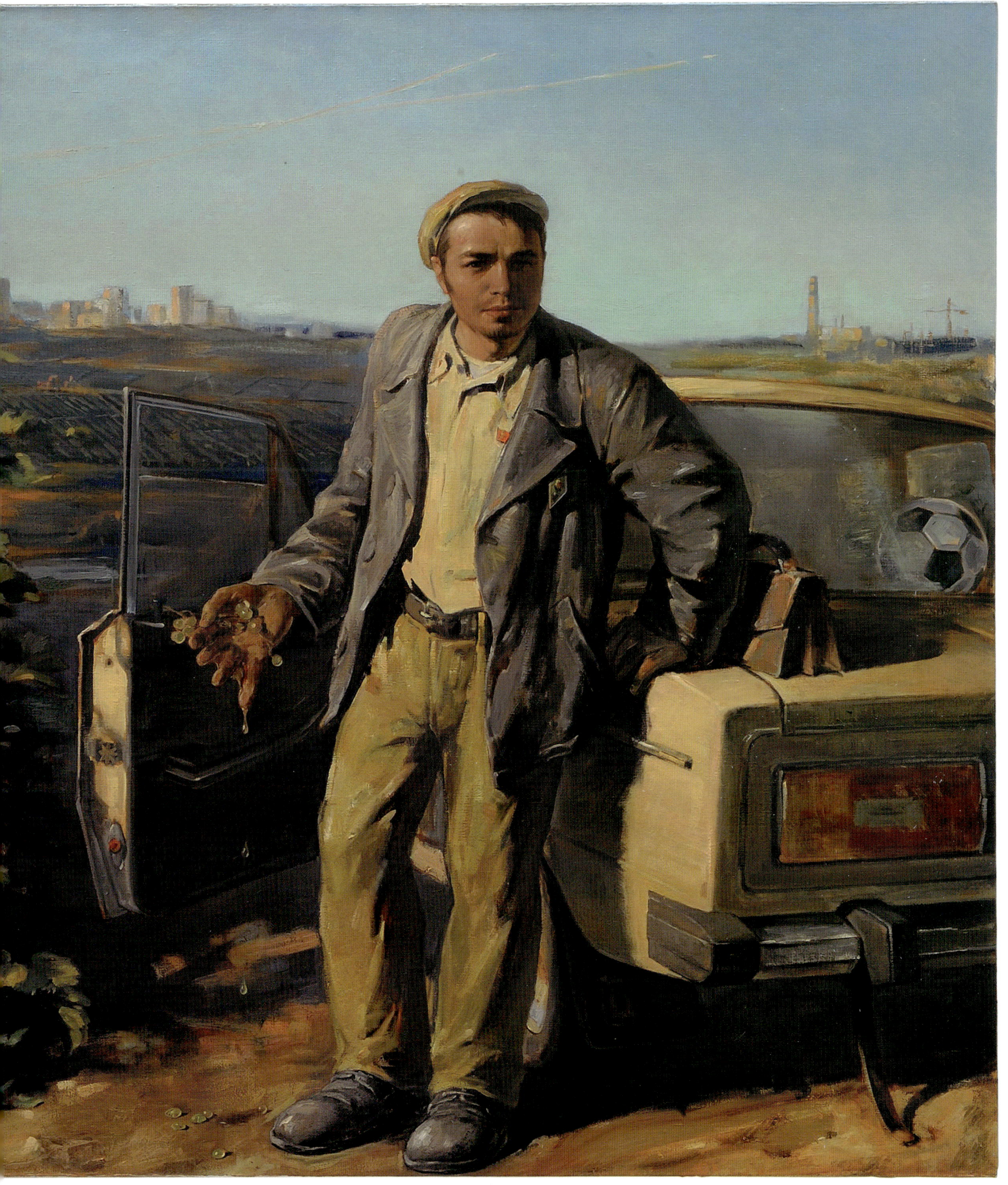

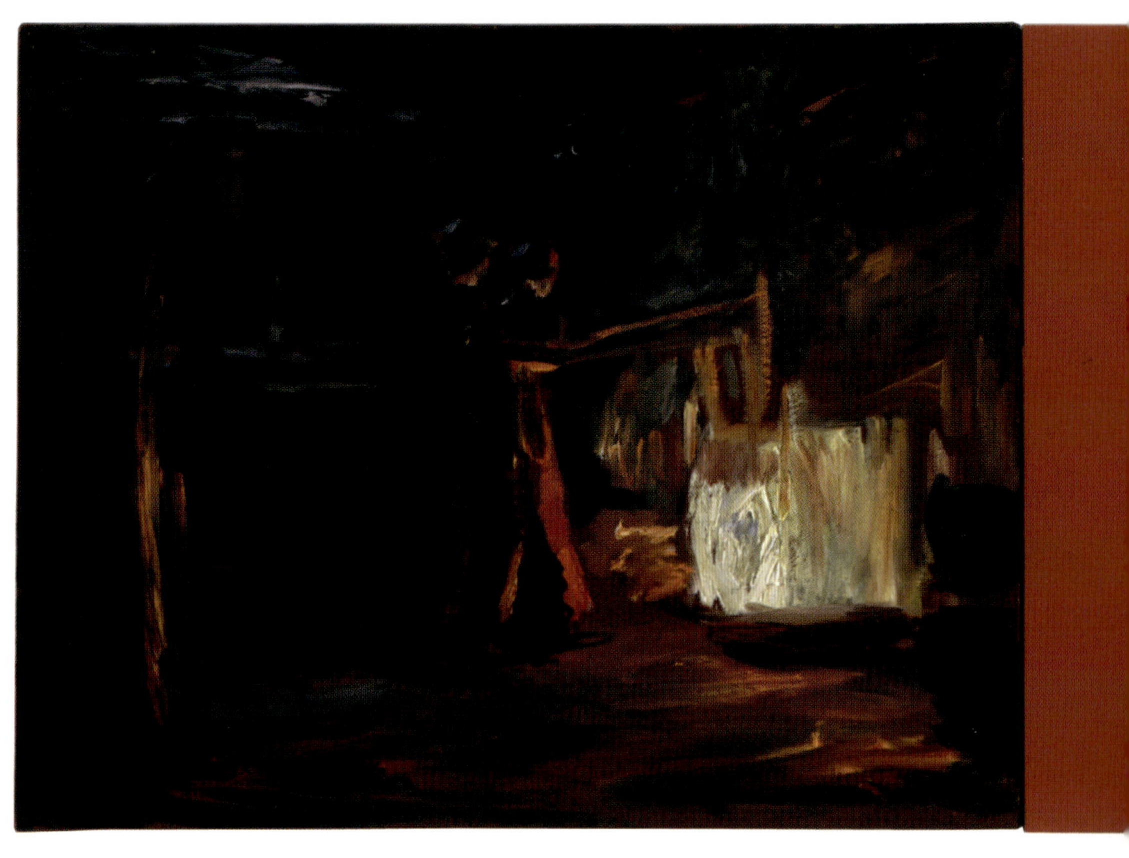

KOMAR AND MELAMID

As students at the Stroganov School of Art and Design, Vitaly Komar and Alexander Melamid forged the artistic bond that became the basis for a 36-year artistic collaboration. In the late 1960s, the duo gained recognition for their own brand of conceptual art that rebelled against the tradition of Soviet Socialist Realism— otherwise known as Sots Art—a Russian movement parallel to the American Pop Art movement. Komar and Melamid became recognised for these satirical paintings, vividly brought to life in a spectrum of colour that appropriated elements of Socialist Realism and Dadaism. Following a number of high profile exhibitions and events, such as the highly publicised Bulldozer Show, 1974, in which theirs and other artist's works were destroyed by Soviet authorities, Komar and Melamid decided to relocate, first to Israel, and then to New York in 1978, and helped to carry the Sots Art movement beyond the borders of Soviet Russia. Though Komar and Melamid's entire oeuvre engages with both Russian and Western politics and visual culture, a shift is visible is the work from this period.

America's Most Wanted is a statistical exploration into America's artistic preferences. The artists produced both an *America's Most Wanted* and an *America's Least Wanted* painting from the results of a professional market research survey—the result of which they considered to be true "people's art"; they then repeated the process with several other countries.

FIRE

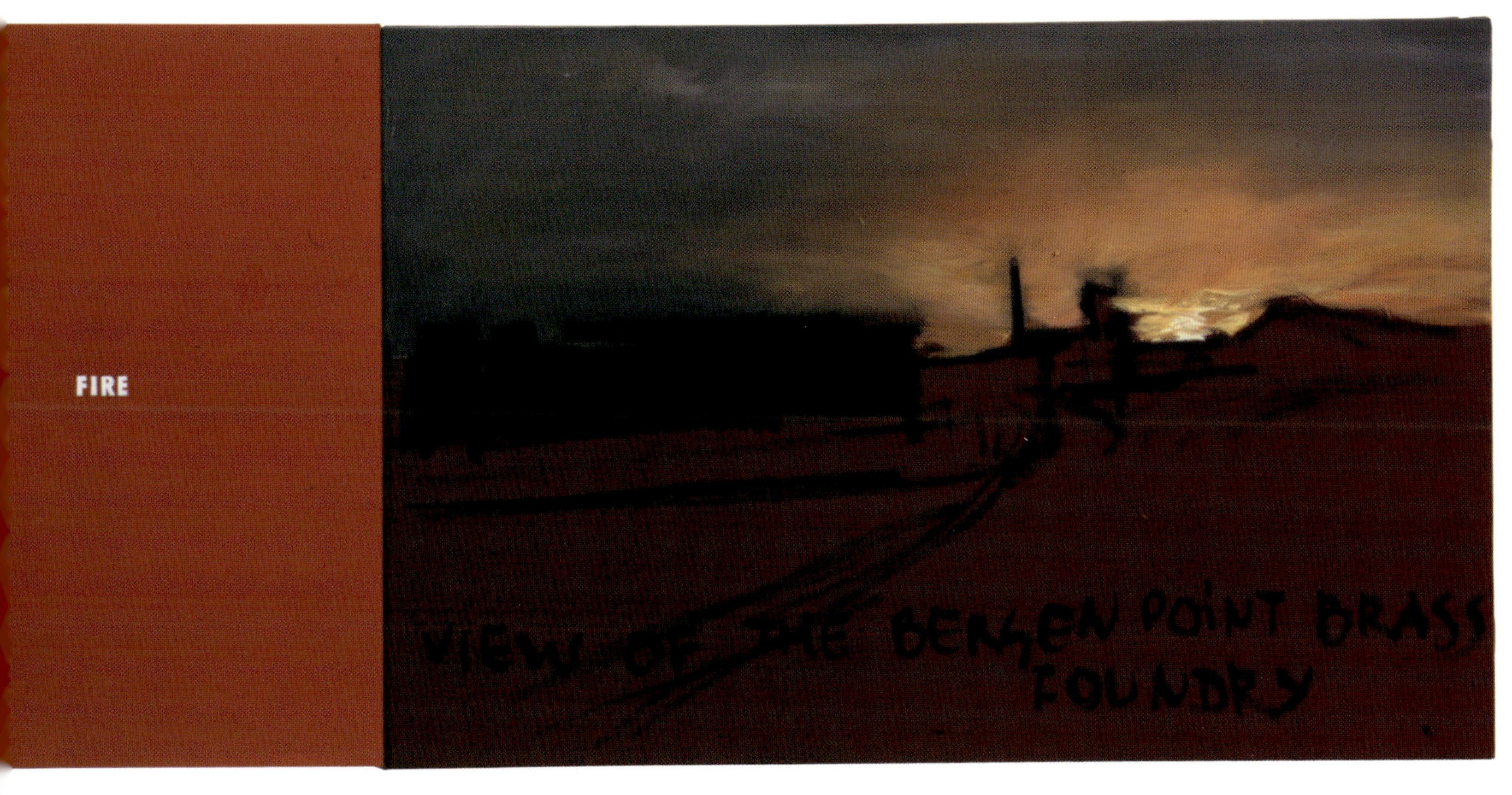

VIEW OF THE BERGEN POINT BRASS
FOUNDRY

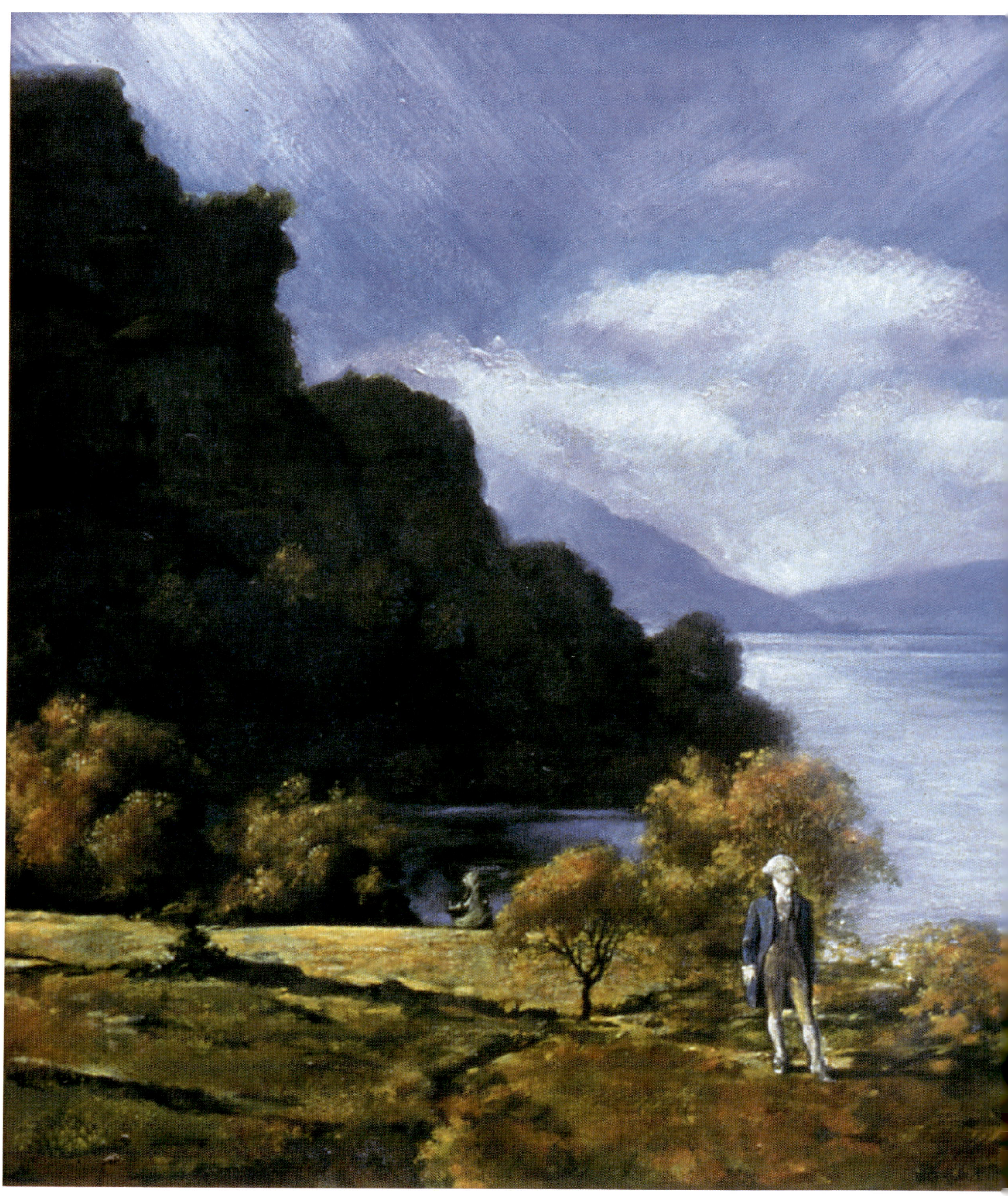

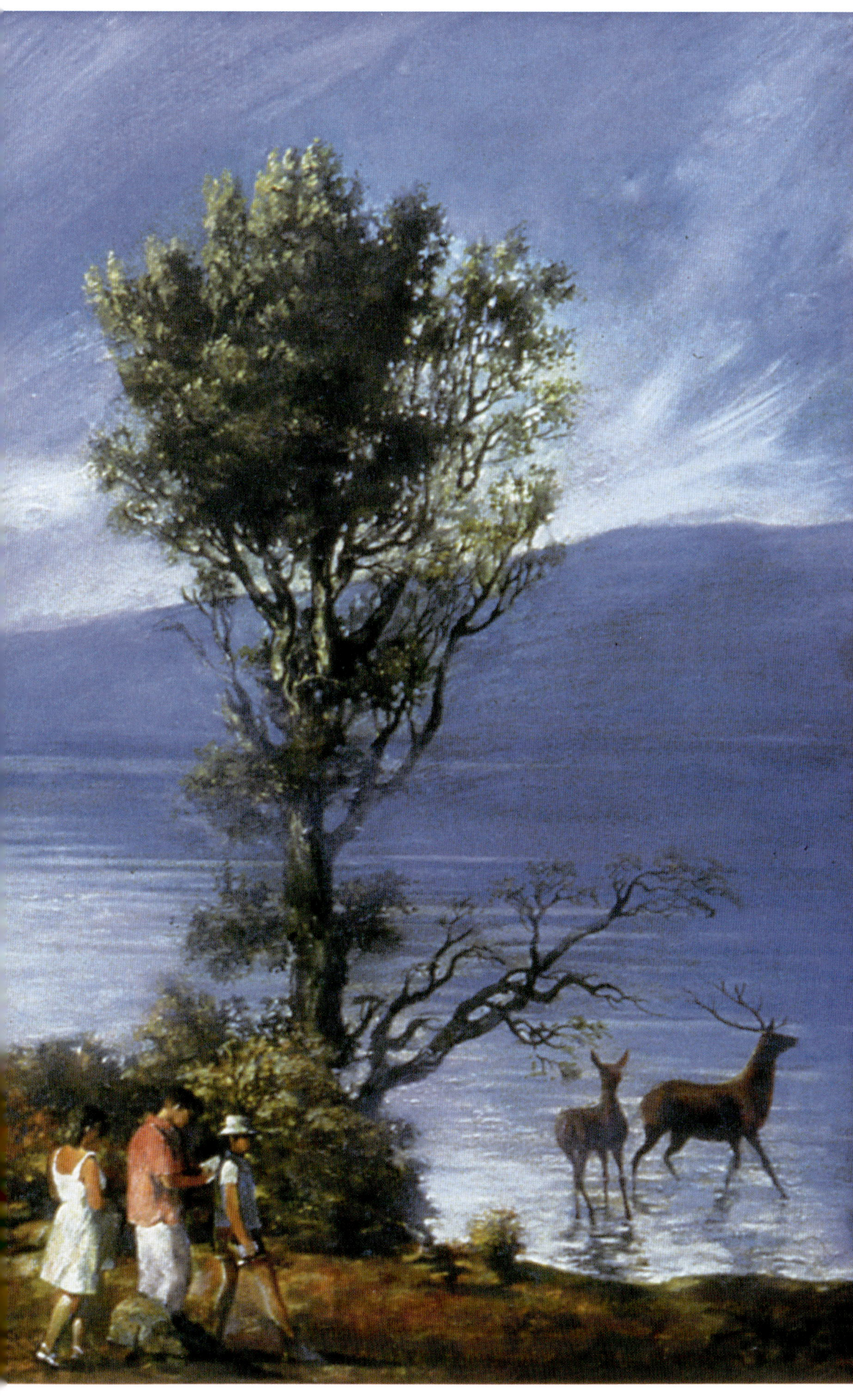

KOMAR AND MELAMID
America's Most Wanted
1994, oil and acrylic on canvas
Courtesy Ronald Feldman Fine Arts
New York, photo: D James Dee

SERBAN SAVU
The Edge of the Empire
2008, oil on canvas, 126 x 190 cm
Courtesy the artist
and David Nolan Gallery, New York

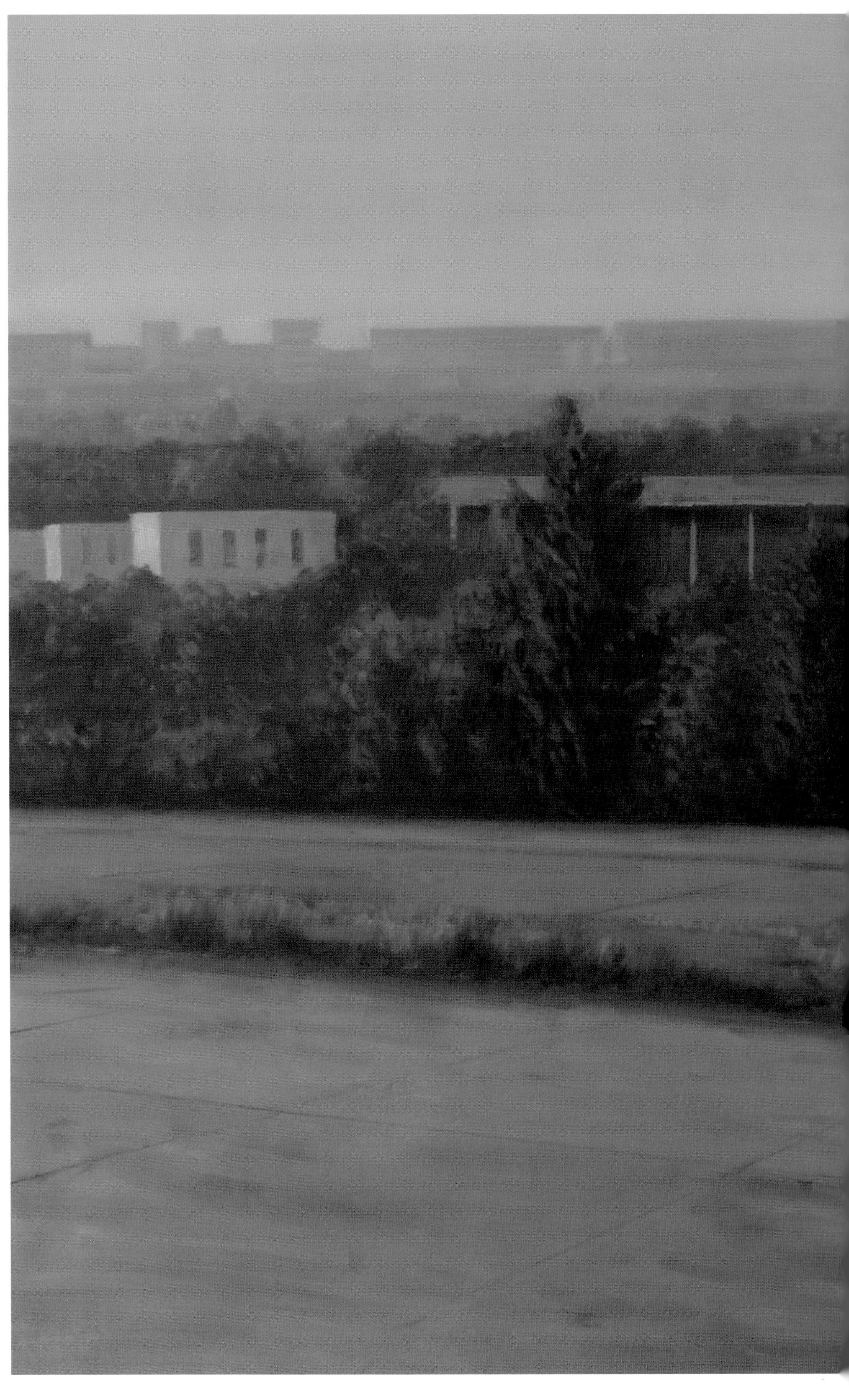

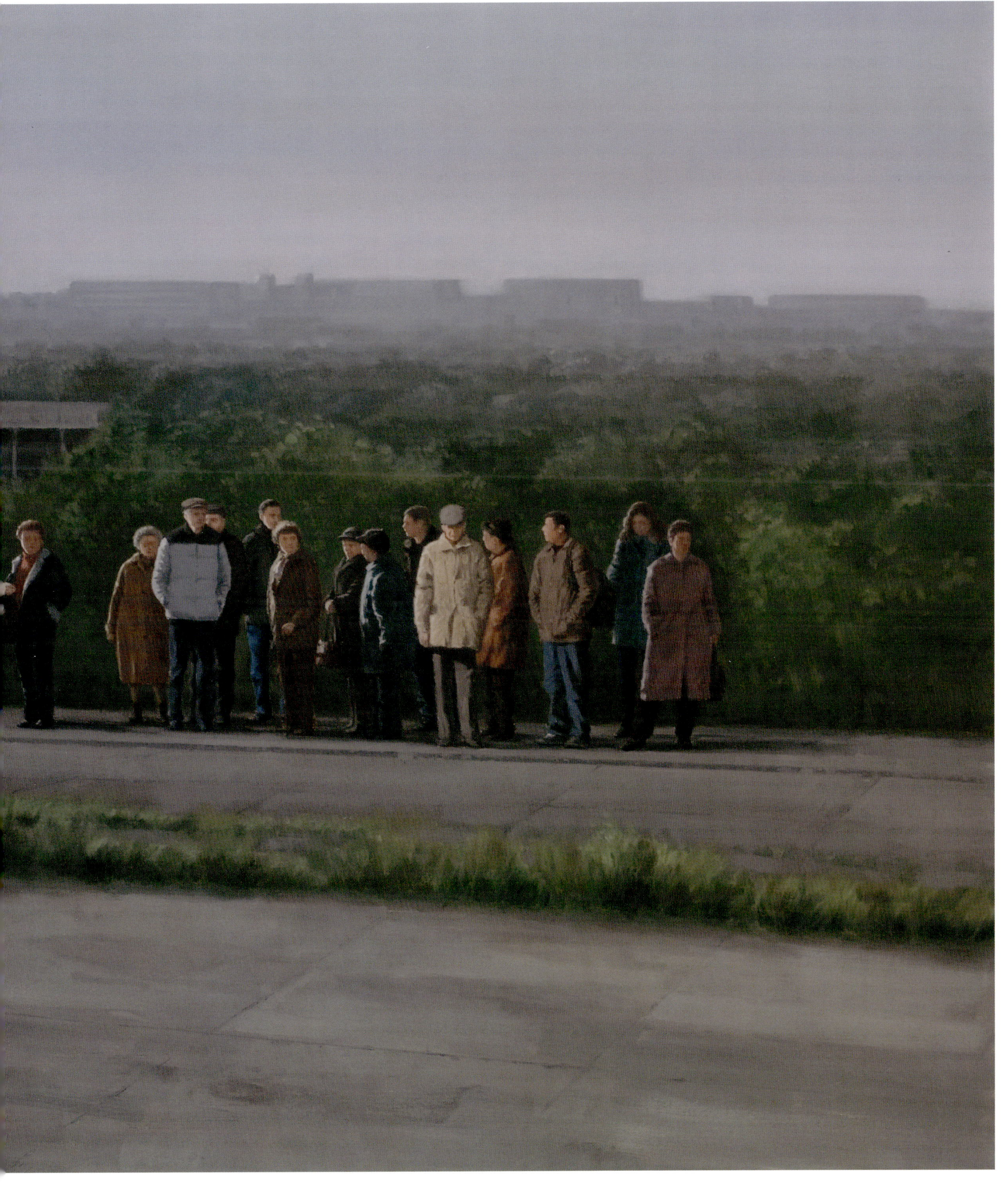

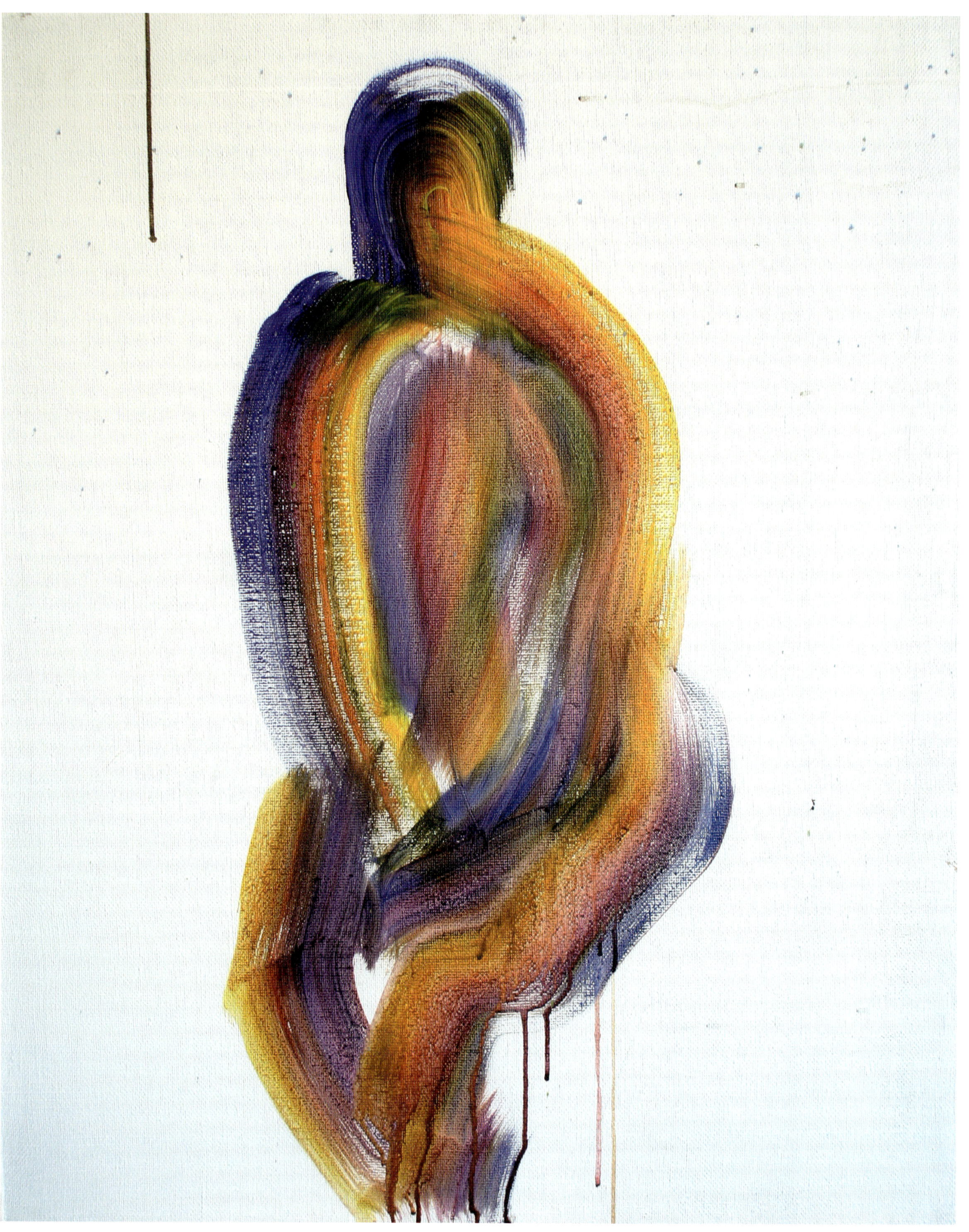

JAAN TOOMIK
Figure (opposite)
2010, acrylic on canvas, 120 x 100 cm
Courtesy the artist

Seagulls (right)
2004, 1.47 minutes , DVD, video installation
Courtesy the artist

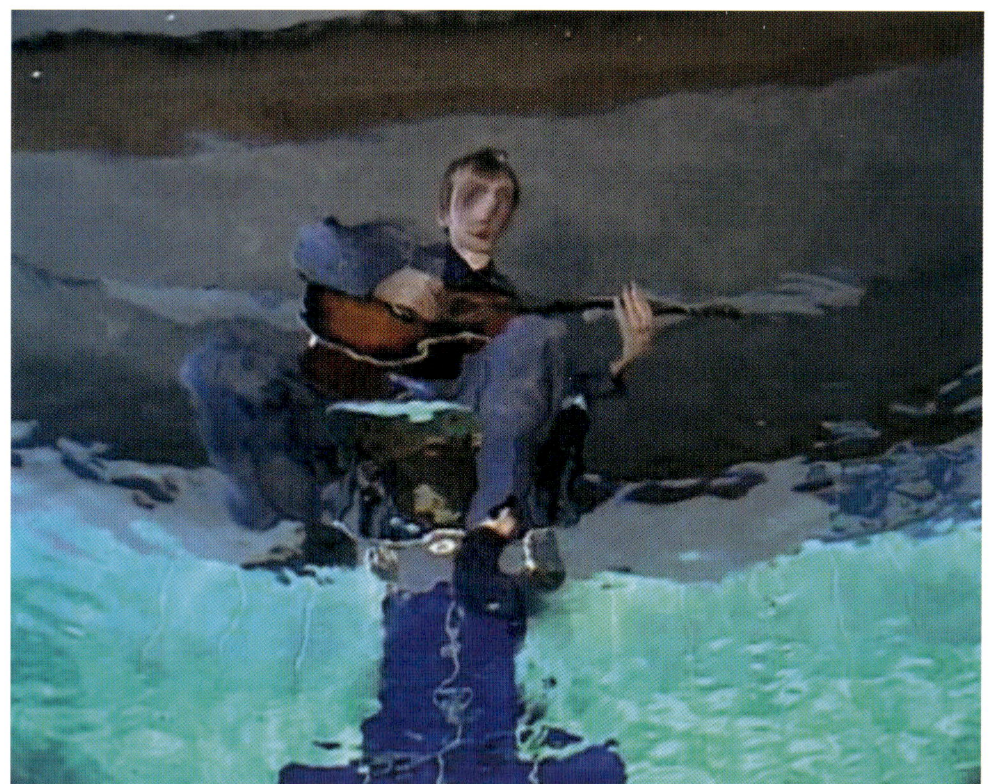

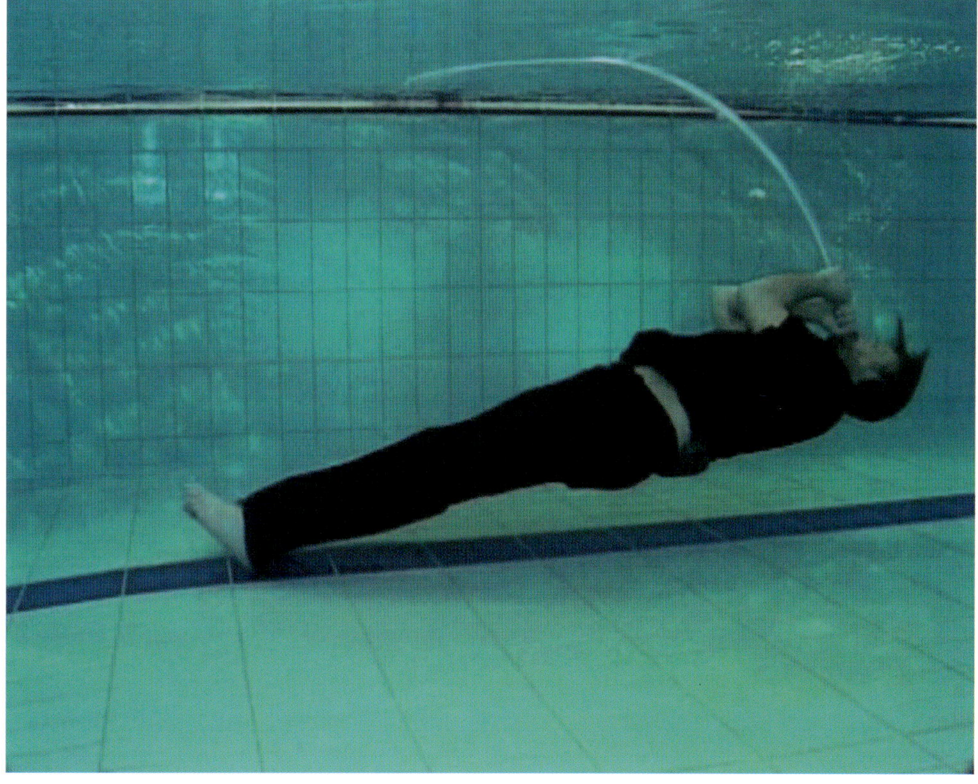

Pie Fight Study 4 (right)
2008, oil on canvas, 52 x 52 cm
Courtesy Tim Van Laere Gallery, Antwerp

The Blue Rain (opposite)
2009, oil on canvas, 240 x 190 cm
Courtesy Tim Van Laere Gallery, Antwerp

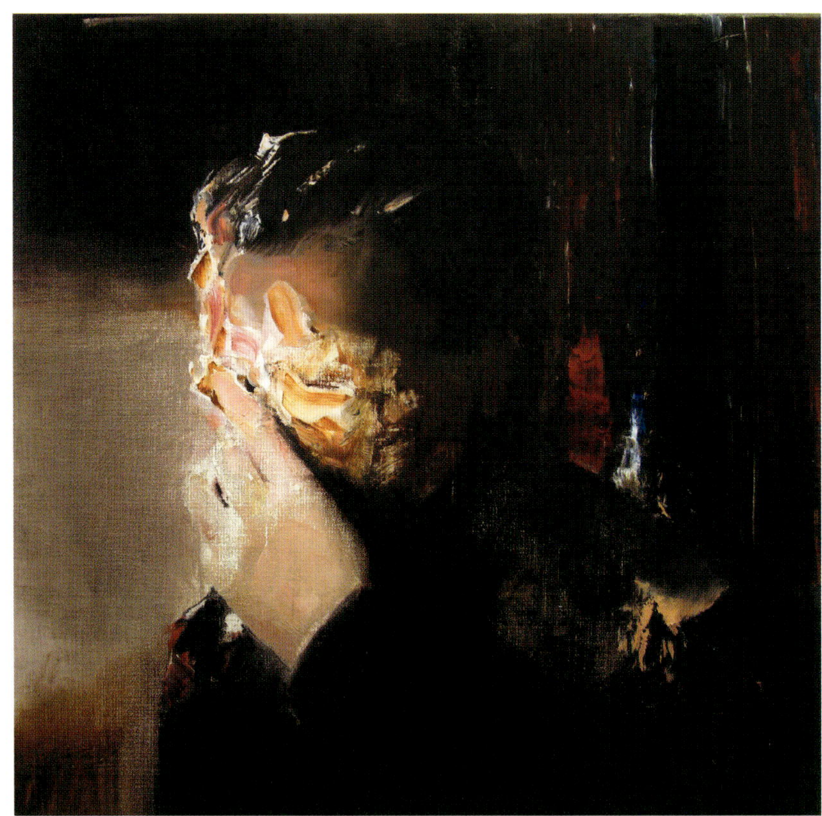

ADRIAN GHENIE

The work of Romanian painter Adrian Ghenie is heavily referential of his home city of Cluj, northern Transylvania—a city closely associated with contemporary painting, which Ghenie staunchly supports. Often likened to the work of Francis Bacon for his brooding and contemplative style, Ghenie's work draws on twentieth century ideas of memory, trauma and extremism—topics which continue to arise in various Eastern European artists' work.

Combining both personal and collective memory in his paintings, Ghenie's work has been interpreted as being at once documentary, yet also fictional; presenting the viewer with a sense of familiarity that lingers somewhat suggestively within their subconscious.

At once representational, the scenes that Ghenie paints possess an acute attention to detail, whilst simultaneously allowing certain parameters for mistakes—a style which has become synonymous with his work. It is for this reason that Ghenie emphasises spatial awareness within his paintings, so as to allow for the mix of colours and accidental brush strokes that arise from these mistakes, a technique evocative of the hazy subject of memory that Ghenie frequently references. It is also this juxtaposition between the representational and the subjective that has given Ghenie his name—a paradox with which Ghenie is fully aware: "On one hand, I work on an image in an almost classical vein: composition, figuration, use of light. On the other hand, I do not refrain from resorting to all kinds of idioms, such as the Surrealist principle of association or the abstract experiments which foreground texture and surface."

The Blue Rain, 2009, is a further exploration into memory—in this case the myth of celebrity culture. Elvis is portrayed throughout the series as a distorted image; highly recognisable by his white suit, however, in most occasions with a blurred facial profile. Ghenie is pointedly questioning the relationship between image and fame and whether the image portrayed by fame is authentic.

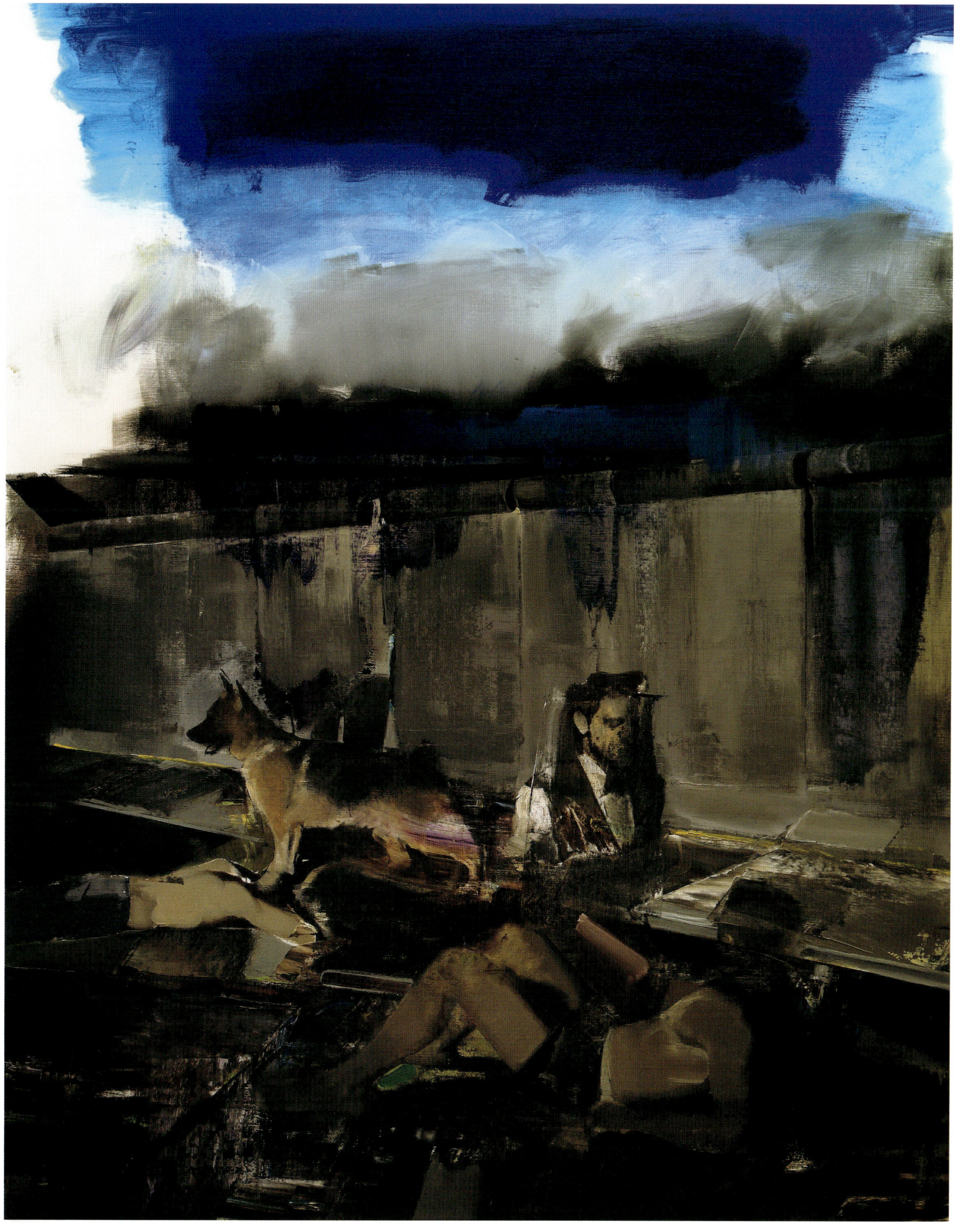

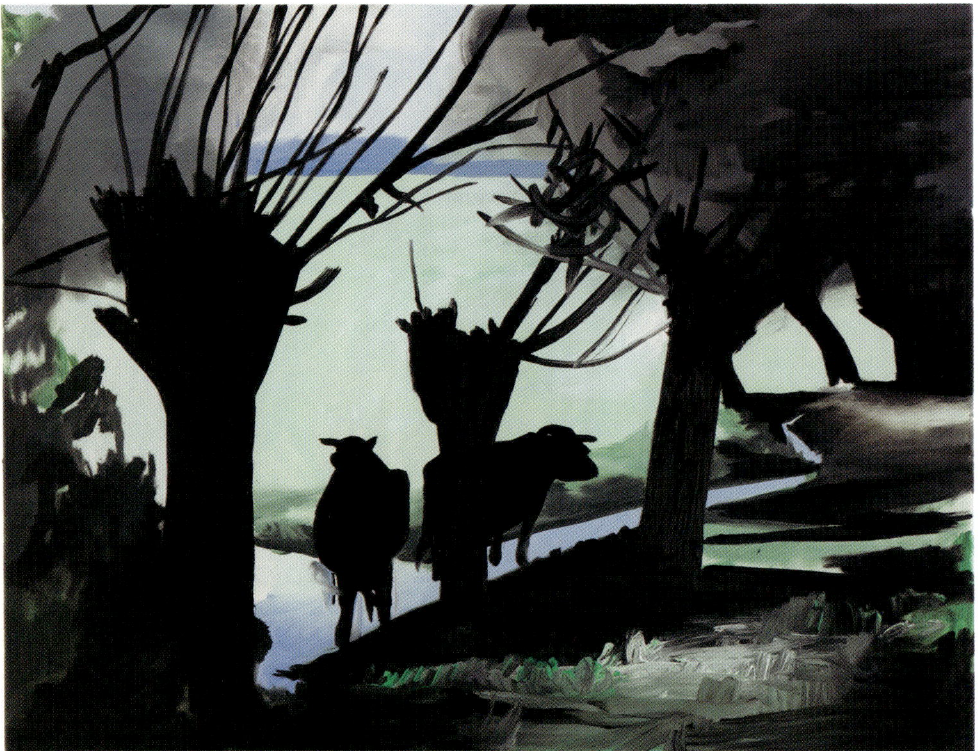

Untitled (right)
2009, oil on canvas, 70 x 90 cm
Copyright Wilhelm Sasnal, courtesy
The Goetz Collection

Swineherd (opposite)
2009, ink on paper, 150 x 105 cm
Copyright Wilhelm Sasnal, courtesy the artist
and Hauser & Wirth

WILHELM SASNAL

Wilhelm Sasnal belongs to a generation of Polish artists who emerged as the country restructured itself around a liberal market economy during its first post-Communist decade. Within an evolving cultural dynamic of production and consumption, and subject to an expanding currency of visual languages, Sasnal and his contemporaries forged their practices in reaction to an absence of adequate means for expressing private realities and responding to broader social experiences.

Originally associated with the Kraków-based Ladnie group of painters—Ladnie meaning "pretty" or "nice"—Sasnal has developed his work with a view to negotiating reality in all its available modes. At the same time as studying the intimate, everyday reality of his immediate surroundings, he has actively engaged with the apparatus of culture that seeks to mediate between individuals and their experience of the world; photojournalism, advertisements and propaganda icons are all confronted and made use of, with Sasnal observing and absorbing their aesthetic devices and allowing these to influence his decisions as a painter. As a result of this decisive attempt at directly relating his practice to this particular context, his paintings exhibit a necessarily antagonistic relationship to art historical precedent.

Employing slick, muted tones and an economic but still tactile handling of paint, Sasnal submits his subject matter to a reductive process that renders content intelligible in its most essential parts. Banal examples of still life—a set of barrels, bags of soil—serve as solid, substantial forms through which the activity of painting can manifest, and exist with the same degree of importance as fragments from culture and history which, divested of any context, become neutralised and suffer a challenge to their original power and meaning. Furthermore, through a considered and deliberate offsetting of various styles of visual description, Sasnal succeeds in animating his work with a critical vocabulary.

In a manner that is composed and practiced, Sasnal approaches an increasingly suffocating abundance of cultural produce and ideology and firmly brings it under his control, establishing a sense of distance from it and reasserting his authority as an individual in the process. In this way—and perhaps ironically—his paintings occupy a position that is entirely coherent with the most significant aspects of the medium's history.

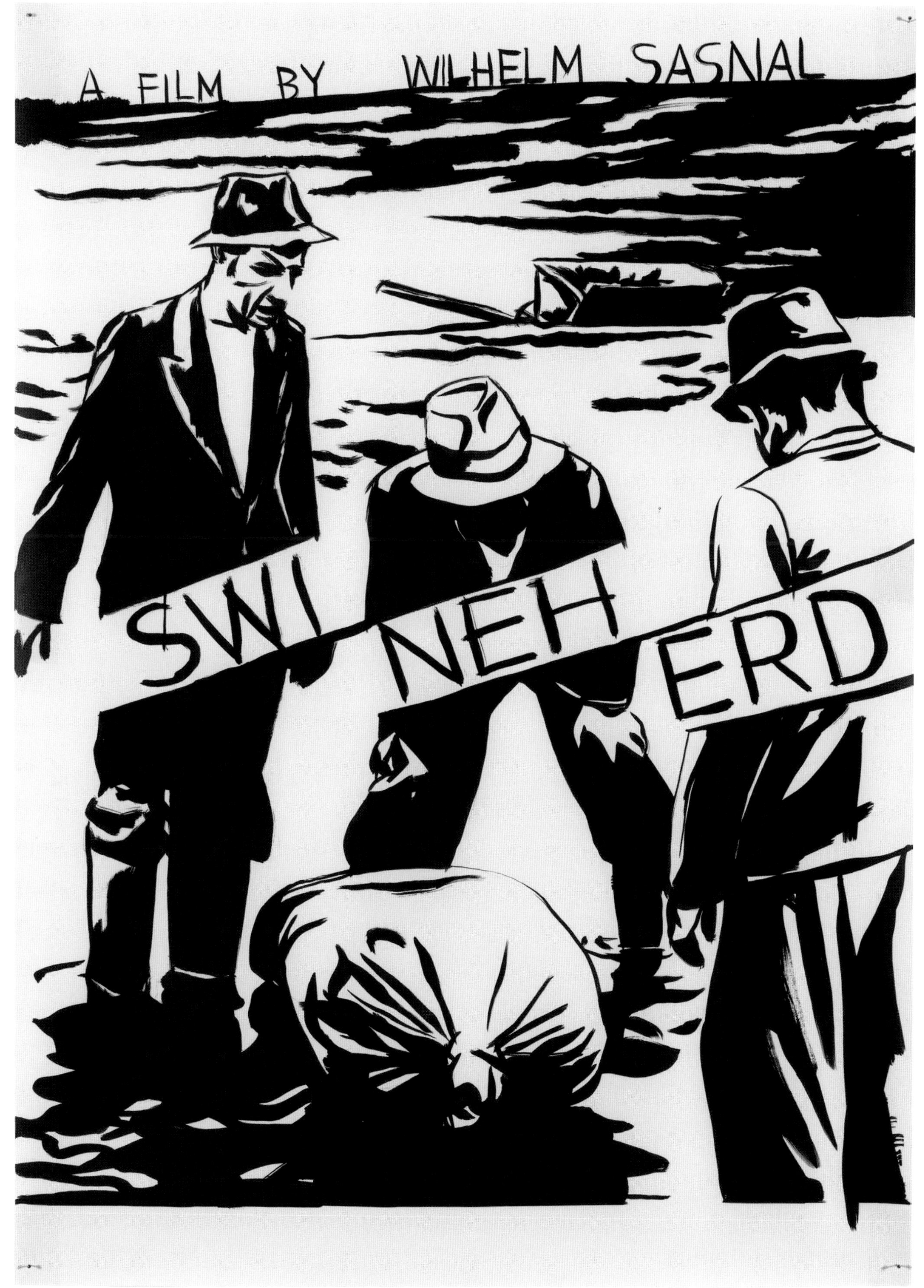

A FILM BY WILHELM SASNAL
SWI NEH ERD

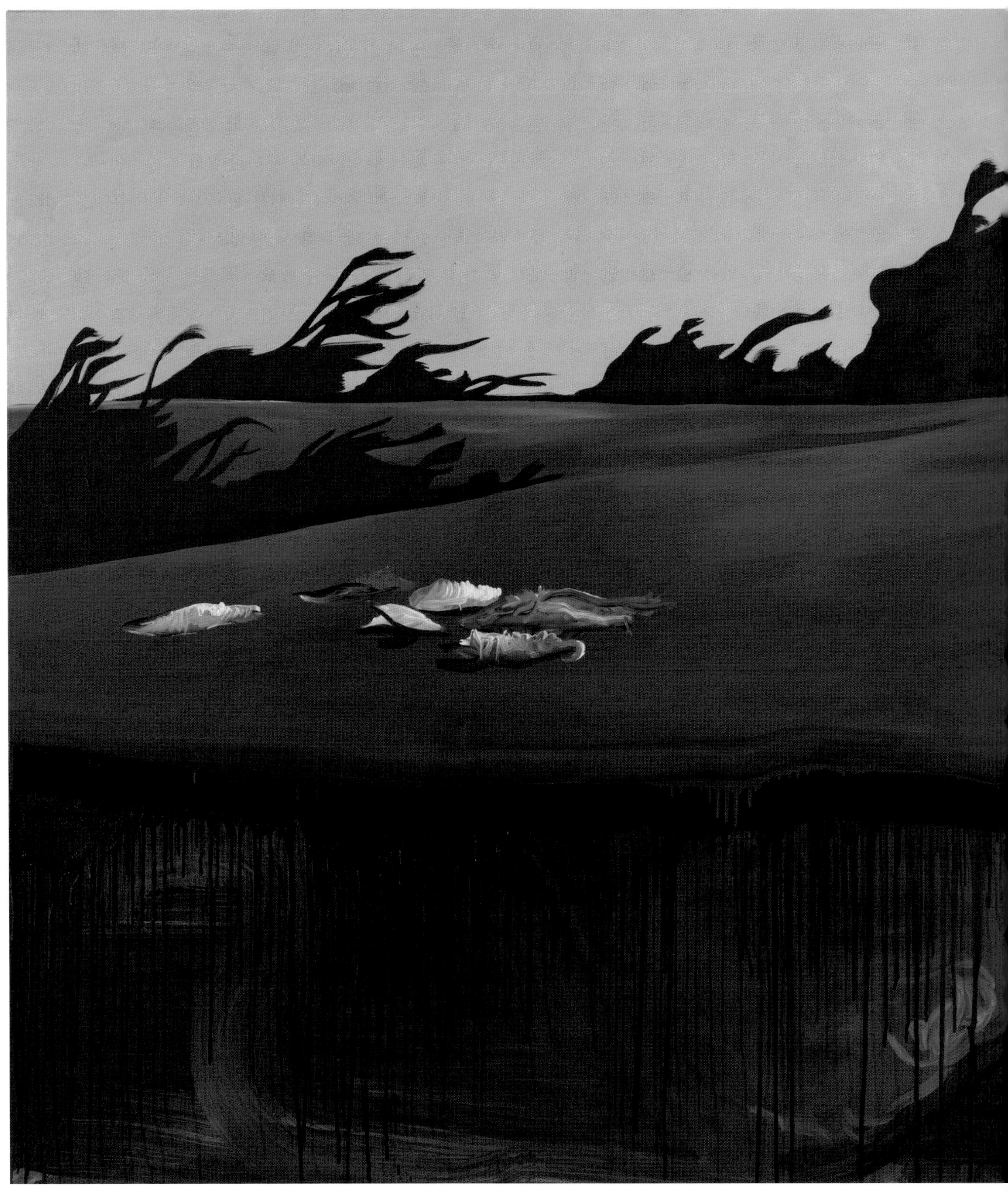

Clothes
2009, oil on canvas, 160 x 220 cm
Copyright Wilhelm Sasnal, courtesy the
artist and Hauser & Wirth

ANDRZEJ JACKOWSKI
Two Narrow Beds (below)
1999, oil on canvas, 152 x 193 cm
Courtesy the artist

Vigilant Dreamer II (opposite)
2009, oil on canvas, 82 x 55 cm
Courtesy the artist

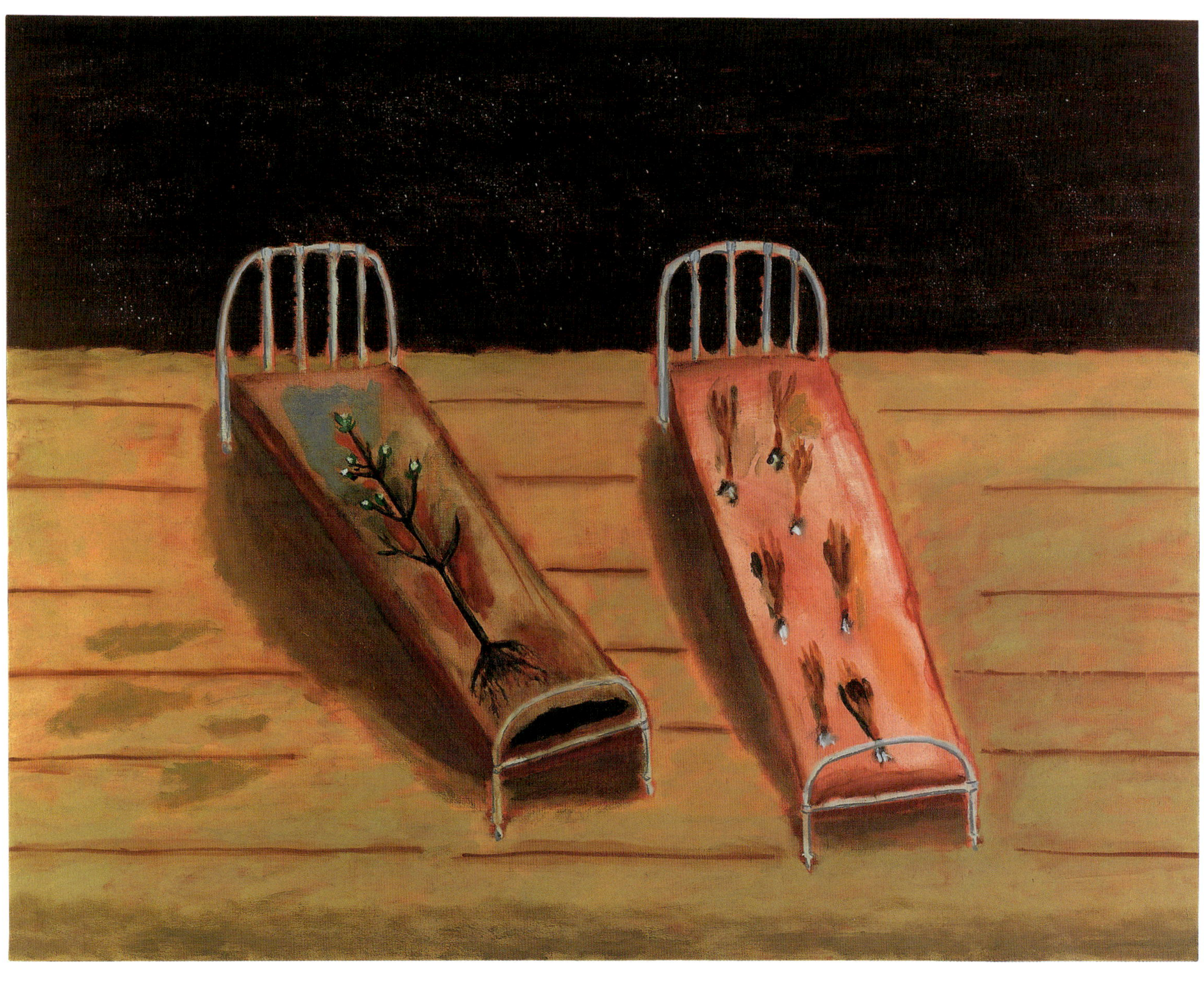

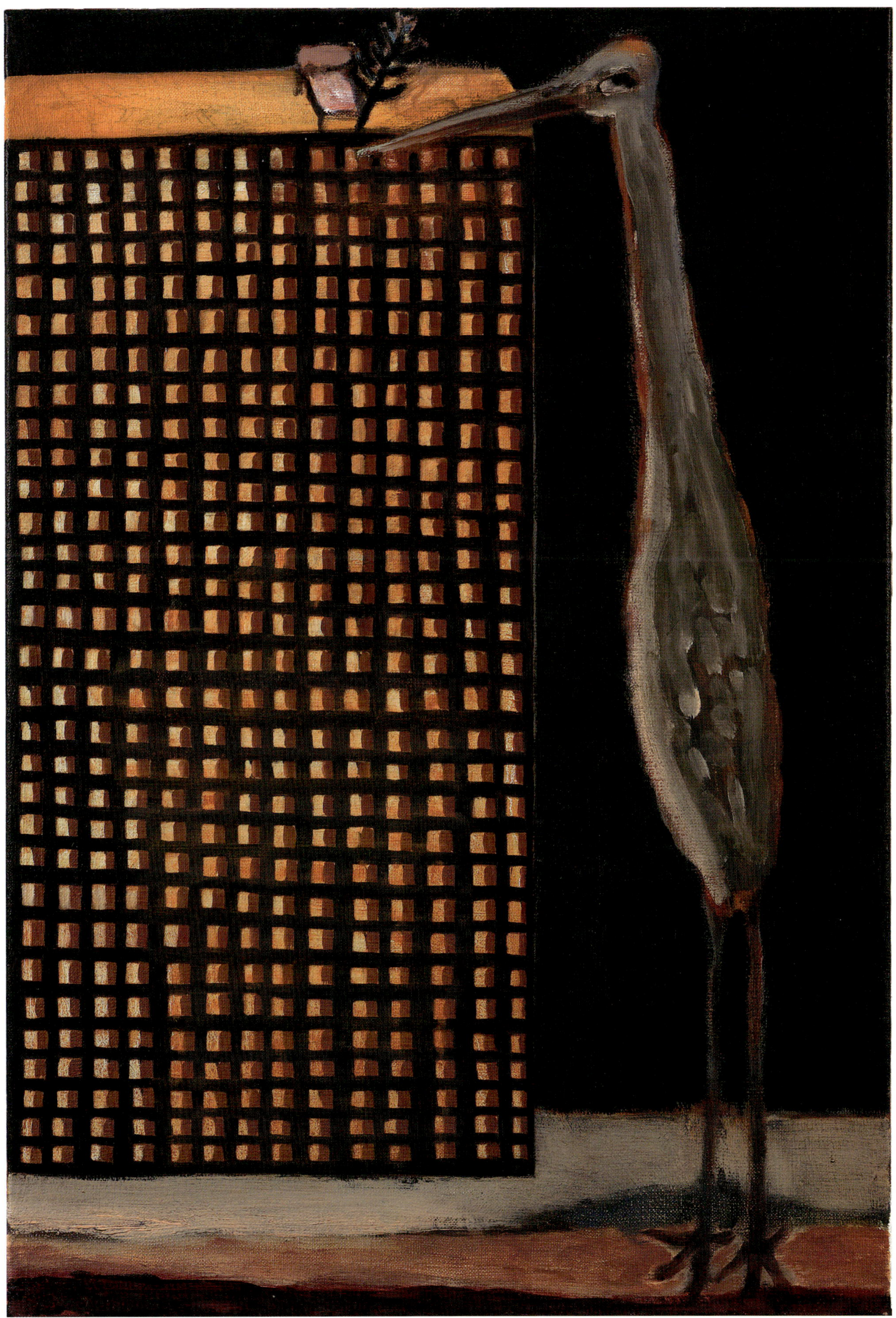

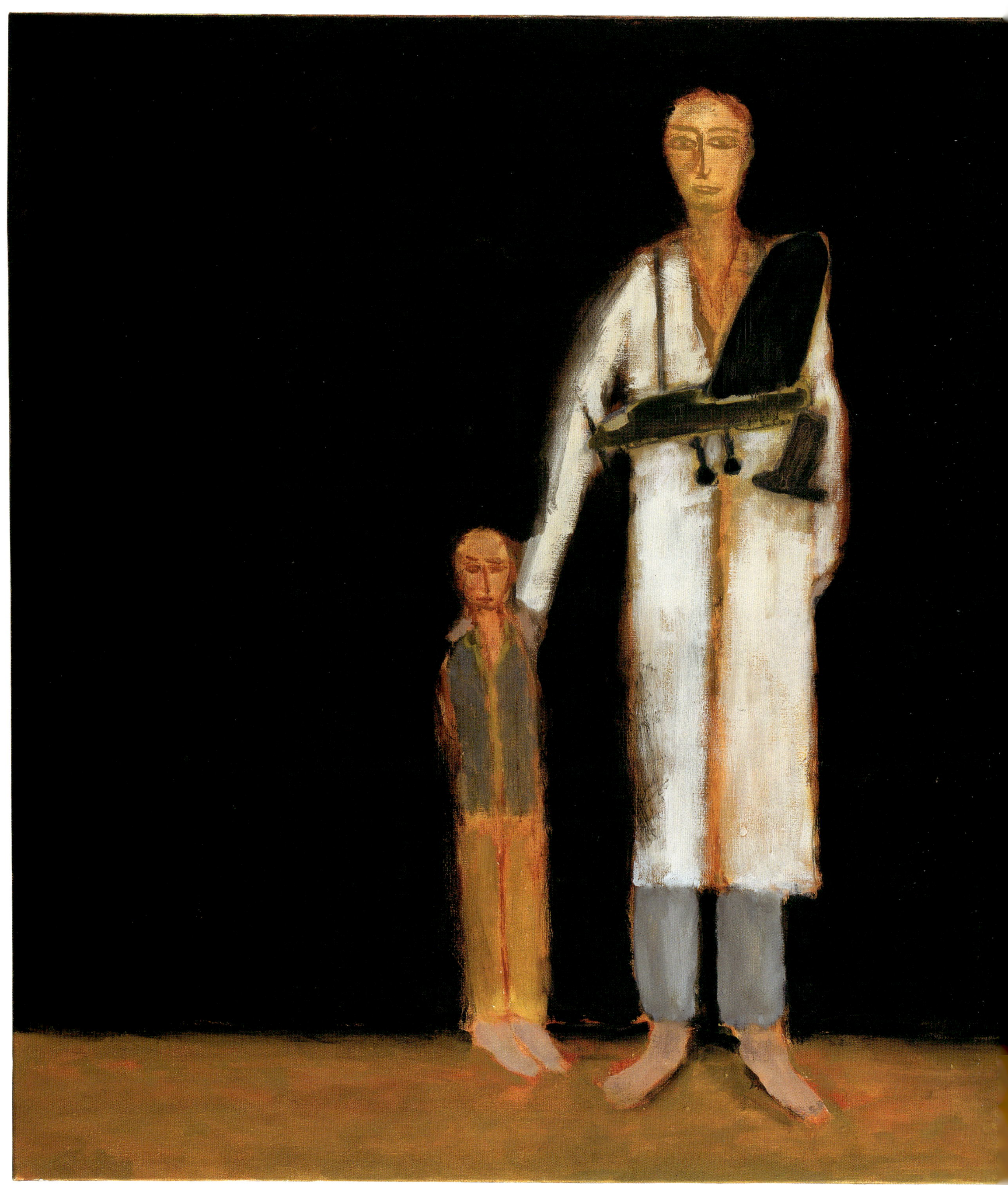

ANDRZEJ JACKOWSKI
Father and Son II
1999, oil on canvas, 152 x 183 cm
Courtesy the artist

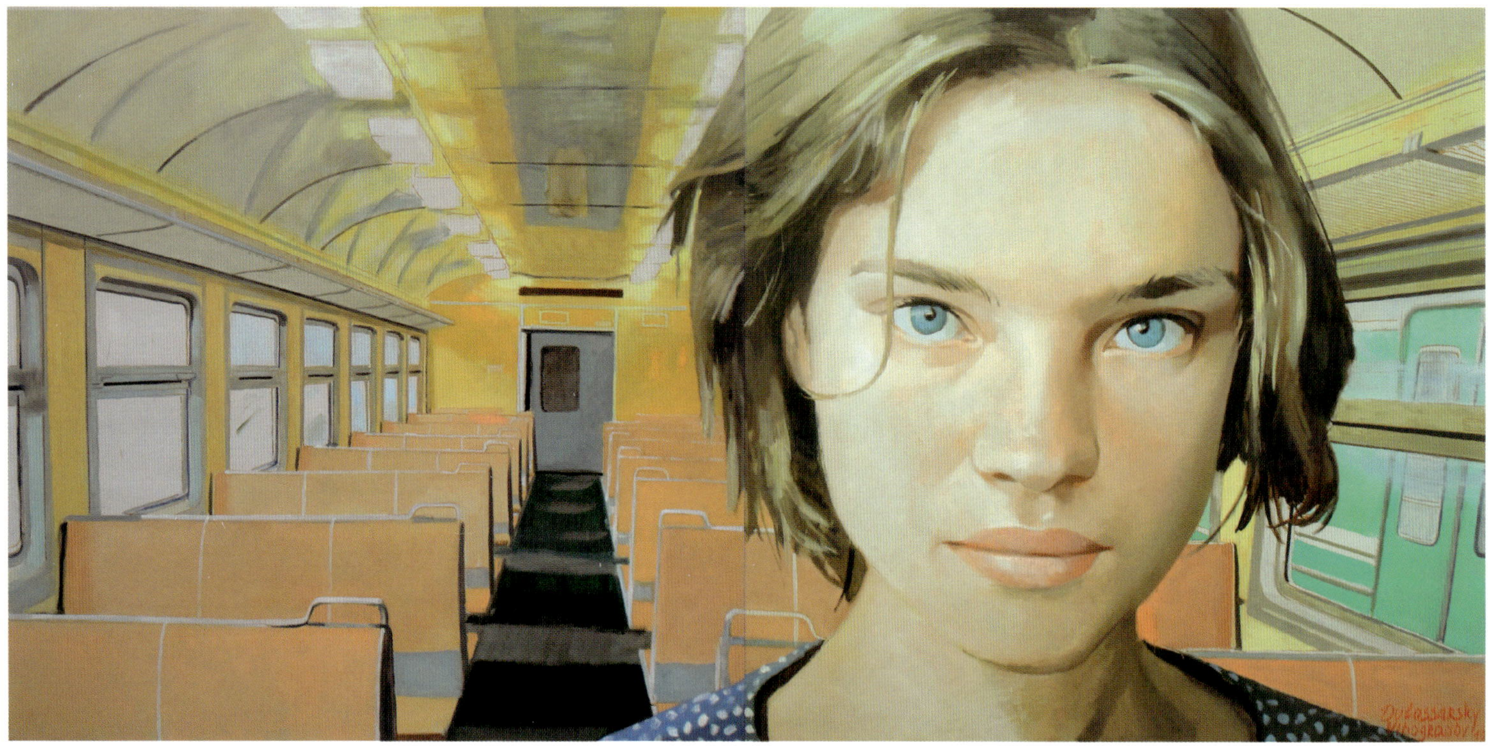

VLADIMIR DUBOSSARSKY
AND ALEKSANDER VINOGRADOV

Amongst the sprawling, absurd allegories, the explicitly sexual pastorals, and the self-conscious paeans to Hollywood icons, the collaborative paintings of Vladimir Dubossarsky and Aleksander Vinogradov clearly display a logic derived from the established traditions of Russian art history, and furthermore mobilised for a modern purpose.

Theirs is a practice shaped by the social and economic conditions that followed the dissolution of the Soviet Union in 1991. In particular, Dubossarsky and Vinogradov have engaged with the developing fabric of a society gutted of its Communist heritage, fitted with the foundations of a free market economy, and subjected to a subsequent influx of Western consumer culture. In addition to acknowledging the prospects offered by this new landscape, Dubossarsky

and Vinogradov's practice evidences a negotiation of the effects of globalisation and the influence of Western hegemony on a Russian cultural identity. The distinctive aesthetic of their paintings combines the most iconic elements of Russian art history—in particular Socialist Realism— to become sites for arrangements of mass media forms.

At the same time, Dubossarsky and Vinogradov have been influenced by the infrastructural decline and social decay that took hold during the post-Soviet era, which led to the unsustainability of past institutions and an emergent need for a legitimate and socially constructive base upon which a new system of art could proceed. In response to this challenge, and in direct contrast to the prescriptive doctrines of Western art, Dubossarsky

and Vinogradov have explicitly sought a position for their work within wider public consciousness. Their relationship to painting can therefore be understood as a calculated and strategic utilisation of the medium's popular potential, and can furthermore be reconciled with their appropriation of a Socialist Realist style and its productivist and democratic associations.

Dubossarsky and Vinogradov typically charge their paintings with a mixture of humour, irreverence and satirical wit. However, in more recent works this has given way to subjective, intimate and more sombre reflections on contemporary existence, compounding a sense that, at its root, Dubossarsky and Vinogradov's practice remains a highly reflexive one acutely sensitive to the changing state of Russian society.

Moscow—Petushki
2010, oil on canvas, 195 x 295 cm
Courtesy the artists

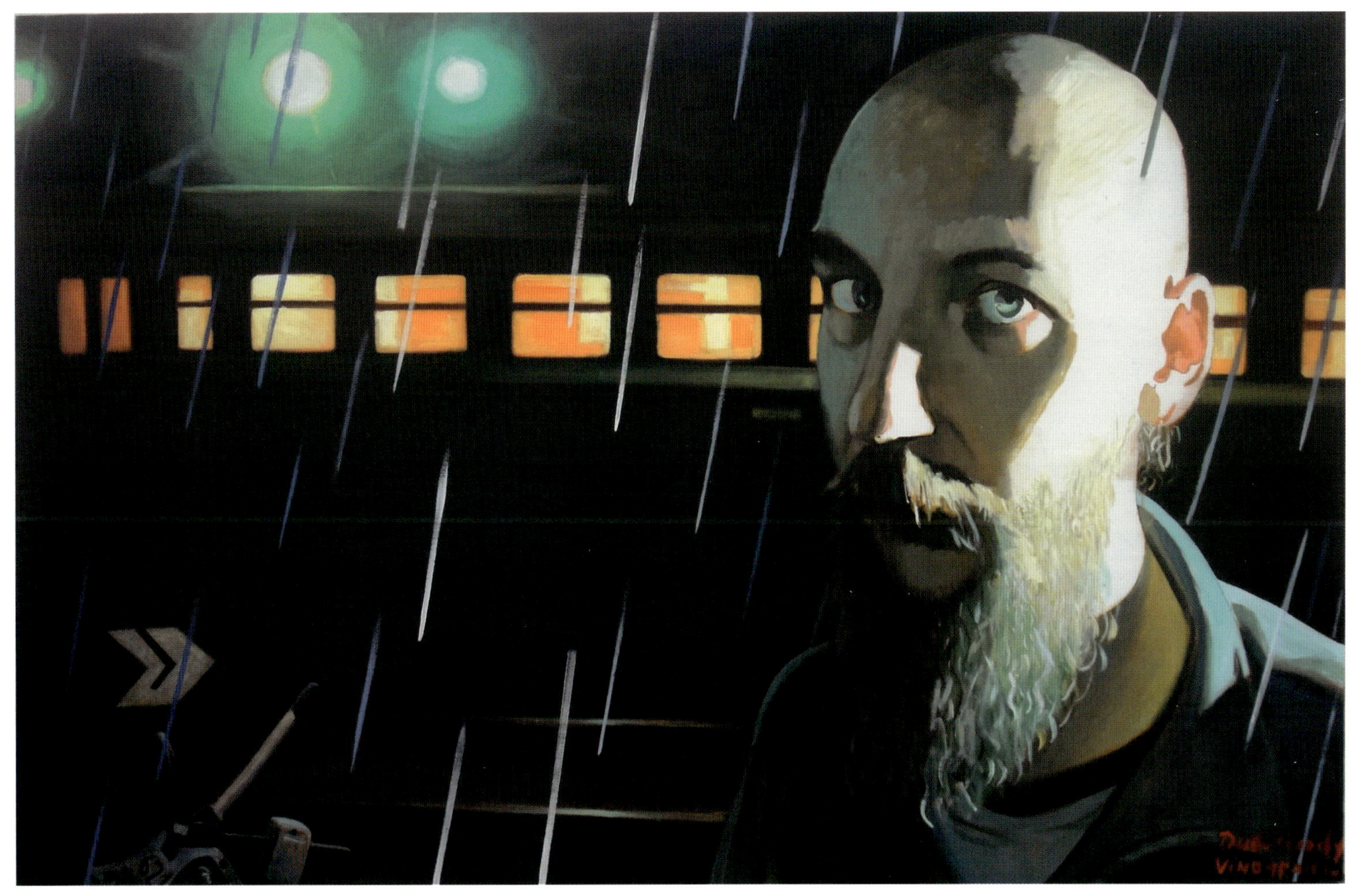

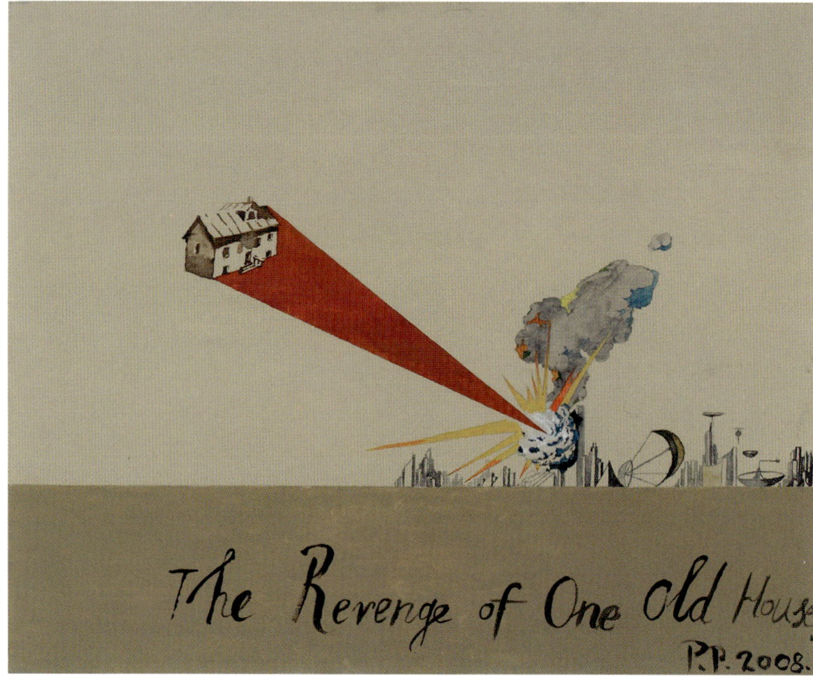

The Revenge of One Old House (right)
2008, acrylic on canvas, 50 x 60 cm
Courtesy of Sutton Lane, London/Paris

Untitled (Prince Oleg the Prophet) (opposite)
2008, acrylic on canvas, 70 x 60 cm
Courtesy of Sutton Lane, London/Paris

PAVEL PEPPERSTEIN

Commended for his unusual drawings and paintings which feature humorous annotations, Pavel Pepperstein is amongst the most influential of a new generation of Russian artists. Born in Moscow in 1966, he is also known outside the contemporary art world for his top selling novels and politically motivated rap performances. Graphic art, installation and film also make up Pepperstein's diverse range of talents, along with his interest in psychoanalytic theory. His own adaptation of Sigmund Freud's *The Interpretation of Dreams* is included in his recent projects and Freudian concepts such as free association inform his seemingly random, surreal works.

During the late 1980s—following the collapse of the Soviet empire—Pepperstein began to work collectively with other artists and authors, calling themselves Inspection Medical Hermeneutics. Since then he has mostly produced candid, sometimes child-like drawings featuring cultural and political symbolism in bizarre alternative contexts. Works akin to these made up his series *Landscapes of Future*, which was featured in the Russian Pavilion of the 2009 Venice Biennale. The series depicts Pepperstein's 'predictions' of mankind's distant future. The piece entitled *The Attack of the Old Houses*, 2008, involves supposedly passé buildings taking revenge on a futuristic city, which is seen obliterated by laser-like beams. Though seemingly off-the-wall and witty, his works often contain more serious undertones and perhaps imply the artist's despair at modern society and culture.

In Pepperstein's 2008 series *Objects above the Sea*, he probed the mystery of UFOs and the often reported sightings over the earth's waters, that perplex and create a sense of mystery. One painting illustrates a murky, yet eerily calm seascape with distant rocks and a lighthouse. An assemblage of bold, coloured shapes rocket across the cloudless sky, introducing panic and uncertainty to the landscape. The works in this series are a continuation of Pepperstein's ongoing exploration into secrecy and the unknown and challenge the viewer to decipher various puzzles, that simultaneously provoke individual interpretation.

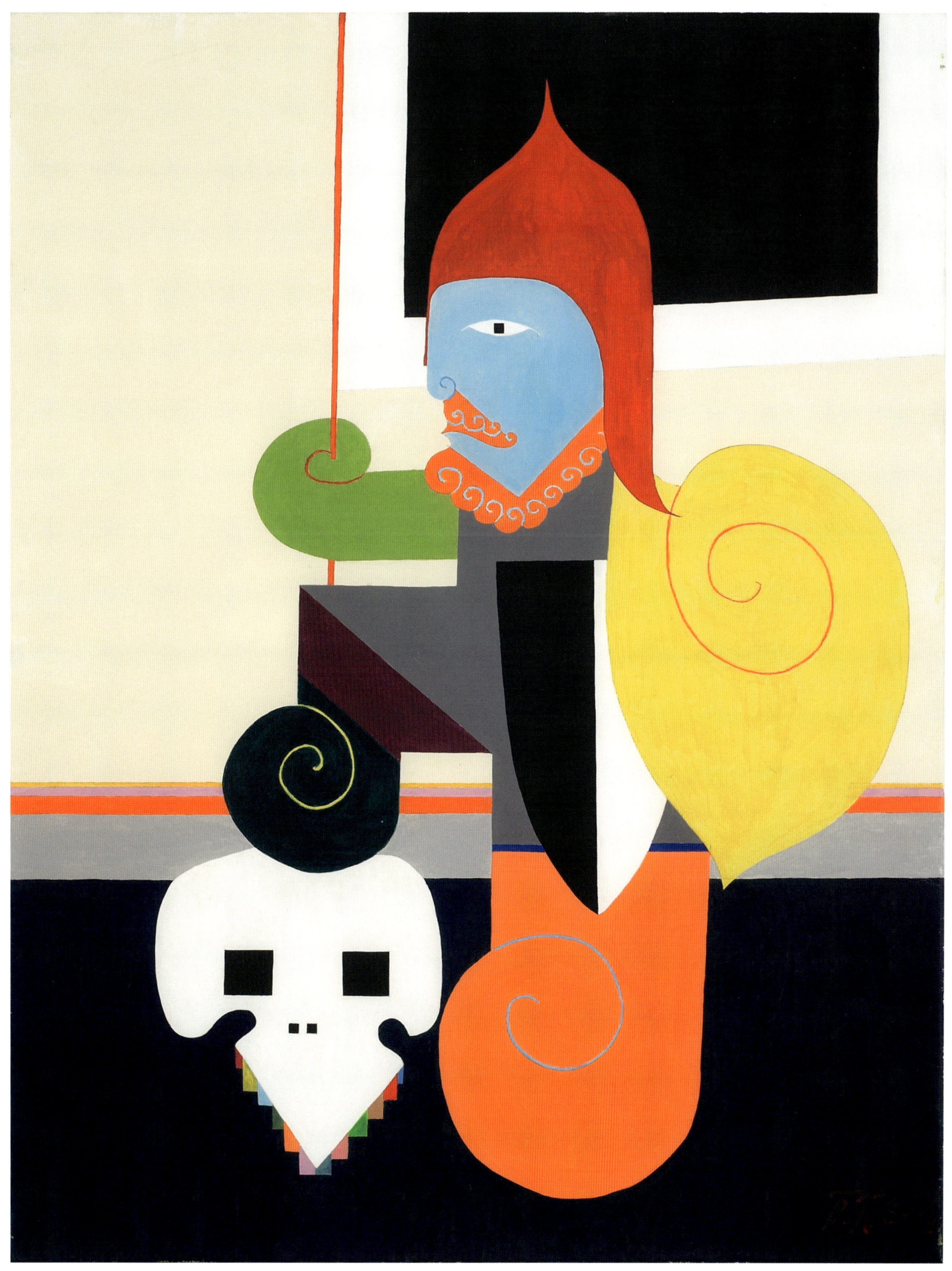

PAVEL PEPPERSTEIN
Untitled (Red Futuristic City)
2008, acrylic on canvas, 50 x 70 cm
Courtesy of Sutton Lane, London/Paris

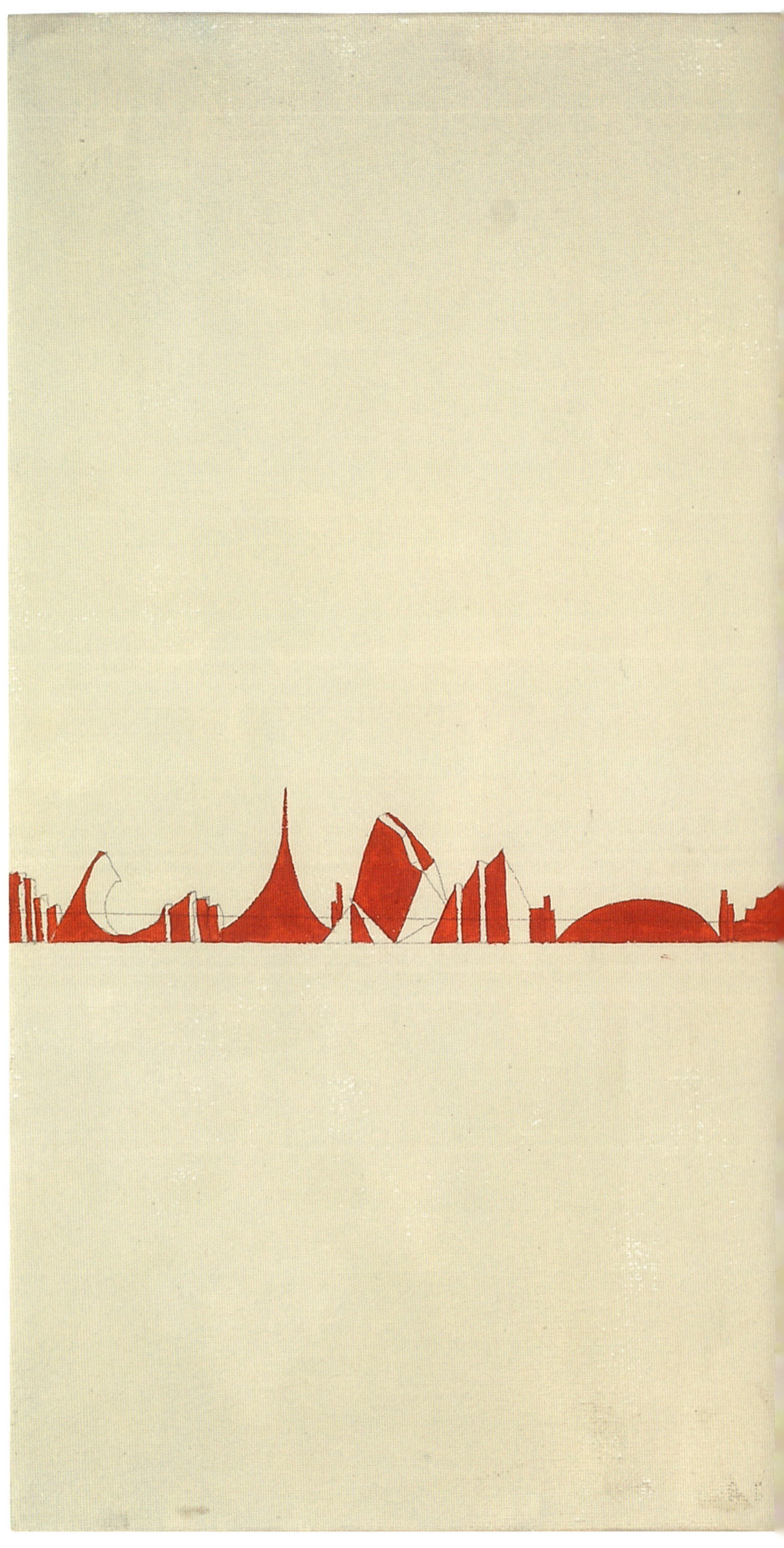

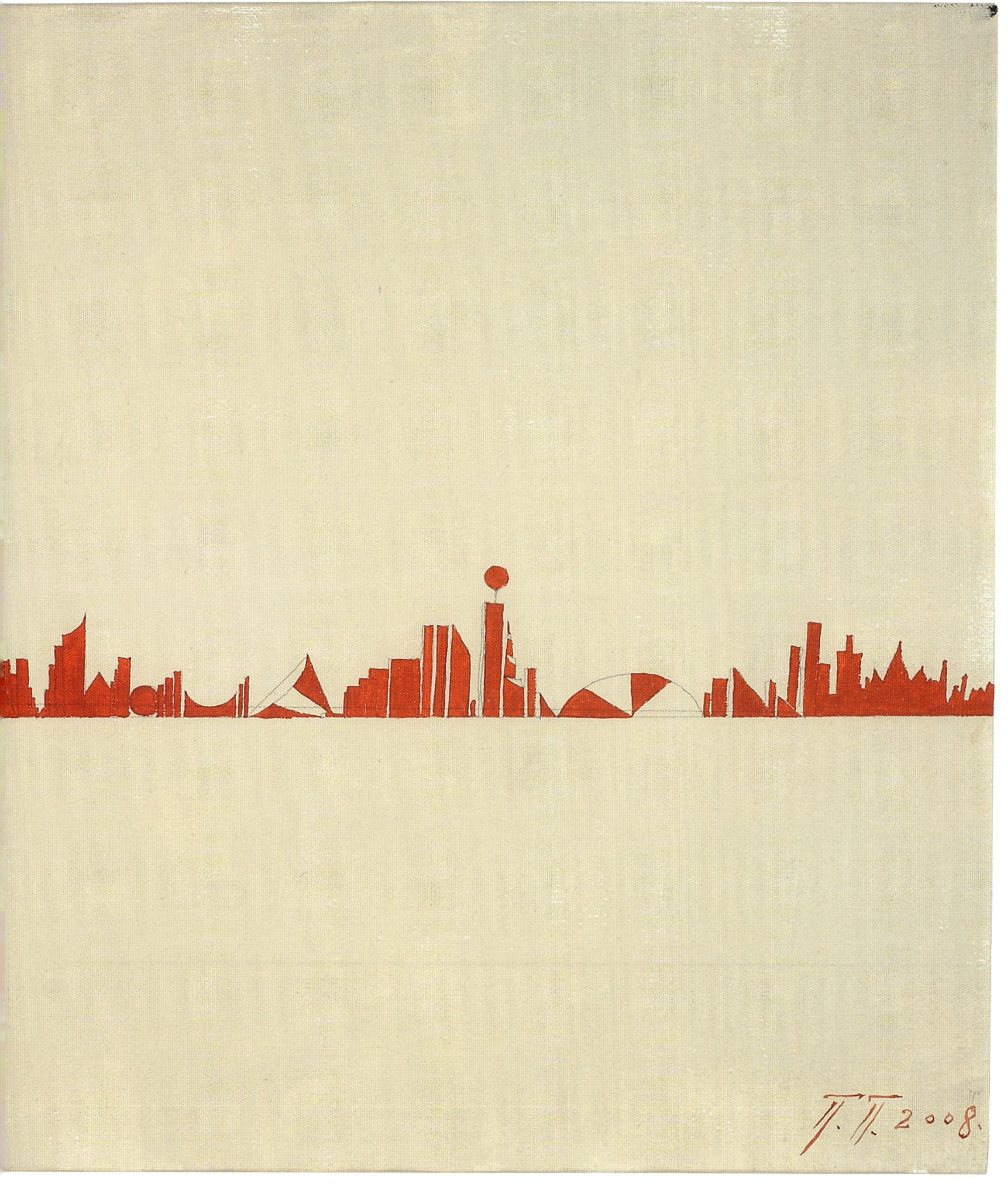

APPENDIX

AN ARTIST'S LIFE MANIFESTO
MARINA ABRAMOVIĆ

1. AN ARTIST'S CONDUCT IN HIS LIFE:
—An artist should not lie to himself
or others
—An artist should not steal ideas from
other artists
—An artist should not compromise
for themselves or in regards to the
art market
—An artist should not kill other
human beings
—An artist should not make themselves
into an idol
—An artist should not make themselves
into an idol
—An artist should not make themselves
into an idol

2. AN ARTIST'S RELATION TO HIS LOVE LIFE:
—An artist should avoid falling in love with
another artist
—An artist should avoid falling in love with
another artist
—An artist should avoid falling in love with
another artist

3. AN ARTIST'S RELATION TO THE EROTIC:
—An artist should develop an erotic point
of view on the world
—An artist should be erotic
—An artist should be erotic
—An artist should be erotic

4. AN ARTIST'S RELATION TO SUFFERING:
—An artist should suffer
—From the suffering comes the best work
—Suffering brings transformation
—Through the suffering an artist
transcends their spirit
—Through the suffering an artist
transcends their spirit
—Through the suffering an artist
transcends their spirit

5. AN ARTIST'S RELATION TO DEPRESSION:
—An artist should not be depressed
—Depression is a disease and should
be cured
—Depression is not productive for an artist
—Depression is not productive for an artist
—Depression is not productive for an artist

6. AN ARTIST'S RELATION TO SUICIDE:
—Suicide is a crime against life
—An artist should not commit suicide
—An artist should not commit suicide
—An artist should not commit suicide

7. AN ARTIST'S RELATION TO INSPIRATION:
—An artist should look deep inside
themselves for inspiration
—The deeper they look inside themselves,
the more universal they become
—The artist is universe
—The artist is universe
—The artist is universe

8. AN ARTIST'S RELATION TO SELF-CONTROL:
—The artist should not have self-control
about his life
—The artist should have total self-control
about his work
—The artist should not have self-control
about his life
—The artist should have total self-control
about his work

9. AN ARTIST'S RELATION WITH TRANSPARENCY:
—The artist should give and receive at the
same time
—Transparency means receptive
—Transparency means to give
—Transparency means to receive
—Transparency means receptive
—Transparency means to give
—Transparency means to receive
—Transparency means receptive
—Transparency means to give
—Transparency means to receive

10. AN ARTIST'S RELATION TO SYMBOLS:
—An artist creates his own symbols
—Symbols are an artist's language
—The language must then be translated
—Sometimes it is difficult to find the key
—Sometimes it is difficult to find the key
—Sometimes it is difficult to find the key

11. AN ARTIST'S RELATION TO SILENCE:
—An artist has to understand silence
—An artist has to create a space for silence
to enter his work
—Silence is like an island in the middle
of a turbulent ocean
—Silence is like an island in the middle
of a turbulent ocean
—Silence is like an island in the middle
of a turbulent ocean

12. AN ARTIST'S RELATION TO SOLITUDE:
—An artist must make time for the long
periods of solitude
—Solitude is extremely important
—Away from home
—Away from the studio
—Away from family
—Away from friends
—An artist should stay for long periods
of time at waterfalls
—An artist should stay for long periods
of time at exploding volcanoes
—An artist should stay for long periods of
time looking at the fast running rivers
—An artist should stay for long periods of
time looking at the horizon where the
ocean and sky meet
—An artist should stay for long periods of
time looking at the stars in the night sky

13. AN ARTIST'S CONDUCT IN RELATION TO WORK:

—An artist should avoid going to the
studio every day
—An artist should not treat his work
schedule as a bank employee does
—An artist should explore life and work
only when an idea comes to him in a
dream or during the day as a vision that
arises as a surprise
—An artist should not repeat himself
—An artist should not overproduce
—An artist should avoid his own
art pollution
—An artist should avoid his own
art pollution
—An artist should avoid his own
art pollution

14. AN ARTIST'S POSSESSIONS:

—Buddhist monks advise that it is best to
have nine possessions in their life:
One robe for the summer
One robe for the winter
One pair of shoes
One begging bowl for food
One mosquito net
One prayer book
One umbrella
One mat to sleep on
One pair of glasses if needed
—An artist should decide for himself the
minimum personal possessions they
should have
—An artist should have more and more
of less and less
—An artist should have more and more
of less and less
—An artist should have more and more
of less and less

15. A LIST OF AN ARTIST'S FRIENDS:

—An artist should have friends that lift
their spirits
—An artist should have friends that lift
their spirits
—An artist should have friends that lift
their spirits

16. A LIST OF AN ARTIST'S ENEMIES:

—Enemies are very important
—The Dalai Lama has said that it is easy
to have compassion with friends but
much more difficult to have compassion
with enemies
—An artist has to learn to forgive
—An artist has to learn to forgive
—An artist has to learn to forgive

17. DIFFERENT DEATH SCENARIOS:

—An artist has to be aware of his
own mortality
—For an artist, it is not only important
how he lives his life but also how he dies
—An artist should look at the symbols
of his work for the signs of different
death scenarios
—An artist should die consciously
without fear
—An artist should die consciously
without fear
—An artist should die consciously
without fear

18. DIFFERENT FUNERAL SCENARIOS:

—An artist should give instructions
before the funeral so that everything
is done the way he wants it
—The funeral is the artist's last art piece
before leaving
—The funeral is the artist's last art piece
before leaving
—The funeral is the artist's last art piece
before leaving

ENJOY ME, ABUSE ME, I AM YOUR ARTIST: CULTURAL POLITICS, THEIR MONUMENTS, THEIR RUINS
EDA CUFER

First published in *East Art Map: Contemporary Art in Eastern Europe*, London: *Afterall*, 2006.
Courtesy Eda Cufer

Every force evolves a form, he thought. Sea and wind had shaped the ship. Shape answers use. And then use modifies the shape. Gulls flew just behind the aft deck, crying 'Tatlin! Tatlin!'
—Guy Davenport, *Tatlin!*

DISPOSITION

If Communism stood behind the narrative of the twentieth century, behind the narrative of the twenty-first century stands its ruin. How, then, should we attempt a new reading of the history of the twentieth century? How will a new politics be articulated—not only on the axes of East and West but also of North and South? How, in the rotation of perspectives, will the perspective of the post-Communist East be included?

Throughout modernity the West and East have been linked.[1] Linked not only through the imaginary of revolution and the historical avant-gardes, but also through a largely unacknowledged and intricate set of co-dependencies and compensations. What happened to one affected the other, not always in the sense of a diagrammable dialectic, but often in terms of a sublimated desire or accelerated dysfunction. For the East, the experience of Communism was an experience grounded in reality. It was not an intellectual exercise or ideological flirtation, but a real engagement with a system that promised to solve the major conflicts and controversies of modern society. On the other hand there is no denying that the East's experiment appeared glamorous to the West. Its external appearance functioned as a mirror in which the West perfected its own image and admired itself as a 'work in progress', where for the best part of a century the solutions and responses relating to the enigma of modernity could be constructed, modelled, rehearsed and

judged. The East, meanwhile, saw its image reflected nowhere outside of the borders of its own social experiment. As Andrei Codrescu has observed, the year 1989 did not bring about the immediate inner transformation of either the historical or the psychological profile of the East formed during the Communist era.[2] What did change was the West's access to this imaginary Communist East. The removal of the "wall of shame", as Bruno Latour has referred to the Berlin Wall, made it possible for this territory to be inundated by a river of goods.[3] Beginning in 1989, the integrated universal world economy, which had developed during the Cold War period, underwent an expansion of explosive proportions and began operating transnationally across state borders previously resistant to Western market influences.[4] It took less than 15 years for the operating conditions and principles of this new stage of globalisation, this new world order, to be established. During this time, the Western model of liberal Capitalism assumed a new reproductive logic, warping the concepts and values of the former territorial West into a spider's web of economic transterritoriality. The West of Cold War times became as much a historical phantom as the former Communist East.

The idea of a de-territorialised West, which, like an empire, is re-territorialising itself within the global framework is a frequent motif of contemporary critical discourse. Globalisation, nationalism and ethnocentrism are not mutually exclusive concepts. Each of them is capable of suppressing class conflict, the prevailing motif of the previous century, in the name of some fictive pre-postmodern unity—global, national or ethnic.[5] The collapse of former multinational states into national and ethnic communities and the regression of already secularised

communities into networks of religious fundamentalism are among the means by which the new 'empire' can reorganise its resources. Many have been forced to take a step backwards in order to achieve a promised leap forwards, as globalisation, the ultimate 'dispositive of power' shapes the new century.[6] Even as attempts to control globalisation seem to come from all possible directions, globalisation operates as a blind force, unpredictable and beyond regulatory order. Regardless of geography or stance, the question that must be addressed is how to use this force—how to 'reorient' it towards some constructive goal, how to turn its abstract universalism, even its transcendentalism, towards particular problems—thereby grounding it in concrete positions, concrete struggles. "Reorientation", Susan Buck-Morss suggests, is the name for "revolution" in the twenty-first century.[7]

As part of the integrated universal world economy, the neo-liberal art system also evolved during the Cold War period into one of the key functional systems of the dispositive of power in Western democracies. This art system, while imperfect, nevertheless became the only one that could provide material and logistical support for the formation of a global culture—the critical culture that accompanies economic and political 'development'. This is not a culture that reveals the virtues or praises the unity of the global order; rather, it points to the differences, inequalities and internal conflicts that arise as a result of economic and technological development and the politics of the powerful. A discourse that would enable a truly constructive response to the controversies surrounding neo-liberal global Capitalism and its art system is still in the process of formation. The existing critical methodologies are no longer sufficient to address, or capable of articulating, the complexities of emerging relations within the new cultural realms and political stratifications—between the dissolving, restructuring centre and the growing number of active, expansive peripheries. As non-Western cultural spaces and subjectivities are assimilated under the wing of systems—economic, technological, cultural—that clearly speak in the idiom of Western hegemony, the need for a tactics of 'reorientation', articulating new languages and positions that challenge the syntax of the dominant idiom becomes acute. Tactics, in other words, that probe the new conditions from thoughtful angles and pose questions derived from constructive intellectual formulations rather than defensive postures. It is important to acknowledge that after all, non-Westerners are not the only ones who have been experiencing post-1989 shocks and transition traumas. The neo-liberal art system, formed within the parameters of the intellectual and political climate of the Cold War, was once a transparent concept, judging itself according to the complacent and self-satisfied premise that art was somehow equated with individual freedom, that it was an 'autonomous zone' where the wounds and pleasures of alienation could be mediated into enlightened forms of modern subjectivity. As long as art was the highly desired product and exclusive property of Western culture, it could be viewed as a necessity, even if the primary function it performed was ensuring the survival of one's own system of belief. But when different notions of art started getting through the Western filters, forcing a critical re-examination of the legitimacy of long held convictions and institutionalised narratives, when the stories coming in from the tributaries started shifting the whole direction and flow of art thinking, this proved frustrating for individuals shaped by laboratory cultural experiences. Many influential intellectual and artistic

circles in the West still defend the principles of Modernism and the Western avant-gardes established during the Cold War without ever having systematically analysed the actual historical conditions under which the dominant art paradigm was produced and practiced in the last century. When nostalgic, academic leftism is applied to the realms of new political and cultural stratifications, the results are no less regressive and pathetic than defensive nationalism or ethnocentrism.

In order to set out a concrete position—one that will itself be in need of reorientation— let us attempt to examine the reasons behind the absence of a synthesised historical narrative about the development of the content, forms and contexts of the cultural and artistic production that took place under Communism in Eastern Europe and the Soviet Union between 1930 and 1989, that is, from the rise of Stalinism in the Soviet Union to the fall of the Berlin Wall. The persisting cultural amnesia of the East with regard to the period of Communism points both to the powerlessness of post-Communist countries to democratise themselves through their own historical, intellectual and creative resources, as well as to the exclusive and ideological character of the historical narrative and discourses of the Western conception of Modernism and avant-garde movements—discourses that evolved for the most part in the second half of the twentieth century, parallel with the formation of the neo-liberal art system.

SITUATION: WEST
Peter Bürger, in *Theory of the Avant-Garde*, makes a crucial distinction between Modernism and the avant-garde movements. He points to a fundamental difference in their respective strategies for negating the basic operative principles of bourgeois society, that is to say, the dominant forms of reception that came about as a consequence of the development of the cultural industry

and the commercialisation of culture.[8] While Modernism may be understood in this process as a strategy of deviation from linguistic norms and *clichés*, as an assault on traditional techniques of writing and painting and a subversion of linguistic norms and structures, avant-garde strategies are something altogether different. They can be understood only as a total assault on the social order, having as their goal the complete transformation of the spaces of organisation. This would include the institutionalised art market and the conditions under which art is produced and distributed in modern industrial society. Whereas Modernism can be understood to have developed within the framework of liberalism, the avant-garde movements operated on the basis of a utopian political imaginary. In their concrete socio-political interventions, they even flirted quite openly with totalitarian political options. The legitimising discourses that functionalised Modernism and avant-gardism as the dominant models of Western culture during the time of post-war democratic Capitalism developed primarily in the 1930s and 1940s, when it was still not clear what the outcome would be in the three-way struggle for political hegemony between National Socialism/Fascism, Communism and Liberal Capitalism. For the first half of the twentieth century, let us remember, there was no retrospective certainty that Communism or Fascism would not prevail. It was precisely the debate between ideologies and value systems during a time when all possibilities were still on the table that made American critical culture matter.

In *How New York Stole the Idea of Modern Art*, Serge Guilbaut provides a detailed analysis of the origin of the discursive formation that was generated within American intellectual and artistic circles in the 1930s and 1940s, parallel with the rise and fall of National Socialism in Germany and Fascism in Italy and the ascendancy of Stalinism in the Soviet Union.[9] Guilbaut's research, which focuses primarily on the critical debates aired in specialised literary and art journals, rescues a short but essential episode in the mythology of modern art. By reminding us of the political, cultural and economic debates that gave shape to and defined the operation of the intellectual public sphere at precisely the time that America's political and economic Cold War doctrine was being constructed, he reveals how the discourses, institutions and professional networks that defined the criteria of art made art such a powerful tool in the post-war political climate of the West.

According to Buck-Morss, the Bolshevik revolution of 1917 presented, from the very beginning, an absolute threat to the Western political imaginary.[10] Operating transterritorially, through the imagination, it inflamed ideas that rang out as a summons to individuals and masses across the entire world. While the West could at any moment prevent the expansion of the Bolshevik army, it could not prevent the expansion of Bolshevism itself, or rather, of all those heterogeneous ideas that sought their meaning in the concept of the October Revolution. This concept not only activated various social classes and segments of the intelligentsia—scientific, artistic, and philosophical—it also operated as a generator of the content and forms of the twentieth century. For that class which held control over politics and economic resources in the West, the primary question of course was how to prevent the virus of revolution from developing enough critical mass to demand change and a redefinition of the principles of property, as had happened in Russia.

The international distribution of twentieth century Western scientific, political and

cultural potential gave rise to the imaginary of the 'internal enemy', an enemy which characterised the homogenising strategy of all three of the dominant ideologies of the last century. The Nazis saw their greatest internal enemy as the Jews; the Communists identified the enemy in bourgeois and anti-Communist 'elements'; while the capitalists saw their internal enemy in the Communist 'elements' operating in their territories. Conservative political and cultural circles in America, as in Nazi Germany, perceived in modern art the virus of Communism. For the actual Communists, however, modern art was the product of the cultural decadence of the Western bourgeoisie.

As Nazism and Stalinism were consolidating their power in Europe in the 1930s, America was trying to recover from the stock market disaster of 1929—it is no coincidence that the Museum of Modern Art (MoMA) was founded in the same year that Wall Street trembled. In the years that followed, there existed in America a massive proletariat movement and a search for the cultural expressions and art forms to legitimise Marxist values. As improbable as it seems today, Communism was at that time still vying to become the 'Americanism' of the twentieth century. Writers, actors and painters played significant roles in the workers' movement guided by the Popular Front and engaged in critical debates about how to integrate social commentary and leftist content into modern literature and painting. In the American debates of the 1930s, the left sharply condemned the attempts of right-wing groups to develop an American national literature and painting. But the unity of the American left was threatened when the conflict between Trotsky and Stalin forced sympathisers to choose sides. While the American Communist Party continued to support Stalinist Russia, most American intellectuals, after hearing reports about

the Moscow Trials of 1936, tended to follow a Trotskyist line. There began to be public debates about how literature and painting could preserve their revolutionary character without, at the same time, having to renounce the achievements and experimental nature of Modernism. The cultural press was full of articles attacking vulgar, mechanical Marxism and the cultural policy of Stalinism, while the crucial debate over modern abstract art continued within the context of Trotskyism. In contrast to MoMA founder and first director Alfred H Barr Jr, who saw abstract art as divorced from social reality and grounded in its own internal formal rules, the influential Marxist art historian Meyer Schapiro asserted that every form of art, even the most abstract, was grounded in social reality and in the conditions under which it was produced. Although Schapiro was critical of abstract artists for living with the illusion of independence from social reality, he nevertheless opened up new possibilities for an interpretation of abstract art by imbuing it with an even loftier meaning than the formalists themselves had given it.

From the second half of the 1930s up to America's intervention in The Second World War at the beginning of the 1940s, there was, according to Guilbaut, a massive turning away from realistic and propagandist painting—on the part of artists on both the left and the right—in favour of Modernist and abstract formal investigation. From 1939 onwards, one can detect in the magazines of the American intelligentsia the crystallisation of new interpretations and discourses that evidenced the de-Marxification and de-politicisation of the anti-Stalinist left. From today's perspective, we know that Clement Greenberg's 1939 essay "Avant-Garde and Kitsch" had a momentous influence on the understanding and development of modern art in the second half of the twentieth century.[11] But in its own time, it was just as important for what it did to ideologically sharpen the terms and stakes of the then prevailing cultural wars. Greenberg managed to reactivate an old opposition, namely, the opposition between the avant-garde and Modernism as a dynamic and vital process on the one hand and a static, mechanically reproduced academicism, or kitsch, on the other—the language of mass culture. Greenberg observed that the masses were more or less uninterested in the development of a dynamic culture:

> Such culture is being abandoned by those to whom it actually belongs— our ruling class. For it is to the latter that the avant-garde belongs. No culture can develop without a social basis, without a source of stable income. And in the case of the avant-garde, this was provided by an elite among the ruling class of that society from which it assumed itself to be cut off, but to which it has always remained attached by an umbilical cord of gold. The paradox is real.[12]

Thus, Greenberg shifted the debate from general political and cultural discourse to the discourse of cultural politics. By identifying the ideological split that lay at the very heart of the concept of culture in industrial society, he neutralised the significance of the political polarisation between right and left. Taking a stance against mass culture and for elite culture in a way that was itself ideological, he eliminated the solutions proposed by the cultural policies of actual Communism and Nazism—which in 1939, when the essay was written, had just entered into a brief alliance with each other under the terms of a pact signed between Hitler and Stalin.

Greenberg wrote:

> Where today a political regime establishes an official cultural policy, it is for the sake of demagogy. If kitsch is the official tendency of culture in Germany, Italy and Russia, it is not because their respective governments are controlled by philistines, but because kitsch is the culture of the masses in these countries, as it is everywhere else.[13]

The linking of kitsch with totalitarian power was compelling for many in the West who still believed in the project of the left. The negation of mass culture on an artistic level, through a formal language, became a new weapon—a means by which the artist, with his exclusive and elite expressive capacities, could fight against degraded political structures.

So what began in the second half of the 1930s as a process of de-Marxifying the American intelligentsia became an ideology of total de-politicisation after The Second World War. By that time, two clear alternatives had emerged: Truman's America was one choice; Stalin's Soviet Union was the other. This impossible choice caused many Leftist intellectuals to withdraw from public debate altogether, while others were motivated to search for a new political doctrine. This doctrine would eventually constitute itself as liberalism, but it was first insinuated in such acts as America's intervention into the war in Europe and in such books as Wendell Wilkie's meaningfully titled *One World*, a popular seller which advocated the policy America was to follow—turning quietly away from isolationism to adopt an almost utopian internationalism.[14]

Ultimately, it was a peculiarly American form of art that became America's most effective foreign policy tool. Enthroned by Clement Greenberg and the new American formalist critics in the 1940s as the updated, American version of the European modern art tradition, there developed around this style an extensive array of interests, coming not only from the art market but also from American foreign policy-makers. Despite the conviction of some of its representatives that it would be "disastrous to name ourselves", the movement took on a name, and it was one that would stick.[15] Indeed, the phrase "abstract expressionism" used to be heard as much in the chambers of Cold War planners as the classrooms of art historians.

Four decades later, the art world was dismayed by what had once been common knowledge among policy experts, when articles by Max Kozloff, Eva Cockcroft and others postulated a political alliance between Abstract Expressionism and the American neo-liberal political doctrine of the Cold War.[16] These stories suggested links between private corporate capital, MoMA and representatives of the Central Intelligence Agency who, bypassing official democratic procedures and congressional authorisation, had apparently devised strategies for the large-scale exportation of American culture to Europe and throughout the world—initially, Abstract Expressionism, then later, examples of all the new, radical and avant-garde cultural trends of the 1950s and 1960s. The connection between American Cold War rhetoric and the manner in which Abstract Expressionist artists set out their existential and individualistic credo was developed by the movement's most influential members, who, according to Cockcroft, controlled museum policies and advocated an enlightened Cold War tactic tailored to the taste of European intellectuals. In Guilbaut's assessment, by 1949 traditional democratic liberalism was already a thing of the past. In its place, a hard-boiled anti-Communism began to permeate the American political spectrum.

Left-leaning editors of magazines and journals, as well as like-minded others in a position to shape public opinion, were quietly removed from influential positions. The neo-liberal ideology—whose manifesto was presented in Arthur Schlesinger's book *The Vital Center*—found no difficulty in adopting an American approach to avant-garde logic, which, after all, propagated the values of individual risk-taking and unrestrained, indomitable energy.[17] As an essential factor in achieving individual freedom, risk-taking was precisely what totalitarian regimes were supposedly trying to nip in the bud. In Schlesinger's ideological reformulation, a victorious liberalism stood behind an unconditional anti-Communism, and established itself as the dominant voice of American politics precisely through the way it instrumentalised the ideal of individual freedom.[18]

This fact—that America's Cold War cultural policies were initially established as a project of the cultural and professional elite, operating outside of the state's official decision-making process and its democratically elected bodies—should not be forgotten. Not only can America's first Cold War cultural practices be read as the early draft of what later became explicit government practice, but lines can be drawn between these times and those. At the end of the 1940s and in the first half of the 1950s, a multitude of cultural connections were being established between America, 'both Europes', and the rest of the world—in the form of art exhibitions, dance tours, film screenings and theatre projects—which met with an ever more positive response abroad. This enthusiasm served to confirm the success of the unofficial cultural policy. It was not only Abstract Expressionism that proved itself an effective cultural signalling device, but radical forms of music, dance and other productions. Finally, in 1954,

President Dwight D Eisenhower decided to legitimise the policy by asking Congress to fund the President's Emergency Fund for International Affairs.[19]

The system for deciding who would represent America abroad adhered to a principle of absolute transparency. The task was entrusted to the American National Theater and Academy (ANTA), which created expert committees made up of informed, progressive critics and intellectuals. Without any interference from politicians, they decided what examples of American culture should be exported, and that meant finding the newest, most radical and experimental artists. Not only the New York City Ballet, not only John Cage, but also Merce Cunningham, the entire generation of Judson Memorial Church artists, minimalists, conceptualists, etc., were all sent abroad as part of America's Cold War art front. The ANTA system eventually evolved into the National Endowment for the Arts, NEA. Established in 1965, the NEA still remains the official funding branch of the United States government for financing American culture.

SITUATION: EAST

While we might criticise the narrative and theory of Western art history as being a unique construct of Cold War cultural policy, that construct could not operate as it did unless it mobilised within the framework of its co-ordinates actual critical, intellectual and creative forms of enjoyment, forms which described and shaped the experience and horizons of the twentieth century.

Critical theory is an integral part of the Western art system. This system is preserved and revitalised through its own criticism. However, modern art and intellectual production in the East during the time of Communism was

neither enjoyed nor abused. That Eastern Europeans had been deprived of the legitimate enjoyment of being modern was a consequence of the inability of the Communist cultural politic to invent a functional use for modern and avant-garde art and culture within the context of its own social political experiment. What attempted to compensate for the usurpation and eradication of modern art was a genuine cultural-political construct that could function only by mobilising repression.

During the Cold War race, the Eastern states could successfully compete with the West in scientific and technical disciplines, where success was measured by instruments, and quality was not reducible to the execution of interpretation. One only has to look at the superior space technology, superb physical culture and sports champions, advanced medicine, well-developed health, energy and educational systems, and other examples of technological and scientific prowess to be reminded of the legendary accomplishments made by Eastern Bloc countries in these realms during the Cold War. In the realm of philosophy, theory and arts, it is another story altogether. Here the institutions and production systems of the East did not recognise genius or skill produced within the East's own political borders. This phenomenon is both a cause and an effect of the brain drain of Eastern humanistic intelligentsia to the West; this fact has been well-documented and acknowledged, but what is far less understood, less tangible, and more damaging was a parallel phenomenon. I am referring to the inner brain drain by which creative expression was prevented and critical articulation discouraged on the part of those who stayed.

The German sociologist Claus Offe has analysed "scientific Socialism" as the official political theory of the socialist countries—a system of interpretation explaining why and how things should be understood, measured and valued in Communist society—the purpose of which was to translate Marxist philosophy into real social practice by inventing the language and ideological formulae that could be spoken and repeated with equal fluency by workers in the factory, teachers in the classroom, journalists in the newspaper, writers in books, painters on canvas, and sociologists or philosophers developing ideas for the scientific institutions for whom they worked.[20] This theory, concludes Offe, was founded on the immense pathos of a system planning its own structures and transformations, as well as on the need for maintaining all social life within the framework of an imaginary entity that would be entirely subject to control. The use of language, the proscribed interpretation of reality, was one of the most powerful means of exercising this control—a control which took place directly through the psyches of the people by telling them what to believe and how to speak—and not to speak what they believed. Paradoxically, however, or rather as a logical consequence, Offe observes, Socialism did not, as a rule, develop reliable methods for controlling what was actually happening in society. In contrast to Socialism, the liberal democracies developed effective control techniques through their support of research and analysis even in the most distant corners and crevices. The socialist regimes were not even able to develop a rational estimation of their capital resources and thus could not calculate their production efficiency. Mainly, however, the socialist regimes did not cultivate the artistic, scientific and political criticality that would have allowed them to articulate and reflect how society was being perceived by its own members.

The validation and interpretation of reality during the time of Communism is the ultimate political complexity of the Eastern post-Communist societies. To look at this issue is to consider how state institutions functioned before and after Communism, what these institutions produced, whom they served, and to what extent the institutions and social bodies of the socialist modern states resemble those of modern democratic states. Indeed, the East has museums, universities, institutes, and academies that, like its Western counterparts, produce history, statistics, theory and other discourses. The question is not one of productivity, but credibility: to what extent can we trust and believe in the narratives they produced? If for Western individuals these institutions represent some kind of prosthetic bodies through which they can extend and fully realise their creative, political or scientific visions and potentials, if for them the institutions are supposed to function as bridges through which individual values become collectivised, and if the history of the institution presents a kind of sum of individual efforts, then for the Easterners, institutions still represent a zone of fear, a source of punishment and frustration, a place where original, subjective inputs get somehow deformed, damned, perverted. Easterners deeply mistrust if not hate their public institutions because those institutions conditioned them to be submissive. On the other hand, paradoxically, it is exactly this hatred that reproduces submissiveness. Constructive critique cannot be born from hatred of the object of criticism, only from the desire to constructively modify it. Although the Communist Party was removed from its central position in the Eastern European countries quite some time ago, and the language of 'scientific Socialism' supposedly survives only in comic strip underground cultures, the dysfunctional, neurotic institutional culture of the East is not so easy to eradicate— its survival perpetuated largely by the memory of fear it instilled. One still finds it wherever one finds bureaucratic systems or authoritarian models discouraging ideas, pleasure or trust—and this can be in museums and academies as easily as in hotels or banks. For this reason, Eastern Europe becomes not only a passive receiver of neo-liberal economic plans and scenarios but also a submissive recipient of Western theory and other contemporary narratives of diverse value, which warrant more differentiation and selection than they receive. Eastern intellectuals and academics cannot help but feel powerful when asked to reproduce some original discourse from Western theory and cultural history, especially when compared to the dysfunctionality and vulnerability they feel when asked to repeat the neurotic formations and unreflected stories that pass as the 'official' Cold War versions of culture in Eastern Europe. The fact is that neither discursive formation is entirely appropriate, and a third narrative still needs to be found—this is the crack in the discursive facade of the East that needs to be explored, not necessarily for gold, but for a moral force that the East needs to regain as its own.

For all the reasons Cold War cultural policy of the East cannot be as clearly reconstructed as that of the West, we will nonetheless attempt to extract some meaning from the East's cultural amnesia and discursive neurosis with respect to its own history from the rise of Stalinism to the fall of Communism—1930–1989.

In the ecstatic, transitional years immediately following the 1917 Revolution in Russia, as in the heady, hopeful years of New Deal America, a struggle for cultural identity unfolded as various cultural groups and artistic movements vied with each other to provide the best interpretation and embodiment of what was supposed to be the sublime ideal of modern revolutionary culture. As Buck-

Morss has written, there was massive support for the events of October 1917, but this support was not of one mind.[21] Utopian dreamers of all types were eager to interpret the revolutionary future as the one they envisaged. Alongside the various avant-garde circles there was also, for example, the Association of Artists of Revolutionary Russia, an umbrella organisation of easel painters founded in 1922 as a reaction to the avant-garde attack on representational art. Proletarian cultural organisations, which in 1917 were centralised in Proletkult, were financed at the local and factory levels in conjunction with workers' organisations. Funding decisions in Proletkult were made independently of the state and the party. Anatoly Lunacharsky, who was responsible for cultural affairs at the party level, focused his cultural policy on the importance of political engagement rather than on any one dominant artistic style. He supported all kinds of artists' groups and encouraged them to compete with each other in demonstrating revolutionary authenticity. While the Russian avant-garde had existed as an art movement before the Revolution, it was only after 1917 that it received official recognition and financial support. The coexistence, even codependence of the Russian avant-garde with more traditional modern and academic groups reveals the complexity of Soviet cultural history before the advent of Stalinism, which Boris Groys has analysed in his book *Gesamtkunstwerk Stalin*.[22] By connecting the birth of Stalinist culture to the spirit of the avant-garde, Groys exposes a deep controversy between art and society in the age of modernity.

As already mentioned, this is the paradox that also occupies Peter Bürger. In his formulation, the avant-garde movements differed from modernism by calling for a total change in the social conditions in which art is produced, not just a revolution in the

understanding of the formal principles of the artwork. It was the avant-garde movements that took the greatest risk in erasing the distinctions between the political and cultural definition of revolution. If we examine avant-garde theories, praxis, and manifestoes carefully, says Groys, we cannot deny the fact that a connection was made between, on the one hand, the artistic will for controlling and organising material in accordance with the artist's own principles, and, on the other, the political will for power. The fact that Western art history has acknowledged avant-garde artists to the point that museums gladly accept their work is, Groys asserts, not a victory for the artist but rather a form of reparation from the victorious democratic state. In this sense, Groys provocatively concludes, the art of Socialist Realism, and Nazi art as well, achieved a position that the avant-garde had sought from the very beginning, that is, a position that placed it beyond the museum, beyond art history, making it absolutely other in relation to any and all cultural norms. The discrepancy between the avant-garde's and the party's interpretations of the Revolution became apparent quite early, around 1919. Buck-Morss locates this discrepancy in a "politics of conflicting temporalities". If an artist chose to accept the cosmological concept of time as constructed by the party through its propagandist imaginary, this meant glorifying the party and concealing all of its failures, which began to accumulate once it started trying to carry out its concrete social projects and plans. The visions of avant-garde artists soon began to diverge drastically from the difficult and dirty reality, and, in the post-Revolutionary climate, began to resemble bourgeois European modernism. In its struggle to win a place in the historical continuum of art, Buck-Morss argues, the avant-garde lost its credibility as a concrete Revolutionary strategy. Groys concludes that Stalin's cultural policies,

which should be studied as an integral part of twentieth century cultural history, fulfilled an inherent demand of the avant-garde movements, namely, to move from the presentation of reality to its transformation. In this way, Stalinist policy crossed a line that avant-garde artists themselves did not dare cross. By the mid-1920s, Suprematism and Futurism were already being regarded as *passé*. Any art that did not develop in the direction outlined by the Party was considered to be historically regressive, bourgeois and counter-revolutionary. The key moment in the temporal unscrolling and establishment of the Party's cosmological time, which was beginning to supplant all other temporalities, was the death of Lenin in 1924. Time stopped with Lenin's death. The committee responsible for arranging Lenin's funeral authorised the mummification and preservation of his body for all time. Artists were invited to collaborate on the design of the corpse's house—the sarcophagus and mausoleum. Tatlin believed that the mausoleum should be a triumph of engineering, while Malevich suggested, on the very day of Lenin's death, that his grave should take the form of a cube: "The cube is no longer a geometric body. It is a new object with which we try to portray eternity, to create a new set of circumstances, with which we can maintain Lenin's eternal life, defeating death."[23] Although neither Tatlin nor Malevich ended up designing the public mortality structure in which Lenin's body now rests, on view for all to see, this building continues to symbolise even today the demonic, impossible bond between revolution and the avant-garde. When in 1992, the IRWIN group, as part of the project NSK Embassy Moscow realised the performance *Black Square on Red Square*, in which a square black cloth, 40 metres by 40 metres, was unfolded on Red Square in Moscow, the action provoked a certain discomfort among Russian artists. At first it seemed that this discomfort was due to territorial resentment—foreign artists were appropriating Russia's historical material as their own—but later it turned out that the reasons were linked to a deeper collective trauma.[24] In 1995, the Bulgarian theoretician Vladislav Todorov confronted the issue of the cultural meaning of Lenin's mausoleum and, in his analysis of the specifically Eastern scientific and theoretical utopian imaginary, illuminated a different, thrillingly transcendentalist face of modernity.[25] The sacrilisation of Lenin heralded a regression from the modern into a pre-postmodern pseudo-religious society in which the party defined—as the church had done previously—the relationship between signifier and signified, or rather, it closed the semiotic gulf and prevented the eruption of the pluralism of interpretations that characterise the modern, alienated, industrial and post-industrial society of the West.

The final shift to the cultural policy of Stalinism was formally announced in 1932 by a decree of the Central Committee of the Communist Party, abolishing all artistic associations. From that point onwards, all Soviet artistic workers would be grouped according to their fields of operation into unified organisations such as the Union of Writers, the Union of Visual Artists, etc. The concurrent termination of the New Economic Policy meant that at the same time the market for artworks was also abolished. As a result, the newly centralised artistic groups were now all forced to work for a single patron: the state. As part of these measures, an officially prescribed artistic style was also formulated, namely Socialist Realism, which, contrary to Greenberg's assertion was not devised to suit the taste of the masses. The masses hated it. Socialist Realism was itself a carefully designed construct of the Soviet Party elite. This centralist, market-less model of cultural policy, which completely blocked the

kind of cultural dynamics and temporal pluralism found in modern Western society was, after The Second World War, also applied to other Eastern Bloc countries. Despite the fact that the Soviet model was grafted in very different ways onto the very different cultural traditions of Eastern Europe, it was nonetheless true that even in the friendliest version of Eastern European Communism—in Tito's Yugoslavia, which in 1948 renounced its allegiance to Stalin—Socialism existed as a system in which the party placed itself above all state interventions and in which the official cultural professional organisations had monopolies in their fields and acted repressively towards any cultural practice that did not wish to submit to their hierarchies. Over time, the monopoly of the unions was not based so much on the idea of maintaining Social Realism as the one legitimate style, as on the principle of maintaining control over the definition of art. In countries like Poland, Czechoslovakia or Yugoslavia, Unions of Visual Artists tolerated or even propagated rigid versions of Greenbergian modernism while remaining intolerant of any approach to art other than the one they prescribed. Today, many official institutions in the East are still very proud of their collections of Eastern modern paintings, as if wanting to say: "Look, we too were modern. Art during the Communist period was not only social realism, but also about modernism, here as well as in the West." Indeed this art was sometimes more fanatically Western than Western art itself. The artist who submitted to the policy of the unions had work and was exhibited, while those who did not were abandoned and dropped into the void of historical amnesia.

Just as we cannot fully equate the post-war cultural policies of Western European countries with those of America, so we cannot fully equate the cultural policies

of Eastern European countries with the policy of the Soviet Union. Both Cold War superpowers were exporting to Europe, which was still trying to reconstitute itself after two World Wars, their own particular model of cultural production forged in the 1930s and 1940s. These two protagonists were the ones who created the political geometry that we still live with today—the idea of West–East as a line and a divide, as opposed to a continuum and a unity.

TALE OF THE (TWO) SQUARE(S)
In the Soviet Union of the 1930s, it was a mortal flaw for an artist to be a 'formalist'. Kasimir Malevich—the inventor of the 'square'—returned to geometrical figurative painting after 1928, a move that even today challenges interpreters of his work. On the other hand, formalism was, as we have already seen, the most valued criterion for political art in America in the late 1930s and 1940s. The stance of apolitical politicality became a weapon in the Cold War when non-representational art was equated with the democratic societies of the West, as opposed to the representational realism of totalitarian regimes—in this regard no difference was made between Nazism/ Fascism and Communism. For this reason, according to Buck-Morss, it is truly revealing to observe the fate of the square as it moved through the complex political landscape of the twentieth century.[26] Of course, the square and abstract art were not the exclusive property of the Russian avant-garde. The Bauhaus, which was also prosecuted for practicing modern art—its closure was forced by the Nazis in 1933— also worked in this idiom, as did the Dutch De Stijl artists. But it was only in the internationalised environments of the West that the square managed to survive.

While the official fate of the square in the East in the 1930s was monumentalised in Red Square in Moscow, crucial debates around this image and its metamorphoses continued in the West right up to the time of conceptualism.[27] Benjamin Buchloh, in his essay "Conceptual Art 1962–1969", while analysing the genealogy of the square and the cube in 1960s American art, refers to the response of minimalist and conceptualist artists to the publication of the first comprehensive history of the Russian avant-garde, Camilla Gray's *The Great Experiment: Russian Art 1863–1922*, in 1962. [28]

> This question is of particular importance, Buchloh writes, since many of the formal strategies of early conceptual art appear at first glance to be as close to the practices and procedures of the constructivist/ productivist avant-garde as minimal sculpture had appeared to be dependent upon its materials and morphologies.

And while there have been some attempts since 1989 to establish a parallel between Western conceptualism and the concurrent conceptual practices in the East, such comparisons, in fact, do more to underscore the differences than to prove equivalence between the two phenomena. These differences will only become clearer as the distinct socio-political contexts in which these works were created and the different positions and manoeuvrability of the artists within the framework of their respective societies is better understood.

Western artists of the 1960s and 1970s, through the deconstruction of the formalist frameworks of modernism, were primarily concerned with the restrictive and repressive features of the art system and the dominant role of the market, in the context of which— as Marcel Duchamp demonstrated at the beginning of the twentieth century—the question "What is art?" becomes the object of legal definition and the consequence of institutional valuation. That which the

artist produces is, as Duchamp posited, only a kind of raw material, "which must be 'refined', as pure sugar from molasses", in the assessment of the public: "The artist may shout from all the rooftops that he is a genius: he will have to wait for the verdict of the spectator in order that his declarations take a social value and that, finally, posterity includes him in the primers of art history."[29]

If we accept Duchamp's persuasive arguments, then how do we define—both within the post-Communist countries of Eastern Europe and in the framework of neo-liberal Capitalism—the cultural or market value of the Eastern European art practices that emerged in the period 1930–1989? The cultural meaning of these practices could hardly be refined "as pure sugar from molasses" by the verdict of the environment in which they developed; or rather, considering the conditions under which the verdict was developed, the work has been preserved in a state of rawness, which must again in today's new context be socially refined and appraised.

In the late 1950s artistic and political undergrounds began to take shape in Eastern Europe, independently and disconnectedly from one another, but in response to similar conditions of repressive cultural politics of the Communist state. These were the years in which the discourses of post-war Eastern art started to gradually develop outside of any state cultural policy and without the benefit of any "umbilical cord of gold" connected to state or private sponsorship.[30] It was during this same time that the West began to rediscover the Russian historical avant-garde. The euphoria over Russian historical avant-garde material was the result of several factors, of which the 1962 publication of Camilla Gray's history was a key one, but not the only one. Also important were a number of studies

published in English, French and Italian by other scholars, both from the Soviet Union and abroad, who during the Khrushchev era gained access to archives and previously banned sources on the basis of which they were able to make reliable historical reconstructions. But as these books and catalogues were printed in the West for the Western marketplace, artists from the Soviet Union remained in the dark about this part of their own cultural heritage. It was only in the 1970s and 1980s, as this narrative was filtered back into Soviet cultural space through the West, that Soviet artists and intellectuals could piece together this narrative for themselves.

The historical codification of the Russian avant-garde is, in a strange way, connected with the incandescent spirit of Western New Left intellectual and artistic trends as well as the student reform movements of the late 1960s. Art historian Eva Forgacs, in her essay "How the New Left Invented East-European Art", argues that the concept of Eastern European art did not even exist until the 1960s, when it was first established through the gaze of the West. Artists from the countries of the Communist East never actually identified themselves with the East, either in the period between the two World Wars or in the Cold War period.[31] While it is possible, as Forgacs states, that political repression created a certain feeling of solidarity among artists who developed strategies of resistance against these regimes, the fact is that no lasting connections or exchanges could be established that would have permitted some sort of common discourse to evolve. In principle, Communism did not have an international cultural policy within the framework of its political bloc, and if cultural exchanges did take place at the state level, we can be sure that those who were at odds with the logic of the regime took no part in them whatsoever. The West's rediscovery of and fascination with the

Russian avant-garde also created an interest, in the art history of other Eastern Bloc countries. In the 1960s and 1970s, during the time that the contemporary art market was being constructed, cultural exchanges and international institutional infrastructure were being developed, and American cultural policies of the Cold War were being exported, numerous exhibitions and exchanges were organised with the East. The idealisation of the Russian avant-garde was embraced by the New Left, which was attempting to rethink the reasons behind the failure of the earlier leftist project in the West and to strategise possible ways of revitalising it. Combusting in the heat of this desire was the Situationist International, viewed by many commentators as the last ultra-left art movement which not only refused to surrender to the hegemony of the marketplace but insisted on analysing, to its last breath, the logic behind this hegemony. Nostalgia for revolution and social utopia was being expressed in American poststructuralist circles as well. When the first issue of *October*, a new American journal of art, theory, criticism and politics appeared in 1976, the editors explained that they had given the journal its name "in celebration of that moment in our century when revolutionary practice, theoretical inquiry and artistic innovation were joined in a manner exemplary and unique. For the artists of that time and place", they wrote, "literature, painting, architecture, film required and generated their own Octobers, radical departures articulating the historical movement which enclosed them, sustaining it through civil war, factional dissension and economic crisis."[32] In the reformist climate of the West in the 1960s and 1970s, the Russian avant-garde represented, then, an unattainable taste or enjoyment which the Western avant-gardes—despite their link to the 'umbilical cord of gold'—had never actually experienced.

Since the West was discovering the Russian avant-garde at a time when the underground movements in the East were already clearly formed, it is worth asking why the critical consciousness of the neo-Left in the West did not seek its pleasure in discovering and analysing these Eastern European movements—its contemporaries —particularly since groups and movements as OHO, Gorgona, Sots-Art, Moscow Conceptualism, Romanian body art and others were neither invisible nor inaccessible; there were enough links between Western intellectual networks and Eastern artistic circles to make contact through any number of channels. But one of the rules of the Western art system's historical narrative in the twentieth century is that it includes only those outsiders who came inside—or who left the outside— who crossed the Cold War's borders and began to operate within the framework of the Western marketplace. For example: Yugoslavia in the 1960s and 1970s was defined by an immensely rich cultural and artistic scene; it prided itself on a policy of open borders and it considered itself to be the most Westernised communist state. But until recently, only two names from this generation—Marina Abramović and Braco Dimitrijević—have had any resonance in the referential frame of the West. Not surprisingly, both live and work in the production framework of Western art. In Forgacs' view, the historical restoration of the Russian avant-garde brought about the recognition of a different narrative, one that was parallel to Western modernism. Within this narrative frame, then, the historical avant-garde of other Eastern European countries could also, and to some degree has been, rehabilitated— Czech cubism, Czech surrealism, Polish constructivism, Hungarian constructivism, Hungarian expressionism, for example. But what about the entire post-war artistic production of Eastern Europe, including the post-Stalinist art of the Soviet Union?

It remains hidden between the cracks of the two great narratives of modernism. What about the fate of the 'other square', the one of the East European post-avant-garde underground movements, to mention but one of many other exciting stories?

With some wit for decoding and some peculiar imagination with which one can read the future from the past, these stories' moralities as well as their formalities speak straight to the problems of the new century. The century where the plurality of interpretations about our global reality becomes centralised through technology as part of an endless mechanical flow, a web of insufferable egalitarianism, which, in a manner completely different from anti-pluralist Stalinist cultural policy, overrides the 'politics of conflicting temporalities', and in doing so, produces a similarly transcendental effect of endless and eternal spectacle. A chimera of a self-generating reality machine which every day asks us to supply our services for some small compensation but rarely for our opinions and judgments. A kind of world, which would seem fine even without us. This situation should finally encourage us to explore and understand how the realities we live in are constructed, and to detect and name their hidden engineers.

1 In this essay, I use the terms "West" and "East" as they were defined by the geopolitics of the Cold War, namely, as Western Europe and the United States of America, on the one hand, and Eastern Europe and the Union of Soviet Socialist Republics, on the other.

2 Codrescu, A, *The Disappearance of the Outside,* Boston: Addison-Wesley, 1990.

3 Latour, B, *We Have Never Been Modern,* Cambridge: Harvard University Press, 1993.

4 *In the Age of Extremes: The Short Twentieth Century 1914–1991,* London: Abacus, 1995, Eric Hobsbawm locates the formation of the integrated world economy between the years 1943 and 1973.

5 Dusan, Bjelic, "Global Aesthetic and the Serbian Cinema", I Imre ed., *East European Cinema,* New York: Routledge, 2005.

6 Michel Foucault defines the term "dispositive of power" as "a thoroughly heterogeneous ensemble consisting of discourse, institutions, architectural forms, regulatory decisions, laws, administrative measures, scientific statements, philosophical, moral and philanthropic propositions." Foucault, M, *Power/Knowledge: Selected Interviews and Other Writings 1972–1977,* New York: Pantheon, 1980.

7 Buck-Morss, S, "Visual Studies and Global Imagination", *Papers of Surrealism,* no. 2, Summer 2004.

8 Bürger, P, *Theory of the Avant-Garde,* Minneapolis: University of Minnesota Press, 1984.

9 Guilbaut, S, *How New York Stole the Idea of Modern Art: Abstract Expressionism, Freedom, and the Cold War,* Chicago: University of Chicago Press, 1983.

10 Buck-Morss, S, *Dreamworld and Catastrophe: The Passing of Mass Utopia in East and West,* Cambridge, MA: MIT Press, 2000.

11 Greenberg's essay was first published in *The Partisan Review,* vol. 6, no. 5, 1939.

12 Greenberg, C, "Avant-Garde and Kitsch", in *The Collected Essays and Criticism,* vol. 1, Chicago and London: University of Chicago Press, 1986, pp. 10–11.

13 Greenberg, "Avant-Garde and Kitsch", pp. 10–11.

14 Guilbaut, *How New York Stole the Idea of Modern Art: Abstract Expressionism, Freedom, and the Cold War.*

15 A frequently quoted comment attributed to Willem de Kooning.

16 Cockcroft, E, "Abstract Expressionism: Weapon of the Cold War", in F Frascina, ed., *Pollock and After,* New York: Harper & Row Publishers, Icon Editions, 1985.

17 Schlesinger, AM, Jr., *The Vital Center: The Politics of Freedom,* Boston: Riverside Press, 1962—originally published in 1949.

18 Guilbaut, *How New York Stole the Idea of Modern Art: Abstract Expressionism, Freedom, and the Cold War.*

19 Prevots, N, *Dance for Export: Cultural Diplomacy and the Cold War,* Middletown: Wesleyan University Press, 1998.

20 Offe, C, *Varieties of Transition: The East European and East German Experience,* Cambridge MA: MIT Press, 1997.

21 Buck-Morss, *Dreamworld and Catastrophe: The Passing of Mass Utopia in East and West.*

22 Groys, B, *Gesamtkunstwerk Stalin: Die gespaltene Kultur in der Sowjetunion,* Munich: Carl Hanser Verlag, 1988.

23 Tumarkin, N, *Lenin Lives! The Lenin Cult in Soviet Russia,* Cambridge MA: Harvard University Press, 1983, p. 190.

24 For a more detailed discussion of this project and documentation of the reaction to it, see E Cufer, ed., *NSK Embassy Moscow: How the East Sees the East,* Loža Gallery, Koper and Obalne Galeije, Piran 1992.

25 Todorov, V, *Red Square, Black Square: Organon for Revolutionary Imagination,* New York: State University of New York Press, 1994.

26 Buck-Morss, *Dreamworld and Catastrophe: The Passing of Mass Utopia in East and West.*

27 The 'secret history' and the fate of the square in Eastern European art must still be explored and analysed.

28 Buchloh, BHD, "Conceptual Art 1962–1969: From the Aesthetic of Administration to the Critique of Institutions", *October,* no. 55, 1990, p. 140; Gray, C, *The Great Experiment: Russian Art 1863–1922,* London: Thames and Hudson, 1962. A new edition of this book, revised and enlarged by M Burleigh-Motley appeared in 1986 as *The Russian Experiment in Art, 1863–1922,* London: Thames and Hudson.

29 Duchamp, M, *The Creative Act,* Brussels: Sub Rosa, 2000, CD.

30 These practices were described under various status labels in the countries of Eastern Europe: 'unofficial', 'alternative', 'subcultural', 'underground', etc.

31 Forgacs, Eva, "How the new Left Invented East- European Art", *Centropa 3,* no. 2, May 2003.

32 *October,* no. 1, Spring 1976, p. 3.

GREY ZONE OF EUROPE
PIOTR PIOTROWSKI

First published in *After the Wall: Art and Culture in Post-Communist Europe*, Stockholm: Moderna Museet, 1999.

In 1960 the congress of AICA, or the International Association of Art Critics, was held in Warsaw for the first time. In fact, it was the first time that the congress of that association had taken place in the territory of the 'Other' Europe, fenced off by the Iron Curtain. There had been one exception to this—the Belgrade congress in 1954, which was a special case, since Yugoslavia had a particular position in Eastern Europe: it was outside the Soviet Bloc. Warsaw was chosen for very specific historic reasons. Artistic processes taking place here, namely, the specific 'modernisation' of artistic culture, which was a reaction to the Soviet Socialist Realist model of culture decreed in the early 1950s, drew the attention of the world to Eastern Europe. The countries of post-Stalinist Europe, in particular those such as Poland, where the 'thaw' brought distinct cultural effects, and also the Soviet Union itself, were perceived in the West as the territories where the influence of modern, hence Western, culture was becoming more solid. The way Eastern Europe perceived Western culture confirmed the effectiveness of the 'colonising' strategy of the West. It should be added, however, that in the East this type of 'colonisation' was received more as a liberalising than colonising force, unlike the earlier indoctrination of Socialist Realism, which was viewed as colonisation *par excellence*.

This relatively insignificant example taken from recent history illustrates the complexity of artistic geography and the ambiguity of some concepts in the historico-geographical map of Europe of the last few decades. Such concepts as, for example, the above-mentioned 'colonisation', which is widely used by the post-colonial postmodernists, means little or nothing without reference to geography. Geography, in turn, carries little meaning too, unless it is understood in terms of the dynamics of the operating vectors, or as Paul Virilio would put it, in the context of the "trajectory", instead of in terms of the statics of rigid political references.[1] The problem of our identity, Virilio suggests, is not reduced to the subjectivity-objectivity question, but should take into account the 'trajectivity' movement, and the 'vectorial nature' of human beings, both physical and cultural. The very concepts of 'East', or 'West' are not neutral. How these concepts are understood 'here' and 'there' depends on many factors and is plotted in different coordinations, which sometimes are totally contradictory. Thus constructed, the dynamic geography of European culture, which in fact uncovers not one but many Europe's, is a great challenge, which is certainly worth taking up so as to understand the place/s where we live. The semiotics of geographical concepts, especially their vectors, reveals the dynamics of the culture of a given place. If we adhere to the example already given here, i.e. the memorable ACIA congress in Warsaw in 1960, we can easily see that the vector of post-Stalinist thaw, not only in Poland but also in many other Central European countries, irrespective of how deep the processes of cultural liberalisation had penetrated each of them, was targeted not only towards the West in general, but precisely at Paris. France was perceived as a mythological centre of modern art, an artistic point of reference, the sublimation of Western culture, and an opposition to the barbarity, which was identified with Socialist Realism from an eastern provenance. Here, in the East, the cultural or political rivalries between various Western centres—e.g. New York versus Paris—were ignored, as were any signals disturbing the idealistic image of the West; no heed was paid to any internal political tensions resulting from opposition motivated by Marxist discourse and Communist liaisons with the bourgeois culture. For instance, on the occasion of the PHASES exhibition in 1959 in Kraków, when André Breton sent an address fraught with political, lofty phraseology and accusations targeted at French culture, it was coldly received.[2] This was because the rhetoric of political involvement in art was associated with a diametrically opposed geographical direction, namely Eastern not Western. The movement from East to West was actually only one-dimensional and selective. However, the opposite direction, i.e. from West to East, was analogous. At that time, the interest of the West in the East focused more on the similarities between them than on their differences, and more on phenomena, which were understandable in the language of the Western artistic paradigm. No wonder then, to keep to the Kraków example of those days, it was Tadeusz Kantor's paintings that gained popularity, and not those of Jerzy Nowosielski. It happened so because, as Igor Zabel writes, the modernist ideology of the Cold War and neo-colonial era was based on the conviction that Western modern forms and values are modern forms *par excellence*, and thus they have a universal value.[3] What is more, this conviction was commonly shared in Eastern Europe.

Today geography seems not less, but actually more complex than 40 years ago. Ten years after pulling down the 'Iron Curtain' and the Berlin Wall, which in the former German Democratic Republic was called the "Anti-Fascist Defense wall", the geography of Europe has undergone significant transformations. Europe is still, as Imre Bukta shows, a subject of many divisions—*Carving the map of Europe* performance in Miscolc, 1989—there are more countries, the borders are longer, more complex divisions are emerging, and Europeans are experiencing new tensions and wars. It is quite surprising that in Europe wars take place at all, as it shows that the binary division of the continent forged after The Second World War and based on the so-called balance of Super Powers has collapsed, or at least has become far more complex.

But already in the post-war period, this binary division of Europe had become a painful simplification. In the so-called Eastern Europe, which took on its shape as a result of the Yalta Agreement, Russia always played a specific role. Even now, after the fall of the Soviet Union, Russia has a particular position on the map of European art. What is more, the process of identification in art there is very complex and specific. The Moscow artists gave me one example of this: trying to avoid to be identified as "Russian"; they prefer to be called "Moscow artists".[4] For them a notion of the "Russian artist" means a fulfilment of Western expectations of "Russianness", and this is exactly what they would like to avoid. This "Russianness" is something like 'exclusion' from global culture and with an exotic label. The notion "Moscow artists", however, has no such connotation; it is identified with a city, a large contemporary metropolis, as one of many in the contemporary global art world. Another state that enjoyed a different status during the Cold War and *détente* was Yugoslavia, which, in Central Europe and in the Soviet Union, was perceived as freer than the rest. In the cultural domain, it was much more open than Poland or Hungary, not to mention Bulgaria, the GDR and Romania, in spite of the fact that the system introduced by Tito did not tolerate any organised opposition or any independent illegal, overt forms of political engagement. At present, however, when the Russian parliament has been drafting a resolution about the expansion of the Union of Russia and Belarus with Serbia, another part of the former Yugoslavia, Slovenia, is clearly steering towards the Western structures and harbours pro-Western ambitions characteristic of Central Europe. Under such circumstances, it is no longer

possible to describe Europe using only the political categories of West and East. The "grey zone" of Europe that emerged from the Soviet world, and "near-Soviet" as in the case of Yugoslavia, which 'already' does not belong to the East, but is not a part of the West 'yet', or in other words the new Central Europe stretching from the Baltic to the Balkans, may not persist for a long time. It will, in the near future, build new borders, new walls running, like the Berlin Wall, across traditional Central Europe; the new border of the newly divided Europe may run across the heart of historical Central Europe— between Slovenia and Croatia, the Czech Republic and Slovakia, between Poland and Lithuania.

There is no doubt that the historico-geographical coordinates of Central Europe are in a state of flux, that we are experiencing both historical and geographical transformation, that we are between two different times, between two different spatial shapes. The "trajectories" of the cultures of Central Europe are changing; their geographic reference points are becoming more complex. The key question to be raised here concerns adding a critical dimension of a new artistic geography, or in other words, if we use Irit Rogoff's words—"critical cartography".[5] We should wonder to what extent this new network of vectors, i.e. this critical geography, is aimed towards disclosing the centre of power, that is the West, and to what extent it rejects its dictatorship and—like feminist, post-colonial and other deconstruction practices—is based on a pluralistic and non-hierarchical concept of the subject, or to be more exact, on the multi-subjectivity of European dimensions. Once we study this problem in the modern art of Central Europe we will be able to answer the question about the identity of this part of the continent.

Critical geography, this time not so much an artistic practice but a theory, enables us to define the space in which we dwell. This space is determined by political and economic globalisation and its ideology, or—as Slavoj Žižek writes—by multiculturalism. This is reminiscent of older colonial discursive practices, yet in this case the West is not only the subject of a peculiar colonisation, as before, but also is its object.[6] Igor Zabel has expressed an analogous view—he writes that global Capitalism colonises not only the rest of the world, but also the place of its origins, i.e. the West itself. It introduces total uniformity. Zabel mentions here the ingenious example of the Benetton advertising campaign—The United Colors of Benetton—in which the allegedly different people, so allegedly the 'Others', look the same.[7]

This is so because the processes of globalisation and multiculturalism seem to be neutral in terms of space; they seem to imply dissemination of the centre, or its dethroning. This spatial transparency can mislead even the most critical minds, since their geographical horizons are, in most cases, exclusively limited to the metropolis. It is rarely pointed out that the subject of the discussion about contemporary multiculturalism concerns only the metropolis, not the places lying outside it. Multiculturalism is presented as a pluralistic doctrine of equality of cultures, yet it is almost entirely devoid of any geographic tensions. An attempt to look at this ideology from the viewpoint of geography clearly shows that cultural equality is an illusion, an illusion based on the alleged transparency of space. In other words, multiculturalism highlights the multi-ethnicity of one place, the metropolis of New York, which then is reproduced and automatically transferred into other places, into other, non-Western, cities as well as into areas lying outside them. When seen from this perspective, the multiculturalism of New York or London in the structural and semiotic sense is analogous to that in Moscow, or Sarajevo. By referring to geography we are able to disclose the spatiality inherent in this concept and to substantiate it, and hence, to undermine the illusion of its non-being; we are able also to deconstruct the concept of the virtuality of the world and subject dislocation, while at the same time revealing its hierarchy.[8]

We should also look with a critical eye at how the ideology of multiculturalism functions at its very centre, let's say in New York or in London, since even there, as Homi Bhabha writes, it poses a threat of "DissemiNation", i.e. deprivation of the subjectivity of the ethnic and national minorities living there.[9] Multiculturalism, thus, apart from its value for defending ethnic minorities living in Western megalopolises and cultural identities, and apart from its particular success in differentiating the education system, still remains a Western doctrine to relevant minorities in the Western world. A perfect example of this process, which clearly grips the imagination of metropolitan intellectuals, is "cuisine multiculturalism", as proposed by Stuart Hall. This is proof of only an apparent pluralism in culture, as it is totally irrelevant whether we eat meals made according to a Chinese, Hindu, Italian or any other recipes as, in each case, we consume them—as Hall writes—in a small territory of Manhattan.[10] The same idea is expressed more tersely and less metaphorically by Rasheed Araeen: globalisation and multiculturalism are manifestations of the dominance of the West, an alibi for its power.[11] If, within the boundaries of one area, in this case New York or London, multiculturalism—as a postmodern sign of culture pluralism and power decentralisation—is questioned, then its centralist character will be more pronounced if seen in terms of spatial

relations. Simply, the multiculturalism of New York, and London, is not the same as the multiculturalism of Sarajevo. In this part of Europe, with an exception of Moscow, which has, however, other problems than those of multiculturalism, there is no megalopolis: the main locus of multiculturalism. Here, in Central and Eastern Europe a more crucial problem is multinationality, rather than multiculturalism. In order to see this, you have to go there, go physically, not via the internet from a comfortable apartment in Greenwich Village. Hence, the virtualisation of space becomes a tool of the dominance of the centre, while any reference to a geographic dimension may undermine its theoretical alibi and, by the same token, reveal the centralist character of globalisation and multiculturalism.

If power is centred in the West, then we may ask about the attitude, "trajectory", formed here, in the "grey zone" of Europe; naturally, we should not generalise. What we can do is to point out tensions or the conflicting directions within East European artistic culture, or in other words, the peculiar dialectics of vectors. Nedko Solakov, a Bulgarian artist, shows his "view to the West" in a humorous way: *View to the West*, 1989, in which a terrace with a fence for security reasons, so as not to be overused for suicide attempts, is protected by a safety barrier bearing a plaque with the title "View to the West". From this one can see a very non-Western architecture of Sophia: the dome of the Orthodox church of Alexander Nevski and—slightly further—a governmental building, which is an exact copy of the Moscow Lomonosov University. However, on the terrace there is a telescope through which, as one might expect, it is possible to view the West. "The Promised Land" is, still, not within one's reach; it is difficult to obtain and visible only by means of optical technology. Moreover, one can try to grasp it only by

using what is available on the spot, and which, in fact, is visible without any telescope: tradition and the post-Soviet reality. In another work, dating from more or less the same time, the artist opens up "top secret" files, as if thus unveiling the omnipotence of the secret police of a totalitarian system—*Top Secret*, 1990. These archives, the currently open drawers, contain "identity records", documents and personal files showing almost every moment of the artist's life.[12] However, after the collapse of the Communist state, should we now empty the drawers and consign their contents to the rubbish dump? Solakov is not sure about that, but he would be inclined to think the reverse; he is actually inquiring about the identity cloaked in the past. Actually, it is not possible to deny the identity. These documents bear our lives, part of our history, an indispensable fragment of our identity. We can see the West through a telescope, but all the time, however, with the ID issued by the People's Republic of Bulgaria, even if, in administrative terms, it has expired. The gaze, the vector of this culture, is focused on the West; the subject, however, is fully aware of the place where the telescope is located.

In the "grey zone" of Europe, the kind of identity that I have defined here is very vulnerable. During the performance festival, organised in 1993 by Ilena Pintilie in Timisoara, a well-known Romanian artist Dan Perjovschi had his arm tattooed with the word "România"—*Romania*, 1993.[13] A year earlier the same artist had employed an ironic method of presenting fears caused by selling off Romanian land, the land of the former state farms, i.e. the 'people's', allegedly belonging to the whole of Romanian society. He decided to sell it in parcels, each 6 x 8 cm in size to highlight the tensions between the two poles at a time of transformation, or in other words, to show the conflict between two complementary slogans: "we want land" and "we do not want to sell away our common good", the former standing for the euphoric atmosphere of privatisation and the latter for the Socialist myth of so-called national property.[14] During the same festival another Romanian artist, Teodor Graur, expressed another type of apprehension: the fears of isolation, of Romania, Central-Eastern Europe, being confined to the Open Air Museum of the "grey zone". Throughout his performance, the artist, enclosed in a cage—which was the title of the work—repeated a sentence in English into a microphone: "Hello, I am speaking to you, can you hear me?" and then expecting the radio, tuned into Western stations, to give him some reply, which—of course—it never did—*The Cage*, 1993. The lack of any reply was a reply enough in itself. At the beginning of the performance, leaflets were dropped, written in English, and what they said, "Speaking to Europe from Europe", was a striking sub-heading to the performance.[15] The conversation was always one-way, and the place from which it was initiated remained a closed cage.

Discussing the dialectics of location, with its contradictory "trajectories", and still keeping to the Romanian example, the group subREAL, one of the most interesting art groups of Central Europe, should also be mentioned. In a very ironic way these artists touch upon the issue of the cultural geography of Europe in their work. One of their installations *1,000 Artists in Europe*, 1991, consisted of two parts. In the first part, 1,000 inflated condoms were hung up to create a curtain 3 x 17 metres in size; while in the second, 1,000 condom packets, each bearing the name of a living Romanian artist, were hammered onto a square black base, thus forming a kind of net—what is important here is that the contraceptive sheaths were manufactured by a company with the very charming

name "Europe".[16] A series of works, under a common and symptomatic name of *Draculaland*, contain a number of often ironic and humourous references not so much to Romanian tradition but rather to certain stereotypical perceptions of the Romanian character. The very title *Prince Dracula* is a perfect example of such a perception. The very confrontation of apparent Transsylvanian physiognomy with a symbol of Western beauty, in da Vinci's painting of Mona Lisa, which additionally refers to the Western, classic work of the avant-garde, to Marcel Duchamp who painted a moustache on the Gioconda, is an element in a perverse game that artists of this group are playing with the Western audience and its culture. The artists of the subREAL group assert that the famous smile of the heroine of Leonardo's painting, together with its mystery that became a myth created by art history, is all of a sudden explained here: the smile of Gioconda is like the shadow of a vampire, and—as the subREAL artists claim—the meaning of this is derived from its absence, *Draculaland 2*, 1993.[17]

In another work from the series, entitled *The Palace*, 1995, which some time ago was displayed in the Warsaw Center for Contemporary Art, the Romanian artists connected the site of the exhibition, the Ujazdowski Castle, with another castle, the famous People's Palace erected by the notorious dictator of the Socialist Republic of Romania, Nicolae Ceaușescu.[18] The very process of constructing the palace was a traumatic experience for Romanians. In order to build it, which apparently was the second largest in the country, a significant part of old Bucharest had to be pulled down, while other parts of the city went to ruin at an unprecedented rate, because all possible resources had been directed towards the construction of this building. A great amount of money was invested in this project, which, for this poor country,

implied a genuine economic catastrophe. To keep the social discipline essential for such a huge architectural enterprise, the dictator introduced a terror unknown since Stalinist times. The culture, economy, and everyday life of Romanians fell prey to the gigantic and sick ambitions of the new embodiment of Dracula, otherwise known as "The Genius of the Carpathians". Following Freud and Lacan, Renata Salecl claimed that this palace is a "wound", which fulfils a significant function in the process of identification of Romanian society.[19] In her opinion, the destruction of the city was as important as the erection of the palace. Creation *ex nihilo* is a manifestation of the impulse of death, and as such it falls into the symbolic dimension of history and into a domain of memory. Trauma cannot then be erased from the identity, since—as part of history and memory—it not only triggers recollections of 'the happy old days' that date back to before the traumatic times, but also prevents one from forgetting about one's involvement in the construction of 'new better days', which were symbolised by this very palace.

The artists of the subREAL group formulate an even deeper problem. They inquire not only about the problem of Romanian identity marked by the dialectics of nostalgia and traumatic experience, wound and identification, but also about the regional and historico-geographical connections that may lead to a discussion not only about national identity but also about a common East European identity. The model exhibited in Warsaw was made of boxes of Carpathians cigarettes. As the Romanian artists point out during periods of martial law in Poland, when there were hardly any goods available there, these cigarettes enjoyed a great popularity on the Black Market.[20] *The Castle of the Carpathians* may be viewed, then, as a common history of Romanians and Poles who are bound together by a common experience of Communist terror and economic catastrophe, or in other words, by a historical and geographical system of coordinates. It should also be mentioned that the Carpathians are not only the name of cigarettes smuggled to Poland during the rule of martial law, but also a mountain chain linking the two countries.

Each nation and each society has its own 'wound', a specific traumatic experience inscribed in historic processes of identification. Whereas for Romanians it is the People's Palace, for Poles it is Siberia, perceived in a long-term perspective, and recently in a more metaphorical than real way. It is a mythological place of national tragedy. It marks the political geography of defeats, repression and oppression, from the point of view of both the history of the nineteenth century and of the post-war occupation. In short, Siberia, a land distant in terms of geography but close in terms of history, triggers for the society a negative vector of space-time identification, and as such it was used in the latest work of Zofia Kulik, shown for the first time in Poznań in a solo exhibition, *From Siberia to Cyberia*, 1999.[21] The former word, "Siberia", begins with "S" and—for sure—refers to what has been said before, i.e. to the historical-geographical resentment of Poles; the latter one, "Cyberia", begins with the letter "C", and—as the artist states—is derived from the name of the first internet cafe in London. The latter, then, is the symbol of a new dimension of identity and can be perceived as a metaphor for a contemporary 'global village', based in virtual space. The question that is bound to arise in that context is the following: do the phonetic similarities imply any similarity in content? Or, in a wider perspective: do they shed any light on the discussion about contemporary Central Europe?

From Siberia to Cyberia is a large tableau, consisting of over 10,000 small photographs taken from a TV screen showing from one to a few frames of a certain programme. That the number of the photographs is so great plays a significant role; it almost is the key to understanding the work. It is not the particular frames, but just their 'infinite' number or the unlimited continuity of their flow that is the point of departure for an interpretation of Kulik's work. They simply suggest a huge amount of TV information or the massive attack of visual culture on people. The range of pictures is indeed diverse, yet the diversity does not actually matter too much. It is the number, or to be precise, the mass that counts and conveys the sense of particular information programmes broadcast in the mass media. What is more, in the 'aesthetic' sense, the individual pictures do not differ: they are emotionless, black and white pictures of a TV screen. Naturally, the monotony is intended, and carries some meaning. It implies the nature of the TV image, its standardisation—irrespective of what is shown, it is shown as if in the same way. The impression of monotony is enhanced by a decorative zigzag running through the whole work. It actually suggests that it is not the content of the pictures that matters, but their standardised form. It often happens that we zap the channels using a remote control, but in fact the images reaching us for a few hours every day are meaningless. We perceive only the "form" of the visual mass: the emotionless, standardised and monotonous visuality. The TV image has lost its contact with reality and the enormous amount of messages have neutralised all content. An apparently active viewer—apparently, as she/he can choose from a great number of world TV stations—has become a victim passively pushing buttons; she/he has become a victim of what W J T Mitchell called "hyper-representation".[22] Instead of being a link, the TV screen separates us from the world; it does so not by its very nature, but through the quantitative explosion of visual information. To use the words of Baudrillard, we actually deal with a simulacrum; we live in a virtual reality, where death, terror, and war, if they do not involve us physically, are confined to a TV screen. Even those who conduct the war do not see their enemies—they sit in an air-conditioned room equipped with a fridge and a coffee-maker, and their perception of reality is confined to "an infrared telescope" of "smart" missiles.

The tension described by Zofia Kulik plays an especially important role in the 'Other' Europe. It indicates a historical and geographical split in this part of the continent, its spatial and temporal entity wedged between geographical dimensions, Siberia and the so-called Euro-America, and between historical periods: on the one hand, repressive police totalitarianism, and on the other, the overwhelming and seductive totalism of virtual and visual media culture. It seems that the most imaginative approach towards this split, this "grey zone" of Europe, which defines its identity in the context of both the traumatic memory of a utopian future and Communist totalitarianism, i.e. of the West and East, has been adopted by the Slovenian group IRWIN. As Alexander Bassin wrote, the slogan of the artistic activity of this group in the 1980s, i.e. "Was ist Kunst?" could *de facto* be paraphrased into a question "Who are we?" and the question addressed their own identity in the context of the changing situation in the Balkans.[23] At the time of the collapse of Yugoslavia, the artists, constituting a part of a larger subculture called in German "Neue Slovenische Kunst" (NSK), did not implement a moralising strategy in their art; in such an approach they did not follow the example of many Central and Eastern European dissidents. Neither was their art that which would be politically involved above all else. Rather, it pursued the critical strategy—as Marina Gržinić put it—of the "denaturalisation" of Socialist culture, of its rituals and signs, by deconstructing a Communist "policy of perception".[24] The strategy boiled down to using the Communist ideology or—as Inke Arns puts it—to extreme "overidentification" with it. The aim of this strategy was to confront the viewer with resentments of both reality and the past, of memory and history. The strategy was not only targeted at overcoming the power of the Communist symbols by means of irony and satire; its primary goal was to indicate that these symbols have power over us, that we are affected by them. As the author further claims, the artists believed that this goal could be achieved only by analysing the aesthetic foundations of the ideology. She then continued, following Slavoj Žižek, whose role in the intellectual development of this group cannot be overestimated, that this was the most effective way of disarming the dominant ideology, and much more effective than moralisation or rebellion. Once a safe distance from ideology was shortened, or eliminated completely, then ideology became powerless. Under these circumstances its covert justification, *jouissance*, the very justification of which provides for enjoyment, without which no ideological system can function, is in question. A consequence of the above is a cynical approach to the values one appreciates, which actually implies that an individual has had no convictions about what one declares, but nonetheless, enjoys the privileges offered by the ideology.[25] The critical denunciation of ideology was the main function of the concerts by the group Laibach, which were fraught with references to totalitarian ideology. This group was related to IRWIN, whose members also used signs derived from the tradition of a totalitarian artistic culture, including the Soviet avant-garde. A spectacular show of this type was *Interior of the Planit*, 1996, in which a space was filled with ironic pictures of diverse totalitarian provenance; it referred to

the conception of "planits" by Kazmir Malevich and to a famous exposition of the Russian avant-garde, *0-10-The Last Futurist Exhibition*, St Petersburg, 1916. Equally unambiguous in its message was the artists' self-portrait called *The Mystery of the Black Square*, 1995. However, the most spectacular manifestation of this type of strategy, typically employed when the historico-artistic and political dimensions overlapped, was the action *The Black Square on the Red Square*, 1992. This encapsulated two zones of the twentieth century history of Eastern Europe: the famous Suprematist painting of Malevich and the Red Square in front of the Moscow Kremlin, the very heart of the Soviet Empire.

When the IRWIN artists visited Moscow they established there an "embassy" of NSK. This was another representation of *NSK State in Time*, a state with no territory but with "citizens" travelling in time and space, a state having its insignia and issuing passports. This project was built within the theoretical framework of the utopian concept of Slavoj Žižek.[26] According to the latter, the tragedy of the former Yugoslavia, and also of the whole of Europe, was a collapse of state structures in favour of ethnic interests and territorial-national claims. Therefore, he proposed to get rid of not only nationalisms but also of anarchistic or even anarcho-liberal ideas of a stateless society. Conversely, it is working for the state, for the abstract and artificial structures of power which repeal the ideologies of rootedness, nation, ethnic ties, etc., that can guarantee safety. The *NSK State in Time* is an embodiment of this utopia. As Inke Arns stresses, it is a "suprematist state"; it is defined by other than "normal" categories: not space but time and movement.[27]

Here, however, we should ask the question if by neutralising spatial relations, the Slovenian artists have not inscribed their actions in the strategy of the centre?

That this suspicion seems justified follows from a simple observation that in the structures of postmodern globalisation and multiculturalism the category of dislocation is used wholeheartedly to mask the character of place. What is more, referring once more to Paul Virilio, we can say that contrary to the "tyranny of distance" tensions between the global and the local, or the transnational and national, describing the world up till now, mean that we are facing the "tyranny of real time", a typical feature of a world organised by "speed".[28] The *NSK State in Time*, thus, could be perceived as an ideal embodiment of this concept. However, when we analyse the art of the IRWIN group from the viewpoint of a critical geography, and in this perspective there is not only a lack of "nobody's voices"—which we know from other critical, postcolonial, and feminist discourses— but "no voices from nowhere" either, then we can define the problem differently. Criticism compels us to ask not only who is speaking, but also from where, since each statement is formulated from a strictly defined place. The discourse of "Cyberia", one of virtual reality, comes from the centre, which as well as the concept of the dislocation of the subject is formulated in the metropolis. The clash of this discourse with the place of its origin, its analysis in geographic terms, unmasks the utopia, which *de facto* is a strategy of the power of the centre, i.e. the West. The message sent by IRWIN comes from a region with a historically painful experience of space. A state with no nation and no territory, in other words, without ethnic definition and without borders, is perhaps the best answer to the present political situation in the Balkans—to the bloody ethnic wars conducted in the territory of the former Yugoslavia in the 1990s—or at least it seems to be best interpreted in terms of such a framework.[29] What is more, the answer has been formulated in an area so far excluded from the space of 'Europe without borders', excluded also from the *Schengenland* which watchfully safeguards its exclusivity; it comes from a place which is experiencing both economic and cultural consequences of this exclusion. The *NSK State in Time* of the IRWIN group reveals the hypocrisy of universalistic discourses of Modernism, or to be exact, of the promises of a "common European home", made during the period of the Cold War and *détente;* it also reveals the hierarchical character of the multicultural 'global village'.

The ultimate recognition of the meaning of the art of the Slovenian artists is facilitated by the sense and status of the utopia they formulate, which, however, is not expressed using the abstract categories of a philosophical discourse, but in the perspective of a critical geography. This utopia is not conjured up to mask power, hierarchy and political, technological and cultural, not to mention military supremacy; the latter being a characteristic of only a part of Europe. Conversely, it is created so as to unmask such power. Furthermore, the connection between geography and art history that the IRWIN artists explicitly refer to, reveals yet another, even deeper, meaning. Numerous artistic utopias and non-place creations formulated in Central-Eastern Europe have always been at dispute with the authorities, even despite their apparent similarities. Let us take the example of Malevich prompted by IRWIN. His art is a utopia of the future, which, in a different way than the strategy of the Slovenian artists, unveils the 'use' by Bolshevik power of its own ideology. As a result of such a strategy, this utopia is clearly anchored in reality. Contrary to what the IRWIN artists suggest, Malevich, by placing his "planits" in the context of a Communist discourse, uncovered, whether consciously or not (this is a separate issue) the cynicism of Bolshevik ideology. The Party did not intend to build the avant-garde, but rather Socialist architecture, which they soon demonstrated. Conflicts

with the systems of power, understood both in a narrower and a wider sense, always differentiated Eastern European utopias from those created in the West, including technological utopias, utopias of ecology, cyberspace, and so on, which, on the contrary, ultimately always find common ground with authorities, and even—as in the case of *Cyberia*—become the dominant ideologies. Following this path, we can see that the Eastern European utopias never threatened to become reality, as this is as much true nowadays as in the case described by Andreas Huyssen who claims, and his opinion is supported by Baudrillard, that we are witnessing times when the utopian vision of a "global village is becoming reality".[30] Paradoxically, in the epistemological sense, this threat is dire. If utopias do become reality, this unequivocally implies the loss of the reference point which is necessary for the description of reality, yet positioned somewhere outside it. To define, describe and think about reality, one has to have an external point of reference; to be understood, a place must be made relative and reduced to a non-place, a utopia, otherwise it becomes unattainable. This danger, which is another paradox, was avoided by the Central and Eastern European artists, from the time of the great avant-garde, through those socially and politically engaged in the 1930s, to the contemporary utopians, including the members of IRWIN. They speak not from the position of virtual metropolis, but, on the contrary, from a small city located on the border line of the "grey zone" of Europe—namely from Ljubljana.

EDITOR'S NOTE

11 years have passed since Piotr Piotrowski wrote "The Grey Zone of Europe". Today, less than a year after the 20th anniversary of the fall of the Berlin Wall—the 10th anniversary a milestone with which Piotrowski measures his discussion—a number of his predictions have materialised. Most notably, in conjunction with Imre Bukta's predisposition, there are "more countries"—Kosovo for one, who declared independence from Serbia in 2008; and indeed "more complex divisions are emerging" with "new tensions and wars" continuing to plague the region, including the 2004 unrest in Kosovo; the South Ossetia War in 2008; and the insurgency in North Caucasus in 2009. As Piotrowski rightly predicted "the new Central Europe…. will, in the near future, build new borders, new walls running." The first explicit reflection of this statement would be the division of the Federal Republic of Yugoslavia into Serbia and Montenegro in 2006, immediately shifting the region's perimeters. Certainly, Piotrowski's foresight of geographic reference points becoming more complex continues today; and until this ceases, will remain highly influential upon East European artistic culture, as seen in the continuing work of artists such as Nedko Solakov and Dan Perjovschi, alongside the new emerging artists from the region; and it is for this reason that Piotrowski's text continues to hold relevance today, hence the inclusion of his essay within this survey of contemporary Eastern European art.

1 Virilio, P, *Open Sky,* London: Verso, 1997, p. 24.

2 Cricot 2, *Grupa Krakowska i Galeria Krzysztofory w latach 1955–1959,* J, Chrobak, ed. Kraków: Grupa Krakowska, 1991, pp. 81–89; JDąbkowska-Zydro, *Surrealizm po surrealizmie. Międzynarodowy ruch PHASES,* Warszawa: Instytut Kultury, 1994, pp. 106–111.

3 Zabel, I, "We and the Others", *Moscow Art Magazine,* no. 22, 1998, p. 29.

4 Degot, K, "Moskaur Aktionismus: Selbstbewusstsein ohne Bewusstsein/ Moscow Actionism: Self-Consciousnes without Cinsciousness", *Kräftemessen,* ed. HG Oroschakoff, Ostfildern bei Stuttgert: Cantz Verlag, 1995, pp. 153/227.

5 Rogoff, I, "The Case for Critical Cartograpies", *Cartographers/Kartografowie/ Kartográfusok/Kartografi,* Ž. Koščevič, ed. Warszawa: Centrum Sztuki Współczesnej "Zamek Ujazdowski", 1998, pp. 144–149.

6 Žižek, S, "Multiculturalism, or, The Cultural Logic of Multinational Capitalism", *New Left Review,* no. 225, September– October 1997, pp. 28–51.

7 Zabel, "We and the Others", p. 33.

8 Rogoff, "The Case for Critical Cartographies", p. 41; the author is referring to the book of H Lefebvre, *The Production of Space,* Oxford: Blackwell Publishers, 1993.

9 Bhabha, H, "DissemiNation: Time, Narrative, and the Margins of the Modern Nation", *Nation and Narration,* HK Bhabha, ed. Routledge: London and New York 1990, pp. 291–322.

10 Hall, S, "The Local and the Global: Globalization and Ethnicity", *Culture, Globalization, and the World-System. Contemporary Conditions for the Representation of Identity,* AD King, ed. Minneapolis: University of Minnesota Press, 1997, p. 33.

11 Araeen, R, "New Internationalism or the Multiculturalism of the Global Bantustans", *Global Visions. Towards a New Internationalism in the Visual Arts,* J Fisher, ed. London: Kala Press, 1994, pp. 3–11.

12 See Nedko Solakov, B Barsch, ed. Berlin: ifa, 1992.

13 *Festival de Performance: Zona Europa de Est,* ed. I Pintilie, Timişoara 1993, pp. 48–49.

14 Marcoci, R, "Romanian Democracy and its Discontents", *Beyond Belief. Contemporary Art from East Central Europe,* L Hoptman, ed. Chicago: Museum of Contemporary Art, 1995, pp. 18–9.

15 Pintilie, *Festival de Performance,* pp. 28–29.

16 *subREAL: Akten/Files,* Berlin: Neuer Berliner Kunstverein & Künstlerhaus Bethanien, 1996, p. 27.

17 *subREAL: Akten/Files,* p. 45.

18 *subREAL: Akten/Files,* pp. 76–81.

19 Salecl, R, "Identity and Memory: the Trauma of Ceauşescu Disneyland", *Related Issues (for "Complexul muzeal"),* CH Kravagna, ed. Arad: Muzeul de Artâ, 1997, pp. 19–20.

20 *subREAL,* pp. 77–81.

21 *Zofia Kulik: Od Syberii do Cyberii [From Syberia to Cyberia],* P Piotrowski, ed. Poznań: Muzeum Narodowe, 1999.

22 Mitchell, WJT, *Picture Theory. Essays on Verbal and Visual Representation,* Chicago: The University of Chicago Press, 1994, p. 423.

23 Bassin, A, "IRWIN/Słowenia: pomiędzy regionalizmem a uniwersalizmem" ["The Local and the Universal"], *Magaszyn Sztuki,* no. 20–21, 1998–1999, p. 62.

24 Gržinič, M, "Art and Culture in the 80s. The Slovenian Situation", *NSK Embassy Moscow: How the East Sees the East,* (project by IRWIN, Apt-Art International, Moscow: Ridzhina Gallery), Koper: Loža Gallery, 1992, pp. 36–38, Gržinič, M, "Neue Slovenische Kunst (NSK): The Art Groups Laibach, IRWIN, and Noordung Cosmokinetica Theater Cabinet—New Strategies in the Nineties", *IRWIN: Interior of the Planit,* Ljubljana: Moderna Galerija, Budapest: Ludwig Museum, 1996.

25 Arns, I, "Mobile States/Shifting Borders/ Moving Entities. The Slovenian Artists' Collective Neue Slovenische Kunst (NSK)", IRWIN. Trzy projekty/Three Projects, Warszawa: Centrum Sztuki Współczesnej "Zamek Ujazdowski", 1998, pp. 70–71. See also: Žižek, S , *The Plague of Fantasies,* London: Verso, 1997 (chapter "Love Thy Neighbour? No, Thanks!", pp. 45–85).

26 Bussman, G, "The Call Reverberated like Hollow Thunder", *IRWIN: Interior of the Planit;* Arns, "Mobile States/Shifting Borders/ Moving Entities. The Slovenian Artists' Collective Neue Slovenische Kunst (NSK)" p. 75. See S Žižek, "Es gibt keinen Staat in Europa", *Padiglione NSK/ IRWIN: Gostujoči umetniki/ Guest Artists,* XLV Biennale di Venezia, Ljubljana: Moderna Galerija, 1993.

27 Arns, "Mobile States/Shifting Borders/Moving Entities. The Slovenian Artists' Collective Neue Slovenische Kunst (NSK)", p. 73.

28 Virilio, *Open Sky,* pp. 18–19.

29 Arns, "Mobile States/Shifting Borders/ Moving Entities. The Slovenian Artists' Collective Neue Slovenische Kunst (NSK)", p. 73; Bussman, "The Call Reverberated like Hollow Thunder".

30 Huyssen, A, *Twilight Memories. Marking Time in a Culture of Amnesia,* Routledge: New York and London, 1995, pp. 90–91.

DIALOGUE
IGOR ZABEL

First presented at the international conference On the Edge, organised by the Croatian section of AICA Zagreb, 1997; published in *Art Press*, no. 226, under the title "Dialogue East-West: East is East".
Courtesy Mateja Kos.

In September 1994, the Russian artist Ilya Kabakov spoke at the AICA Congress in Stockholm. He was describing his experience of a "culturally relocated person". One of the aspects of Western culture he was interested in was the permanent tendency to criticise, provoke and even destroy within this culture. He compared his experience of this tendency to the experience of an orphan living in a children's home who is visiting the family of his friend. This friend is sick of his home and his behaviour is aggressive and insulting, while the visitor himself sees a totally different picture: a nice home and kind and intelligent parents. But there is another thing that is essential, the friend's family is strong enough that it is not in danger because of the boy's outbursts. The same is true of Western culture, says Kabakov, and continues:

> Western culture is so vital, so stable, its roots are so deep and so alive, it is so productive that it, speaking in the language of the parable above, absorbs, recasts and dissolves in itself all destructive actions by its own 'children', and as many believe, it sees in these actions its very own development—what is elegantly referred to here as 'permanent criticism'. But I would like to add a footnote here: this criticism, like the destruction itself, is permitted, if it can be so expressed, only from its own children. That same mom described above would have behaved quite differently if I had started to act up at the table the same way as her son. Most likely she would have called the police.[1]

It did not take too long, less than a year and a half, that the event Kabakov was somehow predicting really happened. It took place during the opening of an exhibition called Interpol in the Färgfabriken Contemporary Art Center in Stockholm; an exhibition trying to establish a 'global network' between Stockholm and Moscow. One of the participants, the Russian performance artist Alexander Brener, destroyed a work of another participant, the Chinese-American artist Wenda Gu; and another Russian artist, Oleg Kulik, who appeared on the show as a dangerous dog on a chain and actually bit some people, was attacked by the audience and was later taken away by the police.

There has been a lot of discussions, and even more rumours and gossip, about the Interpol scandal. I believe that the affair is so attractive because it is not just another scandal in the art world. It implies an extremely serious question: the relationship between East and West, and it indicates that this relationship is far from being idyllic. I believe that it was not the intervention of the police which had made this tension explicit—after all, one should expect such intervention— but *An Open Letter to the Art World*, signed by a group of artists and other participants of the show—all from the West—and broadly distributed.[2] What is surprising is the fact that the letter was written and signed by artists and critics whose position is essentially based on the tradition of "permanent criticism", referred to by Kabakov. Of course, they were not necessarily expected to agree with Kulik's and Brener's actions, but one would at least think they would be more careful in the way they criticise them, since the tradition of twentieth century art offers a number of examples of aggressive, destructive and subversive actions which have, by now, attained a status of historical or even canonical fact.

Some examples of destroying other artists' works are now considered to be major points in the development of modern art. Immediately I can think of at least two examples; the best known is, perhaps, Rauschenberg's *Erased de Kooning*. Another is the so-called "Wolfsburg Affair" from October 1961: "at the opening of the exhibition *Junge Stadt sieht junge Kunst* Arnulf Rainer paints over the etching *Mond und Figuren II* by Helga Pape, which had won second prize, with black paint and attaches a label with the inscription: 'Painted over by Arnulf Rainer'. Rainer is arrested and sentenced to a fine for willfully damaging a work of art."[3] The *Open Letter*, however, is not simply a protest against the two Russian artists and their actions; it attacks them, as well as the Russian curator Viktor Misiano, with direct but, at the same time, very general and imprecise political accusations: "a new form of totalitarian ideology", "hooliganism and skinhead ideology", "a direct attack against art, democracy and the freedom of expression", "speculative and populistic attitude", "classical model of imperialistic behaviour", "attitude that excludes female artists". In short, the *Open Letter* treats the destructive actions of both Russian artists as being eminently political rather than artistic statements.

One could easily dismiss the *Open Letter* as ridiculous and reactionary since it lacks any precise analysis and reflection and because its criticism, as well as the position and the values this criticism implies, is just a set of phrases. I believe, however, that we have to understand this letter as a kind of 'slip', i.e. that we have to recognise its symptomatic value; and it is this value that makes it so very interesting. One has to ask themselves: what made a group of artists and critics who, at least some of them, ascribe to a line of critical and subversive art to write a letter—and distribute it all over the world—in such a style which could easily be used by a representative of any conservative or totalitarian system? What made them blind to the style and form of their own writing? What made them directly and roughly denunciate the artists—as well as the curator who was trying to understand the destructive actions as artistic statements—as being politically incorrect and against art, democracy, freedom of expression and women, only because they did something which is well established in the tradition of twentieth century art as a legitimate means of artistic expression, however radical and problematic?[4]

I do not believe that those who have signed the letter consider Rauschenberg and Rainer to be "hooligans", "skinheads" and "enemies of art, democracy and freedom of expression". We must, therefore, conclude that Brener's action must be seen, in an important aspect, as different from, say, Rainer's. And since they have done exactly the same thing: destroying the work of a fellow artist at the opening of a group show, the difference has to lie elsewhere. I believe that Kabakov is, with his "footnote", indicating the correct answer to this question: the Russians do not belong to the "family". Rainer's action is included in a certain code where it has a precisely determined meaning and value; on the other hand, the position of Brener's action seems to be at the point where two codes clash. Thus, his action could not be legitimised by the code which it was actually questioning and attacking.

There are two sentences in the *Open Letter* which I find essential: "This attitude denies every possibility of a dialogue between the (former) East and the West. It is a speculative and populist attitude that cannot be accepted as the basis of a dialogue." Something has been made very clear here. Brener and Kulik are not two individual artists, they are not even Russians, they represent the 'East'— politically correctly called "the (former) East". The *Open Letter* makes clear that the problematic point of the Interpol scandal is not the behaviour of individual artists. Brener, Kulik and Misiano only represent

an 'attitude', which actually is the 'attitude' of the East. This coincides with the fact reported by Misiano, that only Western artists were invited to sign the letter:

> Nobody asked other Russian artists to sign this letter, though most of them do not identify with the destructive gestures of Kulik and Brener. What's more, the Slovenian artists IRWIN were also excluded. Ridiculous. Ljubljana is the West for Russians, but the logic of confrontation has stated the Western sanction: Ljubljana is the East.[5]

Interpol was obviously more than just a group show. Its main problem was not a network between different artists and different artistic attitudes and practices. The show was about the West–East dialogue. And actually, the result of the 'scandal' at the opening was a sharp division and confrontation between the Eastern and the Western artists. The show, says Misiano in the same text, "was to be a metaphor of the new Europe and post-ideological order (where there is no more East and West)." Nevertheless, the confrontation remains. The East is still the East, although it is now called 'the (former) East'. Does anybody speak about 'the (former) West'? The idea of a global network in the post-ideological new Europe, a model, presumably, replacing the topography of the East–West division, proved to be a veil covering the actual conflicts and confrontations. Even more, such a rhetoric can actually serve as a means in such a conflict. A conflict, that is, which is essentially based on the will to establish a dominant position in the discourse and thus in the practice itself.

A dialogue is only possible on a certain common basis which both parties in the dialogue accept. For example, if I want to discuss with somebody, the meanings of the words we use have to be established

and clear to both of us. The quoted sentences from the *Open Letter* make clear that it was exactly on this level, the level of accepting a common basis, that the West–East dialogue had failed. The Easterners did not accept the terms of the dialogue which were supposed to be "natural" for the Westerners. By not accepting these terms, Brener, Kulik and Misiano—representing the East—"deny every possibility of a dialogue between the, former, East and the West", since their own attitude "cannot be accepted as the basis of a dialogue". I believe that one of the best descriptions of these problems was given by Lewis Carroll in *Through the Looking-Glass*:

> 'When *I* use a word', Humpty Dumpty said, in rather a scornful tone, 'it means just what I choose it to mean—neither more nor less.'
> 'The question is', said Alice, 'whether you 'can' make words mean so many different things.'
> 'The question is', said Humpty Dumpty, 'which is to be master—that's all.'[6]

Thus, one could perhaps say that the struggle for a dialogue, or better, the struggle for the terms of a dialogue, represents the struggle for the position of the master.

The Interpol scandal demonstrated that the West–East division persists and that it was not surpassed with the fall of the Communist regimes. Furthermore, this division is clearly not confined to the area of art. As the ideological oppositions between the capitalist and the socialist systems are no longer functional, it has been replaced, for example, with the idea of the "clash of civilisations". Again, I believe that at the basis of this "clash" lies the struggle over the most basic, 'human' and 'natural' issues which themselves correspond to a certain power structure. For example, Samuel P Huntington, who has introduced the idea of the "clash of civilisations", also describes how the West ensures its domination by presenting its interests as the interests of the "world community" and how it presents its own fundamental values as universal, while in fact they are not valid within most other civilisations.[7] Of course, one may assume that the concept of a world consisting of basically different—and often hostile—civilisations also corresponds to a certain strategy of power and control. The idea of the "clash of civilisations" is actually much more than just an attempt of a neutral scientific description of the contemporary world. It introduces a certain system of interpretation and representation which is directly applicable in international policy. One could, for example, notice how important American specialists in foreign affairs started to use Huntington's terms in describing conflict areas such as Bosnia.

The East–West "conflict", as far as art is concerned, develops in an essential aspect on the level of the fight for codification of the field and thus for its domination. It is this codification which determines the terms of the dialogue or, as Humpty Dumpty has said, which chooses their meaning. The sharp political division between the East and West during the Cold War period also implied a confrontation of two artistic models: Modernist art in the West and Socialist Realism in the East. Western art has presented itself as the 'natural' development of genuine art as opposed to the politically suppressed art of Socialist Realism and its derived forms, which was not supposed to be genuine art, but simply political propaganda. In light of this understanding, Eastern artists have been understood as a kind of underdeveloped and supressed Western artists, and it was thought that they would immediately join the general developments in the West if they would be free to do so.

The identification of Western art of this century with modern art as such—this identification was actually a part of the "Western universalism", as it is described by Huntington— introduced a subtle dialectic of domination. The essential success of this dialectic lies in the fact that it was, to a great extent, accepted by Eastern artists themselves. Modern art was thus located in the West. But, as Western art is universal, Eastern artists also belong to the same idiom; however, they form only its periphery. All the constitutive structures, institutional, conceptual and commercial, are located in the West, thus they are controlled by it. The East more or less accepts, with some delay, and repeats the main currents of Western art; I remember a participant at the CIMAM Congress in Dubrovnik in 1987, who directly said that "all" the important modern art was produced in the West and none in the East. The function of Eastern modernism, inside this constellation, thus was often not to represent an autonomous statement and position, but to serve as a confirmation of the original Western artist or particular movement. In her article "Abstract Expressionism, Weapon of the Cold War", Eva Cockcroft describes an example of using innovative Eastern art for strengthening the position of the West, regardless of the actual role and meaning of this art inside its original context:

> During the post-Stalin era in 1956, when the Polish government under Gomulka became more liberal, Tadeusz Kantor, an artist from Kraków, impressed by the work of Pollock and other abstractionists which he had seen during an earlier trip to Paris, began to lead the movement away from Socialist Realism in Poland. Irrespective of the role of this art movement within the internal artistic evolution of Polish art, this kind of development was seen as a

triumph for 'our side'. In 1961, Kantor and 14 other nonobjective Polish painters were given an exhibition at the MoMA. Examples like this one reflect the success of the political aims of the international programs of MoMA.[8]

Such a constellation permits a very limited acceptance of Eastern artists into the central 'area' of art. An average Eastern artist has, in his effort to produce modern art, remained a kind of "incompletely realized Western artist", and thus a second class artist. It was, of course, only natural that the 'second world' produces second-rate art. Most often, the Eastern artists who have succeeded in the West are those who have actually moved there and became its integral part. Still, some Eastern artists have reached a certain international response, partly due to their quality and the genuine interest of some Western critics and curators, but also because they could serve as evidence of the universal value of modern art and, as mentioned above, as an affirmation of Western artists and artistic developments. Nevertheless, the codification of the field and the construction of its history and tradition, resulted in a marginalisation or total ignorance of important Eastern phenomena. For example, Eastern avant-guard artists of the 1960s and early 1970s simply do not exist in historical surveys of art of this time, except those who have moved to the West.

Establishing itself as the centre, the West has also established itself as a general reference point. East–East communication, in as much as it has existed at all, has been running via the West. This was even present in the recent project, the Europa-Europa exhibition at the Bundeskunsthalle in Bonn. I found this show very important for presenting a number of lesser known or unknown artists and works. Among others, it made us aware of the fact that certain important achievements of, say, Carl Andre, Barnett Newman and others were preceded for more than half a century by the works of artists like Alexander Rodchenko, Olga Rozanova and others. Still, the criteria for selecting the contemporary section, seemed to depend, to a great extent, on the artists' international reputation, which actually means, their reputation in the West.

I believe, that we are witnessing a somehow different situation now, i.e. a change from the Eastern artist as an "incompletely-developed-Westerner" to the Eastern artist as a representative of a different and exotic culture. In the above mentioned speech about the "relocated person", Ilya Kabakov also mentions how an artist who is coming from the East or from the third world is, in advance, committed to represent his origins:

> Belonging to some 'school' now—be it Russian or Mexican, French or Czech— is perceived as a negative ethnographic factor hindering the artist to a certain degree from entering into the Western artistic community on an equal footing. However, the artist who has arrived from these places often himself doesn't know about this circumstance, this 'hump' on his back appears only in the new place upon crossing the border, and as Boris Groys wrote, like a growth on his back, it is visible to everyone except the owner of that back. This is precisely the same thing as when a critic in an offhanded manner writes 'the young artist from India', or 'the famous Mexican painter'—everyone silently understands what this epithet means.[9]

I believe that this change demonstrates an important modification in the field of the East–West relationship, a shift which is connected to the *détente* process and the eventual collapse of the Socialist regimes. During the time of the Cold War, in a situation where the political and ideological confrontations ensured a firm, bipolar structure and therefore balance and control, Western modern art easily claimed to be universal. The post-Cold War era does not supply such controlling mechanisms any more. The necessary result is that the situation of art—as well as other related fields—has to be redefined. The freedom of travelling, for example, could be a universal value and a proclaimed right only as long as the bipolar system made it impossible for a large majority of—Eastern—people to travel freely. As soon as these limitations disappeared, the right of free travel had to be reduced.

As opposed to the proclamation of the universal value of Western modern art during the Cold War period, post-Cold War ideology stresses the differences. On a more global level, a similar development can be observed in the discourse of so-called multiculturalism. As the ideological and political differences disappeared, the East is now established through 'cultural' and 'civilisational' differences, which are by themselves a starting point of conflicts, of the 'clash of civilisations'. In his description of the Interpol incident, Wenda Gu, the artists whose work was destroyed by Brener, spoke very openly about the "cultural war".[10]

The idea of modern art originally did not need the idea of a 'dialogue'; the 'substance', so to speak, was common, the only question was to what extent and how it was realised. Through the idea of "civilisational differences", however, the Easterner is established as the 'Other', thus an inter-cultural and inter-civilisation dialogue is necessary. An Eastern artist now becomes attractive for the West not as somebody producing universal art, but exactly as somebody who reflects his particular condition. He is not only an artist, but particularly a Russian, Polish or Slovene artist, or simply an Eastern artist.[11] This was clearly present in the Interpol incident. Renata Salecl, in her analysis of Kulik's actions, wrote about this question:

> The paradox... is that Kulik was invited as a particularity—as a Russian dog. I am certain that if an American artist were to play a dog, he would be of much less interest for the international art scene than the Russian artist is. We all know that the majority of people in today's Russia live a dog-like life. And the first association a Westerner makes in regard to Kulik's performance is that he is representing this reality of contemporary Russia. Kulik-dog is therefore of interest for the Western art world because of the fact that he is the Russian 'dog'.... And, in regard to Kulik's performance it can be said that the West finds an aesthetic pleasure in observing the Russian 'dog', but only on condition that he does not behave in a truly dog-like manner. When Kulik ceased to be the decorative art-object— the Eastern neighbour who represents the misery of the Russian dog-like life—and started to act in a way that surprised his admirers, he quickly became designated as the enemy.[12]

In short, the idea of the West–East dialogue could be understood as a way of reorganising these relationships after the end of the Cold War era, i.e., as a way of how to deal with the 'Other'. If earlier, the dominant position was achieved through the universal value of Western modern art, it is now achieved through the definition of the 'Other' and, at the same time, through the definition of the basis of communication.[13] As Wenda Gu reports, Misiano said that "this incident creates an essential stage for a dialogue between Eastern and Western Europe."[14] But, it seems clear that this 'stage' includes a reorganisation of the very field of dialogue and thus opens the question "Who is to be master?" Unavoidably, the Western pole of the "global network" could only see mere aggression, imperialism and destruction in this attempt.

1 Kabakov, Ilya, "A Story about a Culturally Relocated Person", Speech at the XXVIII AICA Congress, Stockholm, 22 September 1944, now reprinted in *M'ars*, Ljubljana, 1996, nos. 3–4.

2 The letter was signed by Olivier Zahm, Elein Fleiss, Jan Aman, Catharina Ahlberg, Catti Lindahl, Thomas Lundh, Magnus af Petersens, Matthias Wagner K, Birgitta Muhr, Wenda Gu, Ioanna Theocaropoulou, Ulrika Karlsson, Dan Wolgers, Erns Billgren, Bigert & Bergström, Johannes Albers and Fredrik Wretman.

3 Schwarz, Dieter, "Chronology", *Wiener Aktionismus/Viennese Actionism*, Klagenfurt: Ritter Verlag, 1988, no. 1, p. 168.

4 Recently, Brener has caused another big scandal by attacking a painting by Malevich in the Stedelijk Museum in Amsterdam. This action again, and even more radically, opens up the question of artists attacking and destroying works of other artists. Personally, I think that such actions are highly problematic and not something one could easily agree with. Also, I believe that an artist who has destroyed such a work has to take full responsibility for his action. Attacking a work of art does not necessarily imply a relevant artistic position and statement, but sometimes it does. In such cases, the destructive and unlawful behaviour has a function and meaning, and we have to regard it as a relevant statement—like, I believe, in Brener's case. Personally, I do not agree with Brener's attacks on Wenda Gu's and Malevich's works—no more than I agree with the destruction of the works by de Kooning or Helga Pape, but, of course, these attacks were not meant to be agreed with. They are deliberate hooliganism which, however, has a deep meaning in the context of Brener's artistic position. If those who have written the *Open Letter* would actually read Brener's text in the Interpol catalogue instead of just searching for politically incorrect and compromising quotations in it, they could perhaps understand it.

5 Misiano, Viktor, "The Response", *Flash Art International*, May–June 1996, p. 46. The quotation discloses one of the reasons why I am so interested in this affair. As I am based in Ljubljana, my position is in advance determined by the discourse of the West–East dialogue.

6 Carroll, Lewis, *Alice's Adventures in Wonderland & Through the Looking-Glass*, New York: Bantam Books, 1981, p. 169.

7 Huntington, Samuel P, "The Clash of Civilizations?", *Foreign Affairs*, no. 3, Summer 1993, pp. 22–49. Huntington has expanded and elaborated the questions dealt with in the article, in his recent book, *The Clash of Civilizations and the Remaking of World Order*, New York: Simon & Schuster, 1996.

8 Cockcroft, Eva, "Abstract Expressionism, Weapon of the Cold War", Francis Frascina, ed., *Pollock and After: The Critical Debate*, London: Harper and Row, 1985, p. 132.

9 Kabakov, "A Story about a Culturally Relocated Person"

10 Gu, Wendy, "The Cultural War", *Flash Art International*, Summer 1996, pp. 102–103.

11 In recent Western discussions about contemporary Russian art, especially about artists like Brener and Kulik, such an attitude was often present. One can easily notice how these two artists came to represent the wild, aggressive, irrational, non-understandable, dangerous, animal-like essence of "Russia"—or, perhaps, the "East" in general—and how their actions are received with a mixture of fascination, admiration, fear, hatred and, of course, pleasure.

12 Salecl, Renata, "Love Me, Love My Dog", *Index. Contemporary Scandinavian Art and Culture*, 1996, nos. 3–4, p. 117.

13 It would be, perhaps, more accurate to say that this new strategy is still often combined with the idea of "universalism".

14 Gu, "The Cultural War", p. 103.

BODY AND THE EAST
ZDENKA BADOVINAC

Zdenka Badovinac's essay "Body and the East" was originally written for the catalogue of the exhibition of the same name at the Moderna Galerija, Ljubljana in 1999—*Body and the East: From the 1960s to the Present*, Ljubljana: Moderna Galerija—a major retrospective of Eastern European body art that included work by Marina Abramović and Komar and Melamid, amongst others.

Courtesy Zdenka Badovinac.

I have no concern with any economic criticisms of the Communist system; I cannot enquire into whether the abolition of private property is expedient or advantageous. But I am able to recognize that the psychological premises on which the system is based are an untenable illusion. In abolishing private property we deprive the human love of aggression of one of its instruments, certainly a strong one, though certainly not the strongest; but we have in no way altered the differences in power and influence which are misused by aggressiveness, nor have we altered anything in its nature.[1]

If we talk about art creativity in Eastern Europe, which until recently was relatively isolated from the world, as being a separate phenomenon, we risk pushing it even further into the world of 'Otherness'.[2] We risk making its 'Otherness' even more evident, even within institutionalised frameworks, since we mostly present ourselves—consciously or not—in the way we believe the Other would want to perceive us. But we would be risking more if we simply forgot about its Otherness and presented ourselves—in the spirit of the newly united Europe—as being equal, and if we pointed to those cultural-historical characteristics which comply with the recently very popular slogan that we have always been part of Europe. The idea of the united Europe rests primarily on the Western definition of being European, and it has been politically and economically institutionalised in the European Union, which is now cautiously opening its doors to new members from the East. The position of power in this case is perfectly evident, not at all covert, in contrast with the multiculturalism in culture, which endeavours to hide the "cultural logic of multinational capital".[3] It is true that the Otherness of the East is also already stereotyped and almost

folklorised in the domain of art. In this context I would like to first mention two examples of very popular films made in Yugoslavia during the war, *Underground* by Emir Kusturica and *Before the Rain* by Milče Mančevski, discussed by Žižek in the above paraphrased essay. Žižek writes: "… to the Western liberal view, both films offer precisely what this view would like to see in the Balkan conflict—a spectacle of timeless, incomprehensible, mythical circuit of passion, in contrast with the decadent and anaemic Western life."[4]

It is true, however, that numerous artists from the East have been critical of their own Otherness as the identity constructed through the play of representations. The most outstanding examples of this at the Body and the East exhibition are Aleksander Brener and Oleg Kulik—I shall refer to them later—and there are other examples—not in the context of this exhibition—dealing with the deconstruction of Eastern identity—the work of the Bulgarian artist Nedko Solakov and the Slovene group IRWIN—or its wider collective: Neue Slowenische Kunst (NSK), including the Laibach group presented as a collective body. Solakov creates narrative installations in which he deconstructs the Western art system by shifting its power elsewhere, where it is not expected: to himself, an artist from the East, or even—as in one of his installations—to a chief of an African tribe. The IRWIN group reacted immediately to the political changes in the East at the end of the 1980s and to the newly emerged situation, which culminated in the conflict in the Balkans. They immediately took a critical stance towards the priority of national context into which the artist has been pushed by the new conditions. One of their projects, *Transnationala*, 1996, focused on the issues of the displacement of centre and the circulation of ideas. It was realised by IRWIN, together with

some invited artists, curators and theorists, in a series of discussions and lectures held during their trip from the east coast to the west coast of the United States. The works of these artists leave the relationship between identity and Otherness an open question, a never-ending process of mutual characterisation in countless combinations. The permanent doubt and the deconstruction of the play of representation distinguish the works of contemporary artists from their older colleagues who used ancient practices and esoteric rituals to overcome Otherness. But the creative coupling of Eastern and Western ideas, or their basic principles, has remained a utopia, and one of its most prominent "realisations" was the Eurasienstab action, performed by Joseph Beuys on the basis of anthroposophical ideas and with the participation of the Fluxus member Henning Christiansen in Vienna in 1967.[5] The striving of the different for oneness, be it of different political spaces—whose energetic flows were most drastically broken by the Berlin Wall, and still are by the Great Wall of China, or of man and woman, was expressed in the most monumental manner by Marina Abramović and Ulay in their *The Great Wall Walk Project* in 1988 on the Great Wall of China. The lovers approached each other, walking from the south and the north ends of the wall respectively, for two months, but the project did not end with marriage, but with their intimate divorce.

The captivity of artists in the traps of the multicultural world of Otherness has been questioned primarily by writers from the regions that fall under the patronage of "new internationalism". Ekaterina Dyogot, tells us a lot about the Otherness of the Eastern artist: "The Russian artist perpetually finds him/herself between the Scylla and Charibdis of two representational mechanisms which are switched on automatically and ruthlessly. In Russia… being 'contemporary artist' means to represent Western culture…. In the West, on the other hand, a Russian artist must inevitably represent Russia."[6]

And what is the connection between the above topic and the theme of the Body and the East exhibition, with the issue of the artist's own body as his basic medium of expression, besides the evident intention, of course, to present a segment of creativity of the cultural space that until recently had been quite unknown? This strangeness is starting to be seen as distinctiveness, and the main questions of the present exhibition rotate precisely around these apparent oppositions. We face the question posed on various occasions by Slavoj Žižek, Ekaterina Dyogot, and Igor Zabel: is it possible to avoid the "representational" role of the eastern artist?[7] And why is it that it is precisely art based on the artist's own body that appears to be the best guide if we attempt to answer this question? The answer runs as follows. It is because the artist's body is necessarily defined only in terms of the relation with the other, and because—due to its inherent intersubjectivity and performativeness—it can be a model of another representational economy. The artist's body in body art is not self-sufficient—his/her identity acts within a context, but at the same time his/her body is also the location for projections of viewers' desires. The intersubjectivity and dependence deny directness and the unique presence of the body in body art—and performance.[8]

The presence of the body in art is not a guarantee of truth, nor a reflection of the self, and it does not offer itself to the viewer as a one-way relationship. Body art does not guarantee the truth; its essence is rather in the fact that it upholds the process of the development of truth as an open

structure. This is why the description of body art in the sense of a unique presence of body as subject is the metaphysics of current times, which raises doubts about its reproducibility—this applies primarily to body art performance. Regardless of the fact that a performance loses its totality if reproduced and documented, this proves that the fragmentariness and dependence are inherent to these practices. Postmodern writers also ascribe these properties to photography.

Performativeness or theatricality, critically renounced by Michael Fried, who claimed that it had robbed minimalism of its self-sufficiency and self-reference, emphasises the importance of physical experience and shakes the central position of reason. Body art is counter-formalist, its meaning is not comprised within the limits of an autonomous and fixed object. Instead of a finished self-sufficient artefact we face the process of creation and, equally important, the process of perception. Modernism has replaced a singular artist's body with an object that not only substitutes it, but also surpasses its singularities and thus survives it and preserves the artist's genius forever. We always speak of body art from our contemporary, postmodernist perspective, which places at the forefront its performative character that resists ultimate definitions and always ascribes individual characteristics to particular art practices. The modernist understanding of body art neglects, for example, important implications of performativeness. In modernism, the body is a locus of the subject's unique essence. An artist reaches his/her own essence mainly through physical pain. Under the superficial social codification, which the artist surpasses with the shamanic actionism of body art, the modernist body thus contains a universal essence.

If we now return to the question of whether is it possible to avoid the representative

character of both Eastern and Western European art, we can say—in the language of performative art practices—that if we consider Eastern and Western art in the last 50 years as being two large, long-lasting performances, we can see that the art of both sectors has been interpreted primarily through the represented—i.e. absent— body of performance, in contrast with the performative art practices which always regard the represented body in the relation with the real. To be more concrete: just as Western art has mainly presented itself to the relatively isolated East as reproduced in magazines and books, so the East has been presented in the West with a small quantity of poor-quality documents, with white spots in retrospectives of European art, and with the myths of official art and the suffering dissidents. In this dialogue, the power always remained on the side of the West, which has been constantly producing new trends—ascribed with a universal character— and their interpretations that primarily helped to preserve the political frontiers of the visible. Eastern art was always visible only to the extent to which it figured within the limits of representative economy, that is, in as much as it was either ideological itself, or critical to that ideology, or in as much as it figured within the frameworks dictated by Western European and American trends. When we look at the issue of representativeness, as illuminated by Ekaterina Dyogot with the example of Russian art, we are talking about something already signified and belonging to the ideology of the visible.

Peggy Phelan writes in her book *Unmarked— The Politics of Performance* about the significance and the force of that which is unmarked, and which therefore cannot be confined within the borders of the ideology of the visible. By locating a subject in what cannot be reproduced within the ideology of the visible, I am attempting to revalue a belief in subjectivity and identity which is not visibly representable. This is not the same thing as calling for greater visibility of the hitherto unseen. *Unmarked* examines the implicit assumptions about the connection between representational visibility and political power which have been a dominant force in cultural theory in the last ten years.[9]

Body art and performance are based on the exchange of the visible and invisible, presence and absence. The pain in body art is irreproducible, and precisely this quality makes it one of the significant "means of expression". Peggy Phelan claims in *Unmarked* that the conviction that greater visibility also means greater power is false. Such an observation could bring us to the rather comical conclusion that naked women rule the world. Power is located precisely in what is invisible and irrepresentable. The invisible, the absent, is analogous to the non-articulated, which is manifested in the works by the Russian artists included in the Body and the East exhibition, Oleg Kulik and Aleksander Brener. We could say that the works of these two artists represent "the actively non-signified": "something that does not figure within the borders of the institutionalised and controlled, something that undermines—in the dialogue between East and West—the stable representative economy captured within the frameworks of political power".

The current dialogue between East and West is largely clarified in the example mentioned by Renata Salecl in her paper "Love me, love my dog": "We know from the theory of Foucault as well as from Deleuze and Guattari, that communication, dialogue and exchange of ideas are all means for various forms of power struggle…."[10] In this paper, Renata Salecl refers to the action of Oleg Kulik and Aleksander Brener at the opening of the Interpol exhibition in the Färgfabriken Contemporary Art Center in Stockholm, aimed precisely at the establishment of the dialogue between Eastern and Western artists. Salecl speaks of Oleg Kulik's

performance, in which the artist acted like a dog. Kulik actually assaulted and bit several people at the exhibition, and was taken by the police as a result. Kulik's and Brener's performances caused great disdain among other artists and organisers, and ultimately resulted in an international scandal.

And, in regard to Kulik's performance it can be said that the West finds an aesthetic pleasure in observing the Russian 'dog', but only on condition that he does not behave with truly dog-like behaviour. When Kulik ceased to be a decorative art object— the eastern neighbour who represents the misery of the Russian dog-like life—and started to act in a way that surprised his admirers, he quickly became designated as the enemy. His performance—together with the performance of another Russian artist Aleksander Brener, who at the Interpol show destroyed a work by Chinese-American artist Wenda Gu— was described as 'a direct attack against art, democracy and the freedom of expression', and as a 'classical model of imperialist behaviour'. An open letter to the world.[11]

Aleksander Brener says of his art that it has a centuries-long democratic tradition, the tradition of plebeians, proletarians, slaves, and rebels. Brener speaks of the culture of revolt and destruction, but also of the culture that is not based only in lower strata, but is also practiced by the topmost intellectuals. Brener lists some of his heroes thus: "François Villon and Walt Whitman, the theatre created by Antonin Artaud and Berthold Brecht, films by the Marx Brothers and Buster Keaton".[12] We could continue with the list, and finally we would come to Malevich himself: in 1997, Brener sprayed Andy Warhol's dollar onto one of his paintings. Those who condemned this act were probably

unaware of the fact that Malevich himself, in his essay on museums, argued for the burning of all old pieces of art in order to enjoy the view of ashes.[13] If we look at the actions, as performed by Brener and Kulik, from the contemporary point of view, we must admit that current art uses the language of metonymy much more than that of metaphor. When speaking about the aggression, suffering, and traumas of our civilisation, it does not describe them but embodies them.

BEAUTY AND THE BEAST
Since the very emergence of art practices such as body art, performances and happenings in the 1950s and 1960s, their performative character has provoked embarrassment for its inclusion of elements of the unpredictable, of something continually eluding control. Hence also the problems of performative art practices: throughout their history they called for interpreters. These latter have endeavoured, in the service of their defence and easier understanding, to place them within the bounds of various cultural contexts. Even the anarchistic Brener was urged to defend his work through explanations within what was already known. Thomas McEvilley, in his essay "Art in the Darkness", 1985, saw conceptual and performance genres on the dark side of the Moon, where they constantly alternate the rules of art.[14] McEvilley tried to find the historical context of these practices—particularly those from the 1960s and 1970s—in the Freudian timeless storage of childhood memories, in the Jungian collective unconscious, in shamanic literature, and in discovering exotic cultures. Art in the sense of a kind of psychoanalytic or shamanic practice liberates issues supressed by public morality, and it enables us to get acquainted with these issues and to counterbalance their force with the seemingly distinct identity of the light side. McEvilley speaks in his

essay of the aesthetics of choosing and
will, which has substituted the traditional
aesthetics of idea and execution; he speaks
of the strictness of the oath, which has
replaced the craftmans' tendency for
the perfect form, and of the pureness
of execution without any pragmatism
equivalent to the common quality of an
artwork. McEvilley points out to us that
such art comes close to Arnold Toynbee's
view that the highest cultures are also the
least pragmatic. In fact, McEvilley ascribes
the meaning which Freud saw in beauty
to art from the dark side of the Moon, art
in relation to which we can speak about
the aesthetics of the ugly. Freud also
attributed non-pragmatism to the need for
what is beautiful, and this is why, among
other things, he viewed art and science
as crowning proof of the developmental
level of particular cultures. We can see,
therefore, that non-pragmatism is precisely
the common denominator of both the
aesthetics of the ugly and the aesthetics of
the beautiful, Dionysian and Apollonian.
Non-pragmatism is the quality uniting
both aesthetics under the common roof of
art. The authentic impetuses and motives
of any art lie in both human natures—
beauty and the beast—at the same time.
Slavoj Žižek even speaks of the ontological
primacy of ugliness: "Beauty represents
a kind of defence against the Ugly and its
disgusting existence or, rather, existence
itself, since… what is really ugly is the
brutal fact of existence, of what is real, as
such."[15] Peter Weibel commented critically
on Freud's theory of culture and society
in his paper presented at the Living with
Genocide symposium in the Ljubljana
Museum of Modern Art in 1996. According
to Freud, culture and society are founded
on the function of two drives: Eros and
Thanatos. But while Freud held that the
suppression of destruction and aggression
by means of beauty, purity and order enables
the development of culture, Weibel claims
that the goal of art is to reveal Thanatos as

something belonging not only to nature,
but also to society and its culture. Art which
aims to surpass naive humanism should
not hide the dark sides of human nature;
instead, it should cut into the body of the
society which produces aggression and
destruction and in which it forms a part.

In his paper "Eros and Thanatos of
Communism", the Russian theorist
Alexander Jakimovich refers to Bataille
in pointing to the motives for the work
of totalitarian Communist and Nazi
politicians, and geniuses who create
the highest culture and art: both groups
belong to shamanic, irrational, marginal,
bohemian, and delinquent forces in
society.[16] Yet while after their romantic
revolutionary euphoria the powerful have
adjusted their pedigree and have taken
care to secure appropriate biographies,
the role of art has been more and more
to liberate those issues wrapped in the
Dionysian darkness and to deconstruct
the hidden mechanisms of power. Body
art is the kind of art that treats the body—
at least from the current perspective—
as something perceived by means of
representation. In this sense it is a social
construct, but not exclusively, for we
cannot deny the physical existence of the
body. Both natures of the body are not
necessarily concordant; the body is being
controlled, but at the same time it also
exercises control itself.[17]

In this text, the body represents a metaphor
for numerous other relationships, in which
the games of power and control take place.
Earlier we spoke of the games of control in
the relationships between East and West,
and between body and reason. Now I wish
to discuss this issue from the aspect of the
relationships between body art and Eastern
European institutions of art, between the
individual and the collective as evidenced in
Eastern European body art of the 1960s and
1970s, between identity and the assumed

role of the body in the framework of art
in the 1980s, and between the old and the
new identity of body art in the period of
social and political transitions in the East
in the 1990s.

ON THE MARGIN OF STATE-SUBSIDISED INSTITUTIONS
The beginnings of art based on the artist's
body, also called body art in the East,
go back to the 1960s. The term body art
includes very different art practices based
on the artist's own body as the main bearer
of various socio-political, existential and
cosmological contents. Certain artists have
been constantly inventing new names for
art within this framework, only to emphasise
the importance of their own work and
their independence from Western trends.
Most outstanding in this connection is the
Polish artist Jerzy Beres, whose work is
based primarily on his national tradition.
Beres developed his own concept of
"independence" comprising both the
artist's individual freedom and freedom
of the wider collective.

Body art in Eastern Europe started to
emerge back in the time of McLuhan's
global village, and it certainly belongs
to the developmental line of the broader
European-American art tradition. Hubert
Klocker searched for the genealogy of
European performative practices in the
works of Dadaists, Duchamp, and Pollock,
in the development of desperate social
conditions in Europe in the 1940s and
1950s, and in the works of Alfred Wols
and Antonin Artaud. Klocker emphasised
the importance of turning back—after
the fall of totalitarian regimes, both the
Communists and the Nazi-Fascists—to
pre-war national art traditions.[18]

If we thus discount the wider European
tradition, the pre-war experience of Futurists,
Dadaists and Surrealists, from the context
of Eastern European art, we are left with
the rich tradition of Russian Futurists and

Constructivists, together with numerous local avant-garde movements from the beginning of the century. Particularly where the Communist regime was at its most repressive, the model of the avant-garde and its manner of work helped artists to create a kind of communication network. Even pre-war avant-garde movements had developed ways of connecting with each other, which helped artists to overcome their isolated and marginal position during the totalitarian period. Particularly those artists who relied on new art practices frequently functioned in groups modelled on the avant-garde; they published newspapers, wrote manifestos, prepared joint actions, and internationalised their activities to a workable extent. The Fluxus international movement had great significance also in the East—if nothing else, it enabled Eastern artists to make contacts with the outer world, i.e. via mail art. Prague even had its own Fluxus festival in 1966, organised by Milan Knížák together with Ben Vautier, Alison Knowels, Serge Oldenburg, and Dick Higgins.

Of course, the levels of isolation in the East varied. The most repressive regimes were in Romania, Bulgaria and Russia, while the level of freedom, was highest in the former Yugoslavia. In the countries with the lowest level of personal freedom special conditions emerged for carrying out performative practices. The Romanian artist Ion Gigorescu staged his performances at home, only in front of a photographic camera, since this kind of activity was prohibited in public spaces. In the 1970s and 1980s, a significant culture of actions and rituals developed in private apartments in Moscow, particularly in its suburbs. The Collective Action Group, with its charismatic leader Andrei Monastyrski, performed the biggest number of events for closed circles of people in the 1970s. On the other hand, for instance, artists in the former Yugoslavia functioned in a less isolated way and had more opportunities for cooperation with the outside world, primarily via guest exhibitions of numerous important foreign artists exhibiting particularly in the Belgrade Student Cultural Centre Gallery and at international festivals such as BITEF—Belgrade International Theatre Festival—founded in 1967, or the New Tendencies international exhibitions in Zagreb in the 1960s, and International Biennials of Graphic Art, held in Ljubljana since 1955. Performative practices from the East were only seldom represented at events in the West, e.g. the appearances of individual artists at the Edinburgh Festival and the Biennale of the Young in Paris, and at the "Works and Words" international manifestation at the De Appel Foundation in Amsterdam in 1979 under the label of art from Eastern Europe, introducing artists from Hungary, Czechoslovakia, Poland, and Yugoslavia. The international activity of Eastern European artists multiplied in the 1980s, together with an intensive growth of interest in art from these regions. This was a time when the representative type of Eastern European art was forged; it was virtually dictated by Russian artists, especially Erik Bulatov, Ilya Kabakov, and Komar and Melamid. These artists became real stars in the West, while exhibitions of Russian, Czech, Polish, Croatian, and other national arts helped to create the representative picture of the East. The representative type of Eastern European art was formed in the general atmosphere of the transition of art from modernist universalism to post-modernist particularism.

In the 1990s, after just a few years of young democracies, this interest is now vanishing. The eye of multiculturalism has turned elsewhere, to Latin America, Asia and Africa. However, it will never be as it was. The political and economic exchanges between East and West resulted in cultural exchanges. Networks of state-run galleries, at least a bit less inert nowadays, provide for a larger flow of information in Eastern European countries, together with the Soros Centres for Contemporary Arts, whose role in some countries is decisive. And Manifesta, the new European biennale established in 1996, is now ensuring continuous presentations of Eastern art in the best possible way.

As already mentioned, the art discussed here requires permanent confirmation—despite its decades-long tradition—by emphasising its own history and cultural context. Regardless of this fact, however, we can speak of the marginal status of performative practices in the West only under certain conditions. Despite its liveliness and inherent provocativeness, body art as an art form has already been institutionalised in the West. The highly specialised Western museology has succeeded in finding appropriate ways of collecting, presenting and recording body art and similar art practices. One of the important reasons for the emergence of performative practices—opposition to the commercialisation and musealisation of art—has been long forgotten. And the non-materiality of these works no longer prevents their presentation and circulation in the art market network. One clear example is the 1998 exhibition of Marina Abramović in Bern, in which the artist recycled her best performances from her 30 year history of creative work by means of the latest technology, and thus invested them—in contrast to the claims that only physical presence enables the full meaning of a work—with new life.

But things are still moving slowly in the East. This is evidenced by the simple fact that the bulk of material for the exhibition has been acquired from the artists themselves. Very little of this kind of material can be found in the repositories of state museums. There is probably no need to point out the low technical quality of the material;

a great part of it had to be copied for the needs of the Body and the East exhibition. The fact is, however, that it was precisely and only state institutions that were in a position to support such practices during Socialism. Of course, the main state institutions did not want to occupy themselves with such matters, but the new forms of art were taken care of by marginal, student and youth centres and other alternative spaces, e.g., galleries of the student cultural centres in Zagreb, Belgrade and Ljubljana, the Foksal Gallery in Warsaw, etc., and as mentioned, many of these actions took place in private apartments, out of the control and attention of institutions, while actions in public, particularly on the streets, were most frequently banned—and artists even arrested—by the police. Artists were often condemned for hooliganism, for destroying the sacred icons of Communism and Socialism, and in Slovenia in the 1980s even for Fascism.

From the 1960s on, artists in the West have been acting, in one way or another, against the manipulation of the art market. In the East, where the market was non-existent (nor has it developed to date), artists acted against manipulation by the state-ideological apparatus. If the West knew how to take advantage of the Otherness of artistic practices and prove its own openness, the Eastern regimes succeeded in keeping new art practices constantly on the margin—even today they arouse unease.

Because of the absence of an art market, art in the East has referred to itself and has used its own language, while the artists understood this remoteness as their personal freedom. They took the space on the margins as their oasis of freedom, the only space which allowed the development of artists' autonomous creativity, which elsewhere was under attack from the prevailing spirit of collectivism. In such conditions, art in the East, particularly in the 1960s and

1970s, acquired a special utopian dimension, resulting in the emergence of a special type of bohemian artist marked by a heroic individual stance.

Performative practices in Eastern and Western European art in the 1960s and 1970s did not display—at least superficially, in their appearance—any essential differences. I do not agree with some arguments claiming that the repression in the East was reflected in the greater aggression of Eastern European artists towards their bodies, for example. Chris Burden, Gina Pane, or Günter Brus did not torture their own bodies less than Marina Abramović, Petr Štembera, or Tibor Hajas. We could also look for differences in subjects related to local traditions, particularly in the works of Jerzy Beres and Paul Neagu, but this would not bring us any closer to the essence. In the work of artists living under the Communist regime, such as Raša Todosijevi , Radomir Damnjan, and Jerzy Truszkowski, the stressing of political themes was also not so direct that this could determine our orientation in the search for particularities of body art in the East.

The difference between the practices of these two contrasting spaces lies in something that is actually invisible and non-signified. Thus, for example, the naked men's bodies in the photographs by Ion Grigorescu or Tomislav Gotovac do not tell us much about the particularities of the artist's socio-political surroundings. When Gotovac ran naked through the streets of Belgrade, and Grigurescu photographed his own genitals, these acts bore no direct political message. Nevertheless, if we know the context in which these works were made, we also know that the very fact of the appearance of a naked artist in public had a political dimension. In the East, where the threat of police surveillance and censorship was omnipresent, people were very cautious in their public behaviour and communication.

It is true that the public exposure of what was private was (and still is) also limited in democratic environments, but this is ascribed primarily to public morals. One of the essential differences between East and West lies in the fact that similar gestures are read differently in different spaces. And they are only read at a certain level, for the roots of every human behaviour must be searched for much deeper than the momentary socio-political situation. On the other hand, the messages of the naked man's body in Eastern art and in Western art do not differ to the extent that might be imagined. While it has already been said that the representation of the naked man's body and his genitals in Eastern European art bore the mark of anarchy, Western European art—specifically, Mapplethorpe's photographs with surely the most subversive element, the erect penis—underlined two other dimensions: the "demystification of the patriarchate and exposition of homosexuality as the most frightening element".[19] We must admit that in essence these two identifications are not much different. And the woman's body, depicted in Social Realism as asexual and androgyne, featured in the performative practices primarily as a bearer of freedom and individuality. Be it the ritual body of Marina Abramović, the cosmological bodies in the direct connection with natural rhythms of Natalia LL and Teresa Murak, the intimate body of Sanja Iveković, the erotic body of Vlasta Delimar, the body of Egle Rakauskaite,"treated" with honey and fat, or the disease exhausted body of Katarzyna Kozyra: the works of these artists represent the liberation of the body, they point—at least indirectly—to an active relationship with both society and nature. Despite the fact that the 1970s were prone to individual mythologies, promoted at Szeemann's Documenta 5, it should not be forgotten that autonomy, borne also by the naked body, had another meaning in the

East, where the autonomy of the individual included a political dimension because of the marginalisation of individualism.

In the 1980s, when democratic changes began to take place in the East—most notably in Mikhail Gorbachev's perestroika—the belief in great ideologies started to crumble. Together with this we also saw the decline of the construct of the autonomous individual, the myth of the artist-hero from previous decades. The novelty introduced by performative practices in this decade has been primarily in the distance towards one's own identity, as well as towards pure and coherent modes of expression. The 1980s brought new forms of social behaviour, no longer based on a search for the authentic identity of the individual, but emphasising the formation of personality. In this decade we find theatre everywhere: on the streets, in the subculture scene—with the prevailing punk movement in the East—and in art. Performative practices no longer exposed the artist's body as the bearer of individuality, but emphasised its possibility of transformation into different roles. In the 1980s, performance activity was especially interesting within the 'subculture' scene, combining the domains of visual art, rock music, new media, and theatre. One of the strongest scenes of this kind was certainly in Ljubljana, exemplified in the concerts of the groups Borghesia and Laibach. The play on equating Nazi and Communist iconography (Laibach) and on destroying sexual taboos (Borghesia) was analogous to the unveiling of traumatic issues in psychoanalytic practice. But then the therapeutic effect was directed more towards society and less towards the individual, which was the characteristic of older performance arts. Compare Marina Abramović's performance *Role Exchange* from 1975, in which the artist replaced an Amsterdam prostitute in a shop window, while the latter replaced the artist at the opening of her exhibition, and the

performance by the group Laibach, that is the interview in which members of the group assumed the roles of totalitarians, while the TV Slovenia reporter took them quite seriously. The difference in the acting between the former and the latter is actually the difference between the performative practices of the 1970s and those of the 1980s: while Marina Abramović merely tests her will by acting the role in a rather challenging situation, Laibach's intention is to expose—through their acted behaviour—the mechanisms of power. In the 1980s, artists started to distance themselves from and even satirise the laborious and self-torturing performances of the 1970s. Certain performances in the 1980s (and also in the 1990s)—e.g. by Mare Kovacic, the Autoperforationsartisten, Józef Robakowski, and Jirí Suruvka—show not only irony, but even a parody of body art.

The loss of identity in the 1990s is more disastrous for the artists than the loss in the games of the 1980s. In the 1990s, after the fall of Communist regimes, artists in certain countries have found themselves in even worse conditions. This is not only a time when a new socio-political situation has been emerging, but also a time of formation of new states. In these new states began the development of new spaces of art: in Lithuania and Moldova, for example, where performance practices have no tradition. We can suddenly find artists there, who express the newly-emerged situation with the sovereign languages of performance. In these conditions the artist often feels as if he is being pushed to the edge of civilisation, as evidenced in the work *A Thrown-out Man* by Ceslovas Lukenskas, in which the artist is literally thrown into a rubbish dump. The 1990s is also a time of new socio-political chaos, in certain places only controlled by mafia. I have already pointed to such a situation in the connection with the works of Brener and Kulik. The 1990s is, furthermore, a time

of new nationalistic regimes, particularly in Serbia and Croatia. Artist have been emigrating from these countries, but if they stayed, their presence is felt more as absence. Tanja Ostojic speaks very poetically of such a situation in her work *Personal Spaces*. She first inhabited it with her own body, but then abandoned it, and throughout the exhibition there was only her trace in the white dust on the floor. The 1990s is also a time of the war in the Balkans, reflected in the works of Božidar Jurjevi from Dubrovnik, Slaven Tolj, and Nebojša Šeric-Šoba from Sarajevo as a situation in which the artist finds himself not only without food, but also without communication and language. This is the decade in which artists have been returning to the physical body, which was almost entirely overlooked in the 1980s. The shock experienced in the face of the transition to the new reality, and the direct threat of war to our bodies—for the war in the Balkans was actually directed against the body, employing the most primitive means, i.e. knives and raping—have reminded us that we are captives of our physical existence. Despite the fact that many new things are taking place in the East, we could not speak of a representative type of Eastern art, since art in the West is also returning to the use of the body. It reacts similarly, but not entirely because of the same reasons. In the West, this kind of art is also created because of the threat of death, but even more pronounced reasons are the stronger sense of the disappearance of the real in the virtual, AIDS, racial discrimination, non-liberated women, and bio-engineering. However, all these reasons are not so distant in the East.

In recent years we find the iconography of Life in Eastern European art beside the iconography of Death, which is reflected in the works of younger artists as the enthusiasm for new technologies, new communications and the accelerated flow of energies between East and West. The most notable example of this kind is the work of the Rassim Krastev, who invigorates his work daily with vitamins sent by Ami Barak, a curator from the West.

The East and the West still remain two different spaces, but the plays of representation between them are less and less discernible. The Eastern identity in the performance art of the 1990s is becoming more and more elusive, hovering between local particularities and a mass of identities dispersed in virtual spaces, between the red star of Communism and the new yellow star of the European Community.

EDITOR'S NOTE

First, when reading Zdenka Badovinac's essay "Body and the East" the present membership of the European Union and therefore a "united Europe" must be mentioned. 12 years since the essay was published in 1998, ten Eastern European countries have been accepted into the EU, presumably less "cautiously" than mentioned by Badovinac: the Czech Republic, Estonia, Hungary, Latvia, Lithuania, Poland, Slovakia and Slovenia in 2004; and Bulgaria and Romania in 2007. As these countries previously on the periphery become centralised, it can be considered that this "Otherness" that Badovinac discusses becomes somewhat less salient.

Secondly, there also appears to be greater appreciation for the musealisation of Eastern European art, as new galleries and exhibitions continue to open internationally— but most importantly, within the region itself as borders are dissolved and new countries are borne, each with its own emerging art scene. Also, Manifesta— the new European biennale—remains influential, now in its eighth year; and, poignantly, Marina Abramović's work has once again been recycled in a major retrospective at the Museum of Modern Art (MoMA), New York—Marina Abramović: The Artist is Present, from March–May 2010.

The inclusion of "Body and the East" within this survey of Eastern European contemporary art, even though written over ten years ago, is a considered decision, in reflection of the widespread influence of "body art" that emerged in the early 1960s in Eastern Europe. Appropriated by artists as a response to strict political regimes and their own marginalisation by the authorities, names such as Alexander Brener, Marina Abramović and KwieKulik soon became synonymous with the term, as the use of the body as a

tool with which artist's could articulate their social and political disillusionments gained increasing prevalence over the following years. Therefore, in producing a comprehensive survey on Eastern European contemporary art, body art as a medium must be discussed; its historical and cultural relevance remaining fundamental in any exploration into the subject.

1 Freud, Sigmund, *Civilization and Its Discontents*, New York: W W Norton & Company Inc., 1962, p. 60.

2 Eastern Europe is not meant as a geographical term, but as a term of popular politics, referring to the countries of the various former Socialist regimes.

3 After the title of Slavoj Žižek's essay, "Multiculturalism, or the Cultural Logic of Multinational Capitalism", *Razpol, glasilo freudovskega polja*, no. 10, *Problemi* 5–6, 1997.

4 Žižek, "Multiculturalism, or the Cultural Logic of Multinational Capitalism", p. 107.

5 The fact that Beuys had stretched Eastern Europe as far as China, is entirely irrelevant in this case.

6 Dyogot, E,"The Revenge of the Background", iSilvia Eiblmayr, ed., *Zonen der Ver-Störung/ Zones of Disturbance*, Graz: Steirischer Herbst, 1997, p. 44.

7 Zabel, I, "'We' and 'the Others'". The essay was presented at the *We and the Others* conference, organised in the framework of the ART Manege 97 Moscow International Art Fair, 6–7 December 1997.

8 Here I would like to point to the difference between body art and performance, as stated by Amelia Jones: "The work that emerged during the period—from the 1960s to the mid-1970s—was labelled 'body art' or 'body works' by several contemporaneous writers who wished to differentiate it from a conception of 'performance art' that was at once broader—in that it reached back to *Dada* and encompassed any kind of theatricalised production on the part of a visual artist—and narrower—in that it implied that a performance must actually take place in front of an audience, most often in an explicitly theatrical, proscenium-based setting. I am interested in work that may or may not initially have taken place in front of the audience: in works—as *take place through enactment of the artist's body, whether it be 'performance' setting or in the relative privacy of the studio, that is then documented such that it can be experienced subsequently through photography, film, video* and/or text." Jones, Amelia, *Body Art. Performing the Subject*, Minneapolis, London: University of Minnesota Press, 1998, p. 13. (Italics by the author.)

9 Phelan, Peggy, *Unmarket–The Politics of Performance*, London and New York: Routledge, 1993, p. 1.

10 Salecl, Renata, "Love me, love my dog", *Index. Scandinavian Art and Culture*, 1996, no. 3–4., p. 117.

11 Salecl, "Love me, love my dog", p. 117. Brener, Alexander, *The Dream of Democratic

12 Culture, It's a Better World; Russicher Aktionismus und sein Kontext*, Wiener Secession, Vienna, 6 June–13 July 1997, exhibition catalogue, p. 22.

13 Quoted in the essay by Hubert Klocker, "Gesture and the Object", *Out of Actions– Between Performance and the Object, 1949–1979*, The Museum of Contemporary Art, Los Angeles, 8 Feb–10 May 1998, exhibition catalogue, p. 166.

14 McEvilley, Thomas, "Art in the Dark", Artforum, Summer 1983, pp. 62–71.

15 Žižek, Slavoj, The Plague of Phantasms, Ljubljana: Analecta, 1997, p. 86.

16 Jakimović Aleksandar, "The Eros and Thanatos of Communism", *New Moment*, Belgrade, 4/1995, p. 110.

17 Regarding the body that controls I shall point to the problem of judicial practice. Alan Hyde discusses the issue of the sexual-violence convicts, who defended themselves by stating that they were unable to control their bodies. Hyde, Alan, *Bodies of Law*, New Jersey: Princeton University Press, Princeton, 1997.

18 Klocker, "Gesture and the Object", p.166

19 Pejic, Bojana, "Communism in my mind", *Wounds, Between Democracy and Redemption in Contemporary Art*, Stockholm: Moderna Museet, 1998, exhibition catalogue; Alan Hyde quotes Peter Brook, *Bodies of Law*, p. 150.

CONTRIBUTORS

BORIS GROYS

Boris Groys is an acknowledged authority on late Soviet postmodern art and literature and the Russian avant-garde. A philosopher, art critic and theorist, Groys is Professor of Philosophy and Art Theory at the Academy for Design in Karlsruhe, Germany, and Global Professor of Russian and Slavic Studies at New York University.

EDA CUFER

One of the co-founders of Slovenian art collective NSK, Eda Cufer is a dramaturge, curator and writer, whose essays and articles on theatre, art, dance, culture and politics have appeared in numerous books and journals internationally.

IGOR ZABEL

Igor Zabel, 1958–2005, was a Slovenian curator, writer and cultural theorist, who wrote widely on Eastern European art. Zabel's work as a curator saw him organise numerous exhibitions, including the coordination of Manifesta Three from 1998–2000.

MARINA ABRAMOVIĆ

Serbian performance artist Marina Abramović's prolific career, exploring the relationship between performer, audience and the body's limitations, has recently been celebrated in a retrospective of her work at the Museum of Modern Art, New York. Her manifestos are intended to be performed and give an insight into the artist's guiding principles for her practice.

PIOTR PIOTROWSKI

Polish-born Piotr Piotrowski is Professor Ordinarius at the Art History Department, Adam Mickiewicz University, Poznań, Poland, and Director of the National Museum in Warsaw. An authority on Central and East European modern art, Piotrowski has written extensively on the subject.

ZDENKA BADOVINAC

Zdenka Badovinac is an international curator and writer, as well as the director of the Moderna Galerija, Ljubljana, establishing the first collection of Eastern European art: Moderna galerija's 2000+ Arteast Collection.

ARTIST BIOGRAPHIES

ADRIAN GHENIE
Romanian, b. 1977 in Baia Mare, Romania. Lives and works in Cluj,
Romania and Berlin, Germany
EDUCATION
2001 University of Art and Design, Cluj, Romania
SELECTED GROUP EXHIBITIONS
2009 I've Watered a Horseshoe as if It Were a Flower, Mihai Nicodim Gallery, Los Angeles, USA
2009 Show Me a Hero, Calvert 22, London, UK
2008 Drawings & Other Works on Paper, Tim Van Laere Gallery, Antwerp, Belgium
2007 Across The Trees, David Nolan Gallery, New York, USA
2006 Small Wonder, Andreiana Mihail Gallery, Bucharest, Hungary
SELECTED SOLO EXHIBITIONS
2009 Rainbow at dawn, Tim Van Laere Gallery, Antwerp, Germany
2008 The Flight into Egypt, Nolan Judin Berlin, Germany Dig and Hide, Chung King Project,
       Los Angeles, USA If You Open It You Get Dirty, Galeria Plan B, Cluj, Romania

ADRIAN PACI
Albanian, b. 1969 in Shkoder, Albania. Lives and works in Milan, Italy
SELECTED GROUP EXHIBITIONS
2010 IBRIDO, PAC, Milan
2009 ATOPIA: Art and the City in the 21st Century, Centre de Cultura Contemporània
       de Barcelona, Spain
2009 Post- American L.A., 18th Street Arts Center, Santa Monica, USA
2008 Street and Studio in Urban History of Photography, Tate Modern, London, UK
SELECTED SOLO EXHIBITIONS
2010 Gestures, Francesca Kaufmann, Milan, Italy
2008 Subjects in Transit, Center for Contemporary Art CCA, Tel Aviv
2007 Transculture, Bunkier Sztuki, Kraków, Poland

ALEKSANDRA MIR
Polish, b. 1967 in Lubin, Poland. Lives and works in Palermo, Sicily and New York, USA.
EDUCATION
1996 Cultural Anthropology, The Graduate Faculty, New School for Social Research,
       New York, USA
1992 BFA Media Arts, School of Visual Arts, New York, USA
1987 Communication & Media Studies, Schillerska/Gothenburg University,
       Gothenburg, Sweden
SELECTED GROUP EXHIBITIONS
2010 Star City: The Future Under Communism, Nottingham Contemporary,
       Nottingham, UK
2008 Making a Scene, Fondazione Morra Greco, Naples, Italy
2004 Terminal 5, JFK Airport, New York, USA
1999 Empires without States, Swiss Institute, New York, USA
SELECTED SOLO EXHIBITIONS
2010 Il Sogno e la Promessa, Magazzino d'arte Moderna, Rome, Italy
2007 Newsroom 1986-2000, Mary Boone Gallery, New York, USA
2005 Aeropuerto, Galeria Joan Prats, Barcelona, Spain
1999 First Woman on the Moon, Casco Projects, Utrecht, Netherlands

ALEXANDER BRODSKY
Russian, b. 1955 in Moscow, Former USSR
EDUCATION
1978 The Moscow Architecture Institute, Moscow, Former USSR
SELECTED GROUP EXHIBITIONS
2008 Russian Dreams…, Bass Museum of Art, Miami, USA
2006 Depository of Dreams, White Space Gallery, London, UK
SELECTED SOLO EXHIBITIONS
2007 Alexander Brodsky, Ronald Feldman Fine Arts, New York, USA
2006 Inhabited Locality, Russian Pavillion, Venice Biennale, Italy
2002 The Installation, Aedes Gallery, Berlin, Germany

ALEXANDER KOSOLAPOV
Russian, b. 1943 in Moscow, Former USSR. Lives and works in New York, USA
SELECTED GROUP EXHIBITIONS
2009 Movie Painting, National Center For Contemporary Art (NCCA),
       Moscow Branch, Moscow, Russia
2007 Sots Art. Art politique en Russie de 1972 à aujourd'hui ,
       La Maison Rouge, Paris, France
2006 Arteast Collection 2000+23, Moderna Galerija Ljubljana, Slovenia
SELECTED SOLO EXHIBITIONS
1993 New Post-Communist Billboards oder Bilder aus dem Neuen Rußland, Galerie
       Inge Baecker, Bad Münstereife, Germany

ANDRZEJ JACKOWSKI
Polish, b. 1947 Wales
EDUCATION
1966 Camberwell School of Art, London, UK
1967 Falmouth School of Art, UK
1974 Royal College of Art, London, UK
SELECTED GROUP EXHIBITIONS
2010 Another Country: London Painters in Dialogue with Italian Art, Estorick
       Collection, London, UK
2008 In Drawing, Purdy Hicks Gallery, London, UK
2003 Three from The Royal College of Art, London, New England School of Art
       and Design, Suffolk University, Boston, MA, USA
SELECTED SOLO EXHIBITIONS
2010 The Remembered Present, Purdy Hicks Gallery, London
2008 David Krut Projects, New York, USA

ANDREI MONASTYRSKI
Russian, b.1949.
SELECTED GROUP EXHIBITIONS
2010 Glasnost: Soviet Non-Conformist Art from the 1980s, Haunch of Venison,
       London, UK
2009 Total Enlightenment. Moscow Conceptual Art 1960—1990, Fundación Juan
       March, Madrid, Spain

ANDREI MOLODKIN

Russian, b. 1966 in Boui, Former USSR

EDUCATION

1976 Special School of Arts-Plastiques, Boui, Former USSR

1987 Faculty of Architecture and Interior Design Strogonov Academy, Moscow

SELECTED GROUP EXHIBITIONS

2007 East/West, Orel Art Gallery, Paris, France

2006 Petrodollar, Pierogi and Ronald Feldman Fine Arts, Miami, USA

SELECTED SOLO EXHIBITIONS

2009 Andrei Molodkin: Liquid Modernity (Grid and Greed), Orel Art Gallery, London

2008 Guts a la Russe, Orel Art Gallery, Paris

2007 Sweet Crude American Dream, Daneyal Mahmood Gallery, New York

ANRI SALA

Albanian, b. 1974 in Tirana, Albania. Lives and works in Berlin, Germany

EDUCATION

1996 National Academy of Arts, Tirana, Albania

1998 Ecole Nationale Superieure des Arts Decoratifs, Paris, France

2000 Le Fresnoy, Studio National des Arts Contemporains, Tourcoing, France

SELECTED GROUP EXHIBITIONS

2010 Photo I, Photo You, Calvert 22, London, UK

2007 Absolute Beginners, Isola Art Centre, Milan, Italy

2003 Moving Pictures, Guggenheim Bilbao, Bilbao, Spain
1999 After the Wall: Art and Culture in Post-Communist Europe, Moderna Museet, Stockholm, Sweden

SELECTED SOLO EXHIBITIONS

2009 Answer Me, Johnen Galerie, Berlin, Germany

2007 A Second Look, Hauser & Wirth, London, UK

2002 Ikon Gallery, Birmingham, UK

ARTUR ŻMIJEWSKI

Polish, b. 1966 in Warsaw, Poland. Lives and works in Warsaw

EDUCATION

1995 Department of Sculpture, Warsaw Academy of Fine Arts, Warsaw, Poland

1999 Gerrit Rietveld Academie, Amsterdam, Netherlands

SELECTED GROUP EXHIBITIONS

2010 Promise of the Past, Centre Pompidou, Paris, France

2006 You Won't Feel a Thing, Kunsthaus Dresden, Germany

2001 What Does the Corpse's Glazed Pupil See, Academia Theatre, Warsaw, Poland

1998 Germinations 10, The Factory, Athens, Greece

1991 Cardinal, Supper, Dziekanka Gallery, Warsaw, Poland

SELECTED SOLO EXHIBITIONS

2009 Artur Żmijewski, Museum of Modern Art, New York, USA

2006 Repetition, Wattis Institute for Contemporary Art, California College of Arts, California, USA

2001 Out for a Walk, Foksal Gallery, Warsaw, Poland

1996 Sardines' Song, a.r.t. Gallery, Plock, Poland

BORIS MIKHAILOV

Ukrainian, b. 1938 in Kharkov, Former USSR. Lives and works in Berlin, Germany and Kharkov, Ukraine

SELECTED GROUP EXHIBITIONS

2007 Twilight—Photography in the Magic Hour, Victoria and Albert Museum, London, UK

2003 Cruel + Tender, The Real in Twentieth-Century Photography, Tate Modern, London, UK

1998 Richard Billingham & Boris Mikhailov, Galerie Barbara Gross, Munich, Germany

SELECTED SOLO EXHIBITIONS

2006 Moments/Monuments, Bereznitsky Gallery, Berlin, Germany

2004 Institute of Contemporary Art, Boston, USA

2000 Boris Mikhailov, The Photographers Gallery, London, UK

BRACO DIMITRIJEVIĆ

Bosnian, b. 1977 in Sarajevo, Bosnia and Herzegovina. Lives and works in Paris, France

EDUCATION

1968 MA Academy of Fine Arts, Zagreb, Croatia

1971 Post-graduate at Central Saint Martins School of Art, London, UK

SELECTED GROUP EXHIBITIONS

2009 Who Killed the Painting? Neues Museum, Nuremberg, Germany

2008 Interiors, Oredaria, Rome

2006–2007 Busy Going Crazy, The Parlestein Collection, La Maison Rouge, Paris, France

2005 Open Systems: Rethinking Art c. 1970, Tate Modern, London

SELECTED SOLO EXHIBITIONS

2009 Musée d'Art Moderne Saint-Etienne, France

2008 National Museum of Contemporary Art, Budapest, Hungary

2006 Imperial College of China—Temple of Confucius, Beijing, China

CHRISTO VLADIMIROV JAVACHEFF

American, b. 1935 in Gabrovo, Bulgaria

EDUCATION

1956 Fine Arts Academy, Sofia, Bulgaria

1957 Fine Arts Academy, Vienna, Austria

JEANNE-CLAUDE DENAT DE GUILLEBON

American, b. 1935 in Casablanca, Morocco. d. 2009 in New York City, USA

EDUCATION

1952 Latin and Philosophy, University of Tunis, Tunisia

SELECTED WORKS

2005 The Gates, Central Park. New York City, USA, 1979–2005

1999 The Wall, 13, 000 Oil Barrels, Gasometer, Oberhausen, Germany, 1998–1999

1983 Surrounded Islands, Biscayne Bay, Greater Miami, Florida, USA, 1980–1983

1976 Running Fence, Sonoma and Marine Counties, California, USA, 1972–1976

1969 Wrapped Museum of Contemporary Art, Chicago, USA

CIPRIAN MUREŞAN

Romanian, b. 1977 in Cluj, Romania. Lives and works in Cluj, Romania

EDUCATION

2003 University of Art and Design, Cluj, Romania

SELECTED GROUP EXHIBITIONS

2010 There Is No Alternative, Konsthall C, Hokarangen, Stockholm, Sweden

2007 Across The Trees—Romanian Art Now, David Nolan Gallery, New York, USA

2006 Small Wonder, Andreiana Mihail Gallery, Bucharest, Romania

SELECTED SOLO EXHIBITIONS

2008 Ciprian Mureşan: Compulsory Rules, Prometeogallery, Milan, Italy

2006 Ciprian Mureşan—Karlin Studios, Prague, Czech Republic

DAN PERJOVSCHI

Romanian, b. 1972 in Sibiu, Romania. Lives and works in Bucharest, Romania

EDUCATION

1985 MFA, George Enescu Conservatoire of Fine Arts, Iasi, Romania

SELECTED GROUP EXHIBITIONS

2010 The Promises of the Past, Centre Pompidou, Paris, France

2006 Back to Back, Lombard-Freid Projects, New York, USA

1999 Body and the East, Moderna Galerija, Ljubljana, Slovenia

SELECTED SOLO EXHIBITIONS

2010 Drawing Institute, San Francisco Institute of the Arts, San Francisco, USA

2008 All over, Wiels Centre for Contemporary Art, Brussels, Belgium

2006 The Room Drawing, Tate Modern, London, UK

DAVID MALJKOVIC

Croatian, b. 1973 in Rijeka, Croatia. Lives and Works in Zagreb, Croatia

EDUCATION

1996 Art Department, Faculty of Philosophy, University of Rijeka, Croatia,

1999 Multimedia Alternative, Academy of Fine Arts, University of Zagreb, Croatia

2000 Department of Painting, Academy of Fine Arts, University of Zagreb, Croatia

SELECTED GROUP EXHIBITIONS

2010 Star City: The Future Under Communism, Nottingham Contemporary, Nottingham, UK

2008 Cohabitation, Galleria Francesca Kaufmann, Milan, Italy

2004 Painting and Object, Museum of Modern Art, Dubrovnik, Croatia

SELECTED SOLO EXHIBITIONS

2009 Retired Compositions, Metro Pictures, New York, USA

2005 Waiting Tomorrow, Annet Gelink Gallery, Amsterdam, Netherlands

2002 Paintings for everyday use, Miroslav Kraljevic Gallery, Zagreb, Croatia

DEIMANTAS NARKEVIČIUS

Lithuanian, b. 1964 in Utena, Lithuania

SELECTED GROUP EXHIBITIONS

2010 Into the Unknown, Ludlow 38, New York City, USA

2008 Yes, No and Other Options, S1 Artspace, Sheffield, UK

2005 Do Not Interrupt Your Activities, Royal College of Art Galleries, London, UK

SELECTED SOLO EXHIBITIONS

2010 Deimantas Narkevičius: The Unanimous Life of Art, Kunsthallen Brandts, Odense, Denmark

2007 Among the things we touched, Wiener Secession, Vienna, Austria

2002 GB Agency, Paris, France

DÓRA MAURER

Hungarian, b. 1937 in Budapest, Hungary. Lives and works in Budapest, Hungary and Vienna, Austria

EDUCATION

1955 Akademie der Bildenden Künste, Budapest, Hungary

SELECTED GROUP EXHIBITIONS

2009 Phases of Movement, Dominik Art Projects, Kraków, Poland

2008 Richtig Farbe, Galerie Linde Hollinger, Ladenburg, Germany

2007 For a Special Place, Generali Foundation Collection, Austrian Cultural Forum, New York, USA

SELECTED SOLO EXHIBITIONS

2008–2009 Dóra Maurer—Concise Oeuvre, Ludwig Museum, Budapest, Hungary

2007 Fotoworks, Vintage Galéria, Budapest, Hungary

2004 Farbräume, Galerie Lindner, Vienna, Austria

EDWARD KRASINSKI

Polish, b. 1925 in Luck, Poland. D. 2004 in Warsaw, Poland

EDUCATION

1942 School of Arts and Crafts, Kraków, Poland

1948 Academy of Fine Arts, Kraków, Poland

SELECTED GROUP EXHIBITIONS

2009 Target Practice: Art Under Attack 1949-1978, Seattle Art Museum, Seattle, USA

2004 Collected Views from East or West, Generali Foundation, Vienna, Austria

1995 Galeria Zacheta, Warsaw, Poland

SELECTED SOLO EXHIBITIONS

2006 Edward Krasinski—Les mises en scene, Generali Foundation, Vienna, Austria

2003 Anton Kern Gallery, New York, USA

1997 Galeria Zacheta, Warsaw, Poland

GOSHKA MACUGA

Polish, b. 1967 in Warsaw, Poland. Lives and works in London, UK

EDUCATION

1987 Diploma in Exhibition Design, Wojciech Gerson's School of Art, Warsaw, Poland

1991 Foundation, City of London Polytechnic, London, UK

1995 BA Hons Fine Art, Central St Martins, London, UK

1996 MA Fine Art, Goldsmith College, London, UK

SELECTED GROUP EXHIBITIONS

2009 Berlin2000, Pace Wildenstein, New York, USA

2005 Can Buildings Curate?, Architectural Association, London, UK

2002 The New Religious Art, Liverpool Biennale, Liverpool, UK

1999 The mountain and a valley, Cubitt Gallery, London, England

SELECTED SOLO EXHIBITIONS

2009 The Nature of the Beast, Whitechapel Gallery, London, UK

2007 Objects in Relation, Art Now, Tate Britain, London, UK

2002 Homeless Furniture, Transmission Gallery, Glasgow, Scotland

1999 Cave, Sali Gia, London, UK

ILYA KABAKOV

Russian, b. 1933 in Dnipropetrovsk, Former USSR. Lives and works in New York, USA

EDUCATION

1957 Graphic Design and Book Illustration, VI Surikov State Art Institute, Moscow, Russia

1951 Art School, Moscow, Russia

EMELIA KABAKOV

Russian, b. 1945 in Dnipropetrovsk, Former USSR. Lives and works in New York, USA

EDUCATION

1972 Spanish Language and Literature, Moscow University, Russia

1966 Irkutsk Music College, Dnipropetrovsk, Ukraine

1959 Moscow Music School, Russia

SELECTED GROUP EXHIBITIONS

2010 The Two Cabinets, Nottingham Gallery of Contemporary Art, Nottingham, UK

2006 Blackwood Gallery, University of Toronto, Toronto, Canada

2000 Visions of the Future: A History of Fears and Hopes of Mankind, Galeries Nationales du Grand Palais, Paris, France

SELECTED SOLO EXHIBITIONS

2010 Vertical Opera, Guggenheim Museum, New York, USA

2005 The House of Dreams, Serpentine Gallery, London, UK

2001 20 Ways to Get an Apple, Listening to the Music of Mozart, Columbus Museum of Art, Columbus, Ohio, USA

JAAN TOOMIK

Estonian, b. 1961 in Tartu, Estonia. Lives and works in Tallinn, Estonia

EDUCATION

1991 MA, Faculty of Painting, Estonian Academy of Arts, Estonia

SELECTED GROUP EXHIBITIONS

2010 A Pair of Left Shoes—Reality Check in Eastern Europe, Museum of Contemporary Art, Zagreb, Croatia

2004 Instant Europe, Vila Manin Centro d'Contemporanea, Codroipo, Italy

2000 L'autre moi tie de L'europe. Galerie Nationale du Jeu de Paume, Paris, France

SELECTED SOLO EXHIBITIONS

2008 Invisible Pearls, Riga Art Space, Riga, Latvia

2005 Videoworks, National Museum of Contemporary Art, Bucharest, Romania

2004 Dancing with Dad, IBID Gallery, London, UK

JAN MANČUŠKA

Slovakian, b. 1972 in Bratislava, Slovakia. Lives and works in Prague, Czech Republic and Berlin, Germany

EDUCATION

1990 Secondary School of Applied Arts, Prague, Czech Republic

1998 Academy of Fine Arts, Prague, Czech Republic

SELECTED GROUP EXHIBITIONS

2009 4 + 4 Days in Motion, 14th International Theatre Festival, Prague, Czech Republic

2005 Wall Pieces, Galerie Jan Mot, Brussels. Belgium

2003 Things You Don't Know, K&S Galerie, Berlin, Germany

SELECTED SOLO EXHIBITIONS

2010 Everything that really is, but has been forgotten, Meyer-Riegger, Berlin, Germany

2005 True Story, Andrew Kreps Gallery, New York, USA
Me, Gallery MXM, Prague, Czech Republic

JIŘÍ KOVANDA

b. 1953 in Prague, Former Czechoslovakia. Lives and works in Prague, Czech Republic

SELECTED GROUP EXHIBITIONS

2010 If Space Meant Nothing, Condotto C, Rome, Italy

2004 Strategies of Desire, Kunsthaus Baseland, Basel, Switzerland

2001 Body and the East, Exit Art, New York, USA

SELECTED SOLO EXHIBITIONS

2009 Galerie Krobath, Berlin, Germany

2006 Krobath Wimmer Gallery, Vienna, Austria

2002 Walled Sausage, Gallery CO 14, Prague, Czech Republic

JOANNA MALINOWSKA

Polish, b. 1972 in Gdynia, Poland. Lives and works in New York, USA

EDUCATION

1998 BFA Rutgers, the State University of New Jersey, New Brunswick, USA

2001 MFA Sculpture, Yale University, New Haven, USA

SELECTED GROUP EXHIBITIONS

2010 Star City ; The Future Under Communism, Nottingham Contemporary, Nottingham, UK

2006 Polyphony of Images, The Consulate General of Poland, New York, USA

2003 In Practice, Sculpture Centre, Long Island City, USA

SELECTED SOLO EXHIBITIONS

2009 Time of Guerrilla Metaphysics, Canada, New York, USA

2007 Umanaqtuaq, Venetia Kapernekas Gallery, New York, USA

2006 In Search of The Miraculous, Continued, Galeria, Okna, Contemporary Art Centre, Warsaw, Poland

JÚLIUS KOLLER

Slovakian, b. 1939 in Piestany, Former Czechoslovakia. d. 2007 in Bratislava, Slovakia

EDUCATION

1958 School of Industrial Arts, Bratislava, Slovakia, Former Czechoslovakia

1965 Academy of Applied Arts and Design, Bratislava, Slovakia

SELECTED GROUP EXHIBITIONS

2010 Star City: The Future Under Communism, Nottingham Contemporary, Nottingham, UK

2003 Links, gb agency, Paris, France

1997 Face a L'Histoire (1933-96), Centre Georges Pompidou, Paris, France

1993 The 1st Floor, Municipal Gallery, Bratislava, Slovakia

SELECTED SOLO EXHIBITIONS

2007 Space is the Place, gb agency, Paris, France

2003 Július Koller Univerzaine Futurologicke Operacie, Kolnischer Kunstverein, Cologne, Germany

1999 Gallery SOGA, Bratislava, Slovakia

1991 Post-Komunikacia, The Art Gallery, Zilina, Slovakia

KAREL MALICH

Czech, b. 1924 in Holice, Czech Republic. Lives and works in Prague, Czech Republic

SELECTED GROUP EXHIBITIONS

2010 Salcman School, Galeria mesta Plzne, Pilsen Municipal Gallery, Pilsen, Czech Republic

2006 Feeling the Line, Marian Goodman Gallery, New York, USA

2002 Beyond Preconceptions, Berkeley Art Museum and Pacific Film Archive, Berkeley, USA

SELECTED SOLO EXHIBITIONS

2008 Diving in beauty, Galeria, Zdenek Sklenar, Prague, Czech Republic

1995 Kunsthalle, Krems, Austria

1989 Gallery of Modern Art, Roudnice, nad Labem, Czech Republic

KATERINA ŠEDÁ

Czech, b. 1972 in Brno, Former Czechoslovakia. Lives and works in Brno and Prague, Czech Republic

EDUCATION

1995 Secondary School of Applied Arts, Hodonin, Czech Republic

1999 Graphic Department, Secondary School of Applied Arts, Brno, Czech Republic

2005 Academy of Fine Arts, Prague, Czech Republic

SELECTED GROUP EXHIBITIONS

2010 A Pair of Left Shoes—Reality Check in Eastern Europe, Museum of Contemporary Art, Zagreb, Croatia

2007 Stalking With Stories, Apexart, New York City, USA

2006 Local Stories, Modern Art Oxford, UK

SELECTED SOLO EXHIBITIONS

2008 The Renaissance Society at the University of Chicago, USA

2007 The Granddaughter, Czech Centre, New York, USA

2006 Arrivals:Czech Republic, Modern Art Oxford, UK

VITALY KOMAR

Russian, b, 1943 in Moscow, Former USSR

EDUCATION

1960 Moscow Art School, Moscow, Former USSR

1967 Stroganov Institute of Art and Design, Moscow, Former USSR

ALEXANDER MELAMID

Russian, b. 1945 in Moscow, Former USSR

EDUCATION

1960 Moscow Art School, Moscow, Former USSR

1967 Stroganov Institute of Art and Design, Moscow, Former USSR

SELECTED GROUP EXHIBITIONS

2009 Contemporary Russian Art, Egon Schiele Art Centrum, Cesky Krumlov, Czech Republic

2006 Artists Against The State: Perestroika Revisited, Ronald Feldman Fine Arts Inc, New York, USA

2001 Democratic Art?, Sprovieri Gallery, London, UK

SELECTED SOLO EXHIBITIONS

2003 Desperately Seeking A Masterpiece, Kawamura Memorial Museum of Art. Chiba, Japan

2000 Asian Elephant Art and Conservation Project, Moore College of Art and Design, Philadelphia, USA

1996 Monumental Propaganda, Kemper Museum of Contemporary Art, Kansas City, USA

KRZYSZTOF WODICZKO

Polish, b. 1943 in Warsaw, Poland. Lives and works in
New York and Cambridge, USA

EDUCATION

1968 MFA, Academy of Fine Arts, Warsaw, Poland

SELECTED GROUP EXHIBITIONS

2007 Open City: Tools for Public Action, Eyebeam, New York, USA

2002 Designs for the Real World, Generali Foundation, Vienna, Austria

1999 Conceptual Reflections in Polish Art, Experience of Discourse 1965–1975,
Contemporary Art Centre, Warsaw, Poland

SELECTED SOLO EXHIBITIONS

2005 Monument Therapy, Zacheta National Gallery of Art, Warsaw, Poland

2001 Projection a Tijuana, Galerie Gabrielle Maubrie, Paris, France

1996 Xenology: Immigrant Instruments, Galerie Lelong, New York, USA

LALA MEREDITH-VULA

Kosovan, b.1966 in Sarajevo, Former Yugoslavia

EDUCATION

1985 Art Foundation, Trent University, Nottingham, UK

1988 Goldsmith College, University of London, UK

1988 Yugoslav Government Post Graduate Scholarship, Pristina University, Kosovo,
former Yugoslavia

SELECTED GROUP EXHIBITIONS

2009 London East Festival, August Gallery, London, UK

2003 Dead Bird Show, Whitechapel Project Space, London, UK

1988 Freeze, London, UK

SELECTED SOLO EXHIBITIONS

2007 Shifting Borders, National Gallery of Art, Tirana, Albania

2003 Homeland, Ruskin Impromptu, Ruskin School of Drawing and Fine Art,
University of Oxford, UK

1991 Photographers' Gallery, London, UK

MARINA ABRAMOVIĆ

Serbian, b. 1946 in Belgrade, Former Yugoslavia. Lives and works in New York, USA

EDUCATION

1970 Academy of Fine Arts, Belgrade, Former Yugoslavia

1972 Academy of Fine Arts, Zagreb, Former Yugoslavia

SELECTED GROUP EXHIBITIONS

2010 Haunted: Contemporary Photographs/Videos/Performances, Guggenheim
Museum, New York, USA

2005 The Artist's Body. Then and Now, Centre d'Art, Contemporain,
Geneva, Switzerland

2000 Performing Bodies. Tate Modern, London, UK

SELECTED SOLO EXHIBITIONS

2010 Marina Abramović: Personal Archaeology, Sean Kelly Gallery, New York, USA

2003 The Star, Contemporary Art Museum, Kumamoto, Japan

1998 Artist Body—Public Body, Museum of Contemporary Art, Valencia, Spain

MILICA TOMIĆ

Serbian, b. 1960 in Beograd, Serbia. Lives and works in Belgrade, Former Yugoslavia

EDUCATION

1990 University of Arts, Belgrade, Former Yugoslavia

SELECTED GROUP EXHIBITIONS

2010 MyWar, Foundation for Art and Creative Technology, Liverpool, UK

2007 Global Feminisms, Brooklyn Museum of Art, New York, USA

2003 Independence, South London Gallery, London, UK

SELECTED SOLO EXHIBITIONS

2010 Museum of Contemporary Art, Belgrade, Serbia

2006 Alone/Reading Capital, Artspace. Sydney, Australia

2001 Dossier, Charim Galerie, Vienna, Austria

MIRCEA CANTOR

Romanian, b. 1977 in Oradea, Romania. Lives and works in Paris, France
and Cluj, Romania

EDUCATION

1999 Ion Andreescu Academy of Visual Arts, Cluj, Romania

2000 Ecole Regionale des Beaux Arts, Nantes, France

2000 Advanced Course of Visual Arts, Fondazione Antonio Ratti, Como, Italy

SELECTED GROUP EXHIBITIONS

2009 Universal Code, The Power Plant, Toronto, USA

2007 Airs de Paris, Centre Pompidou, Paris, France

2004 Quick Sand, De Appel, Amsterdam, the Netherlands

SELECTED SOLO EXHIBITIONS

2009 Which light kills you, The Common Guild, Glasgow, Scotland

2006 The Title Is the Last Thing, Philadelphia Museum of Art, Philadelphia, USA

2005 Dvir Gallery, Tel Aviv, Israel

MIROSŁAW BAŁKA

Polish, b. 1958 in Warsaw, Poland. Lives and works in Warsaw and Otwock, Poland

EDUCATION

1985 Sculpture Department, Warsaw Academy of Fine Arts, Poland

SELECTED GROUP EXHIBITIONS

2008 Minimum—Maximum, BWA Gallery, Lublin, Poland

2004 Eclipse: Towards the Edge of the Visible, White Cube, London, UK

1999 Still, Alexander and Bonin, New York, USA

SELECTED SOLO EXHIBITIONS

2009 Turbine Hall, Tate Modern, London, UK

2006 Force of Light, K21, Düsseldorf, Germany

2000 Quit, White Cube, London, UK

MONIKA SOSNOWSKA

Polish, b. 1972 in Ryki, Poland. Lives and works in Warsaw, Poland

EDUCATION

1993   Schola Posnaniensis, Poznań, Poland

1998   Painting Department, Academy of Fine Arts, Poznań, Poland

2000   Rijksakademie van Beeldende Kunsten, Amsterdam, Belgium

SELECTED GROUP EXHIBITIONS

2010   Les Promesses du Passe, Centre Pompidou, Paris, France

2006   Satellite of Love, Witte de With, Rotterdam, the Netherlands

2003   Architectures of Gender: Contemporary Women's Art in Poland, Sculpture Centre, New York, USA

SELECTED SOLO EXHIBITIONS

2008   The Wind House, Primrose Hill, London, UK

2005   The Tired Room, Freud Museum, Vienna, Austria

2004   Serpentine Gallery, London, UK

NATALIA LL

Polish, b. 1937 in Zywiec. Lives and works in Wroclaw, Poland

EDUCATION

1963   National University of Fine Arts, Wroclaw, Poland

SELECTED GROUP EXHIBITIONS

2009   Gender Check—Femininity and Masculinity in the Art of Eastern Europe, Museum of Modern Art foundation Ludwig Vienna, Austria

2003   Architectures of Gender—Contemporary Women's Art in Poland, Sculpture Centre, New York, USA

1996   Body as Membrane, The Nordic Arts Centre, Helsinki, Finland

1982   Polish Photography, Centre National d'Art et de Culture Georges Pompidou, Paris, France

1976   Foto Idea, Galeria d'Arte Moderna, Parma, Italy

SELECTED SOLO EXHIBITIONS

2008   Natalia LL, Galeria Art NEW Media, Warsaw, Poland

2003   Volucres Coeli, Galeria Sztuki Wozownia, Torun, Poland

1994   Paintings and Installations, Silesian Museum, Katowice, Poland

1980   Pyramid, Galeria Spojrzenia, Wroclaw, Poland

1972   Word, Galeria Permafo, Wroclaw, Poland

NEDKO SOLAKOV

Bulgarian, b. 1957 in Cherven Briag, Bulgaria. Lives and works in Sofia, Bulgaria

EDUCATION

1981   Mural Painting, Academy of Fine Arts, Sofia, Bulgaria

1986   National Hoger Instituut voor Schone Kunsten, Antwerp, Belgium

SELECTED GROUP EXHIBITIONS

2009   For the Use of Those Who See, Kunstwerke, Berlin

2006   Forms of Classification, Cisneros Fontanals Art Foundation, Miami, USA

1999   After the Wall, Moderna Museet, Stockholm, Sweden

SELECTED SOLO EXHIBITIONS

2008   Emotions, Kunstmuseum, Bonn, Germany

2005   Dead—Lock Stories, Galleria Continua, San Gimignano, Italy

1998   Sea Show, Ted Gallery, Varna, Bulgaria

NEUE SLOWENISCHE KUNST (NSK)

Founded in 1984 in Ljubljana, Slovenia

SELECTED GROUP EXHIBITIONS

2009   Outlook: Words from Africa in Utopics,11th Swiss Sculpture Exhibition, Biel/Bienne, Switzerland

SELECTED SOLO EXHIBITIONS

2010   2000 Gesamtkunst Laibach, Fundamentals1980—1990, International Centre of Graphic Arts, Ljubljana, Slovenia

2010   The Eye of the State, Irwin Exhibition at the Israeli Centre for Digital Art, Holon, Israel

2009   Ausstellung Laibach Kunst—Recapitulation 2009, Muzeum Sztuki, Łodz, Poland

OLEG KULIK

Russian, b. 1961 in Kiev, Former USSR. Lives and works in Moscow, Russia

EDUCATION

1979   Kiev Art School, Kiev, Former USSR

1982   Geological Institute, Kiev, Former USSR

SELECTED GROUP EXHIBITIONS

2010   Russian Utopias, Garage Centre for Contemporary Culture, Moscow, Russia

2007   Depository of Dreams, White Space Gallery, London, UK

2005   The Gravity in Art, De Appel, Amsterdam, the Netherlands

SELECTED SOLO EXHIBITIONS

2008   Galerie Rabouan Moussion, Paris, France

2003   Universal Strangers, Galeria Filomena Soares, Lisbon, Portugal

2001   Two Kuliks, Ikon Gallery, Birmingham, UK

OLGA CHERNYSHEVA

Russian, b. 1962 in Moscow, Former USSR. Lives and works in Moscow, Russia

EDUCATION

1986   Moscwo Cinema Academy, Moscow, Former USSR

1996   Rijksakademie van Beeldende Kunsten, Amsterdam, the Netherlands

SELECTED GROUP EXHIBITIONS

2006   Contested Spaces in Post-Soviet Art, Russia Redux 2, Sidney Mishkin Gallery, Barucb College, New York, USA

2004   System of Coordinates: Russian Art Today, Museum of Contemporary Art, Zagreb, Croatia

1995   I don't actually have to go, Lumen Travo Gallery, Amsterdam, the Netherlands

SELECTED SOLO EXHIBITIONS

2006   Panorama, Stella Art Gallery, Moscow, Russia

2004   Zone of Happiness, Heckenhauer Gallery, Berlin, Germany

1993   Krings—Ernst Gallery, Cologne, Germany

PAULINA OLOWSKA

Polish, b. 1976 in Gdansk, Poland. Lives and works in Berlin, Germany and Warsaw, Poland

EDUCATION

1996 BFA, School of the Art Institute of Chicago, Chicago, USA

2000 MFA, Academy of Fine Arts, Gdansk, Poland

SELECTED GROUP EXHIBITIONS

2010 Early Years. KW Institute for Contemporary Art, Berlin, Germany

2006 Between the Lines, Daniel Reich Gallery, New York, USA

2002 Hotel Sub Rosa, Marc Foxx Gallery, Los Angeles, USA

SELECTED SOLO EXHIBITIONS

2010 Accidental Collages, Tramway, Glasgow, Scotland

2006 Cabinet Gallery, London, UK

2004 Arriviste, Galerie Akinci, Amsterdam, the Netherlands

PAVEL BRAILA

Moldovan, b. 1971 in Chisinau, Republic of Moldova. Lives and works in Berlin, Germany and Chisinau, Republic of Moldova

EDUCATION

1994 State Technical University, Chisinau, Republic of Moldova

1997 State University of Moldova, Chisinau, Republic of Moldova

2001 Jan van Eyck Academie, Maastricht, the Netherlands

SELECTED GROUP EXHIBITIONS

2010 A Pair of Left Shoes — Reality Check in Eastern Europe, Museum of
      Contemporary Art, Zagreb, Croatia

2006 Through the Rabbit Hole, 21c Museum, Louisville, USA

2001 Body and the East, Exit Art, New York, USA

SELECTED SOLO EXHIBITIONS

2006 Baltic Art Centre, Visby, Sweden

2005 MIT List Visual Arts Center, Cambridge, USA

2004 33 Revolutions per minute, Yvon Lambert, Paris, France

PAVEL PEPPERSTEIN

Russian, b. 1966 in Moscow, Russia. Lives and works in Moscow, Russia and Tel Aviv, Israel

EDUCATION

1987 Scholarship at Academy of Fine Arts, Prague, Czech Republic

SELECTED GROUP EXHIBITIONS

2010 Diary of a Madman. Regina Gallery, Moscow, Russia

2001 Body of Art, Biennale de Valencia, Valencia, Spain

1996 Exhibition of Projects, Aiden Galerie, Moscow, Russia

SELECTED SOLO EXHIBITIONS

2005 Riders of the Storm, Sutton Lane, London, UK

2003 Flowers and Flags, Galerie Kamm, Berlin, Germany

2000 Russian Novel 2000, Ridzina Gallery, Moscow, Russia

PAWEL ALTHAMER

Polish, b. 1967 in Warsaw. Lives and works in Warsaw

EDUCATION

1993 Warsaw Academy of Fine Arts, Poland

SELECTED GROUP EXHIBITIONS

2008 Double Agent, Institute of Contemporary Arts, London, UK

2005 9th International Istanbul Biennial, Istanbul, Turkey

1999 Fauna, Galeria Zacheta, Warsaw, Poland

1993 Unvollkommen, Museum Bochum, Bochum, Germany

SELECTED SOLO EXHIBITIONS

2007 One of Many, Fondazione Nicola Trussardi, Milan, Italy

2003 Neugerriemschneider, Berlin, Germany

2000 Brodno 2000, Galeria Foksal, Warsaw, Poland

1994 Bajka, Galeria WOK, Warsaw, Poland

ROBERT KUŚMIROWSKI

Polish, b. 1973 in Lodz, Poland. Lives and works in Lublin

EDUCATION

2002 Institute of Fine Arts, Marie Curie—Sklodowska University, Lublin, Poland

2003 Ecole des Beaux-Arts, University of Rennes 2, Rennes, France

SELECTED GROUP EXHIBITIONS

2010 Star City: The Future Under Communism, Nottingham Contemporary,
Nottingham, UK

2007 Against Time, Bonniers Konsthall, Stockholm, Sweden

2003 Jusqu'au bout du mone, Galerie de L'Esapace International et Orangerie du
      Thabor, Rennes, France

SELECTED SOLO EXHIBITIONS

2009 Bunker, The Curve, Barbican Art Gallery, London, UK

2006 Kanal, Johnen & Schottle, Cologne, Germany

2003 Fountain, XX1 Gallery, Warsaw, Poland

ROMAN ONDÁK

Slovakian, b. 1966 in Zilina, Slovakia. Lives and works in Bratislava, Slovakia

EDUCATION

1994 Academy of Fine Arts, Bratislava, Slovakia

1993 Slippery Rock University, Pennsylvania, USA

SELECTED GROUP EXHIBITIONS

2010 In the face of spatial grandeur, Circuit, Lausanne, Switzerland

2008 I am never at home, Johnen Galerie, Berlin, Germany

2005 Do Not Interrupt Your Activities, Royal College of Art Galleries, London, UK

SELECTED SOLO EXHIBITIONS

2009 Rear Room, Johnen Galerie, Berlin, Germany

2006 Tate Modern, London, UK

2003 Talker, gb agency, Paris, France

SERBAN SAVU
Romanian, b. 1978 in Sighisoara, Romania. Lives and works in Cluj, Romania
EDUCATION
2001   University of Art and Design, Cluj, Romania,
2004   Nicolae Iorga Postgraduate Research Grant, Venice, Italy
SELECTED GROUP EXHIBITIONS
2008   Re-construction, Biennial of Young Artists, Bucharest, Romania
2007   Across the Trees: Romanian Art Now, David Nolan Gallery, New York, USA
2006   Cluj Connection, Haunch of Venison, Zurich, Switzerland
SELECTED SOLO EXHIBITIONS
2009   The Edge of the Empire, David Nolan Gallery, New York USA
2007   Along the River, FA Projects, London, UK
2006   The New Man, Mie Lefever Gallery, Gent, Belgium

STANO FILKO
Slovakian, b. 1937 in Velka Hradna, Former Czechoslovakia. Lives and works in
Bratislava, Slovakia
SELECTED GROUP EXHIBITIONS
2010   Star City: The Future Under Communism, Nottingham Contemporary, Nottingham, UK
2007   Contemporary Slovak Art 1960–2000, Varosi Muveszeti Muzeum, Gyor, Hungary
2006   22 minutes 58 seconds, Gallery Art Factory, Prague, Czech Republic

TOMISLAV GOTOVAC
Serbian, b, 1937 in Sombor, Serbia. Lives and works in Zagreb, Croatia
SELECTED GROUP EXHIBITIONS
2009   Performing the East, Salzburger Kunstverein, Salzburg, Austria
2005   First Person Singular, Museum of Modern Art, Dubrovnik, Croatia
2004   Flipside, Artists Space, New York, USA

VLADIMIR DUBOSSARSKY
Russian, b. 1964 in Moscow, Former USSR. Lines and works in Moscow, Russia
EDUCATION
1991   Moscow State Art Institute, Former USSR
1984   Moscow Art College, Former USSR
ALEXANDER VINOGRADOV
Russian, b. 1963 in Moscow, Former USSR. Lives and works in Moscow, Russia
EDUCATION
1995   Moscow State Art Institute, Former USSR
1984   Moscow Art College, Former USSR
SELECTED GROUP EXHIBITIONS
2009   From A Study to An Art-Object, Moscow Museum of Modern Art, Moscow, Russia
2006   The Triumph of Painting, Part 6, The Saatchi Gallery, London, UK
2002   Urgent Painting, Musee d'Art Modern de la Ville de Paris, Paris, France
1998   Summer Vacation, Moscow Fine Art Gallery, Moscow, Russia
SELECTED SOLO EXHIBITIONS
2007   Four Seasons of Russian Painting, The State Tretyakov Gallery, Moscow, Russia
2003   Our Best World, Deitch Projects, New York, USA
1999   Just Pictures, Moscow Fine Art Gallery, Moscow, Russia

WILHELM SASNAL
Polish, b. 1972 in Tarnow, Poland. Live and works in Kraków, Poland
EDUCATION
1999   Department of Painting, Kraków Academy of Fine Arts, Kraków, Poland
SELECTED GROUP EXHIBITIONS
2007   Very Abstract and Hyper Figurative, Thomas Dane Gallery, London, UK
2004   From My Window, Artists and their Teritorries, Ecole Nationale Superieure des
          Beaux-Arts, Paris, France
2000   In Between: Art From Poland 1945-2000, Chicago Cultural Centre, Chicago, USA
SELECTED SOLO EXHIBITIONS
2007   Anton Kern Gallery, New York, USA
2004   Camden Arts Centre, London, UK
2001   Everyday life in Poland in 1999-2000, Raster, Warsaw, Poland
1999   One hundred pieces, Zderzak Gallery, Kraków, Poland

ZOFIA KULIK
Polish, b. 1947 in Wroclaw, Poland. Lives and works in Warsaw
EDUCATION
1971   Academy of Fine Arts, Warsaw, Poland
SELECTED GROUP EXHIBITIONS
2006   Interrupted Histories, Museum of Modern Art, Ljubljana, Slovenia
2005   Warsaw—Moscow/Moscow—Warsaw 1900–2000, Zacheta National Gallery,
          Warsaw, Poland
1996   New Histories, The Institute of Contemporary Art, Boston, USA
SELECTED SOLO EXHIBITIONS
2005   From Siberia to Cyberia, Museum Bochum, Bochum, Germany
2004   Self-portraits and the Garden, Le Guern Gallery, Warsaw, Poland
1998   The Human Motif IV, National Gallery, Prague, Czech Republic

BIBLIOGRAPHY

SUGGESTED READING

AMAN, ANDERS, *Architecture and Ideology in Eastern Europe During the Stalin Era: An Aspect of Cold War History*, Cambridge, MA: MIT Press, 1992

BARNETT, DENNIS, AND ARTHUR SKELTON, eds., *Theatre and Performance in Eastern Europe: The Changing Scene*, Lanham, MD: Scarecrow Press, 2007

BENTON, CHARLOTTE, ed., *Figuration/Abstraction: Strategies for Public Sculpture in Europe 1945–1968*, Aldershot: Ashgate Publishing Group, 2004

CROWLEY, DAVID, AND SUSAN E. REID, eds., *Style and Socialism*, Oxford: A & C Black Publishers Ltd, 2000

CROWTHER, PAUL A., *New Art From Eastern Europe: Identity and Conflict*, London: John Wiley and Sons Ltd, 1994

DAVIES, NORMAN, *Europe East and West*, London: CCV, 2007

ERJAVEC, ALES, ed., *Postmodernism and the Postsocialist Condition: Politicized Art under Late Socialism*, Berkeley and Los Angeles, CA: University of California Press, 2003

GROYS, BORIS, *Art Power*, Cambridge, MA: MIT Press, 2008

HERMAN, NICHOLAS, ELENA SOROKINA AND EUGENE RAIKHEL, *Russian Art in Translation*, New York, NY: Ante Projects, 2007

HOPTMAN, LAURA J, ed., *Beyond Belief: Contemporary Art from East Central Europe*, Chicago: Museum of Contemporary Art, 1995

HOPTMAN, LAURA, AND TOMAS POSPISZYL, ed., *Primary Documents: A Sourcebook for Eastern and Central European Art since the 1950s*, Cambridge, MA: MIT Press, 2002

HOWARD, JEREMY, *East European Art 1650–1950*, Oxford and New York: Oxford University Press, 2006

IMRE, ANIKO, ed., *East European Cinemas*, London: Taylor and Francis Ltd, 2005

IRWIN, ed., *East Art Map*, London: Afterall, 2006

JORDAN, MEL, AND MALCOLM MILES, *Art and Theory After Socialism*, Bristol: Intellect Books, 2008

LEACH, NEIL, ed., *Architecture and Revolution: Contemporary Perspectives on Central and Eastern Europe*, London: Taylor and Francis Ltd, 1999

MAGGIA, FILIPPO, *Contemporary Photography from Eastern Europe*, Milan: Skira, 2010

MANSBACH, S A, *Modern Art in Eastern Europe: from the Baltic to the Balkans, ca. 1890–1939*, Cambridge: Cambridge University Press, 2001

PIKE, DAVID, *The Politics of Culture in Soviet Occupied Germany 1945–1949*, Palo Alto: Stanford University Press, 1993

PIOTROWSKI, PIOTR, *In the Shadow of Yalta: Art and the Avant-garde in Eastern Europe 1945–1989*, London: Reaktion Books, 2009

ROSENFELD, ALLA, AND N T DODGE, eds., *Art of the Baltics: The Struggle for Freedom of Artistic Expression Under the Soviets 1945–1991*, New Brunswick, NJ: Rutgers University Press, 2001

SANDQVIST, TOM, *Dada East*, Cambridge, MA: MIT Press, 2006

SLATER, THOMAS J, ed., *Handbook of Soviet and East European Films and Film Makers*, Westport: ABC-CLIO, 1991

SVASEK, MARUSKA, *Postsocialism: Politics and Emotions in Central and Eastern Europe*, Oxford: Berghahn Books, 2008

WACHTEL, ANDREW BARUCH, *Remaining Relevant After Communism: The Role of the Writer in Eastern Europe*, Chicago, IL: The University of Chicago Press, 2006

ESSAYS AND ARTICLES

AYERZA, JOSEPHINE, "Hidden Prohibitions and the Pleasure Principle", in *Flash Art*, March/April 1992

BADOVINAC, ZDENKA, "Contemporaneity as Points of Connection", www.e-flux.com, 2010

BEKE, LÁSZLÓ, "East Central Europe from the Perspective of a Hungarian Curator", in Laura J Hoptman ed., *Beyond Belief: Contemporary Art from East Central Europe*, Chicago: Museum of Contemporary Art, 1995

EFIMOVA, ALLA, "Idea Against Materia: On the Consumption of Post-Soviet Art", www.artmargins.com, 1999

HLAVAJOVÁ, MÁRIA, "Towards the Normal: Negotiating the 'Former East' ", in Vanderlinden and Filipovic eds., *The Manifesta Decade: Debates on Contemporary Art Exhibitions and Biennials in Post-Wall Europe*, Cambridge, MA: Roomade and MIT Press, 2005

HOPE, SOPHIE and MARK STAMENKOVIC, "Exploring Critical and Political Art in the UK and Serbia" in Jordan and Miles eds., *Art and Theory After Socialism*, Chicago: Intellect Books, 2008

MOCNIK, RASTKO, "East!", in IRWIN, eds. *East Art Map*, 2002

PIOTROWSKI, PIOTR, "Central Europe in the Face of Unification", in eds., Maria Hlavajova and Jill Winder, *Who if not we should at least try to imagine the future o f all this*, Amsterdam: Artimo, 2004

SORBELLO, MARINA, "Eastwards—A Panel Discussion About the Emerging Art Markets of the New Europe", www.artmargins.com, 2006

ŽIŽEK, SLAVOJ, "Can Lenin Tell Us About Freedom Today?" in *Rethinking Marxism*, vol 3, no. 2, 2001

EXHIBITION CATALOGUES

ANDRAS, EDIT, KETI CHUKROV and BRANKO DIMITRIJEVIA, *Gender Check: Femininity and Masculinity in the art of Eastern Europe*, Buchhandlung Walther Konig GmbH & Co. KG. Abt. Verlag, 2009

BADOVINAC, ZDENKA, *Body and the East: From the 1960s to the Present,* Ljubljana: Moderna Galerija Ljubljana/Museum of Modern Art, 1998

BRENER, ALEXANDER, *The Dream of Democratic Culture, It's a Better World; Russicher Aktionismus und sein Kontext*, Vienna: Wiener Secession,

ELLIOT, DAVID and BOJANA PEJIC, *After the Wall: Art and Culture in Post-Communist Europe,* Stockholm: Moderna Museet, 1999

FOWKES, MAJA and REUBEN FOWKES, *Revolution is Not a Garden Party*, Manchester: Miriad, 2006

HAVRANEK, VIT, JAN VERWOERT, IGOR ZABEL, CHRISTINE MACEL and NATASA PETRESIN, *Promises of the Past: A Discontinuous History of art in Former Eastern Europe*, JRP Ringier, 2010

MARCOCI, ROXANA, *Beyond Belief: East Central European Contemporary Art,* Chicago, IL: Museum of Contemporary Art, Chicago, 1995

Wounds, Between Democracy and Redemption in Contemporary Art, Stockholm: Moderna Museet, 1998

Under the Red and White Flag: New Art from Poland, Warsaw: Zacheta National Galery of Art, 2004

SELECTED BIBLIOGRAPHY CITED IN THE BOOK

CODRESCU, A, *The Disappearance of the Outside*, Boston: Addison-Wesley, 1990

GROYS, BORIS, *History Becomes Form: Moscow Conceptualism*, Cambridge, MA: MIT Press, 2010

ŁUKASZ, RONDUDA,"Polish Art of the 70s", Warsaw: Polski Western, 2009

BÜRGER, P, *Theory of the Avant-Garde*, Minneapolis: University of Minnesota Press, 1984

GREENBERG, C, "Avant-Garde and Kitsch", in *The Collected Essays and Criticism*, vol. 1, Chicago and London: University of Chicago Press, 1986

HUYSSEN, A, *Twilight Memories. Marking Time in a Culture of Amnesia*, Routledge: New York & London, 1995

KABAKOV, ILYA "A Story about a Culturally Relocated Person", Speech at the XXVIII AICA Congress, Stockholm, 22 September 1944, now reprinted in *M'ars*, Ljubljana, 1996

OFFE, C, *Varieties of Transition: The East European and East German Experience*, Cambridge MA: MIT Press, 1997

PHELAN, PEGGY, *Unmarket—The Politics of Performance*, London and New York: Routledge, 1993

SALECL, RENATA, "Love me, love my dog", *Index. Scandinavian Art and Culture,* 1996, no. 3–4

ZABEL, I, "We and the Others", *Moscow Art Magazine*, No. 22, 1998

ŽIŽEK, S "Multiculturalism, or, The Cultural Logic of Multinational Capitalism", *New Left Review*, No. 225, Sept–Oct 1997

WEBSITES

Transitland—Video Art from Central and Eastern Europe 1989–2009
www.transitland.eu

ARTMargins: Central and Eastern European Visual Culture
www.artmargins.com

SocialEast Forum on the Art and Visual Culture of Eastern Europe
www.socialeast.org

Polish Culture
www.culture.pl

Calvert22 Foundation
www.calvert22.org

Beyond East European Art
www.beyondeast.wordpress.com

INDEX

ACKNOWLEDGEMENTS

First and foremost our gratitude must go to *Contemporary Art in Eastern Europe*'s advisors—Neil Gall and Rut Blees Luxemburg—who generously lent their time and expert advice, from the initial research stages of the book, right through to its completion. A particular thanks must also go to Boris Groys, not only for his insightful introductory essay, but also for his words of advice; as with Eda Cufer and Zdenka Badovinac.

Many thanks to each of the artist's profiled, all of whom showed considerable enthusiasm and support towards the project—this volume certainly would not have been possible without the eclectic range of work displayed throughout the book's pages. Also, to the many representative galleries who were more than accommodating in sending images and information on their artists. Thank you especially to Walter Seidl and Karolina Radenkovic at Kontakt: The Arts and Civil Society Program of Erste Group; Melissa Morales at the Sean Kelly Gallery, and Solene Guillier at the GB Agency; alongside those at the Foksal Gallery Foundation.

Finally, a special thanks to those here at Black Dog—in particular to the book's designers Lottie Crumbleholme and Fred Birdsall, along with Matt Bucknall for his original template design for the ARTWORLD series and Johanna Bonnevier for the design of the volume's map. In editorial, thank you to Nikolaos Kotsopoulos for his initial research; also many thanks to Jon Aye and Grace Beaumont for their dedicated assistance throughout, along with help from Jonno Ovans. And, on behalf of Rut Blees Luxemburg, thank you to Karel Cisar and Benjamin Beker for their knowledgeable contributions.

COLOPHON

© 2010 Black Dog Publishing Limited, London, UK,
the authors and artists. All rights reserved.

Edited by Phoebe Adler and Duncan
McCorquodale at Black Dog Publishing.
Designed by Fred Birdsall with thanks
to Lottie Crumbleholme and Matt Bucknall
at Black Dog Publishing.

Black Dog Publishing Limited
10A Acton Street
London WC1X 9NG
info@blackdogonline.com

All opinions expressed within this publication are those
of the authors and not necessarily of the publisher.

British Library Cataloguing-in-Publication Data. A CIP
record for this book is available from the British Library.

ISBN 978 1 906155 84 1

Black Dog Publishing Limited, London, UK, is an
environmentally responsible company. *Contemporary Art
in Eastern Europe: Artworld* is printed on FSC certified paper.

Cover image: Christo and Jeanne-Claude, *Wall of
Oil Barrels-Iron Curtain-Rue Visconti, Paris*, 1961–62,
oil barrels. Copyright Christo 1962, courtesy the
artists, Photo: Jean-Dominique Lajoux.

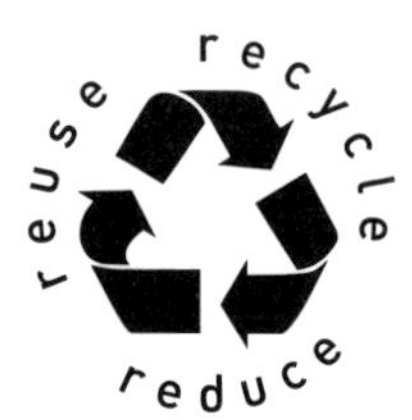

architecture art design
fashion history photography
theory and things

www.blackdogonline.com   london uk